W9-BKR-069

EXPANDED 2ND EDITION

Picture-Perfect SCIENCE Lessons

USING CHILDREN'S BOOKS TO GUIDE INQUIRY, 3–6

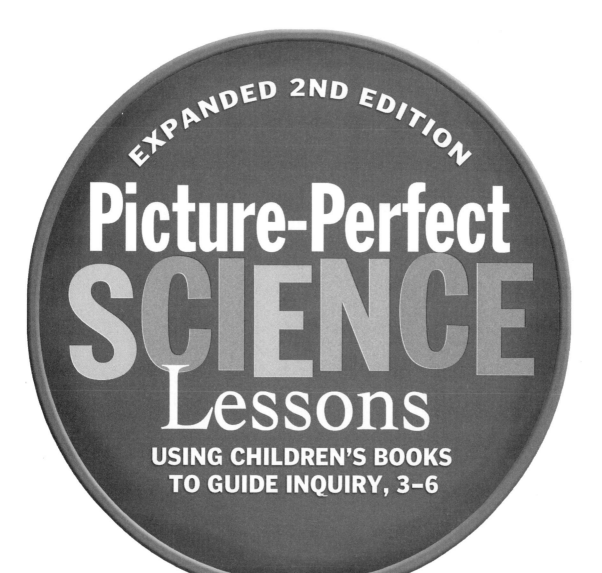

EXPANDED 2ND EDITION

Picture-Perfect SCIENCE Lessons

USING CHILDREN'S BOOKS TO GUIDE INQUIRY, 3–6

By Karen Ansberry
and Emily Morgan

NSTApress
National Science Teachers Association

Arlington, Virginia

DiPietro Library
Franklin Pierce University
Rindge, NH 03461

NSTA press®
National Science Teachers Association

Claire Reinburg, Director
Jennifer Horak, Managing Editor
Andrew Cooke, Senior Editor
Judy Cusick, Senior Editor
Wendy Rubin, Associate Editor
Amy America, Book Acquisitions Coordinator

Art and Design
Will Thomas Jr., Director
Linda Olliver, Cover, Interior Design, Illustrations

Printing and Production
Catherine Lorrain, Director

National Science Teachers Association
Francis Q. Eberle, PhD, Executive Director
David Beacom, Publisher

1840 Wilson Blvd., Arlington, VA 22201
www.nsta.org/store
For customer service inquiries, please call 800-277-5300.

Copyright © 2010 by the National Science Teachers Association.
All rights reserved. Printed in the United States of America.
18 17 16 15 8 7 6 5

NSTA is committed to publishing material that promotes the best in inquiry-based science education. However, conditions of actual use may vary, and the safety procedures and practices described in this book are intended to serve only as a guide. Additional precautionary measures may be required. NSTA and the authors do not warrant or represent that the procedures and practices in this book meet any safety code or standard of federal, state, or local regulations. NSTA and the authors disclaim any liability for personal injury or damage to property arising out of or relating to the use of this book, including any of the recommendations, instructions, or materials contained therein.

Permissions
Book purchasers may photocopy, print, or e-mail up to five copies of an NSTA book chapter for personal use only; this does not include display or promotional use. Elementary, middle, and high school teachers may reproduce forms, sample documents, and single NSTA book chapters needed for classroom or noncommercial, professional-development use only. E-book buyers may download files to multiple personal devices but are prohibited from posting the files to third-party servers or websites, or from passing files to non-buyers. For additional permission to photocopy or use material electronically from this NSTA Press book, please contact the Copyright Clearance Center (CCC) (*www.copyright.com*; 978-750-8400). Please access *www.nsta.org/permissions* for further information about NSTA's rights and permissions policies.

Library of Congress Cataloging-in-Publication Data
Ansberry, Karen Rohrich, 1966-
Picture-perfect science lessons, expanded 2nd edition : using children's books to guide inquiry, 3-6 / by Karen Ansberry and Emily Morgan.
p. cm.
Includes bibliographical references and index.
ISBN 978-1-935155-16-4
1. Science--Study and teaching (Elementary) 2. Children's books. I. Morgan, Emily R. (Emily Rachel), 1973- II. Title.
LB1585.A58 2010
372.3'5044--dc22

2010014284

eISBN 978-1-936137-72-5

BV-SFICOC-210043
SUSTAINABLE FORESTRY INITIATIVE
Certified Fiber Sourcing
www.sfiprogram.org

Contents

Foreword

I had the good fortune to meet the authors of *Picture-Perfect Science Lessons,* Karen Ansberry and Emily Morgan, in the fall of 2003 at a workshop I facilitated on inquiry-based science. At that event, we had a lively discussion about the nature of science and how the teachers in attendance might impart their love of science to elementary-age children. The authors then took me aside and told me of their plans to write a book for teachers (and parents, too) using children's literature to engage children in scientific inquiry. I have always believed that children in the elementary grades would experience more science if elementary teachers were provided with better ways to integrate literacy and science. So, of course, I was intrigued.

As I reviewed this manuscript, I was reminded of one of my favorite "picture books" as an adult—*The Sense of Wonder,* by Rachel Carson. In that book, Ms. Carson expresses her love of learning and how she helped her young nephew discover the wonders of nature. As she expressed,

> *I sincerely believe that for the child, and for the parent seeking to guide him, it is not half so important to know as to feel. If facts are the seeds that later produce knowledge and wisdom, then the emotions and the impressions of the senses are the fertile soil in which the seeds must grow. The years of early childhood are the time to prepare the soil. Once the emotions have been aroused—a sense of the beautiful, the excitement of the new and the unknown, a feeling of sympathy, pity, admiration or love—then we wish for knowledge about the object of our emotional response. Once found, it has lasting meaning. It is more important to pave the way for the child to want to know than to put him on a diet of facts he is not ready to assimilate.* (Carson 1956)

Rachel Carson used the natural environment to instill in her nephew the wonders of nature and scientific inquiry, but I believe, along with the authors, that picture books can have a similar emotional effect on children and inspire their wonder and their curiosity. Then, when teachers and parents couple scientific inquiry experiences with the content of the picture books, science really comes to life for children. *Picture-Perfect Science Lessons* provides an ideal framework that encourages children to read first; explore objects, organisms, and events related to what they've read; discern relationships, patterns, and explanations in the world around them; and then read more to gather more information, which will lead to new questions worth investigating.

In addition, *Picture-Perfect Science Lessons* is the perfect antidote to leaving science behind in the elementary classroom. As elementary teachers struggle to increase the basic literacy of all students, they often cannot find the time to include science in the curriculum, or they are discouraged from teaching science when literacy scores decline. Teachers need resources such as *Picture-Perfect Science Lessons* to genuinely integrate science and literacy. There is no doubt that inquiry-based science experiences motivate children to learn. Through this book, teachers have the best of both worlds—they will have the resources to motivate children to read and to "do science." What could be better?

As one of the developers of the BSCS 5E Instructional Model, I was gratified to learn that the authors intended to use the "5Es" to structure their learning experiences for children and teachers. These authors, as with many teachers across the country, had become acquainted with the 5Es and used the model extensively to promote learning in their own classrooms; however, they did not know the origin of the model until we had a conversation about BSCS and the 5Es. This book helps set the record straight—the 5E Instructional Model was indeed developed at BSCS in the late 1980s in conjunction with an elementary curriculum project and thus is appropriately titled "The BSCS 5E Instructional Model" in this book. The authors' iterative use of the BSCS 5Es is appropriate because the model is meant to be fluid, where one exploration leads to a partial explanation that invites further exploration before a child has a grasp of a complete scientific explanation for a phenomenon. As the authors mention, the final E—evaluate—is applied more formally at the end of a unit of study, but the BSCS 5E model by no means implies that teachers and students do not evaluate, or assess, student learning as the students progress through the model. Ongoing assessment is an integral part of the philosophy of the BSCS 5Es and the authors appropriately weave formative assessment into each lesson.

Once you place your toe into the waters of this book, I guarantee that you will dive right in! Whether you are a teacher, a parent, or both, you will enjoy this inviting approach to inquiry-based science. If you follow the methods outlined in *Picture-Perfect Science Lessons,* you and the children with whom you interact will have no choice but to learn science concepts through reading and scientific inquiry.

I don't know about you, but I'm rather curious about those sheep in a jeep. Enjoy!

Nancy M. Landes
Senior Science Educator
Center for Professional Development
Biological Sciences Curriculum Study

Reference

Carson, R. 1956. *The sense of wonder.* Berkeley, CA: The Nature Company. (Copyright renewed 1984 by Roger Christie. Text copyright 1956 by Rachel Carson.)

Preface

A class of fifth-grade students laughs as their teacher reads Jeanne Willis's *Dr. Xargle's Book of Earth Hounds*. Students are listening to the alien professor, Dr. Xargle, teach his pupils about Earth Hounds (puppies): "Earth Hounds have fangs at the front and a waggler at the back. To find out which is which, hold a sausage at both ends." The fifth-grade class giggles at this outrageous lesson as Dr. Xargle continues to lecture. Students then begin sorting cards containing some of the alien professor's "observations" of Earth Hounds. The teacher asks her students, "Which of Dr. Xargle's comments are truly observations?" Students review their cards and realize that many of his comments are not observations but rather hilariously incorrect inferences. They re-sort their cards into two groups: observations and inferences. This amusing picture book and word sorting activity guide students into hands-on inquiry where they make observations about sealed mystery samples Dr. Xargle collected from Earth. Eventually students develop inferences about what the mystery samples might be. Through this exciting lesson, students construct their own understanding of the difference between an observation and an inference, how scientists use observations and inferences, and how to make good observations and inferences.

What Is Picture-Perfect Science?

This scenario describes how a children's picture book can help guide students through an engaging, hands-on inquiry lesson. *Picture-Perfect Science Lessons* contains 20 science lessons for students in grades 3 through 6, with embedded reading comprehension strategies to help them learn to read and read to learn while engaged in inquiry-based science. To help you teach according to *A Framework for K–12 Science Education*, the lessons are written in an easy-to-follow format for teaching inquiry-based science: the Biological Sciences Curriculum Study 5E Instructional Model (Bybee 1997, used with permission from BSCS). This learning cycle model allows students to construct their own understanding of scientific concepts as they cycle through the following phases: Engage, Explore, Explain, Elaborate, and Evaluate. Although *Picture-Perfect Science Lessons* is primarily a book for teaching science, reading comprehension strategies are embedded in each lesson. These essential strategies can be modeled throughout while keeping the focus of the lessons on science.

Use This Book Within Your Science Curriculum

We wrote *Picture-Perfect Science Lessons* to supplement, not replace, an existing science program. Although each lesson stands alone as a carefully planned learning cycle based on clearly defined science objectives, the lessons are intended to be integrated into a more complete unit of instruction in which concepts can be more fully developed. The lessons are not designed to be taught sequentially. We want you to use *Picture-Perfect Science Lessons* where appropriate within your school's current science curriculum to support, enrich, and extend it. And we want you to adapt the lessons to fit your school's curriculum, your students' needs, and your own teaching style.

Special Features

1. Ready-to-Use Lessons With Assessments

Each lesson contains engagement activities, hands-on explorations, student pages, suggestions for student and teacher explanations, opportunities for elaboration, assessment suggestions, and annotated bibliographies of more books to read on the topic. Assessments range from poster sessions with rubrics to teacher checkpoint labs to formal multiple choice and extended response quizzes.

2. Reading Comprehension Strategies

Reading comprehension strategies based on the book *Strategies That Work* (Harvey and Goudvis 2000) and specific activities to enhance comprehension are embedded throughout the lessons and clearly marked with an icon. Chapter 2 describes how to model these strategies while reading aloud to students.

3. Standards-Based Objectives

All lesson objectives are from *A Framework for K-12 Science Education* (NRC 2012) and are clearly identified at the beginning of each lesson. Chapter 5 outlines the *Framework* for those grade ranges, and Appendix 1 (p. 393) shows the correlation between the lessons and the *Framework*. In addition, Appendix 2 (p. 395) shows the correlation to the *Common Core State Standards, English Language Arts* (NGAC and CCSSO 2010).

4. Science as Inquiry

As we said, the lessons in *Picture-Perfect Science Lessons* are structured as guided inquiries following the 5E Model. Guiding questions are embedded throughout each lesson and marked with an icon ?. The questioning process is the cornerstone of good teaching. A teacher who asks thoughtful questions arouses students' curiosity, promotes critical-thinking skills, creates links between ideas, provides challenges, gets immediate feedback on student learning, and helps guide students through the inquiry process. Each lesson includes an "Inquiry Place," a section at the end of the lesson that suggests ideas for developing open inquiries. Chapters 3 and 4 explore science as inquiry and the BSCS 5E Instructional Model.

References

Bybee, R. W. 1997. *Achieving scientific literacy: From purposes to practices.* Portsmouth, NH: Heinemann.

Harvey, S., and A. Goudvis. 2000. *Strategies that work: Teaching comprehension to enhance understanding.* York, ME: Stenhouse Publishers.

National Governors Association Center for Best Practices and Council of Chief State School Officers (NGAC and CCSSO). 2010. *Common core state standards.* Washington, DC: NGAC and CCSSO.

National Research Council (NRC). 2012. *A framework for K-12 science education: Practices, crosscutting concepts, and core ideas.* Washington, DC: National Academies Press.

Children's Book Cited

Willis, J. 2011. *Dr. Xargle's book of Earth hounds.* London, UK: Anderson Press Ltd.

Editors' Note: *Picture-Perfect Science Lessons* builds on the texts of 38 children's picture books to teach science. Some of these books feature animals that have been anthropomorphized—sheep crash a jeep, a hermit crab builds his house. While we recognize that many scientists and educators believe that personification, teleology, animism, and anthropomorphism promote misconceptions among young children, others believe that removing these elements would leave children's literature severely underpopulated. Furthermore, backers of these techniques not only see little harm in their use but also argue that they facilitate learning.

Because *Picture-Perfect Science Lessons* specifically and carefully supports scientific inquiry—"The Changing Moon" lesson, for instance, teaches students how to weed out misconceptions by asking them to point out inaccurate depictions of the Moon—we, like our authors, feel the question remains open.

Acknowledgments

We would like to give special thanks to science consultant Carol Collins for sharing her expertise in teaching inquiry-based science, for giving us many wonderful opportunities to share *Picture-Perfect Science Lessons* with teachers, and for continuing to support and encourage our efforts.

We would also like to express our gratitude to language arts consultant Susan Livingston for opening our eyes to the power of modeling reading strategies in the content areas and for teaching us that every teacher is a reading teacher.

We appreciate the care and attention to detail given to this project by Claire Reinburg, Jennifer Horak, Betty Smith, and Linda Olliver at NSTA Press.

And these thank-yous as well:

- To Bill Robertson for reviewing the teacher background section for each lesson.
- To the Ohio Department of Education for funding our very first teacher workshop.
- To NSTA and Toyota Motor Corporation for giving us a jump start with the Toyota Tapestry Grant in 2002.
- To all the wonderful teachers and students of Mason City Schools for trying our lessons and giving us feedback for improvement.
- To the administration of Mason City Schools for supporting our efforts.
- To Nancy Landes at BSCS for helping us better understand the 5Es and guiding us with her advice.
- To Diana Hunn and Katie Kinnucan-Welsh for their help with our research study.
- To Patricia Quill and her students at Western Row Elementary for piloting our lessons in their classroom.
- To Krissy Hufnagel for sharing her expertise in teaching reading.
- To Jean Muetzel and Sil Bobinski, wonderful librarians at Western Row Elementary, for going to the ends of the Earth to find picture books for us.
- To Ray Bollhauer and John Odell for their legal and business advice.
- To Christopher Canyon for inspiring us with his beautiful artwork and for encouraging us with kind words.
- To Jeff Alt for advising us to keep calling, keep calling, keep calling ...
- To Jenni Davis for the opportunities to share *Picture-Perfect Science Lessons* with teachers.
- To Jodee Seibert with Heinemann Library for supplying us with books to preview.

- To John R. Meyer at North Carolina State University Department of Entomology and Don Koller and Mike Wright at Miami University of Ohio for having the "gall" to review our "Close Encounters" dichotomous key.
- To Linda Sutphin for reviewing "Close Encounters."
- To Chris Lucas for proofreading sections of the book.
- To Amy Bleimund for sharing *Seven Blind Mice* with us.
- To Shirley Hudspeth and her class at Mason Intermediate School for trying out the turtle fortune-tellers.
- To Kim Rader and her class at Mason Intermediate School for their popcorn investigations.
- To Julie Wellbaum for her "instrumental help" with the "Sounds of Science" lesson.
- To Sheri Hill, John Hutton, Sandra Gross, and all the good people at the Blue Manatee Children's Bookstore in Cincinnati for helping us in our search for fabulous picture books.
- To Michelle Gallite and Erica Poulton for help in "cleaning up" our "Oil Spill!" lesson, and to Mrs. Gallite's third graders for their help with "The Perfect Pet" lesson.
- To Theresa Gould and the research staff at RiceTec for their advice on growing rice in the classroom.
- To Gerald Skoog for reviewing material in Chapter 11.
- To Keith Summerville at Drake University for his help in answering our questions about insects.
- To Patricia Eastin and her students at Evendale Elementary for trying out the "Batteries Included" lesson.
- To Kevin Gale and his students at Van Gorden Elementary and Patricia Quill and her students at Mason Intermediate School for trying out the "If I Built a Car" lesson.
- To our husbands, families, and friends for their moral support (and for keeping an eye on our kids!).
- And to our parents, who were our very first teachers.

The contributions of the following reviewers are also gratefully acknowledged: Mariam Jean Dreher, Nancy Landes, Christine Anne Royce, Carol Collins, Lisa Nyberg, Chris Pappas, and Ken Roy.

About the Authors

Karen Ansberry is an elementary science curriculum leader and a former fifth- and sixth-grade science teacher at Mason City Schools, in Mason, Ohio. She has a bachelor of science in biology from Xavier University and a master of arts in teaching from Miami University. Karen lives in historic Lebanon, Ohio, with her husband, daughter, twin boys, two dogs, and two cats.

Emily Morgan is the science leader for the High AIMS Consortium in Cincinnati, Ohio. She is a former elementary science lab teacher at Mason City Schools in Mason, Ohio, and a seventh-grade science teacher at Northridge Local Schools in Dayton, Ohio. She has a bachelor of science in elementary education from Wright State University and a master of science in education from the University of Dayton. Emily lives in West Chester, Ohio, with her husband, son, dog, and two cats.

Karen and Emily, along with language arts consultant Susan Livingston, received a Toyota Tapestry grant for their Picture-Perfect Science grant proposal in 2002. Since then, they have enjoyed facilitating teacher workshops at elementary schools, universities, and professional conferences across the country. They are also the authors of *More Picture-Perfect Science Lessons: Using Children's Books to Guide Inquiry, K–4.*

Karen Ansberry, right, and Emily Morgan developed *Picture-Perfect Science Lessons* based on their workshops supported by a Toyota Tapestry grant.

About the Picture-Perfect Science Program

The Picture-Perfect Science program originated from Emily Morgan's and Karen Ansberry's shared interest in using children's literature to make science more engaging. In Emily's 2001 master's thesis study involving 350 of her third-grade science lab students at Western Row Elementary, she found that students who used science trade books instead of the textbook scored significantly higher on district science performance assessments than students who used the textbook only. Convinced of the benefits of using picture books to engage students in science inquiry and to increase science understanding, Karen and Emily began collaborating with Susan Livingston, the elementary language arts curriculum leader for the Mason City Schools in Ohio, in an effort to integrate literacy strategies into inquiry-based science lessons. They received grants from the Ohio Department of Education (2001) and Toyota Tapestry (2002) to train all third-grade through sixth-grade science teachers, and in 2003 they also trained seventh- and eighth-grade science teachers with district support. The program has been presented both locally and nationally, including at the National Science Teachers Association national conferences.

For more information on Picture-Perfect Science teacher workshops, go to *www.pictureperfectscience.com.*

Lessons by Grade

Chapter		Grade	Picture Books
6	Earth Hounds	3–6	*Dr. Xargle's Book of Earth Hounds* *Seven Blind Mice*
7	Name That Shell!	3–5	*Next Time You See a Seashell* *A House for Hermit Crab*
8	Rice Is Life	3–6	*Rice Is Life* *Rice*
9	What's Poppin'?	5–6	*Popcorn!*
10	Mystery Pellets	3–6	*White Owl, Barn Owl* *Butternut Hollow Pond*
11	Close Encounters of the Symbiotic Kind	3–6	*What's Eating You? Parasites–The Inside Story* *Weird Friends: Unlikely Allies in the Animal Kingdom*
12	Turtle Hurdles	3–5	*Turtle Watch* *Turtle, Turtle, Watch Out!*
13	Oil Spill!	3–5	*Prince William* *Oil Spill!*
14	Sheep in a Jeep	3–5	*Sheep in a Jeep*
15	Sounds of Science	3–6	*Sound* *The Remarkable Farkle McBride*
16	Chemical Change Café	3–5	*Pancakes, Pancakes!*
17	The Changing Moon	3–5	*Next Time You See the Moon* *Papa, Please Get the Moon for Me*
18	Day and Night	3–5	*Somewhere in the World Right Now*
19	Grand Canyon	3–6	*Erosion* *Grand Canyon: A Trail Through Time*
20	Brainstorms: From Idea to Invention	5–6	*Imaginative Inventions* *Girls Think of Everything: Stories of Ingenious Inventions by Women*

Chapter		Grade	Picture Books
21	Bugs!	3–5	*The Perfect Pet* *Bugs Are Insects* *Ant, Ant, Ant! (An Insect Chant)*
22	Batteries Included	3–5	*Electrical Circuits* *Too Many Toys*
23	The Secrets of Flight	3–6	*How People Learned to Fly* *Kids' Paper Airplane Book*
24	Down the Drain	3–6	*Down the Drain: Conserving Water* *A Cool Drink of Water*
25	If I Built a Car	3–6	*If I Built a Car* *Inventing the Automobile*

Activity-specific safety guidelines are highlighted throughout the lessons. For a more thorough discussion of safety procedures, see *The NSTA Ready-Reference Guide to Safer Science* or *Exploring Safely.* The National Science Teachers Association has also created a convenient *Safety in the Elementary Science Classroom* flipchart. This colorful and student-friendly safety resource can be hung on the wall for easy reference or a quick refresher.

Resources

Kwan, T., and J. Texley. 2002. *Exploring safely: A guide for elementary teachers.* Arlington, VA: NSTA Press.

National Science Teachers Association (NSTA). 2003. *Safety in the elementary science classroom* flipchart. Arlington, VA: NSTA Press.

Roy, K. R. 2007. *The NSTA ready-reference guide to safer science.* Arlington, VA: NSTA Press.

Why Read Picture Books in Science Class?

Think about a book you loved as a child. Maybe you remember the zany characters and rhyming text of Dr. Seuss classics such as *Green Eggs and Ham* or *The Lorax*. Perhaps you enjoyed the page-turning suspense of *The Monster at the End of This Book* or the fascinating facts found in Joanna Cole's *Dinosaur Story*. You may have seen a little of yourself in *Where the Wild Things Are, Curious George,* or *Madeline*. Maybe your imagination was stirred by the detailed illustrations in *Jumanji* or the stunning photographs in Seymour Simon's *The Moon*. You probably remember the warm, cozy feeling of having a treasured book such as *The Snowy Day* or *Goodnight Moon* being read to you by a parent or grandparent. But chances are your favorite book as a child was *not* your fourth-grade science textbook! The format of picture books offers certain unique advantages over textbooks and chapter books for engaging students in a science lesson. More often than other books, fiction and nonfiction picture books stimulate students on both the emotional and intellectual levels. They are appealing and memorable because children readily connect with the imaginative illustrations, vivid photographs, and engaging storylines, as well as the experiences and adventures of characters, the fascinating information that supports them in their quest for knowledge, and the warm emotions that surround the reading experience.

What characterizes a picture book? We like what *Beginning Reading and Writing* says: "Picture books are unique to children's literature as they are defined by format rather than content. That is, they are books in which the illustrations are of equal importance as or more important than the text in the creation of meaning" (Strickland and Morrow 2000). Because picture books are more likely to hold children's attention, they lend themselves to reading comprehension strategy instruction and to engaging students within an inquiry-based cycle of science instruction. "Picture books, both fiction and nonfiction, are more likely to hold our attention and engage us than reading dry, formulaic text. ... Engagement leads to remembering what is read, acquiring knowledge and enhancing understanding" (Harvey and Goudvis 2000). We wrote *Picture-Perfect Science Lessons* so teachers can take advantage of the positive features of children's picture books by supplementing the traditional science textbook with a wide variety of high-quality fiction and nonfiction science-related picture books.

The Research

1. Context for Concepts

Literature gives students a context for the concepts they are exploring in the science classroom. Children's picture books, a branch of literature, have interesting storylines that can help students understand and remember concepts better than they would by using textbooks alone, which tend to present science as lists of facts to be memorized (Butzow and Butzow 2000). In addition, the colorful pictures and graphics in picture books are superior to many texts for explaining abstract ideas (Kralina 1993). As more and more content is packed into the school day, and higher expectations are placed on student performance, it is critical for teachers to cover more in the same amount of time. Integrating curriculum can help accomplish this. The wide array of high-quality children's literature available today can help you model reading comprehension strategies while teaching science content in a meaningful context.

2. More Depth of Coverage

Science textbooks can be overwhelming for many children, especially those who have reading problems. They often contain unfamiliar vocabulary and tend to cover a broad range of topics (Casteel and Isom 1994; Short and Armstrong 1993; Tyson and Woodward 1989). However, fiction and nonfiction picture books tend to focus on fewer topics and give more in-depth coverage of the concepts. It can be useful to pair an engaging fiction book with a nonfiction book to round out the science content being presented.

For example, the Chapter 13 lesson "Oil Spill!" features both *Prince William*, a fictionalized account of a young girl's experience rescuing an oil-covered baby seal, and *Oil Spill!*, a nonfiction book detailing causes and effects of oil spills. The emotion-engaging storyline and the realistic characters in *Prince William* hook the reader, and the book *Oil Spill!* presents facts and background information. Together they offer a balanced, in-depth look at how oil spills affect the environment.

3. Improved Reading and Science Skills

Research by Morrow, Pressley, Smith, and Smith (1997) on using children's literature and literacy instruction in the science program indicated gains in science as well as literacy. Romance and Vitale (1992) found significant improvement in both science and reading scores of fourth graders when the regular basal reading program was replaced with reading in science that correlated with the science curriculum. They also found an improvement in students' attitudes toward the study of science.

4. Opportunities to Correct Science Misconceptions

Students often have strongly held misconceptions about science that can interfere with their learning. "Misconceptions, in the field of science education, are preconceived ideas that differ from those currently accepted by the scientific community" (Colburn 2003). Children's picture books, reinforced with hands-on inquiries, can help students correct their misconceptions. Repetition of the correct concept by reading several books, doing a number of experiments, and listening to scientists invited to the classroom can facilitate a conceptual change in children (Miller, Steiner, and Larson 1996).

But teachers must be aware that scientific misconceptions can be inherent in picture books. Although many errors are explicit, some of the misinformation is more implicit or may be inferred from text and illustrations (Rice 2002). This problem is more likely to occur within fictionalized material. Mayer's (1995) study demonstrates that when both inaccuracies and science facts are presented in the same book, children do not necessarily remember the correct information.

Scientific inaccuracies in picture books can be useful for teaching. Research shows that errors in picture books, whether identified by the teacher or the students, can be used to help children learn to question the accuracy of what they read by comparing their own observations to the science presented in the books (Martin 1997). Scientifically inaccurate children's books can be helpful when students analyze inaccurate text or pictures after they have gained understanding of the correct scientific concepts through inquiry experiences.

For example, in "The Changing Moon" lesson, Chapter 17, students analyze the inaccurate moon phases in Eric Carle's *Papa, Please Get the Moon for Me* and then correct them through their own illustrations of the story. This process takes students to a higher level of thinking as they use their knowledge to evaluate and correct the misinformation in the picture book.

Use With Upper Elementary Students

Picture-Perfect Science Lessons is designed for students in grades 3 through 6. Although picture books are more commonly used with younger children, we have good reasons to recommend using them with upper elementary students. In *Strategies That Work* (2000), reading experts Harvey and Goudvis maintain that "the power of well-written picture books cannot be overestimated... picture books lend themselves to comprehension strategy instruction at every grade level." The benefits of using picture books to teach science and reading strategies are not reserved for younger children. We have found them effective for engaging students, for guiding scientific inquiry, and for teaching comprehension strategies to students in kindergarten through eighth grade. We believe that the wide range of topics, ideas, and genres found in picture books reaches all readers, regardless of their ages, grades, reading levels, or prior experiences.

Selection of Books

Each lesson in *Picture-Perfect Science Lessons* focuses on one or more of the National Science Education Standards. We selected one to three fiction and/or nonfiction children's picture books that closely relate to the Standards. An annotated "More Books to Read" section is provided at the end of each lesson. If you would like to select more children's literature to use in your science classroom, try the Outstanding Science Trade Books for Students K–12 listing, a cooperative project between the National Science Teachers Association (NSTA) and the Children's Book Council (CBC). The books are selected by a book review panel appointed by the NSTA and assembled in cooperation with the CBC. Each year a new list is featured in the March issue of NSTA's elementary school teacher journal, *Science and Children*. See *www.nsta.org/ostbc* for archived lists.

When you select children's picture books for science instruction, you should consult with a knowledgeable colleague who can help you check them for errors or misinformation. You might talk with a high school science teacher, a retired science teacher, or a university professor. To make sure the books are developmentally appropriate or lend themselves to a particular reading strategy you want to model, you could consult with a language arts specialist.

Finding the *Picture-Perfect* Books

Each activity chapter includes a "Featured Picture Books" section with titles, author names, summaries, and other publication details. The years and publisher names listed are for the most recent editions available—paperback, wherever possible—as of the printing of *Picture-Perfect Science Lessons, Expanded 2nd Edition*.

All of the trade books featured in *Picture-Perfect Science Lessons* are currently in print and can be found at your local bookstore or online retailer. There are also handy collections of the books featured in *Picture-Perfect Science Lessons* available at *www.nsta.org/store* for a reduced cost.

Considering Genre

Considering genre when you determine how to use a particular picture book within a science lesson is important. Donovan and Smolkin (2002) identify four different genres frequently recommended for teachers to use in their science instruction: story, nonnarrative information, narrative information, and dual purpose. *Picture-Perfect Science Lessons* identifies the genre of each featured book at the beginning of each lesson. Summaries of the four genres, a representative picture book for each genre, and suggestions for using each genre within the BSCS 5E learning cycle we use follow. (The science learning cycle known as the BSCS 5E Model is described in detail in Chapter 4.)

Storybooks

Storybooks center on specific characters who work to resolve a conflict or problem. The major purpose of stories is to entertain, not to present factual information. The vocabulary is typically commonsense, everyday language. An engaging storybook can spark interest in a science topic and move students toward informational texts to answer questions inspired by the story. For example, "Earth Hounds," Chapter 6, uses the storybook *Dr. Xargle's Book of Earth Hounds* to hook learners and engage them in an inquiry about mystery samples from Planet Earth.

Scientific concepts in stories are often implicit, so teachers must make the concepts explicit to students. As we mentioned, be aware that storybooks often contain scientific errors, either explicit or implied by text or illustrations. Storybooks with scientific errors should not be used in the introduction of a topic, but may be used later in the lesson to teach students how to identify and correct the misconceptions. For example, "The Changing Moon," Chapter 17, features Eric Carle's *Papa, Please Get the Moon for Me*, a storybook that contains many scientific inaccuracies. This book would not be appropriate for introducing how the Moon seems to change shape, but it can be a powerful vehicle for assessing the ability of learners to analyze the scientific accuracy of a text.

Nonnarrative Information Books

Nonnarrative information books are factual texts that introduce a topic, describe the attributes of the topic, or describe typical events that occur. The focus of these texts is on the subject matter, not specific characters. The vocabulary is typically technical. Readers can enter the text at any point in the book. Many contain features found in nonfiction such as a table of contents, bold-print vocabulary words, a glossary, and an index. Young children tend to be less familiar with this genre and need many opportunities to experience this type of text. Using nonnarrative information books helps students become familiar with the structure of textbooks, as well as "real-world" reading, which is primarily expository. Teachers may want to read only those sections that provide the concepts and facts needed to meet particular science objectives.

We wrote the articles included in some of the lessons (see Chapters 8, 11, 14, and 16) in nonnarrative information style to give students more opportunity to practice reading this type of text. For example, "Close Encounters of the Symbiotic Kind," Chapter 11, includes an article written in an expository style that shows key words in bold print. Another example of nonnarrative information writing is the book *Rice*, which contains nonfiction text features such as a table of contents, bold-print words, diagrams, a glossary, and an index. *Rice* is featured in "Rice Is Life," Chapter 8. The appropriate placement of nonnarrative information text in a science learning cycle is after students have had the opportunity to explore concepts through hands-on activities. At that point, students are engaged in the topic and are motivated to read the nonnarrative informational text to learn more.

Narrative Information Books

Narrative information books, sometimes referred to as "hybrid books," provide an engaging format for factual information. They communicate a sequence of factual events over time and sometimes recount the events of a specific case to generalize to all cases. When using these books within science instruction, establish a purpose for reading so that students focus on the science content rather than the storyline. In some cases, teachers may want to read the book one time through for the aesthetic components of the book and a second time for specific science content. *Butternut Hollow Pond*, an example of a narrative information text, is used in "Mystery Pellets," Chapter 10. This narrative presents the dynamics of survival and competition in a pond ecosystem and contains factual information about a pond food web. The narrative information genre can be used at any point within a science learning cycle. This genre can be both engaging and informative.

Dual-Purpose Books

Dual-purpose books are intended to serve two purposes: present a story and provide facts. They employ a format that allows readers to use the book like a storybook or to use it like a nonnarrative information book. Sometimes information can be found in the running text, but more frequently it appears in insets and diagrams. Readers can enter on any page to access specific facts, or they can read it through as a story. You can use the story component of a dual-purpose book to engage the reader at the beginning of the science learning cycle. For example, Chapter 8 features the book *Rice Is Life*, which is used to engage the students in an investigation about rice.

Dual-purpose books typically have little science content within the story. Most of the informational ideas are found in the insets and diagrams. If the insets and diagrams are read, discussed, explained, and related to the story, these books can be very useful in helping students refine concepts and acquire scientific vocabulary *after* they have had opportunities for hands-on exploration. *White Owl, Barn Owl* is a dual-purpose book used in Chapter 10, "Mystery Pellets."Although the story part is about a girl and her grandfather's search for an owl, the insets can be read to give students factual information about the characteristics and life cycles of barn owls.

Using Fiction and Nonfiction Texts

As we mentioned previously, pairing fiction and nonfiction books in read alouds to round out the science content being presented is effective. Because fiction books tend to be very engaging for students, they can be used to hook students at the beginning of a science lesson. But most of the reading people do in everyday life is nonfiction. We are immersed in informational text every day, and we must be able to comprehend it to be successful in school, at work, and in society. Nonfiction books and other informational text such as articles should be used frequently in the elementary classroom. They often include text structures that differ from stories, and the opportunity to experience these structures in read alouds can strengthen students' abilities to read and understand informational text. Duke (2004) recommends four strategies to help teachers improve students' comprehension of informational text. Teachers should

- increase students' access to informational text;
- increase the time they spend working with informational text;
- teach comprehension strategies through direct instruction; and
- create opportunities for students to use informational text for authentic purposes.

Picture-Perfect Science Lessons addresses these recommendations in several ways. The lessons expose students to a variety of nonfiction picture books and articles on science topics, thereby increasing access to informational text. The lessons explain how word sorts, anticipation guides, pairs reading, and the use of nonfiction features all help improve students' comprehension of the informational text by increasing the time they spend working with it. Each lesson also includes instructions for explicitly teaching comprehension strategies within the learning cycle. The inquiry-based lessons provide an authentic purpose for reading informational text, as students are motivated to read or listen to find the answers to questions generated within the inquiry activities.

References

Butzow, J., and C. Butzow. 2000. *Science through children's literature: An integrated approach.* Portsmouth, NH: Teacher Ideas Press.

Casteel, C. P., and B. A. Isom. 1994. Reciprocal processes in science and literacy learning. *The Reading Teacher* 47: 538–544.

Colburn, A. 2003. *The lingo of learning: 88 education terms every science teacher should know.* Arlington, VA: NSTA Press.

Donovan, C., and L. Smolkin. 2002. Considering genre, content, and visual features in the selection of trade books for science instruction. *The Reading Teacher* 55: 502–520.

Duke, N. K. 2004. The case for informational text. *Educational Leadership* 61: 40–44.

Harvey, S., and A. Goudvis. 2000. *Strategies that work: Teaching comprehension to enhance understanding.* York, ME: Stenhouse Publishers.

Kralina, L. 1993. Tricks of the trades: Supplementing your science texts. *The Science Teacher* 60 (9): 33–37.

Martin, D. J. 1997. *Elementary science methods: A constructivist approach.* Albany, NY: Delmar.

Mayer, D. A. 1995. How can we best use children's literature in teaching science concepts? *Science and Children* 32 (6): 16–19, 43.

Miller, K. W., S. F. Steiner, and C. D. Larson. 1996. Strategies for science learning. *Science and Children* 33 (6): 24–27.

Morrow, L. M., M. Pressley, J. K. Smith, and M. Smith. 1997. The effect of a literature-based program integrated into literacy and science instruction with children from diverse backgrounds. *Reading Research Quarterly* 32: 54–76.

National Research Council (NRC). 1996. *National science education standards.* Washington, DC: National Academies Press.

Rice, D. C. 2002. Using trade books in teaching elementary science: Facts and fallacies. *The Reading Teacher* 55 (6): 552–565.

Romance, N. R., and M. R. Vitale. 1992. A curriculum strategy that expands time for in-depth elementary science instruction by using science-based reading strategies: Effects of a year-long study in grade four. *Journal of Research in Science Teaching* 29: 545–554.

Short, K. G., and J. Armstrong. 1993. Moving toward inquiry: Integrating literature into the science curriculum. *New Advocate* 6 (3): 183–200.

Strickland, D. S., and L. M. Morrow, eds. 2000. *Beginning reading and writing*. New York: Teachers College Press.

Tyson, H., and A. Woodward. 1989. Why aren't students learning very much from textbooks? *Educational Leadership* 47 (3): 14–17.

Children's Books Cited

Bemelmans, L. 1958. *Madeline*. New York: Viking Press.

Berger, M. 1994. *Oil spill!* New York: HarperTrophy.

Brown, M. W. 1976. *Goodnight moon*. New York: HarperCollins.

Carle, E. 1986. *Papa, please get the moon for me*. New York: Simon & Schuster.

Cole, J. 1974. *Dinosaur story*. New York: William Morrow.

Davies, N. 2007. *White owl, barn owl*. Cambridge, MA: Candlewick Press.

Gelman, R. G. 2000. *Rice is life*. New York: Henry Holt.

Heinz, B. J. 2000. *Butternut hollow pond*. Brookfield, CT: Millbrook Press.

Keats, E. J. 1963. *The snowy day*. New York: Viking Press.

Rand, G. 1992. *Prince William*. New York: Henry Holt.

Rey, H. A. 1973. *Curious George*. Boston: Houghton Mifflin.

Sendak, M. 1988. *Where the wild things are*. New York: HarperCollins.

Seuss, Dr. 1960. *Green eggs and ham*. New York: Random House Books for Young Readers.

Seuss, Dr. 1971. *The lorax*. New York: Random House Books for Young Readers.

Simon, S. 1984. *The Moon*. Salem, OR: Four Winds.

Spilsbury, L. 2001. *Rice*. Chicago: Heinemann Library.

Stone, J. 2003. *The monster at the end of this book*. New York: Golden Books.

Van Allsburg, C. 1981. *Jumanji*. Boston: Houghton Mifflin.

Willis, J. 2011. *Dr. Xargle's book of Earth Hounds*. London: Anderson Press.

Reading Aloud

READ-ALOUD TIME IS A SPECIAL PART OF MRS. WILSON'S CLASS.

This chapter addresses some of the research supporting the importance of reading aloud, tips to make your read-aloud time more valuable, descriptions of Harvey and Goudvis's six key reading strategies (2000), and tools you can use to enhance students' comprehension during read-aloud time.

Why Read Aloud?

Being read to is the most influential activity for building the knowledge required for eventual success in reading (Anderson et al. 1985). It improves reading skills, increases interest in reading and literature, and can even improve overall academic achievement. A good reader demonstrates fluent, expressive reading and models the thinking strategies of proficient readers, helping to build background knowledge and fine-tune students' listening skills. When a teacher does the reading, children's minds are free to anticipate, infer, connect, question, and comprehend (Calkins 2000). In addition, being read to is risk free. In *Yellow Brick Roads: Shared and Guided Paths to Independent Reading 4-12* (2000), Allen says, "For students who struggle with word-by-word reading, experiencing the whole story can finally give them a sense of the wonder and magic of a book."

Reading aloud is appropriate in all grade levels and for all subjects. It is important not only when children can't read on their own but also even after they have become proficient readers (Anderson et al. 1985). Allen supports this view: "Given the body of research supporting the importance of read-aloud for modeling fluency, building background knowledge, and developing language acquisition, we should remind ourselves that those same benefits occur when we extend read-aloud beyond the early years. You may have to convince your students of the importance of this practice, but after several engaging read-alouds they will be sold on the idea" (2000). Just as students of all ages enjoy a good picture book, none of them is too old to enjoy read-aloud time.

Ten Tips for Reading Aloud

We have provided a list of tips to help you get the most from your read-aloud time. Using these suggestions can help set the stage for learning, improve comprehension of science material, and make the read-aloud experience richer and more meaningful for both you and your students.

1 Preview the Book

Select a book that meets your science objectives *and* lends itself to reading aloud. Preview it carefully before sharing it with the students. Are there any errors in scientific concepts or misinformation that could be inferred from the text or illustrations? If the book is not in story form, is there any nonessential information you could omit to make the read-aloud experience better? If you are not going to read the whole book, choose appropriate starting and stopping points before reading.

2 Set the Stage

Because reading aloud is a performance, you should pay attention to the atmosphere and physical setting of the session. Gather the students in a special reading area, such as on a carpet or in a semicircle of chairs. Seat yourself slightly above them. Do not sit in front of a bright window where the glare will keep students from seeing you well or in an area where students can be easily distracted. You may want to turn off the overhead lights and read by the light of a lamp or use soft music as a way to draw students into the mood of the text. Establish expectations for appropriate behavior during read-aloud time, and before reading, give the students an opportunity to settle down and focus their attention on the book.

3 Celebrate the Author and Illustrator

Always announce the title of the book, the author, and the illustrator before reading. Build connections by asking students if they have read other books by the author or illustrator. Increase interest by sharing facts about the author or illustrator from the book's dust jacket or from library or internet research. This could be done either before or after the reading. The following resources are useful for finding information on authors and illustrators:

Books

- Kovacs, D., and J. Preller. 1991. *Meet the authors and illustrators: Volume one.* New York: Scholastic.
- Kovacs, D., and J. Preller. 1993. *Meet the authors and illustrators: Volume two.* New York: Scholastic.
- Peacock, S. 2003. *Something about the author: Facts and pictures about authors and illustrators of books for young people.* Farmington Hills, MI: Gale Group.

- Preller, J. 2001. *The big book of picture-book authors and illustrators.* New York: Scholastic.

Websites

- *www.teachingbooks.net*—Teaching Books continually identifies, catalogs, and maintains reliable links to children's books' author and illustrator websites and organizes them into categories relevant to teachers' needs.
- *www.cbcbooks.org*—The Children's Book Council (CBC) is a nonprofit trade organization encouraging literacy and the use and enjoyment of children's books. Its website has a feature titled "About Authors and Illustrators" with links to author and illustrator websites.

4 Read with Expression

Practice reading aloud to improve your performance. Try listening to yourself read on a tape recorder. Can you read with more expression to more fully engage your audience? Try louder or softer speech, funny voices, facial expressions, or gestures. Make eye contact with your students every now and then as you read. This strengthens the bond between reader and listener, helps you gauge your audience's response, and cuts down on off-task behaviors. Read slowly enough that your students have time to build mental images of what you are reading, but not so slowly that they lose interest. When reading a nonfiction book aloud, you may want to pause after reading about a key concept to let it sink in, then reread that part. At suspenseful parts in a storybook, use dramatic pauses or slow down and read softly. This can move the audience members to the edge of their seats!

5 Share the Pictures

Don't forget the power of visual images to help students connect with and comprehend what you are reading. Make sure you hold the book in such a way that students can see the pictures on each page. Read captions if appropriate. In some cases, you may want to hide certain pictures so students can infer from the reading before you reveal the illustrator's interpretation of the text.

6 Encourage Interaction

Keep chart paper and markers nearby in case you want to record questions or new information. Try providing students with "think pads" in the form of sticky notes to write on as you read aloud. Not only does this help extremely active children keep their hands busy while listening, but it also encourages students to interact with the text as they jot down questions or comments. After the read aloud, have students share their questions and comments. You may want students to place their sticky notes on a class chart whose subject is the topic being studied. Another way to encourage interaction without taking the time for each student to ask questions or comment is to do an occasional "Turn and Talk" during the read aloud. Stop reading, ask a question, allow thinking time, and have each student share answers or comments with a partner.

7 Keep the Flow

Although you want to encourage interaction during a read aloud, avoid excessive interruptions that may disrupt fluent, expressive reading. Aim for a balance between allowing students to hear the language of the book uninterrupted and providing them with opportunities to make comments, ask questions, and share connections to the reading. As we have suggested, you may want to read the book all the way through one time so students can enjoy the aesthetic components of the story. Then go back and read the book for the purpose of meeting the science objectives.

8 Model Reading Strategies

Use read-aloud time as an opportunity to model questioning, making connections, visualizing, inferring, determining importance, and synthesizing. Modeling these reading comprehension strategies when appropriate before, during, and/or after reading helps students internalize the strategies and begin to use them in their own reading. These six key strategies are described in detail later in this chapter.

9 Don't Put It Away

Keep the read-aloud book accessible to students after you read it. They will want to get a close-up look at the pictures and will enjoy reading the book independently. Don't be afraid of reading the same book more than once. Younger children especially benefit from the repetition.

10 Have Fun

Let your passion for books show. It is contagious! Read nonfiction books with interest and wonder. Share your thoughts and questions about the topic and your own connections to the text. When reading a story, let your emotions show—laugh at the funny parts and cry at the sad parts. Seeing an authentic response from the reader is important for students. If you read with enthusiasm, read-aloud time will become special and enjoyable for everyone involved.

Reading Comprehension Strategies

A common misconception about reading is that students are fully capable of reading to learn in the content areas by the time they reach the upper elementary grades. But becoming a proficient reader is an ongoing, complex process, and people of all ages must develop strategies to improve their reading skills. In *Strategies That Work,* Harvey and Goudvis (2000) identify six key reading strategies that are essential for achieving full understanding when we read. These strategies are used where appropriate in each lesson and are seamlessly embedded into the 5E Model. The strategies should be modeled as you read aloud to students from both fiction and nonfiction texts. Research shows that explicit teaching of reading comprehension strategies can foster comprehension development (Duke and Pearson 2002). Explicit teaching of the strategies is the initial step in the gradual-release-of-responsibility approach to delivering reading instruction (Fielding and Pearson 1994). During this first phase of the gradual-release method, the teacher *explains* the strategy, demonstrates *how* and *when* to use the strategy, explains *why* it is worth using, and *thinks aloud* to model the mental processes used by good readers. Duke (2004) describes this process: "I often discuss the strategies in terms of good readers, as in 'Good readers think about what might be coming next.' I also model the uses of comprehension strategies by thinking aloud as I read. For example, to model the importance of monitoring understanding, I make comments such as, 'That doesn't make sense to me because ...' or 'I didn't understand that last part—I'd better go back.'" Using the teacher modeling phase within a science learning cycle reinforces what students do during reading instruction, when the gradual-release-of-responsibility model can be continued. After teacher modeling, students should be given opportunities in the reading classroom for both guided and independent practice until they are ready to apply the strategy in their own reading.

Descriptions of the six key reading comprehension strategies featured in *Strategies That Work* (Harvey and Goudvis 2000) follow. The icon highlights these strategies here and within the lessons.

Making Connections

Making meaningful connections during reading can improve comprehension and engagement by helping learners better relate to what they read. Comprehension breakdown that occurs when reading or listening to expository text can come from a lack of prior information. These three techniques can help readers build background knowledge where little exists:

- *Text-to-Self* connections occur when readers link the text to their past experiences or background knowledge.
- *Text-to-Text* connections occur when readers recognize connections from one book to another.
- *Text-to-World* connections occur when readers connect the text to events or issues in the real world.

Questioning

Proficient readers ask themselves questions before, during, and after reading. Questioning allows readers to construct meaning, find answers, solve problems, and eliminate confusion as they read. It motivates readers to move forward in the text. Asking questions is not only a critical reading skill, but it is also at the heart of scientific inquiry and can lead students into meaningful investigations. To help you model the questioning strategy, we suggest writing your questions on sticky notes before the read aloud and placing them on the appropriate pages of the book.

Visualizing

Visualizing is the creation of mental images while reading or listening to text. Mental images are created from the learner's emotions and senses, making the text more concrete and memorable. Imagining the sensory qualities of things described in a text can help engage learners and stimulate their interest in the reading. When readers form pictures in their minds, they are also more likely to stick with a challenging text. During a reading, you can stop and ask students to visualize the scene. What sights, sounds, smells, and colors are they imagining?

Inferring

Reading between the lines, or inferring, involves learners merging clues from the reading with prior knowledge to draw conclusions and interpret the text. Good readers make inferences before, during, and after reading. Inferential thinking is also an important science skill and can be reinforced during reading instruction.

Determining Importance

Reading to learn requires readers to identify essential information by distinguishing it from nonessential details. Deciding what is important in the text depends on the purpose for reading. In *Picture-Perfect Science Lessons*, the lesson's science objectives determine importance. Learners read or listen to the text to find answers to specific questions, to gain understanding of science concepts, and to identify science misconceptions.

Synthesizing

In synthesizing, readers combine information gained through reading with prior knowledge and experience to form new ideas. To synthesize, readers must stop, think about what they have read, and contemplate its meaning before continuing on through the text. The highest level of synthesis involves those "Aha!" moments when readers gain new insights and, as a result, change their thinking.

Tools to Enhance Comprehension

We have identified several activities and organizers that can enhance students' science understanding and reading comprehension in the lessons. These tools, which support the Harvey and Goudvis reading comprehension strategies, are briefly described on the following pages and in more detail within the lessons.

Anticipation Guides

Anticipation guides (Herber 1978) are sets of questions that serve as a pre- or post-reading activity for a text. They can be used to activate and assess prior knowledge, determine misconceptions, focus thinking on the reading, and motivate reluctant readers by stimulating interest in the topic. An anticipation guide should revolve around four to six key concepts from the reading that learners respond to before reading. They are motivated to read or listen carefully to find the evidence that supports their predictions. After reading, learners revisit their anticipation guide to check their responses. In a revised extended anticipation guide (Duffelmeyer and Baum 1992), learners are required to justify their responses and explain why their choices were correct or incorrect.

Chunking

Chunking is dividing the text into manageable sections and reading only one section at any one time. This gives learners time to digest the information in a section before moving on. Chunking is also a useful technique for weeding out essential from nonessential information when reading nonfiction books. Reading only those parts of the text that meet your learning objectives focuses the learning on what is important.

Cloze Paragraph

Cloze is an activity to help readers infer the meanings of unfamiliar words. In the cloze strategy, key words are deleted in a passage. Students then fill in the blanks with words that make sense and sound right. (See Chapter 22 for an example of a cloze paragraph.)

Visual Representations

Organizers such as T-charts; I Wonder/I Learned charts; O-W-L charts ("**O**bservations, **W**onderings, **L**earnings"); the Frayer Model (Frayer, Frederick, and Klausmeier 1969); semantic maps (Billmeyer and Barton 1998); and personal vocabulary lists (Beers and Howell 2004) can help learners activate prior knowledge, organize their thinking, understand the essential characteristics of concepts, or see relationships among concepts. They can be used for pre-reading, assessment, or summarizing or reviewing material. Visual representations are effective because they help learners perceive abstract ideas in a more concrete form. Examples of these visual representations, with instructions for using them within the lesson, can be found throughout the book. (See Chapters 6, 8, and 14 for examples of T-charts. See Chapter 9 for an example of an I Wonder/I Learned chart. See Chapters 6 and 16 for examples of the Frayer Model. See Chapters 7, 10, and 11 for examples of O-W-L charts. See Chapter 8 for an example of a semantic map. See Chapter 19 for a variation of a personal vocabulary list.)

Pairs Read

Pairs read (Billmeyer and Barton 1998) requires the learners to work cooperatively as they read and make sense of a text. While one learner reads aloud, the other listens and then makes comments ("I think ..."), asks questions ("I wonder ..."), or shares new learnings ("I didn't know ..."). Encourage students to ask their partners to reread if clarification is needed.

Benefits of pairs read include increased reader involvement, attention, and collaboration. In addition, students become more independent and less reliant on the teacher.

Rereading

Nonfiction text is often full of unfamiliar ideas and difficult vocabulary. Rereading content for clarification is an essential skill of proficient readers, and you should model this frequently. Rereading content for a different purpose can aid comprehension. For example, you might read aloud a text for enjoyment and then revisit the text to focus on specific science content.

Sketch to Stretch

During sketch to stretch (Seigel 1984), learners pause to reflect on the text and do a comprehension self-assessment by drawing on paper the images they visualize in their heads during reading. They might illustrate an important event from the text, sketch the characters in a story, or make a labeled diagram. Have students use pencils so they understand that the focus should be on collecting their thoughts rather than creating a piece of art. You may want to use a timer so students understand that sketch to stretch is a brief pause to reflect quickly on the reading. Students can share and explain their drawings in small groups after sketching.

Stop and Jot

Learners stop and think about the reading and then jot down a thought. They may write about something they've just learned, something they are wondering about, or what they expect to learn next. If they use sticky notes for this, the notes can be added to a whole-class chart to connect past and future learning.

Turn and Talk

Learners each pair up with a partner to share their ideas, explain concepts in their own words, or tell about a connection they have to the book. This method allows each child to respond so that everyone in the group is involved as either a talker or a listener. Saying "Take a few minutes to share your thoughts with someone" gives students an opportunity to satisfy their needs to express their own thoughts about the reading.

Word Sorts

Word sorts (Gillett and Temple 1983) help learners understand the relationships among key concepts and help teach classification. They can also reveal misconceptions if you use them as a pre-reading activity. Ask learners to sort vocabulary terms, written on cards, into different categories. In an *open sort,* learners sort the words into categories of their own making. They can classify and reclassify to help refine their understanding of concepts. In a *closed sort,* you give them the categories for sorting. Learners can also use the vocabulary words to build sentences about specific concepts before and after reading. (See Chapters 10 and 11 for examples of word sorts.)

Using Features of Nonfiction

Many nonfiction books include a table of contents, index, glossary, bold-print words, picture captions, diagrams, and charts that provide valuable information. Because children are generally more used to narrative text, they often skip over these text structures. It is important to model how to interpret the information these features provide the reader. To begin, show the cover of a nonfiction book and read the title and table of contents. Ask students to predict what they'll find in the book. Show students how to use the index in the back of the book to find specific information. Point out other nonfiction text structures as you read and note that these features are unique to nonfiction. Model how nonfiction books can be entered at any point in the text, because they generally don't follow a storyline.

Why Do Picture Books Enhance Comprehension?

Students should be encouraged to read a wide range of print materials, but picture books offer many advantages when teaching reading comprehension strategies. Harvey and Goudvis (2000) not only believe that interest is essential to comprehension, but also maintain that because picture books are extremely effective for building background knowledge and teaching content, instruction in reading comprehension strategies during picture book read alouds allows students to better access that content. In summary, picture books are invaluable for teaching reading comprehension strategies because they are extraordinarily effective at keeping readers engaged and thinking.

References

Allen, J. 2000. *Yellow brick roads: Shared and guided paths to independent reading 4-12.* Portland, ME: Stenhouse Publishers.

Anderson, R. C., E. H. Heibert, J. Scott, and I. A. G. Wilkinson. 1985. *Becoming a nation of readers: The report of the commission on reading.* Champaign, IL: Center for the Study of Reading; Washington, DC: National Institute of Education.

Beers, S., and L. Howell. 2004. *Reading strategies for the content areas: An action tool kit, volume 2.* Alexandria, VA: Association for Supervision and Curriculum Development.

Billmeyer, R., and M. L. Barton. 1998. *Teaching reading in the content areas: If not me, then who?* Aurora, CO: Mid-continent Regional Educational Leadership Laboratory.

Calkins, L. M. 2000. *The art of teaching reading.* Boston: Pearson Allyn & Bacon.

Duffelmeyer, F. A., and D. D. Baum. 1992. The extended anticipation guide revisited. *Journal of Reading* 35: 654–656.

Duke, N. K. 2004. The case for informational text. *Educational Leadership* 61: 40–44.

Duke, N. K., and P. D. Pearson. 2002. Effective practices for developing reading comprehension. In *What research has to say about reading instruction,* ed. A. E. Farstrup and S. J. Samuels, 205–242. Newark, DE: International Reading Association.

Fielding, L., and P. D. Pearson. 1994. Reading comprehension: What works? *Educational Leadership* 51 (5): 62–67.

Frayer, D. A., W. E. Frederick, and H. J. Klausmeier. 1969. *A schema for testing the level of concept mastery.* Madison, WI: University of Wisconsin Research and Development Center for Cognitive Learning.

Gillett, J. W., and C. Temple. 1983. *Understanding reading problems: Assessment and instruction.* Boston: Little, Brown.

Harvey, S., and A. Goudvis. 2000. *Strategies that work: Teaching comprehension to enhance understanding.* York, ME: Stenhouse Publishers.

Herber, H. 1978. *Teaching reading in the content areas.* Englewood Cliffs, NJ: Prentice Hall.

Seigel, M. 1984. Sketch to stretch. In *Reading, writing, and caring,* ed. O. Cochran, 178. New York: Richard C. Owen.

Teaching Science Through Inquiry

The word *inquiry* brings many different ideas to mind. For some teachers, it may evoke fears of giving up control in the classroom or spending countless hours preparing lessons. For others, it may imply losing the focus of instructional objectives while students pursue answers to their own questions. And for many, teaching science through inquiry is perceived as intriguing but unrealistic. But inquiry doesn't have to cause anxiety for teachers. Simply stated, inquiry is an approach to learning that involves exploring the world and that leads to asking questions, testing ideas, and making discoveries in the search for understanding. There are many degrees of inquiry, and it may be helpful to start with a variation that emphasizes a teacher-directed approach and then gradually builds to a more student-directed approach. As a basic guide, the National Research Council (2000) identifies five essential features for classroom inquiry, shown in Figure 3.1.

Figure 3.1. Five Essential Features of Classroom Inquiry

1. Learners are engaged by scientifically oriented **questions**.
2. Learners give priority to **evidence**, which allows them to develop and evaluate explanations that address scientifically oriented questions.
3. Learners formulate **explanations** from evidence to address scientifically oriented questions.
4. Learners **evaluate** their explanations in light of alternative explanations, particularly those reflecting scientific understanding.
5. Learners **communicate** and justify their proposed explanations.

From *Inquiry and the National Science Education Standards: A Guide for Teaching and Learning* (NRC 2000).

Essential Features of Classroom Inquiry

The following descriptions illustrate each of the five essential features of classroom inquiry using Chapter 11, "Close Encounters of the Symbiotic Kind." Any classroom activity that includes all five of these features is considered to be inquiry.

1. *Learners are engaged by scientifically oriented questions.* In "Close Encounters of the Symbiotic Kind," students are given "mystery objects" (plant galls) that engage them in the initial question, "What are these objects?" In this case, the mystery objects pique students' curiosity, stimulating additional questions.
2. *Learners give priority to evidence, which allows them to develop and evaluate explanations that address scientifically oriented questions.* Students use measuring tools and hand lenses to make quantitative and qualitative observations about the mystery objects and use the observations as evidence to develop answers to questions.
3. *Learners formulate explanations from evidence to address scientifically oriented questions.* Students develop explanations about the mystery objects based on their observations.
4. *Learners evaluate their explanations in light of alternative explanations, particularly those reflecting scientific understanding.* After using a dichotomous key to identify their objects and reading an article about plant galls, students evaluate, and possibly eliminate or revise, their explanations.
5. *Learners communicate and justify their proposed explanations.* Students show their mystery objects to the rest of the class, share their explanations, and justify the explanations with evidence. This provides other students the opportunity to ask questions, examine the evidence, identify faulty reasoning, and suggest alternative explanations.

Benefits of Inquiry

Developing an inquiry-based science program is a central tenet of the *National Science Education Standards* (NRC 1996). So what makes inquiry-based teaching such a valuable method of instruction? Many studies state that it is equal or superior to other instructional modes and results in higher scores on content achievement tests. *Inquiry and the National Science Education Standards* (NRC 2000) summarizes the findings of *How People Learn* (Bransford, Brown, and Cocking 1999), which support the use of inquiry-based teaching. Those findings include the following points:

- Understanding science is more than knowing facts. Most important is that students understand the major concepts. Inquiry-based teaching focuses on the major concepts, helps students build a strong base of factual information to support the concepts, and gives them opportunities to apply their knowledge effectively.
- Students build new knowledge and understanding on what they already know and believe. Students often hold preconceptions that are either reasonable in only a limited context or scientifically incorrect. These preconceptions can be resistant to change, particularly when teachers use conventional teaching strategies (Wandersee, Mintzes, and Novak 1994). Inquiry-based teaching uncovers students' prior knowledge and, through concrete explorations, helps them correct misconceptions.
- Students formulate new knowledge by modifying and refining their current concepts and by adding new concepts to what they already know. In an inquiry-based model, students give priority to evidence when they prove or disprove their pre-

conceptions. Their preconceptions are challenged by their observations or the explanations of other students.

- Learning is mediated by the social environment in which learners interact with others. Inquiry provides students with opportunities to interact with others. They explain their ideas to other students and listen critically to the ideas of their classmates. These social interactions require that students clarify their ideas and consider alternative explanations.
- Effective learning requires that students take control of their own learning. When teachers use inquiry, students assume much of the responsibility for their own learning. Students formulate questions, design procedures, develop explanations, and devise ways to share their findings. This makes learning unique and more valuable to each student.
- The ability to apply knowledge to novel situations, that is, transfer of learning, is affected by the degree to which students learn with understanding. Inquiry provides students a variety of opportunities to practice what they have learned and connect to what they already know, and therefore moves them toward application, a sophisticated level of thinking that requires them to solve problems in new situations.

Inquiry learning not only contributes to better understanding of scientific concepts and skills but, because science inquiry in school is carried out in a social context, also contributes to children's social and intellectual development (Dyasi 1999). Within an inquiry-based lesson, students work collaboratively to brainstorm questions, design procedures for testing their predictions, carry out investigations, and ask thoughtful questions about other students' conclusions. This mirrors the social context in which "real science" takes place.

What Makes a Good Question?

Questioning lies at the heart of inquiry and is a habit of mind that should be encouraged in any learning setting. According to *Inquiry and the National Science Education Standards* (NRC 2000), "Fruitful inquiries evolve from questions that are meaningful and relevant to students, but they also must be able to be answered by students' observations and scientific knowledge they obtain from reliable sources." One of the most important skills students can develop in science is understanding which questions can be answered by investigation and which cannot. The teacher plays a critical role in guiding the kinds of questions the students pose. Students often ask *why* questions, which cannot be addressed by scientific investigations. For example, "Why does gravity make things fall toward Earth?" is a question that would be impossible to answer in the school setting.

Testable questions, on the other hand, generally begin with *how can, does, what if,* or *which* and can be investigated using controlled procedures. For example, encouraging students to ask questions such as "How can you slow the fall of an object?" "Which object falls faster, a marble or a basketball?" or "What materials work best for constructing a toy parachute?" guides them toward investigations that can be done in the classroom.

Helping students select developmentally appropriate questions is also important. For example, "What will the surface of the Moon look like in a hundred years?" is a question that is scientific but much too complex for elementary students to investigate. A more developmentally appropriate question might be "How does the size of a meteorite affect the size of the crater it makes?" This question can be tested by dropping different-size marbles into a pan of sand, simulating how meteors hit the Moon's surface. It is essential to help students formulate age-appropriate and testable questions to ensure that their investigations are both engaging and productive.

Variations Within Classroom Inquiry

Inquiry-based teaching can vary widely in the amount of guidance and structure you choose to provide. Table 3.1 describes these variations for each of the five essential features of inquiry.

The most open form of inquiry takes place in the variations on the right-hand column of the Inquiry Continuum. Most often, students do not have the abilities to begin at that point. For example, students must first learn what makes a question scientifically oriented and testable before they can begin posing such questions themselves. The extent to which you structure what students do determines whether the inquiry is *guided* or *open* inquiry. The more responsibility you take, the more guided the inquiry. The more responsibility the students have, the more open the inquiry. Guided inquiry experiences, such as those on the left-hand side of the Inquiry Continuum, can be effective in focusing learning on the development of particular science concepts. Students, however, must have open inquiry experiences, such as those in the right column of the Inquiry Continuum, to develop the fundamental abilities necessary to do scientific inquiry.

One common misconception about inquiry is that all science subject matter should be taught through inquiry. It is neither possible nor practical to teach all science subject matter through inquiry (NRC 2000). For example, you would not want to teach lab safety through inquiry. Good science teaching requires a variety of approaches and models. *Picture-Perfect Science Lessons* combines a guided inquiry investigation with an open inquiry investigation. Dunkhase (2000) refers to this approach as "coupled inquiry." In *Picture-Perfect Science Lessons,* the guided inquiries are the lessons presented in each chapter. The lessons generally fall on the left-hand (teacher-guided) side of the Inquiry Continuum. The Inquiry Place suggestion box (discussed in depth later in this chapter) at the end of each lesson produces experiences falling more toward the right-hand, or student self-directed, side of the Inquiry Continuum.

Checkpoint Labs in Guided Inquiry

One way to manage a guided inquiry is to use a "checkpoint lab." This type of lab is divided into sections, with a small box located at the end of each section for a teacher check mark or stamp. Six lessons in this book contain checkpoint labs to guide teams of students through an inquiry (Chapters 9, 13, 14, 19, 20, and 22). In a checkpoint lab, each team works at its own pace. A red cup and a green cup taped together at the bottoms are used to signal the teacher. When teams are working, they keep the green cup on top. When teams have a question or when they reach a checkpoint, they signal the teacher by flipping their cups so that red is on top.

Tips for Managing a Checkpoint Lab

- Give students task cards (like those provided in "Sheep in a Jeep," Chapter 14) to assign each student a job.
- Tell students that every member of the team is responsible for recording data and writing responses. All team members must be at the same checkpoint in order to get the stamp or check mark and continue on to the next section.
- Explain how to use the red-green cup. Tell students that when the green cup is on top, it is a signal to you that the team is

Table 3.1. Inquiry Continuum

Teacher Guided* ◄——► *Learner Self-Directed

ESSENTIAL FEATURE	VARIATIONS			
1. Learners are engaged in scientifically oriented questions.	Learner engages in question provided by teacher or materials.	Learner sharpens or clarifies the question provided.	Learner selects among questions, poses new questions.	Learner poses a question.
2. Learners give priority to evidence, which allows them to develop and evaluate explanations that address scientifically oriented questions.	Learner is given data and told how to analyze.	Learner is given data and asked how to analyze.	Learner is directed to collect certain data.	Learner determines what constitutes evidence and collects it.
3. Learners formulate explanations from evidence to address scientifically oriented questions.	Learner is provided with explanations.	Learner is given possible ways to use evidence to formulate explanations.	Learner is guided in process of formulating explanations from evidence.	Learner formulates explanation after summarizing evidence.
4. Learners evaluate their explanations in light of alternative explanations, particularly those reflecting scientific understanding.	Learner is told connections.	Learner is given possible connections.	Learner is directed toward areas and sources of scientific knowledge.	Learner independently examines other resources and forms the links to explanations.
5. Learners communicate and justify their proposed explanations.	Learner is given steps and procedures for communication.	Learner is provided broad guidelines to sharpen communication.	Learner is coached in development of communication.	Learner communicates and justifies explanations.

Teacher Guided* ◄——► *Learner Self-Directed

Adapted from *Inquiry and the National Science Education Standards: A Guide for Teaching and Learning* (NRC 2000).

SIGNALING THE TEACHER WITH A RED-GREEN CUP

progressing with no problems or questions. When the red cup is on top, it is a signal that the team needs you.

- Explain that there are only two situations in which students should flip the red cup on top:
  - Everyone on the team is at a checkpoint, or
  - The team has a question.
- Tell students that before they flip the cup to red for a question, they must first ask everyone else on the team the question ("Ask three, then me"). Most of the time, the team will be able to answer the question without asking you.
- When a team reaches a checkpoint and signals you, make sure every member of the team has completed all of the work in that section. Then ask each member a probing question about that part of the lab. Asking each student a question holds each one accountable and allows you to informally assess each student's learning. Examples of probing questions are
  - ? How do you know?
  - ? What does this remind you of?
  - ? What do you think will happen next?

Inquiry Place

As we mentioned earlier, a box called Inquiry Place is provided at the end of each lesson to help you move your students toward more open inquiries. The Inquiry Place lists questions related to the lesson that students may select to investigate. Students may also use them as sample questions for writing their own scientifically oriented and testable questions. After selecting one of the questions in the box or formulating their own questions, students can make predictions, design investigations to test their predictions, collect evidence, devise explanations, examine related resources, and communicate their findings.

The Inquiry Place boxes suggest that students share the results of their investigations with one another through a poster session. Scientists, engineers, and researchers routinely hold poster sessions to communicate their findings. Here are some suggestions for poster sessions:

- Posters should include a title, the researchers' names, a brief description of the investigation, and a summary of the main findings.
- Observations, data tables, and/or graphs should be included as evidence to justify conclusions.
- The print should be large enough that people can read it from a distance.
- Students should have the opportunity to present their posters to the class.
- The audience in a poster session should examine the evidence, ask thoughtful questions, identify faulty reasoning, and suggest alternative explanations to presenters in a polite, respectful manner.

Not only do poster sessions mirror the work of real scientists, but they also provide you with excellent opportunities for authentic assessment.

Implementing the guided inquiries in this book along with the Inquiry Place suggestions at the end of each lesson provides a framework for moving from teacher-guided to learner-self-directed inquiry. The Inquiry Place Think Sheet on page 25 (Figure 3.2) can help students organize their own inquiries.

An example of how the Inquiry Place can be used to give students the opportunity to engage in an open inquiry follows. This particular example is from "The Changing Moon," Chapter 17. In that lesson, students learn about the Moon's phases by observing them for a month, modeling the phases with a foam ball and lamp, and reading about the Moon. This is how one teacher chose to use the Inquiry Place following a guided inquiry lesson:

After "The Changing Moon" lesson, Mrs. Bell begins a discussion about the Moon's surface. She and her students talk about the craters on the Moon and the fact that they are caused by meteorites.

Mrs. Bell: *There are so many different-size craters on the Moon. I wonder, does the speed of the meteorite affect the size of the crater it makes? I have some supplies we can use as a model: a pan of sand to represent the surface of the Moon and marbles to represent the meteorites. How can we use these supplies to find the answer to the question?*

Mrs. Bell writes the question on the board: "Does the speed of a meteorite affect the size of the crater it makes?"

Pedro: *We can drop the marbles in the pan at different speeds and measure the craters.*

Mrs. Bell: *How can we get the marbles to hit at different speeds?*

Hannah: *We can drop one from high and one from low and measure the craters.*

Mrs. Bell: *Is there a way we can measure the height of the drop?*

Rudy: *We can use a meterstick. We'll drop one from 50 centimeters and the other from 1 meter.*

Mrs. Bell: *Good. Is there a way we can collect even more data than just two drops?*

Julia: *We can drop it from 25 centimeters, 50 centimeters, 75 centimeters, and 100 centimeters.*

Mrs. Bell: *How can we record our data?*

Eva: *We can make a table with the height on one side and the size of the crater on the other side.*

Mrs. Bell: *Great idea! Let's make a data table on the board. Now, what do we need to keep the same to make this a fair experiment? (Silence.)*

Mrs. Bell: *For example, should we use four different-size marbles?*

Jeff: *No, we should use the same marble each time to keep it fair.*

Mrs. Bell: *Good. Is there anything else we need to do to keep it fair?*

Mikayla: *We should use the same pan of sand each time.*

Mrs. Bell: *Yes! I think we are ready to begin the experiment. Let's make some predictions first.*

Mrs. Bell and her class make predictions and then perform the experiment together and record their data on the board. They use their data as evidence to answer the question and reach the conclusion that faster-moving meteorites make larger craters than slower-moving meteorites.

Mrs. Bell: *Now that we have answered my question, I wonder if you have any questions about meteorites and craters that we could investigate using the pan and marble model.*

Mrs. Bell passes out the Inquiry Place Think Sheet to each student. She instructs them to answer number 1: "My questions about moon craters." After providing students time to write down some questions, Mrs. Bell asks them to share some of their questions.

Rudy: *Where do meteorites come from?*

Mrs. Bell: *That's a good question, Rudy. Can we use this model to find the answer?*

Rudy: *No.*

Mrs. Bell: *How could we find the answer to that question?*

Rudy: *Maybe at the library or on the computer.*

Mrs. Bell: *Yes. Maybe we can look for that answer next time we are in the library. Let's try to think of questions that we can answer using the sand and marble model.*

Yushi: *We could find out if bigger meteorites make bigger craters.*

Marcus: *Do square meteorites make square craters?*

Hannah: *Do heavier meteorites make bigger craters?*

Julia: *Does it matter what kind of moon dirt it hits?*

Mrs. Bell rephrases the questions and writes them on the board.

- Does the size of a meteorite affect the size of the crater?
- Does the shape of a meteorite affect the shape of the crater?
- Does the mass of the meteorite affect the size of the crater?
- Does the type of surface the meteorite lands on affect the size of the crater?

Mrs. Bell: *Excellent! These four questions can be answered by investigating with the marble and pan model. Choose one of the questions that you would like to investigate and write it down for number 2.*

Mrs. Bell provides time for students to think about which question they want to investigate and to write it down. She then forms teams of students who have chosen the same question.

Mrs. Bell: *Now that you have formed your teams, complete the rest of the Inquiry Place Think Sheet together. When your experiment is planned and you are ready for the teacher checkpoint, signal by placing the green cup on top.*

Mrs. Bell circulates to ask questions and check progress as teams complete the Inquiry Place Think Sheet. Students finish planning the investigations and look forward to completing them the next day. They will share their findings during a poster session later in the week.

Figure 3.2. Inquiry Place Think Sheet

Name: ____________________

Inquiry Place Think Sheet

1 My questions about:

____

____

2 My testable question:

____

3 My prediction:

____

4 Steps I will follow to investigate my question:

____

____

____

____

____

5 Materials I will need:

____

6 How I will share my findings:

____

____

____

Checkpoint ☐

Performing the investigation designed on the Inquiry Place Think Sheet

References

Bransford, J. D., A. L. Brown, and R. Cocking, eds. 1999. *How people learn: Brain, mind, experience, and school.* Washington, DC: National Academies Press.

Dunkhase, J. 2000. Coupled inquiry: An effective strategy for student investigations. Paper presented at the Iowa Science Teachers Section Conference, Des Moines, IA.

Dyasi, H. 1999. What children gain by learning through inquiry. In *Foundations Volume II: Inquiry–thoughts, views, and strategies for the K-5 classroom,* 9–13. Arlington, VA: Division of Elementary, Secondary, and Informal Education in conjunction with the Division of Research, Evaluation, and Communication, National Science Foundation.

National Research Council (NRC). 1996. *National science education standards.* Washington, DC: National Academies Press.

National Research Council (NRC). 2000. *Inquiry and the national science education standards: A guide for teaching and learning.* Washington, DC: National Academies Press.

Wandersee, J. H., J. J. Mintzes, and J. D. Novak. 1994. Research on alternative conceptions in science. In *Handbook of research on science teaching and learning,* ed. D. L. Gable, 177–210. New York: Macmillan.

BSCS 5E Instructional Model

The guided inquiries in this book are designed using the BSCS 5E Instructional Model, commonly referred to as the 5E Model (or the 5Es). Developed by the Biological Sciences Curriculum Study (BSCS), the 5E Model is a learning cycle based on a constructivist view of learning. Constructivism embraces the idea that learners bring with them preconceived ideas about how the world works. According to the constructivist view, "learners test new ideas against that which they already believe to be true. If the new ideas seem to fit in with their pictures of the world, they have little difficulty learning the ideas ... if the new ideas don't seem to fit the learners' picture of reality then they won't seem to make sense. Learners may dismiss them ... or eventually accommodate the new ideas and change the way they understand the world" (Colburn 2003). The objective of a constructivist model, therefore, is to provide students with experiences that make them reconsider their conceptions. Then students "redefine, reorganize, elaborate, and change their initial concepts through self-reflection and interaction with their peers and their environment" (Bybee 1997). The 5E Model provides a planned sequence of instruction that places students at the center of their learning experiences, encouraging them to explore, construct their own understanding of scientific concepts, and relate those understandings to other concepts. An explanation of each phase of the BSCS 5E Model—Engage, Explore, Explain, Elaborate, and Evaluate—follows.

Engage

The purpose of this introductory stage, *engage*, is to capture students' interest. Here you can uncover what students know and think about a topic as well as determine their misconceptions. Engagement activities might include a reading, demonstration, or other activity that piques students' curiosity.

ENGAGE: MRS. RADER GAVE EACH OF HER STUDENTS A BOWL OF POPCORN TO EAT WHILE SHE WROTE WHAT THEY KNOW AND WHAT THEY ARE WONDERING ABOUT POPCORN ("WHAT'S POPPIN'?" CHAPTER 9).

explore

In the *explore* stage, you provide students with cooperative exploration activities, giving them common, concrete experiences that help them begin constructing concepts and developing skills. Students can build models, collect data, make and test predictions, or form new predictions. The purpose is to provide hands-on experiences you can use later to formally introduce a concept, process, or skill.

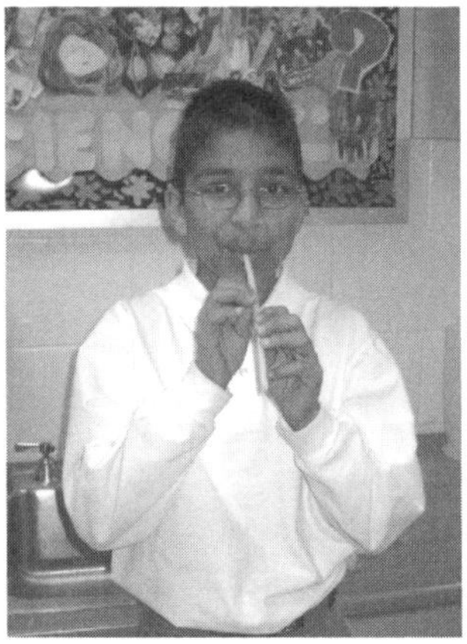

EXPLORE: BEFORE FORMALLY INTRODUCING THE TERM *PITCH*, MISS SCHULTZ HAD HER STUDENTS TEST THEIR IDEAS AFTER BRAINSTORMING WAYS TO MAKE THEIR STRAW INSTRUMENTS PRODUCE HIGH AND LOW SOUNDS ("SOUNDS OF SCIENCE," CHAPTER 15).

explain

In the *explain* stage, learners articulate their ideas in their own words and listen critically to one another. You clarify their concepts, correct misconceptions, and introduce scientific terminology. It is important that you clearly connect the students' explanations to experiences they had in the engage and explore phases.

EXPLAIN: STUDENTS IN MR. MICHALAK'S CLASS ARE JUSTIFYING HOW THEY SORTED THEIR CARDS IN THE CLOSE ENCOUNTER WORD SORT ("CLOSE ENCOUNTERS OF THE SYMBIOTIC KIND," CHAPTER 11).

elaborate

At the *elaborate* point in the model, some students may still have misconceptions, or they may understand the concepts only in the context of the previous exploration. Elaboration activities can help students correct their remaining misconceptions and generalize the concepts in a broader context. These activities also challenge students to apply, extend, or elaborate on concepts and skills in a new situation, resulting in deeper understanding.

ELABORATE: A STUDENT IN MRS. HUDSPETH'S CLASS ELABORATES ON WHAT HE HAS LEARNED ABOUT MOTION BY DESIGNING A PARACHUTE FOR A TOY ANIMAL ("SHEEP IN A JEEP," CHAPTER 14).

EVALUATE: A STUDENT IN MRS. MANN'S CLASS HAS DESIGNED AN EXPERIMENT TO TEST THE EFFECTIVENESS OF AN INVENTION. MRS. MANN WILL EVALUATE THE STUDENT'S SKILLS IN DESIGNING AND CARRYING OUT AN EXPERIMENT ("BRAINSTORMS," CHAPTER 20).

evaluate

At the *evaluate* phase, you evaluate students' understanding of concepts and their proficiency with various skills. You can use a variety of formal and informal procedures to assess conceptual understanding and progress toward learning outcomes. The evaluation phase also provides an opportunity for students to test their own understanding and skills.

Although the fifth phase is devoted to evaluation, a skillful teacher evaluates throughout the 5E model, continually checking to see if students need more time or instruction to learn the key points in a lesson. Ways to do this include informal questioning, teacher checkpoints, and class discussions. Each lesson in *Picture-Perfect Science Lessons* also includes a formal evaluation such as a written quiz or poster session. These formal evaluations take place at the end of the lesson.

Cycle of Learning

The 5Es are listed above in linear order—engage, explore, explain, elaborate, and evaluate—but the model is most effective when you use it as a cycle of learning as in Figure 4.1.

Figure 4.1. The BSCS 5Es as a Cycle of Learning

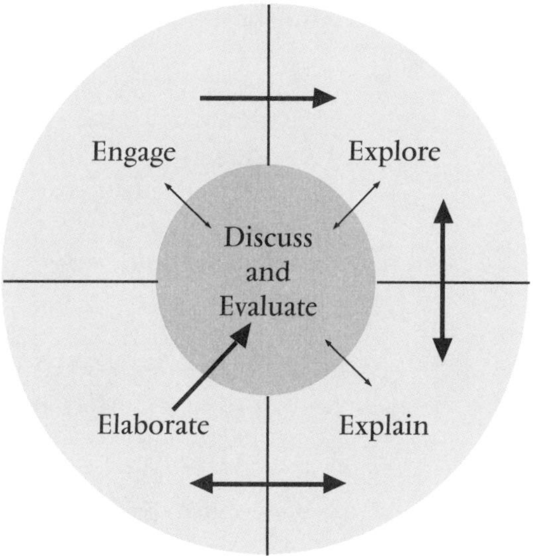

Adapted from Barman, C. R. 1997. *The learning cycle revised: A modification of an effective teaching model.* Arlington, VA: Council for Elementary Science International.

Table 4.1. The BSCS 5Es Teacher

What the Teacher Does		
	CONSISTENT **with the BSCS 5E Model**	***INCONSISTENT*** **with the BSCS 5E Model**
engage	• Generates interest and curiosity • Raises questions • Assesses current knowledge, including misconceptions	• Explains concepts • Provides definitions and conclusions • Lectures
explore	• Provides time for students to work together • Observes and listens to students as they interact • Asks probing questions to redirect students' investigations when necessary	• Explains how to work through the problem or provides answers • Tells students they are wrong • Gives information or facts that solve the problem
explain	• Asks for evidence and clarification from students • Uses students' previous experiences as a basis for explaining concepts • Encourages students to explain concepts and definitions in their own words, then provides scientific explanations and vocabulary	• Does not solicit the students' explanations • Accepts explanations that have no justification • Introduces unrelated concepts or skills
elaborate	• Expects students to apply scientific concepts, skills, and vocabulary to new situations • Reminds students of alternative explanations • Refers students to alternative explanations	• Provides definite answers • Leads students to step-by-step solutions to new problems • Lectures
evaluate	• Observes and assesses students as they apply new concepts and skills • Allows students to assess their own learning and group process skills • Asks open-ended questions	• Tests vocabulary words and isolated facts • Introduces new ideas or concepts • Promotes open-ended discussion unrelated to the concept

Adapted from *Achieving Scientific Literacy: From Purposes to Practices* (Bybee 1997).

Table 4.2. The BSCS 5Es Student

What the Student Does		
	CONSISTENT **with the BSCS 5E Model**	***INCONSISTENT*** **with the BSCS 5E Model**
engage	• Asks questions such as "Why did this happen?" "What do I already know about this?" "What can I find out about this?" • Shows interest in the topic	• Asks for the "right" answer • Offers the "right" answer • Insists on answers and explanations
explore	• Thinks creatively, but within the limits of the activity • Tests predictions and hypotheses • Records observations and ideas	• Passively allows others to do the thinking and exploring • "Plays around" indiscriminately with no goal in mind • Stops with one solution
explain	• Explains possible solutions to others • Listens critically to explanations of other students and the teacher • Uses recorded observations in explanations	• Proposes explanations from "thin air" with no relationship to previous experiences • Brings up irrelevant experiences and examples • Accepts explanations without justification
elaborate	• Applies new labels, definitions, explanations, and skills in new but similar situations • Uses previous information to ask questions, propose solutions, make decisions, and design experiments • Records observations and explanations	• "Plays around" with no goal in mind • Ignores previous information or evidence • Neglects to record data
evaluate	• Demonstrates an understanding of the concept or skill • Answers open-ended questions by using observations, evidence, and previously accepted explanations • Evaluates his or her own progress and knowledge	• Draws conclusions, not using evidence or previously accepted explanations • Offers only yes-or-no answers and memorized definitions or explanations • Fails to express satisfactory explanations in his or her own words

Adapted from *Achieving Scientific Literacy: From Purposes to Practices* (Bybee 1997).

Each lesson begins with an engagement activity, but students can reenter the 5E Model at other points in the cycle. For example, in "Name That Shell!" Chapter 7, students *explore* the characteristics of shells and sort them. Then they *explain* the characteristics they used to sort the shells and the teacher introduces the scientific terms *bivalve* and *gastropod*. Next the students re-enter the *explore* phase by sorting the shells into bivalves and gastropods. Moving from the *explain* phase back into the *explore* phase gives students the opportunity to add to the knowledge they have constructed so far in the lesson by participating in additional hands-on explorations.

The traditional roles of the teacher and student are virtually reversed in the 5E Model. Students take on much of the responsibility for learning as they construct knowledge through discovery, whereas in traditional models the teacher is responsible for dispensing information to be learned by the students. Table 4.1 shows actions of the teacher that are consistent with the 5E Model and actions that are inconsistent with the model.

In the 5E Model, the teacher acts as a guide: raising questions, providing opportunities for exploration, asking for evidence to support student explanations, referring students to existing explanations, correcting misconceptions, and coaching students as they apply new concepts. This model differs greatly from the traditional format of lecturing, that is, leading students step-by-step to a solution, providing definite answers, and testing isolated facts. The 5E Model requires the students to take on much of the responsibility for their own learning. Table 4.2 shows the actions of the student that are consistent with the 5E Model and those that are inconsistent with the model.

References

Bybee, R. W. 1997. *Achieving scientific literacy: From purposes to practices*. Portsmouth, NH: Heinemann.

Colburn, A. 2003. *The lingo of learning: 88 education terms every science teacher should know*. Arlington, VA: NSTA Press.

Connecting to Standards

In each chapter of this book, we have clearly identified connections between the lesson and *A Framework for K–12 Science Education*. On the first page of each chapter, you will find a box titled "Lesson Objectives: Connecting to the *Framework*," which lists the science and engineering practices, disciplinary core ideas, and crosscutting concepts that the lesson supports. This chapter provides some background information about those three dimensions, as well as about the *Common Core State Standards, ELA* (*CCSS ELA*) and how the lessons address them.

A Framework for K–12 Science Education

Published by the National Research Council (NRC) in 2012, *A Framework for K–12 Science Education* summarizes the most current research on how science is both taught and learned and identifies what all students should know from grades K–12. The overarching goal of the writing committee was

> *to ensure that by the end of 12th grade,* all *students have some appreciation of the beauty and wonder of science; possess sufficient knowledge of science and engineering to engage in public discussions on related issues; are careful consumers of scientific and technological information related to their everyday lives; are able to continue to learn about science outside school; and have the skills to enter careers of their choice, including (but not limited to) careers in science, engineering, and technology. (NRC 2012, p. 1)*

The committee recommended that K–12 science education be developed around three major dimensions: (1) science and engineering practices, (2) disciplinary core ideas, and (3) crosscutting concepts. These three dimensions are the key components of the *Next Generation Science Standards (NGSS)* and many other state standards.

Dimension 1: Science and Engineering Practices

This dimension describes fundamental practices that scientists use as they investigate phenomena in the world and that engineers use as they design solutions (NRC 2012, p. 42). The eight science and engineering practices are

1. Asking questions (for science) and defining problems (for engineering),
2. Developing and using models,

3. Planning and carrying out investigations,
4. Analyzing and interpreting data,
5. Using mathematics and computational thinking,
6. Constructing explanations (for science) and designing solutions (for engineering),
7. Engaging in argument from evidence, and
8. Obtaining, evaluating, and communicating information.

Throughout *Picture-Perfect Science Lessons,* we offer suggestions for how to engage students in these practices in both teacher-guided and student-directed ways. For example, in Chapter 8, "Rice Is Life," students plan an investigation and design an experiment in which they manipulate variables to determine which type of rice will grow into rice plants (white, brown, or rice in the hull). Students are then encouraged to plan and carry out their own investigations of rice by using suggestions in the "Inquiry Place" box.

Some lessons in this book focus more explicitly on the engineering practices. For example, in Chapter 23, "The Secrets of Flight," students learn about how the forces of lift, drag, gravity, and thrust are involved in flight. They are deeply immersed in the practices of engineers as they design, test, and redesign paper gliders. In Chapter 25, "If I Built a Car," students learn how the invention of the moving assembly line allowed automobiles to be manufactured more cheaply and efficiently. Using engineering practices, students design and test assembly lines to produce toy race cars. Engineering is sometimes referred to as the "stealth" profession because although we use many designed objects, we seldom think about the engineering practices involved in the creation and production of these objects. It is important to not only give students an awareness of the work of engineers but also provide them with opportunities to think like engineers.

Picture-Perfect Science Lessons engages students in these science and engineering practices to capture their interest, motivate their continued study, and, above all, instill in them a sense of wonder about the natural and designed world. The end result is that by actually doing science and engineering rather than merely learning about it, students will recognize that the work of scientists and engineers is a creative and rewarding endeavor that deeply affects the world in which they live.

Dimension 2: Disciplinary Core Ideas

Disciplinary core ideas are grouped in four domains: (1) physical sciences; (2) life sciences; (3) Earth and space sciences; and (4) engineering, technology, and applications of science. Each discipline contains between one and four core ideas, which are then broken down into component ideas.

The lesson objectives in this book support a variety of the disciplinary core ideas. At the beginning of each lesson, we provide the disciplinary core idea the lesson addresses, as well as the grade levels the lesson targets.

Dimension 3: Crosscutting Concepts

Seven crosscutting concepts outlined by the *Framework* and listed below underlie the lessons in this book:

1. Patterns
2. Cause and effect
3. Scale, proportion, and quantity
4. Systems and system models
5. Energy and matter
6. Structure and function
7. Stability and change

As you implement the lessons in this book, you can use these concepts to help students make connections between disciplines and recognize that the same concept is relevant across different contexts. For example, the crosscutting concept of patterns underlies several lessons. In Chapter 17, "The Changing Moon," students learn that the pattern of the Moon phases is regular and predictable. In Chapter 18, "Day and Night," students observe the pattern of the daily changes of the position of the Sun in the sky. Noticing patterns is often a first step to organizing and asking scientific questions about why and how the patterns occur. It is important for students to develop ways to recognize, classify, and record patterns in the phenomena they observe, such as life cycles, weather, or patterns of change in Earth and sky.

Because students often do not make the connections on their own, it is important for the teacher to make these seven crosscutting concepts explicit for students to help them connect knowledge from different science fields into a coherent and scientifically based view of the world.

Appendix 1 (p. 393) summarizes the correlations between the lessons in this book and the *Framework*.

Common Core State Standards, English Language Arts

The Common Core State Standards Initiative (*www.corestandards.org*) is a state-led effort to define the knowledge and skills students should acquire in their K–12 mathematics and ELA courses. This initiative came from an extended, broad-based effort to fulfill the charge issued by the states to craft the next generation of K–12 standards to ensure that all students are college- and career-ready by the end of high school. The standards are research- and evidence-based, aligned with college and work expectations, rigorous, and informed by other countries' standards. The *Common Core* suggests that the ELA standards be taught in the context of history/social studies, science, and technical subjects (NGAC and CCSSO 2010). Grade-specific K–12 standards in reading, writing, speaking, listening, and language are included. Many of these grade-specific standards are used in *Picture-Perfect Science Lessons* through the use of high-quality children's fiction and nonfiction picture books, research-based reading strategies, poster presentations, vocabulary development activities, and various writing assignments.

Appendix 2 (p. 395) summarizes the correlations between the lessons presented in *Picture-Perfect Science Lessons* and the *Common Core State Standards, ELA*.

You can access the complete *Common Core State Standards* documents for ELA at *www.corestandards.org/ELA-Literacy*.

References

National Governors Association Center for Best Practices and Council of Chief State School Officers (NGAC and CCSSO). 2010. *Common core state standards.* Washington, DC: NGAC and CCSSO.

National Research Council (NRC). 2012. *A framework for K–12 science education: Practices, crosscutting concepts, and core ideas.* Washington, DC: National Academies Press.

Chapter 6

Earth Hounds

Description

Learners develop understandings of the differences between observations and inferences by analyzing Dr. Xargle's comical, yet misguided, attempts to teach his extraterrestrial students about dogs. Learners then make observations and inferences of "mystery samples" collected from Earth by Dr. Xargle.

Suggested Grade Levels: 3–6

Lesson Objectives Connecting to the *Framework*

Science and Engineering Practices

- Obtaining, evaluating, and communicating information

Crosscutting Concepts

- Scale, Proportion, and Quantity

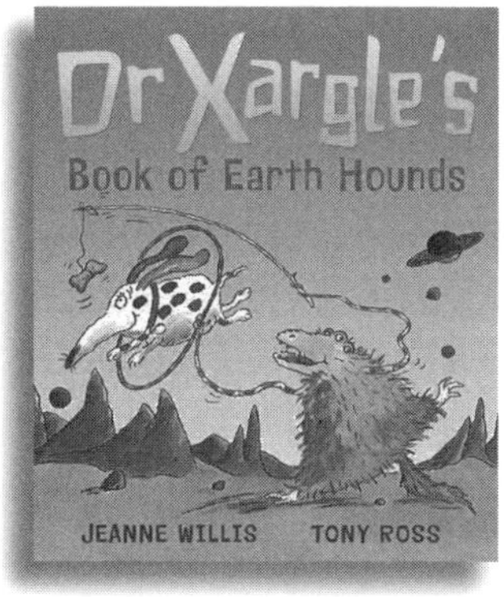

Featured Picture Books

Title	***Dr. Xargle's Book of Earth Hounds***
Author	**Jeanne Willis**
Illustrator	**Tony Ross**
Publisher	**Andersen Press**
Year	**2011**
Genre	**Story**
Summary	**Dr. Xargle, a green, five-eyed alien, teaches a lesson about strange creatures called Earth Hounds.**

Title	***Seven Blind Mice***
Author	**Ed Young**
Illustrator	**Ed Young**
Publisher	**Puffin Books**
Year	**2002**
Genre	**Story**
Summary	**Retells the fable of the blind men discovering the different parts of an elephant and arguing about its appearance**

Time Needed

This lesson will take several class periods. Suggested scheduling is as follows:

Day 1: **Engage** with read aloud of *Dr. Xargle's Book of Earth Hounds,* **Explore** with word sorts, and **Explain** with observation versus inference and Inference Frayer Model

Day 2: **Explore** and **Explain** with mystery samples from Planet Earth

Day 3: **Elaborate** with *Seven Blind Mice,* **Evaluate** with Observation and Inference Practice and Quiz

Day 4: **Evaluate** with review and Observation and Inference Quiz

Materials

- Black film canisters or small opaque containers with lids (1 per student) to make mystery samples: Make the mystery samples in sets of 2 so you can randomly distribute 2 identical samples of each kind. Be sure to put in equal amounts, such as 1 tbs. popcorn kernels in each, 1 of the same size marble in each, and so on. Put in familiar, everyday household items that make sound when shaken, such as
    - 5 small paper clips
    - 1 tbs. popcorn kernels
    - 1 marble
    - 1 screw
    - 1 small disc magnet or magnetic marble
    - 3 pennies
    - 2 plastic centimeter cubes
    - 1 key chain
    - 1 salt packet
    - 1 pencil eraser
    - 1 tbs. water
    - 1 button
    - 5 rubber bands
    - 1 tbs. sand or small gravel
    - 1 crayon, broken in half
    - 1 piece of chalk, broken in half
- Magnets for testing magnetic properties
- Balances or electronic kitchen scales for measuring mass

Student Pages

- Earth Hounds Word Sort Cards
- Inference Frayer Model
- Mystery Sample From Planet Earth Data Sheet
- Observation and Inference Practice
- Observation and Inference Quiz

Background

When learning to work and think scientifically, students need to use both observation and inference to construct explanations for phenomena. Making an *observation* involves using one or more of the senses to gather evidence about objects or events. Making an *inference* involves logical reasoning–drawing a conclusion using prior knowledge to interpret our observations. Students can observe many things directly, for example, a weather vane on top of a building. However, they cannot see moving air, so they must make inferences about wind by noting the direction the weather vane is pointing, feeling the breeze against their skin, and observing tree branches moving in the wind. They can see the lightbulbs in a circuit, but they must make inferences about the electric current going through them by observing the bulbs' brightness. They can see tracks in the snow, but they must infer what type of animal made them by studying their shape and size and comparing that information to what is already known about animal footprints. Children quite naturally make inferences from their observations, but it is important for science teachers to help them understand the difference between the two to fine-tune these skills.

It is also important for students to understand how scientists make observations and inferences in their work. Sometimes scientists gather information using their senses; other times, direct observation is not possible. For example, the inside of an atom is much too small to be seen, even with the most powerful microscope. Scientists have had to make inferences about atomic structure based on their observations of how atoms behave. For many years, the "plum pudding" model was the widely accepted model of atomic structure. In this model, negatively charged particles were thought to be scattered throughout an atom. However, in 1909 a scientist by the name of Ernest Rutherford conducted a famous experiment in which he observed how particles of matter behaved as they passed through a thin layer of gold foil. From his observations, he inferred that atoms had a small nucleus, with a positive charge, surrounded by electrons. By combining his experimental results with what was already known about subatomic particles, Rutherford was able to propose a new model of atomic structure without ever seeing an atom.

In this lesson, students make observations and inferences about the unseen properties of mystery objects and, in doing so, learn the difference between observations and inferences and how scientists generate knowledge using both.

Engage

Inferring

Show students the cover of the book, and ask the following questions:

- Who do you think Dr. Xargle is?
- What do you think Earth Hounds are?

Earth Hounds Read Aloud

Introduce the author and illustrator of *Dr. Xargle's Book of Earth Hounds*. Then read *Dr. Xargle's Book of Earth Hounds* to the class.

Explore

Ask students the following questions after reading the book:

- Who is Dr. Xargle? (a teacher or professor from another planet)
- What are Earth Hounds? (dogs)
- What observations did Dr. Xargle make about dogs? (Responses will vary.)
- What is an observation? (information taken in directly through the senses)

Word Sorts

Word sorts help learners understand the relationships among key concepts and help teach classification.

Open Sort: Pass out the Earth Hounds Word Sort Cards student page to each pair of students. Have them cut out the cards containing several statements made by Dr. Xargle about Earth Hounds. Then ask them to sort the cards any way they wish. At this point, it should be an open sort, in which students group the cards into categories of their choice and then create their own labels for each category. As you move from pair to pair, ask students to explain how they categorized the cards. Then ask

- Do you notice any differences among the kinds of statements Dr. Xargle makes on the cards?
- Which statements are truly observations, or information Dr. Xargle got directly through his eyes or ears?

Closed Sort: Tell students that now you want them to classify the cards into only two groups: statements that are *observations* and those that aren't. Give them time to sort the cards.

Next make a T-chart on the board. Don't label it yet. Discuss the statements the students have identified as observations. As students give answers, write them (or attach the cards) on the left side of the T-chart if they are truly observations with the corresponding (incorrect) inferences on the right. Then ask

- Does anyone know what the statements on the right-hand side of the T-chart are called? (inferences)

Next label the T-chart with "Observations" on the left and "Inferences" on the right.

Sample T-Chart

Observations	Inferences
Earth Hounds have eyes and tongues.	The eyes of the Earth Hounds are made of buttons, and their tongues are made of flannel.
Earth Hounds are taken for walks.	Earth Hounds are attached to strings so they can be pulled along in the sitting position.
Earth Hounds roll in compost.	Earth Hounds roll in compost to dry themselves after a bath.
The Earthlings place newspapers on the floor.	The Earthlings place newspapers on the floor for the Houndlets to read.

explain

Observation Versus Inference

Discuss the differences between observations and inferences using the following explanation: "Making an *observation* involves using one or more of the senses to find out about objects or events. Making an *inference* involves logical reasoning–drawing a conclusion using prior knowledge to explain our observations. A problem Dr. Xargle has is that he makes incorrect inferences to explain his observations. Dr. Xargle observes people putting newspapers on the floor. Dr. Xargle infers that people do that so that puppies can read them.

? Why do people really put newspapers down for puppies? How do you know? (People put newspapers down so puppies can "potty" on them. We know this from our past experiences with puppies.)

Use the following example to further illustrate the concept of inference: "Inferences are always based on observations. When you make an inference, you use your observations combined with your past experiences to draw a conclusion. Think about this example: You are walking on the grass barefoot. It is a warm, sunny day. You reach the end of the grass and have a choice between walking barefoot on blacktop or on a sidewalk. You notice heat waves rising from the blacktop. You choose to walk on the sidewalk because you *infer* from the heat waves and your prior knowledge about dark surfaces that the blacktop is too hot. This is an inference because you did not directly observe the temperature of the blacktop by stepping on it, but your observations, combined with past experience, led you to the conclusion that the blacktop is hotter than the sidewalk.

"Dr. Xargle, being from another planet, doesn't have any past experiences with dogs. So, he makes inferences that are incorrect. For example, Dr. Xargle makes an incorrect inference about why people put newspapers down for puppies. He does not base his inference on past experience with puppies (perhaps dogs on his planet can read!). Sometimes scientists have to reject their first inferences when observations later disprove them. If Dr. Xargle went back to Earth to make more observations, he would be able to revise his incorrect inferences."

Lead students to more examples of inferences by asking the following questions:

? Your dog comes in from outside and you observe its fur is wet. What inferences could you make from your observation? Turn and talk. (It is raining outside; your dog jumped in a creek; someone gave it a bath.)

? You walk into your backyard and you observe feathers all over the ground. What inferences could you make from your observation? Turn and talk. (An animal caught a bird; someone had a pillow fight; birds were fighting.)

? A paleontologist observes a fossil of a fish in the desert. What inferences could she make from her observation? Turn and talk. (The desert was covered with water at one time; someone dropped the fossil there.)

explain

Inference Frayer Model

The Inference Frayer Model is a tool used to help students develop their vocabularies. Students write a particular word in the middle of a box and proceed to list characteristics, examples, nonexamples, and a definition in other quadrants of the box.

Give each student an Inference Frayer Model student page. Explain that the Frayer Model is a way to help them understand the meaning of concepts such as *inference*. Have students formulate a definition for inference in their own words in the top left box of the Inference Frayer Model

Sample Frayer Model for "Inference"

Definition	Characteristics
Conclusion you draw to explain your observations	• Uses your past experiences • Always based on observations
Inference	
Examples	**Nonexamples**
• I inferred that it was raining outside because people came in carrying wet umbrellas	• I saw an umbrella

student page. Then have students write some characteristics of inferences in the top right box. Have students work in pairs to come up with examples and nonexamples from their own lives. Encourage them to use their previous experiences as a basis for their inference examples. Refer back to the blacktop example and encourage them to think of similar experiences from their lives. For nonexamples, encourage students to think of direct observations they have made using their senses. Students can then present and explain their models to other groups. As they present to each other, informally assess their understanding of the concept and clarify as necessary.

Explore

Mystery Samples From Planet Earth

Tell students that they are scientists from Dr. Xargle's planet and that he has asked for their help in identifying certain samples that have been collected from Earth. The problem is that students cannot look directly at the samples to make observations. The samples must be kept sealed in small black containers because Dr. Xargle believes they could contain radiation or harmful microorganisms. Tell students that under no circumstances can they open the containers. Discuss the properties of the objects that they might be able to observe without looking at them (sound, mass, and magnetic properties). Then pass out the Mystery Sample From Planet Earth Data Sheet and the sealed mystery samples.

Procedure for Mystery Samples From Planet Earth Activity

1. Before the lesson, prepare one film canister for each student. Put in items that make sounds, such as water, a paper clip, popcorn kernels, a marble, or a penny. Make pairs of canisters so that you can randomly distribute two of each kind: two canisters with popcorn in them, two with marbles in them, and so forth. Make sure you put equal amounts of materials in each pair of canisters, such as 1 tablespoon popcorn in each, and one of the same-size marble in each.
2. Students can calculate the mass of the samples in their canisters by subtracting the mass of an empty canister from the mass of their full canisters.
3. Ask students to make observations of the sounds the samples make. Walk around and check their descriptions. Are they making observations or inferences? They may find it difficult to make an observation of sound without inferring based on past experience. Accept observations such as "swishy," but do not accept inferences such as "It is water" at this point. Students should be using their sense of sound to describe what they hear without making inferences as to the identities of the samples.

4 Students can slide a magnet against the side of the film canister to observe whether the contents move with the magnet.

5 Have students make an inference about the contents of their canisters. "I think the mystery sample is ___________ because ________________________."

6 Ask some of the students to share their inferences with the class.

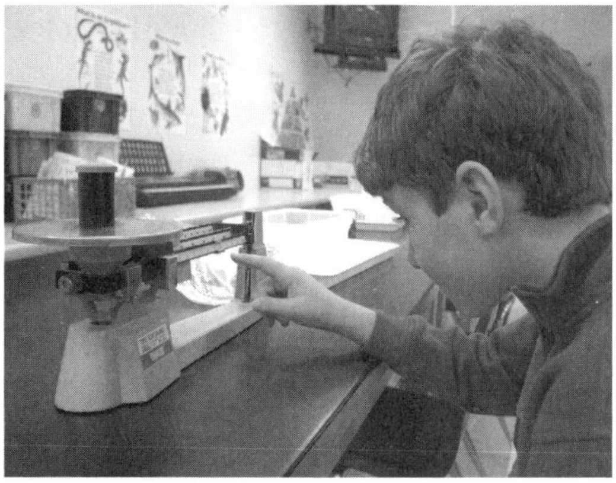

FINDING THE MASS OF A "MYSTERY SAMPLE"

explain

After all students have finished the Mystery Sample From Planet Earth Data Sheet, have them stand, holding their containers. They will want to open their samples to see if their inferences are correct, but don't let them yet! Instead have them form two groups—the students holding magnetic mystery samples should go to one side of the room and those holding nonmagnetic mystery samples should go to the other side of the room. Tell them to listen to the sounds that the samples make as they are gently shaken, and then try to find the person with an identical sample. When they find a "match," have them sit down with the person holding that sample and discuss their observations and inferences. Remind them not to open their containers, as they may contain radiation or harmful microorganisms.

When all students have found their match, discuss the following:

"There are many things in the world that cannot be directly observed by scientists because they no longer exist, they are too small or too far away, or (like our mystery samples) it is too dangerous to observe them. For example, has anyone ever seen a live dinosaur? (No.) Why not? (They have been extinct for millions of years.) So how do we know so much about dinosaurs? (Paleontologists observe fossils to make inferences about dinosaurs.) What kind of inferences can paleontologists make by looking at fossil evidence? (They can measure the bones to infer the size, look at the teeth to infer what they ate, look at the footprints to infer how they moved, and so on.) *But paleontologists will never see a live dinosaur, just as you may never see what is inside your container!*

Has anyone ever seen the inside of an atom? (No.) Why not? (Atoms are too small to be seen, even with the most powerful microscopes.) So how do we know so much about atoms? (Physicists observe how matter behaves in all kinds of chemical reactions. They have to make inferences about atoms and build models of atoms based on this indirect evidence rather than by directly observing them.) *But physicists may never see the inside of an atom, just as you may never see what is inside your container!*

Has anyone ever directly observed the center of the Earth? (No.) Why not? (It is too dangerous or difficult to go there.) So how do we know that the Earth's core is made of iron? (Geologists are able to use a variety of observations, including measurements of earthquake waves, to come up with inferences about the composition of Earth's core.) *But geologists may never see the center of the Earth, just as you may never see what is inside your container!"*

Next ask students to think about their mystery sample inferences. Ask

- How many of you are absolutely certain that your inference is correct?
- How many of you are fairly certain that your inference is correct?
- How many of you have no idea whether or not your inference is correct?

Explain that in science, there's often not absolute certainty. But making careful repeated observations, performing controlled experiments that can be replicated by others, and analyzing research thoroughly can reduce uncertainty and decrease the chances of making incorrect inferences.

Let students open their containers now, or make them wait until the next class period. If you really want to make your point (and you aren't afraid of a mob of angry kids), never let your students open them!

elaborate

Seven Blind Mice

Questioning

Introduce the author and illustrator of the book *Seven Blind Mice*. Show students the cover of the book.

- What do you think this book might be about?

As you read the book aloud, do not show the illustrations of the elephant so that students can infer what the "something" is. Only show the pages of the pillar, spear, etc. After reading, ask

- What was the "something" the blind mice observed?

After student share their inferences, show the illustrations of the elephant's parts. Then ask the following questions:

- What did the first mouse observe? (He felt the elephant's foot.)
- What did he infer from his observation? (He thought it was a pillar.)
- What did the seventh mouse do before making an inference? (She ran from one end of the elephant to the other and made observations of each part.)
- Why is it a good idea to make multiple observations before making an inference? (When you base your inference on more observations, you are less likely to make an incorrect inference.)
- The mouse moral is, "Knowing in part may make a fine tale, but wisdom comes from seeing the whole." How does this apply to making good observations and inferences? (Making only one observation may allow you to make an inference, but it is not likely to give you the big picture. Making multiple observations is more likely to give you the wisdom to draw an accurate conclusion about something.)

Making Connections: Text-to-Text

- What advice could White Mouse give Dr. Xargle about his study of Earth Hounds? (Dr. Xargle should go back to Earth to make more observations, reject his original ideas about dogs, and make new inferences.)

evaluate

Observation and Inference Practice

Have students practice making observations and inferences using the Observation and Inference Practice. Check for understanding by having students explain their thinking.

evaluate

Review and Observation and Inference Quiz

After reviewing the differences between observations and inferences, have students complete the Observation and Inference Quiz. Answers are below:

1 Answers will vary but should be based on what can be directly observed in the picture. Responses may include the following: Water or another liquid is dripping from the fish bowl; water or another liquid is on the floor; there is no fish in the bowl; the cat is "smiling."

2 Answers will vary but should be based on the observation in question number 1. Responses may include the following: The cat put its head in the fishbowl; the cat ate the fish; the cat is happy.

3 b.

4 b.

5–6 Answers may include any two of the following: Mealworms prefer dark places or enclosed places; mealworms are attracted to cardboard; mealworms do not like water; mealworms do not like light; mealworms can't climb; and so on.

7 c.

8 Answers will vary, but they should suggest that Dr. Xargle make more observations on which to base his inferences.

Inquiry Place

Have students investigate animal tracks in a natural area. A good time to do this is when the ground is wet or snow covered. Students can place food in the area to attract animals. A cast of a track can be made by encircling it with a dam made of a strip of poster paper taped together at the ends, and then pouring plaster of paris into the track.

If a natural area is not available, you can construct a simulation by placing two or more different kinds of animal footprints made of paper on the floor of the classroom. Arrange them in a pattern that suggests how the animals interacted. For example, place rabbit and fox footprints in a pattern that implies there was a chase. When students enter the room, they can try to figure out what happened. As they work to solve the mystery, assess their ability to distinguish observations from inferences.

? What observations can you make about the footprints?

? What inferences can you make from your observations?

Students can present their findings in a poster session.

More Books to Read

Banyai, I. 1995. *Zoom*. New York: Puffin Books.
Summary: This wordless picture book presents a series of scenes, each one from farther away, showing, for example, a girl playing with toys, which is actually a picture on a magazine cover, which is then revealed to be part of a sign on a bus, and so on. Students will enjoy making observations about each page and then inferring what might really be happening in each scene.

Banyai, I. 1998. *Re-Zoom*. New York: Puffin Books.
Summary: This book reprises the wordless format of *Zoom*, beginning with a cave painting

and ending with the lights of a subway train disappearing into a tunnel.

George, L. B. 1995. *In the snow: Who's been here?* New York: Greenwillow Books.
Summary: Two children, on their way to go sledding, see evidence of animal life. Readers must infer what animals had been in each location. Each time, the answer is revealed on the next page.

Kramer, S. 2001. *Hidden worlds: Looking through a scientist's microscope.* Boston: Houghton Mifflin Co.
Summary: This book for upper elementary students provides a wealth of information about how scientists study the world using powerful electron microscopes. The book features the work of microscopist Dennis Kunkel, who has examined and photographed objects ranging from a mosquito's foot to a crystal of sugar to the delicate hairs on a blade of grass. It describes how he became interested in microscopes as a boy, how he prepares specimens for study, and how different kinds of microscopes work.

Pallotta, J. 2002. *The skull alphabet book.* Watertown, MA: Charlesbridge Publishing.
Summary: A detailed painting of an animal's skull represents each letter of the alphabet. The name of the animal isn't revealed, but visual tips to its identity are given in the background and through clues in the text. Readers will enjoy using their observational skills and prior knowledge to make inferences about the identity of the animals.

Selsam, M. E. 1998. *Big tracks, little tracks: Following animal prints.* New York: HarperCollins Children's Books.
Summary: This picture book for lower elementary students leads readers through the process of identifying animals and animal activities by their tracks. Explaining that scientists use clues to investigate the natural world, the book tells readers to make observations of a set of tracks, collect information about the animals that left those tracks, and finally infer what happened based on information revealed by the tracks.

Earth Hounds

Word Sort Cards

Earth Hounds have eyes and tongues.	Earthlings place newspapers on the floor for the Houndlets to read.
Earth Hounds are attached to strings so they can be pulled along in the sitting position.	Earth Hounds roll in compost.
Earthlings place newspapers on the floor.	The eyes of Earth Hounds are made of buttons, and their tongues are made of flannel.
Earth Hounds roll in compost to dry themselves after a bath.	Earth Hounds are taken for walks.

Name: ______________________________

Inference Frayer Model

Definition	Characteristics

Inference

Examples	Nonexamples

Name: ______________________

Mystery Sample From

Planet Earth

Data Sheet

Mass	Sample + Container = _____ g Empty Container = _____ g Sample = _____ g
Sound	Make an observation of the sound your sample makes when you shake the container: ______________________ ______________________
Magnetic Property	Use a magnet against the side of the container to determine if the sample is attracted to a magnet. _____ YES _____ NO
Inference	I think the mystery sample is ______________________ because ______________________ ______________________

Name: ______________________________

Observation and Inference Practice

Look at the picture. List in the chart below three observations and three inferences that can be made from those observations. An example of each is given for you.

Observation	Inference
The man is sitting by a fireplace.	The man is warm.

Name: ________________________________

Observation and Inference Quiz

Look at the picture above. Write one observation about the picture. Then write one inference based on that observation.

1 Observation: ________________________________

2 Inference: ________________________________

3 Scientists must be able to tell the difference between observations and inferences. Which of the following is an **inference?**

a The bird has blue feathers and a yellow beak that measures 3 cm long.

b The rodent might be nocturnal because it has large eyes and long whiskers.

c The snake is wrapping its body around its prey.

d The leaf measures 12.4 cm long.

Name: ______________________________

Observation and Inference Quiz cont.

Rainforest Journal 2/16/15 Today I found the body of an unusual frog. The frog might be poisonous because it is very brightly colored.	It has a mass of 22.4 grams. The frog is probably a tree climber because it has large, round toe pads. I think the frog is a species of poison dart frog because of its size and color.

4 A scientist discovers the body of an unknown species of frog in the rain forest of Brazil. She writes several statements in her journal about the animal shown above. Which of the following is an **observation** about the frog?

a The frog might be poisonous because it is very brightly colored.

b It has a mass of 22.4 grams.

c The frog is probably a tree climber because it has large, round toe pads.

d I think the frog is a species of poison dart frog because of its size and color.

Name: ______________________________

Observation and Inference Quiz cont.

Trial	Number of mealworms under light	Number of mealworms in cardboard tube	Number of mealworms in water dish
1	12	37	1
2	6	44	0
3	7	43	0

A student placed 50 mealworms in the middle of an aquarium containing a light, a cardboard tube, and a water dish. He waited 5 min. and then recorded the data for the first trial in the table above. The student repeated this procedure two more times, and recorded the results. Read the results of all three trials. Then write two inferences you could make about mealworms based on the results.

5 Inference: ______________________________

6 Inference: ______________________________

Name: ______________________________

Observation and Inference Quiz cont.

7 A scientist finds the skeleton of an animal that lived long ago. He observes that the animal had broad, flat teeth and feet with hooves. What is the best **inference** he could make from his observations?

a The animal lived in an area with few trees.

b The animal was a good swimmer.

c The animal was probably a plant eater.

d The animal was probably a meat eater.

8 When Dr. Xargle visits Earth and observes Earthlings placing newspapers on the floor, he infers that the newspapers are for the Houndlets to read. What is incorrect about his inference, and what advice would you give Dr. Xargle about making inferences?

____

____

____

____

____

____

____

____

____

Name That Shell!

Description

Learners make observations and inferences about seashells, generate questions about seashells, create and use categories to organize seashells, and use dichotomous keys to identify shells and other sea creatures by their characteristics.

Suggested Grade Levels: 3–5

Lesson Objectives Connecting to the *Framework*

Science and Engineering Practices

- Constructing explanations (for science) and designing solutions (for engineering)
- Obtaining, evaluating, and communicating information

Disciplinary Core Ideas

LS1.A: Structure and Function

Crosscutting Concepts

- Structure and Function

Featured Picture Books

Title	***Next Time You See a Seashell***
Author	**Emily Morgan**
Publisher	**NSTA Kids**
Year	**2013**
Genre	**Nonnarrative Information**
Summary	**Simple text and vivid photographs explain how seashells are made by mollusks.**

Title	***A House for Hermit Crab***
Author	**Eric Carle**
Illustrator	**Eric Carle**
Publisher	**Aladdin**
Year	**2002**
Genre	**Story**
Summary	**A hermit crab who has outgrown his old shell moves into a new one, which he decorates with the sea creatures he meets in his travels.**

Time Needed

This lesson will take several class periods. Suggested scheduling is as follows:

Day 1: **Engage** with read aloud of *Next Time You See a Seashell*, **Explore** with Seashell O-W-L and Shell Sorting

Day 2: **Explain** with Let's Learn About Shells, **Explore** and **Explain** with Name That Shell! Dichotomous Key

Day 3: **Elaborate** with *A House for Hermit Crab*, **Evaluate** with Under the Sea Dichotomous Key and Seashell Poster

Materials

- Assorted seashells
- Rulers or tape measures
- Balances
- Hand lenses
- Resealable plastic sandwich bags containing 6 or 7 different kinds of the numbered shells (1 bag per student pair)
- Poster board

Label the following shells A-G with a permanent marker (you will need 1 of each kind of shell per student pair):

- Cockle
- Whelk
- Olive
- Kitten's Paw
- Auger
- Scallop
- Jingle

Collect empty seashells from a beach, or purchase assorted seashells from a craft store. Using real shells is better, but if you are unable to get them, you can use the drawings on the Shell Drawings student page.

Student Pages

- Seashell O-W-L
- Shell Sorting Sheet
- *Next Time You See a Seashell* Anticipation Guide
- Name That Shell! Dichotomous Key
- Name That Shell! Shell Drawings
- Under the Sea Dichotomous Key

Background

A key concept in biology is the classification of living things. In this lesson, students classify seashells by their characteristics and learn how to use a dichotomous key to identify them. In the process, they learn about the structures of mollusks, the animals that make seashells. This lesson focuses on how scientists use these characteristics to classify living things, particularly mollusks.

Some mollusks—such as slugs, octopi, and squid—do not have shells, but most of these animals do have an exterior shell that can provide their soft bodies with shape and rigidity, protection, and sometimes camouflage from predators. When a mollusk hatches from its egg, it already has a tiny shell. Mollusk shells are made from calcium the animals derive from their environment. The shell is actually a part of the animal and grows as the mollusk grows. Each species of mollusk makes a shell that is unique to its species alone, but there can be variations in texture and color within a species due to a mollusk's food and environment.

Scientists can classify seashells into two groups: bivalve and gastropod. *Bivalves* include clams, oysters, and scallops. The shells of these animals have two parts connected by a muscular hinge. When you find a bivalve shell washed up on the beach, you are usually seeing only half of the original shell. After the mollusk that lived in the shell decomposed, the two halves of the bivalve came apart. You can tell if a shell is a bivalve by locating the hinge where the other half was connected. *Gastropods* include whelks, conchs, and snails. Gastropod shells are made up of one piece, so they do not have a hinge. Some gastropods also have a spiral shape.

In the elaborate portion of this lesson, students learn about the characteristics of other marine animals, including hermit crabs. Hermit crabs are not mollusks, though they live in a shell. They are actually crustaceans like lobsters and shrimp. Because their long, soft abdomens are unprotected, they salvage empty mollusk shells to carry on their backs. The tips of their abdomens are adapted to clasp strongly onto the spiral part of gastropod shells. When a hermit crab is threatened, it withdraws into its shell until the danger has passed. Hermit crabs must find progressively larger shells to live in as their bodies grow and they molt their exoskeleton. Suitable gastropod shells are a limited resource, so competition for shells can be fierce! Some hermit crab species, like the one featured in *A House for Hermit Crab,* have a symbiotic relationship with sea anemones. These anemones specialize in attaching themselves to the shell of the hermit crab. Then they protect and camouflage the crab and, in turn, may share fragments of the hermit crab's meals. The sea anemone is able to migrate to a new shell along with the hermit crab. This type of symbiosis is known as *mutualism,* meaning both organisms benefit.

For more information on seashells, go to *www.conchologistsofamerica.org* or *www.shellmuseum.org.*

Engage

Seashell O-W-L

Read aloud pages 6 to 7 of *Next Time You See a Seashell,* then pass out one shell and a copy of the Seashell O-W-L (observations, wonderings, learnings) student page to each student. Provide rulers or tape measures, hand lenses, and balances. Ask students to draw and observe their shells carefully and write both quantitative observations (numbers) and qualitative observations (words) about the shells. Quantitative observations involve counting and measuring, such as "The shell is 6.2 cm long"; qualitative observations involve using the senses to describe the properties of the object, such as "The shell has grooves on one side." Then ask students to generate a list of wonderings about their shells.

When students are finished drawing, writing observations, and generating questions, collect all the shells and place them in a pile where all the students can see them. Ask a volunteer to come up and, using another student's Seashell O-W-L page, try to locate that student's shell from its drawing and description. Repeat with several other students. Then have students find their own shells using their observations and return to their seats. Discuss the following questions:

- ? How well does your description and drawing distinguish your shell from other shells?
- ? How could you describe your shell better?
- ? What are some characteristics that make your shell different from the rest?
- ? What are some questions you have about your shell?

Tell students they will be learning the answers to some of their questions about shells over the next few days. Encourage them to continue to add wonderings and learnings to their Seashell O-W-L page.

Explore

Shell Sorting

STUDENTS SORTING SEASHELLS

Give pairs of students an assortment of seashells. Have them examine the characteristics of the shells—such as shape, size, texture, and structure—and make observations. Ask them to use the Shell Sorting Sheet to sort the shells into two groups using one characteristic. After the shells are sorted, pairs can switch places with other pairs and guess what characteristic the other pairs used to sort the shells.

Explain

Next Time You See a Seashell Read Aloud

First have students explain to one another what characteristics they used to sort the shells and why.

Anticipation Guide

Then tell students you are going to read the rest of the book *Next Time You See a Seashell* to learn more about shells. Have students complete the "before reading" column on the *Next Time You See a Seashell* Anticipation Guide.

Next take students to a reading corner—or have them stay at their seats but turn their anticipation guides over—and read the rest of the book aloud. Tell them to signal —"touch your ear"—when they hear answers to the questions on the anticipation guide.

Have students return to their seats and fill out the "after reading" column on the anticipation guide. Discuss each question as a class and ask students to cite evidence from the text that supports their answers. The correct answers to the anticipation guide are

1. True—page 11
2. True—page 15
3. True—page 18
4. False—page 25
5. True—page 27
6. False—page 28

Have students add any new information from the reading to the Learnings column of their Seashell O-W-L.

Then write the words *bivalve* and *gastropod* on the board. Explain that scientists group mollusks into several classes, the two largest of which are bivalves (also called pelecypods, such as clams, oysters, and scallops) and gastropods (also called univalves, such as whelks, conchs, and snails).

HINGE

Show examples of bivalves, and point out the hinge. Shells that have a hinge had another shell connected at the hinge at one time. Place two bivalve shells of the same species together to show how they were once connected by a hinge.

Explain that after the animal that lived in the shell died and decomposed, the two halves of the bivalve came apart.

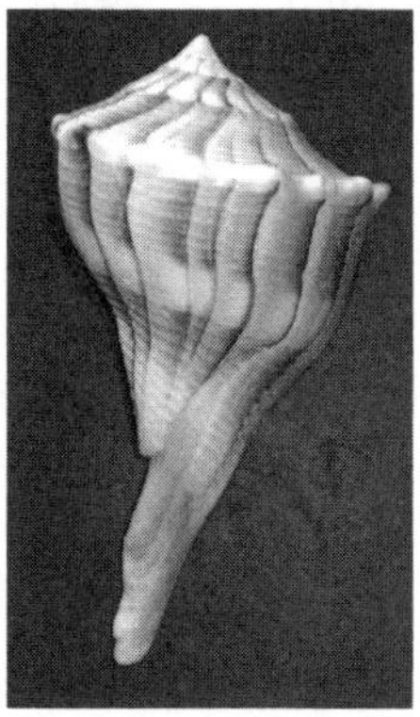

SPIRAL GASTROPOD

If there is no hinge, the shell is a gastropod. Show examples of gastropods and point out that there is no hinge. Many gastropods also have a spiral shape.

Then ask the following questions about shells:

- ? Why do mollusks need shells? (for protection, to aid in their survival)
- ? Do you think mollusks ever outgrow their shells? (Students should recall from the read aloud that a mollusk's shell grows along with it.)

Again, have students add to the Learnings column of their Seashell O-W-L if they have learned any new information about shells.

Explore & Explain

Name That Shell! Dichotomous Key

Note: The dichotomous key was designed to be used only with the set of shells used in the Materials section. It will not be helpful in identifying other shells.

Now students are ready to classify their shells as gastropods and bivalves. They can use the Shell Sorting Sheet again for this task—gastropods in group A, bivalves in group B.

Introduce the Name That Shell! Dichotomous Key as a special tool that scientists can use to identify organisms. Explain that the word *dichotomous* means "dividing into two parts." A dichotomous key has two choices at every step. Direct students' attention to the pictures and labels at the top of the dichotomous key. Tell students that the first thing they should do when using a dichotomous key is look at the pictures and read the labels. This information will help them identify their objects. Discuss the different characteristics used in the key such as knobs, grooves, dome-shaped side view, and rounded hinge. Have students hold up a shell that has knobs on it, have them hold up a shell that has grooves, and so forth.

Read the directions for the dichotomous key together. Lead the students through the process of using the dichotomous key to find the name of shell A. Students should now try to identify each shell using the dichotomous key and mark their answers on the answer sheet.

Have students explain their thought processes when they determined the correct name for each shell. Correct the answer sheets as a class.

If you use the Shell Drawings student page instead of real shells, the answers are as follows: A. scallop; B. auger; C. whelk; D. cockle; E. jingle; F. kitten's paw; and G. olive.

elaborate

A House for Hermit Crab

Inferring

Show students the cover of *A House for Hermit Crab* and read the title.

? What can you infer from the cover? (The book is about hermit crabs; hermit crabs live in a shell; and so forth.)

Discuss their inferences and ask them to explain their thinking.

? What do you know about hermit crabs?

Then read the book aloud, beginning with the information opposite the title page. After reading, discuss Hermit Crab's home.

? Why does Hermit Crab need a shell? (for protection)

? Does Hermit Crab choose bivalve shells or gastropod shells to make his home? Why? (gastropod shells because he can hide inside them; gastropods because they have a smaller opening; bivalves are only half of a shell after the animals inside them die; and so forth)

Then discuss some of the other ocean animals in the book:

? What are some of the animals that Hermit Crab encountered? (sea anemone, starfish, sea urchin, and others)

? What characteristics might scientists use to classify them? (number of body parts, how they move, type of body covering, and so forth)

? What tool could you use to identify the animals if you didn't know what they were called? (a key or a dichotomous key)

Then read and discuss the last page of *A House for Hermit Crab* about the various animals featured in the book.

evaluate

Under the Sea Dichotomous Key

As a final evaluation, have students use the Under the Sea Dichotomous Key to identify a variety of sea creatures. The answers are listed below:

A. Octopus
B. Jellyfish
C. Nautilus
D. Sea anemone
E. Sea urchin
F. Sea cucumber

evaluate

Seashell Research

Assign further research on seashells or the animals that make them. Students can research unanswered questions from their Seashell O-W-L or research questions you assign, focusing on the different structures that serve different functions in the growth and survival of mollusks. Determine the criteria you would like students to meet, and then assign a poster project. Alternately, have students create *Next Time You See a ...* books using the format of *Next Time You See a Seashell.* Make sure students are aware of the criteria you will be using to assess their work.

Inquiry Place

Have students brainstorm questions about mollusk shells such as

- ? Which type of shell has the most space for the mollusk that lives inside? (How could you measure the capacity of a shell?)
- ? Do larger scallop shells have more grooves than smaller ones?
- ? What are seashells made of? Research it!
- ? When you hold seashells up to your ear, what causes the sounds in them? Research it!

Students can select a question to investigate as a class, or groups of students can vote on the question they want to investigate as teams. Students can design an investigation to test their predictions or do research to find the answer. They can present their findings at a poster session.

More Books to Read

Arthur, A. 2000. *Eyewitness: Shell.* New York: Dorling Kindersley Publishing.
Summary: The authors provide fascinating photographs and information about different kinds of shells.

Frasier, D. 1998. *Out of the ocean.* New York: Voyager Books.
Summary: A young girl and her mother walk along the beach and marvel at the treasures cast up by the sea and the wonders of the world around them.

Lember, B. H. 1997. *The shell book.* Boston: Houghton Mifflin.
Summary: This book features fourteen shells commonly found along the shores of the United States and includes a stunning hand-tinted photograph of each shell with a brief information-packed description.

Roach-Evans, J. 2013. *Seashells: Treasures from the Northeast coast.* Yarmouth, ME: Islandport Press.
Summary: This beautifully illustrated pocket guide helps children identify shells of animals commonly found on the northeastern shores of the United States.

Silver, D. M. 1997. *One small square series: Seashore.* New York: McGraw-Hill.
Summary: This book examines the rich diversity of sea life from algae to manatees and includes activities as well as journal keeping.

Zoehfeld, K. W. 1994. *What lives in a shell?* New York: HarperTrophy.
Summary: Children in different settings observe various shelled creatures. The book also provides information about shell growth, locomotion, and the shells as protection for the animals that live in them.

References

Alvarado, A. E., and P. R. Herr. 2003. *Inquiry-based learning using everyday objects.* Thousand Oaks, CA: Corwin Press.

Ostlund, K., and S. Mercier. 1996. *Rising to the challenge of the National Science Education Standards.* Fresno, CA: S&K Associates.

Name: ______________________________

Seashell O-W-L

Drawing

O W L

Observations about My Seashell	**Wonderings** about My Seashell	**Learnings** about My Seashell

Name: ______________________________

Shell
Sorting Sheet

Directions: Sort your shells into two groups based on one characteristic.

Group A	Group B

Name: ______________________________

Next Time You See a *Seashell* Anticipation Guide

Before Reading True or False		After Reading True or False
________	**1** Seashells are made by animals.	________
________	**2** Seashells grow as the creature inside grows.	________
________	**3** Some shells are made of two pieces.	________
________	**4** Shells can only be found on beaches.	________
________	**5** A shell is part of an animal's body.	________
________	**6** Hermit crabs make their own shells.	________

Name: ______________________________

Name That Shell!

Dichotomous Key

Gastropod

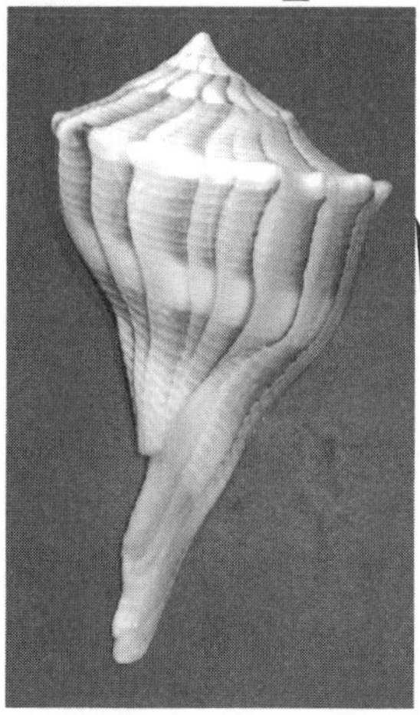

Bivalve

Starting with one of the shells in your set, use the key below to identify the shell. Write the name of the shell on your answer sheet. Remember to go back to #1 on the key each time you start with a new shell!

1 Bivalve.. go to 2
Gastropod.. go to 5

2 Straight line across hinge.. SCALLOP
Rounded hinge.. go to 3

3 Outer surface smooth and shiny.. JINGLE
Outer surface rough with grooves.. go to 4

4 Fairly flat side view.. KITTEN'S PAW
Dome-shaped side view.. COCKLE

5 Many knobs on closed end.. WHELK
No knobs on closed end.. go to 6

6 Small opening on one end.. AUGER
Long slit along length.. OLIVE

Name: ______________________________

Name That Shell!

Shell Drawings

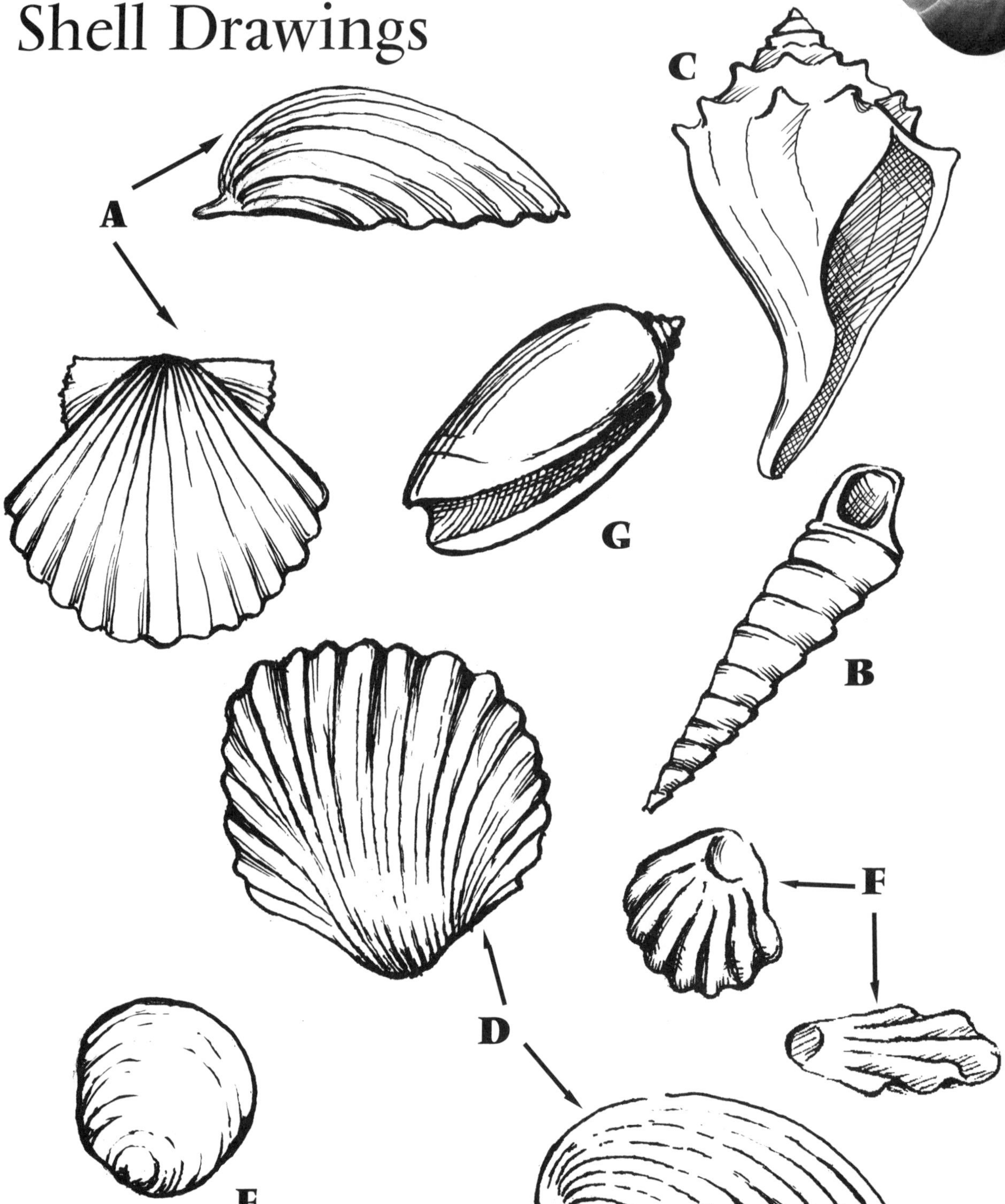

Name: ______________________________

Name That Shell!

cont.

A ______________________________

B ______________________________

C ______________________________

D ______________________________

E ______________________________

F ______________________________

G ______________________________

Name: ______________________________

Under the Sea

Dichotomous Key

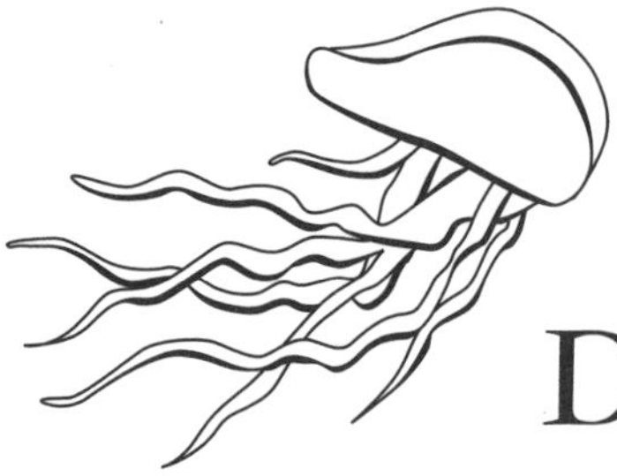

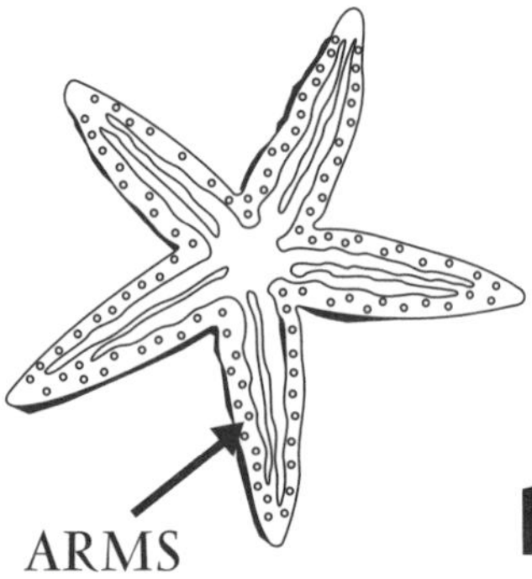

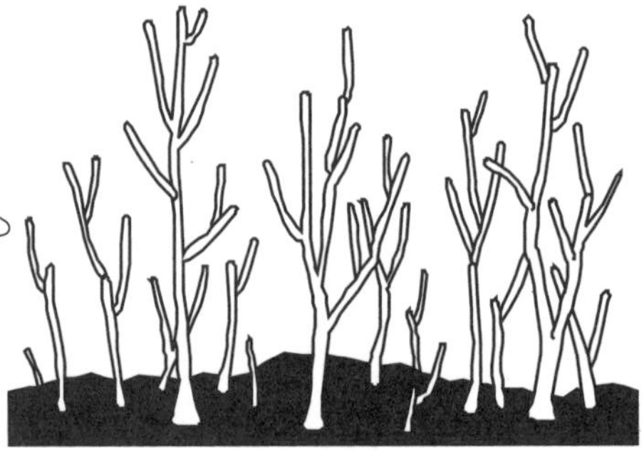

Starting with one of the animals on the next page, use the key below to identify the animal. Write the name of the animal on your answer sheet. Remember to go back to #1 on the key each time you start with a new animal!

1 Animal has eyes .... go to 2
Animal has no eyes .... go to 4

2 Outer shell present .... NAUTILUS
No outer shell .... go to 3

3 Rounded head and 8 arms .... OCTOPUS
Long narrow head and 10 arms .... SQUID

4 Animal is spherical with spikes .... SEA URCHIN
Not spherical .... go to 5

5 Animal has tentacles .... go to 6
Animal has no tentacles .... go to 7

6 Tentacles point upward or outward from tubelike body .... SEA ANEMONE
Tentacles dangle downward from "umbrella"-shaped body .... JELLYFISH

7 Animal has 5 arms coming off center of body .... SEA STAR
Animal has no arms .... SEA CUCUMBER

Name: ______________________________

Under the Sea

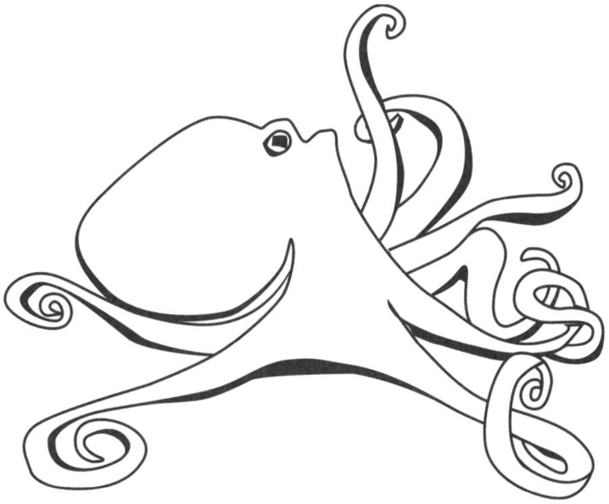

A

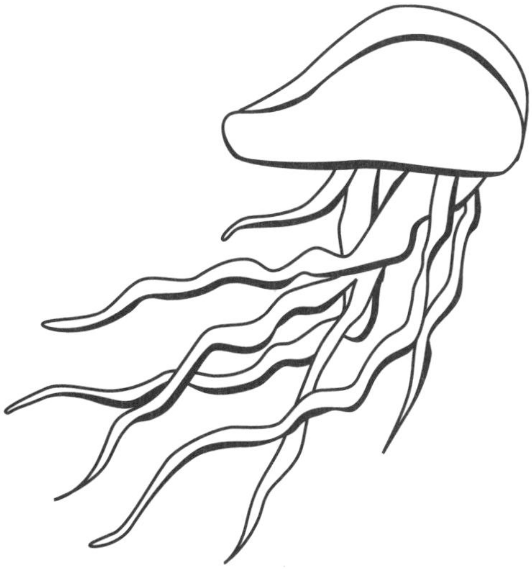

B

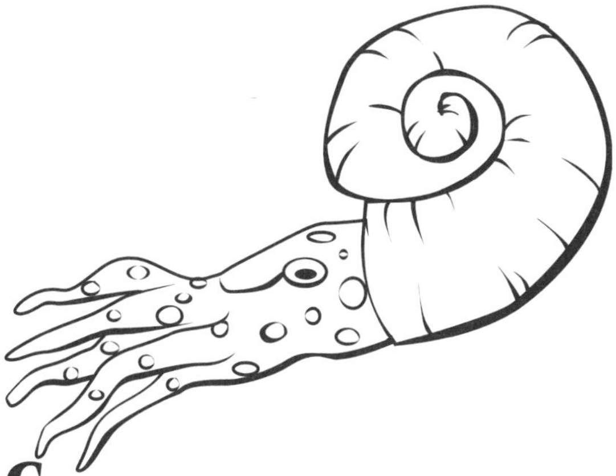

C

D

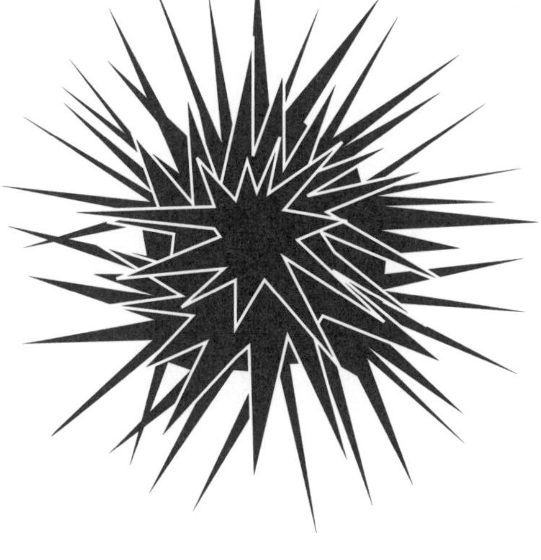

E

F

Name: ______________________________

Under the Sea cont.

A ______________________________

B ______________________________

C ______________________________

D ______________________________

E ______________________________

F ______________________________

Rice Is Life

Description

Learners explore the importance of rice as a food source, the differences among types of rice, the life cycle of rice, and rice production methods. Learners also explore controls, variables, and experimental design by investigating how rice grows and by designing their own plant growth experiments.

Suggested Grade Levels: 3–6

Lesson Objectives Connecting to the *Framework*

Science and Engineering Practices
- Planning and carrying out investigations
- Analyzing and interpreting data

Disciplinary Core Ideas

LS1.A: Structure and Function
LS1.B: Growth and Development of Organisms

Crosscutting Concepts
- Structure and Function
- Patterns

Featured Picture Books

Title	***Rice Is Life***
Author	**Rita Golden Gelman**
Illustrator	**Yangsook Choi**
Publisher	**Henry Holt and Company**
Year	**2000**
Genre	**Dual Purpose**
Summary	**Poetic text, factual information, and charming illustrations demonstrate the importance of rice to life on the island of Bali.**

Title	***Rice***
Author	**Louise Spilsbury**
Illustrator	**Barry Atkinson**
Publisher	**Heinemann Library**
Year	**2001**
Genre	**Nonnarrative Information**
Summary	**Describes how rice is grown and what happens to it on its way from the field to your table**

Time Needed

This lesson will take several class periods. Suggested scheduling is as follows:

Day 1: **Engage** with Semantic Map and *Rice Is Life* read aloud, and **Explore** with observing rice grains

Day 2: **Explain** with Let's Learn About Rice article and Rice Journals

Day 3-7: **Explore** with Rice Experiment and Rice Journals

Day 8: **Explain** with *Rice* read aloud, and **Elaborate** with Journey Through a Rice Mill

Day 9: **Explain** with investigatable questions, and **Evaluate** with Design a Plant Experiment

Day 10: **Evaluate** with Experimental Design Quiz

Materials

- Bowls of cooked rice (1 per student)
- Chopsticks (optional, 1 pair per student)
- Chart paper (1 sheet)
- "Think pads" (several sheets of sticky notes per student)
- Hand lenses (1 per student)
- White rice (about ½ cup per class)
- Brown rice (about ½ cup per class)
- Rice in the husk, also called rice in the hull or unmilled rice seed (1 seed packet)
- Clear plastic cups (3 per group)
- Centimeter rulers (1 per group)
- Thermometer (1 per class)
- Water

Rice seed in the husk is available from

Kitazawa Seed Co.
P.O. Box 13220
Oakland, CA 94661-3220
Phone 510-595-1188
Fax 510-595-1860
www.kitazawaseed.com

For Journey Through a Rice Mill

- Instant white rice (a few grains per student)
- Rice in the husk (a few grains per student)
- 2 in. sandpaper squares (2 per student)

For Design a Plant Experiment

- Small plants of the same type (beans, radishes, cucumbers, and marigolds work well; 2 per student)
- Cups for growing plants (2 per student)
- Potting soil for growing plants

Student Pages

- Let's Learn About Rice Anticipation Guide
- Rice article
- Rice Journal (Copy the cover on a separate sheet, and then copy page 1 back-to-back with pages 2 and 7; copy pages 6 and 3 back-to-back with pages 4 and 5. Fold and staple along spine.)
- Journey Through a Rice Mill
- Design a Plant Experiment
- Experimental Design Quiz

Background

Rice is the most important food staple for more than half the world's population. About 90% of the world's rice is grown in Asia. China, India, and Indonesia are the top rice producers. Rice is a type of grass that belongs to the same family as barley, oats, rye, and wheat. The edible portion of the rice plant is part of the seed. The outer covering of the rice seed is called the *hull,* or husk. Rice undergoes various degrees of processing before it ever reaches your table. First harvesters cut the ripe grain from the stalk, then, after it has dried, they thresh it to separate the grains from the rice straw. Milling then removes each grain's hull to reveal the part of the rice plant that eventually ends up on your plate. Brown rice has the hull removed but still retains a bran layer; milling both the hull and bran layers of the kernel renders white rice; and "instant" rice is milled, completely cooked, and dried to create a quicker cooking time. White rice may also be enriched by adding nutrients lost during processing.

It is often assumed that rice plants require a lot of water to grow because rice is most often grown in flooded fields. The primary reason rice is grown under flooded conditions is because the water provides control of weeds and pests. Rice is able to grow in standing water because its leaves and stems have internal air spaces that can pass air down to the roots. However, rice plants will die if all of the leaves are covered with water for too long, so the water level in rice paddies is carefully monitored. Rice paddies can be complete ecosystems unto themselves.

In this lesson, students learn about some of the organisms involved in the rice paddy ecosystem, such as eels that live in the slippery mud and are eaten by egrets, bats that feed on mosquitoes, ducks that eat the rice and grubs, and so on. Students then investigate rice germination through a controlled experiment. Within these experiments, students should make observations, take accurate measurements, and identify and control variables. A *variable* is something that can change during the course of an experiment. In the Explore activity for this lesson, the variable that is changed by the student investigators is the type of rice: brown, white, or rice in the husk. The *controlled variables* are those things that the investigators attempt to keep constant—in this case, temperature, amount of water, number of rice grains, size and color of the cups, and amount of sunlight.

engage

Semantic Map and Read Aloud

Serve students some cooked rice (chopsticks optional) and begin creating a semantic map as they eat. A semantic map is a tool that helps activate prior knowledge, determine misconceptions, and show relationships among concepts. Discussion of a semantic map helps students become aware of new words, create new meanings for terms, and recognize the relationships among numerous words related to the science content. As students are eating their rice, ask

? What are some terms you think of when you hear the word *rice*?

? What do you know about rice?

Give groups of two or three students some sticky notes and ask them to write one word about rice on each sticky note. Give them time to generate a dozen or so sticky note words per group. Then ask them to sort the sticky notes into categories. Write the word *rice* in the center of a sheet of chart paper or on the board, and circle it. Have students share their categories and terms. Discuss the categories and terms, choose several main categories to write on the map, and have students place their sticky notes on the board or chart paper under the corresponding categories. Display the map throughout the lesson, adding new categories and terms as students learn more about rice.

Semantic Map Template

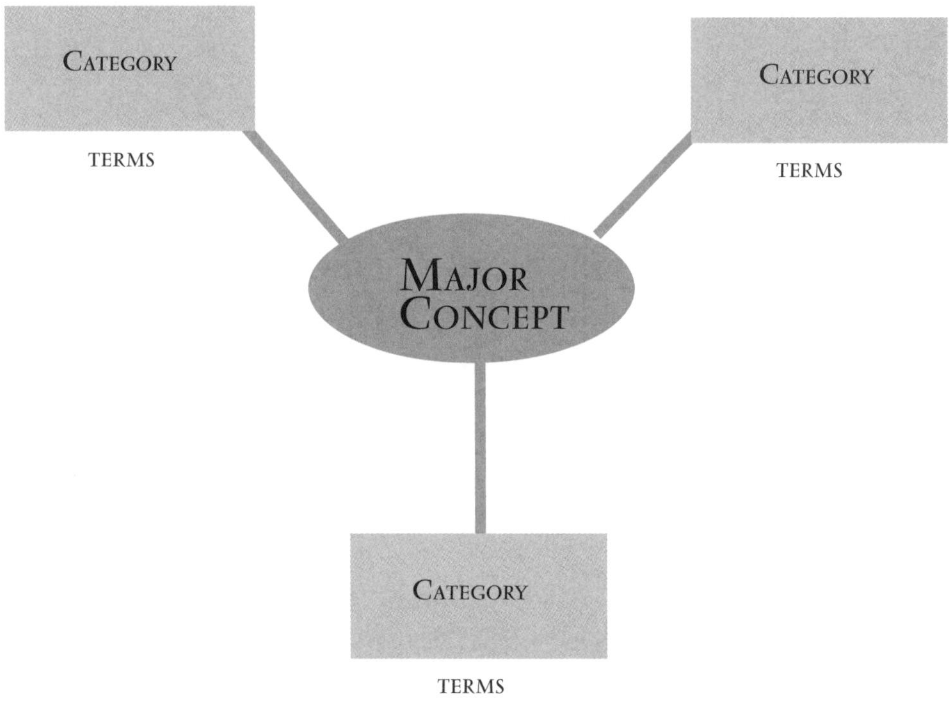

Sample Semantic Map for Rice

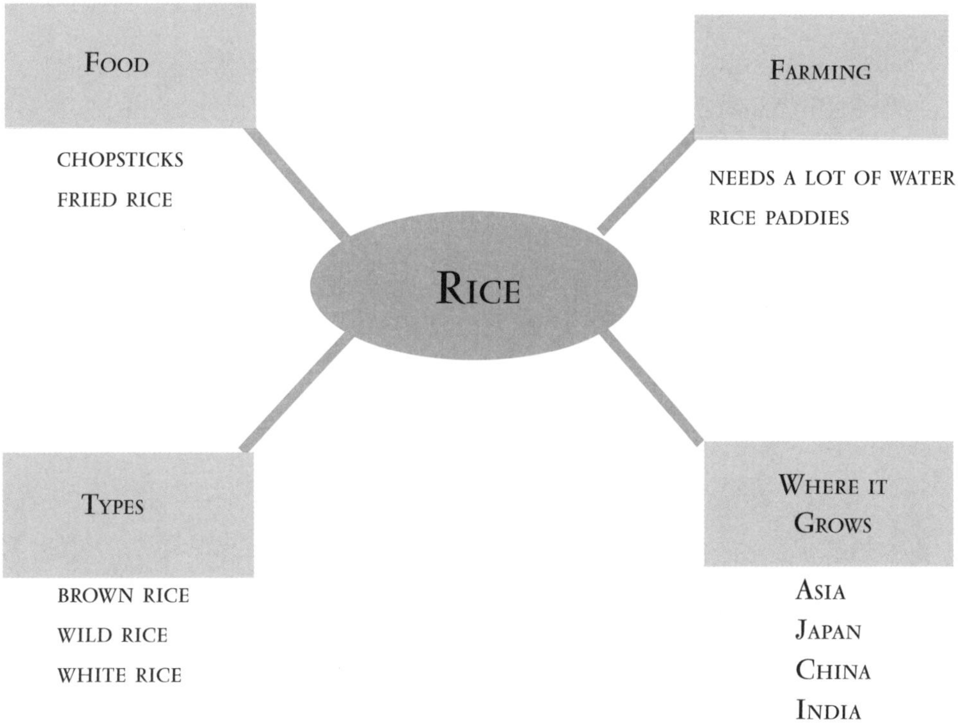

Inferring

Before you read *Rice Is Life* to students, write the comprehension activities suggested below on sticky notes and then insert them into the appropriate places in the text. This will help you avoid disrupting the flow of the poetic text.

Ask students to examine the cover of the book *Rice Is Life* and infer what the title might mean. Introduce the author and the illustrator. (You can find out more about this fascinating author at *www.ritagoldengelman.com*.) Then read *Rice Is Life* to the students.

Inferring: Stop and Jot

On pages 6 and 7 (about the boys and girls "fishing" for dragonflies), read the verses and ask students to stop and jot on their sticky note "think pads" why they think the boys and girls are catching dragonflies.

Visualizing: Sketch to Stretch

Don't show the picture (of the people scaring away the birds) on pages 14 and 15. Tell students to visualize as you read and draw a picture on their sticky note "think pads" of what they think that scene might look like.

Synthesizing

Ask students what they think the title *Rice Is Life* means after reading the book. Have them support their ideas with examples from the book. Then go back to the semantic map and add any new categories or terms they learned from the book. You can also have students correct any misconceptions that might have been written on the map. Continue adding to and revising the semantic map throughout the lesson to show relationships and correct misconceptions.

Explore

Observing Rice Grains

Give each group of students a plate with a few grains each of brown rice, white rice, and rice in the husk, but don't tell them what they are at this point. Give them hand lenses and have them make observations. After students have had plenty of time to observe and infer what the samples are, point out the one that is white rice, the one that is brown rice, and the one that is rice in the *husk* (seed coat, also called hull). Ask students to predict which type of rice would *germinate* (sprout): rice in the husk, brown rice, or white rice.

Explain

Let's Learn About Rice Article

Anticipation Guide

Tell students that they are going to explore the question "What does rice need to grow?" Pass out the Let's Learn About Rice Anticipation Guide. Have students fill in the "before reading" column.

Pairs Read

Pass out the Rice article. Put students in pairs and have them take turns reading aloud from the article. While one person reads a paragraph, the other listens and then makes comments ("I think ..."), asks questions ("I wonder ..."), or shares new learnings ("I didn't know ..."). Have students read for the answers and mark the correct answers in the "after reading" column.

Answers to the Let's Learn About Rice Anticipation Guide are

1. T
2. T
3. F
4. F
5. T
6. F

Explain

Rice Journals

Pass out the Rice Journals to students and tell them they are going to investigate which of the three types of rice (brown rice, white rice, and rice in the husk) will germinate. Have students fill in their predictions on page 1 of the journals.

The question at the bottom of page 1 asks what the experimental variable is in this experiment. Tell students that when scientists design an experiment, the first thing they do is determine what it is they want to test. The one thing in the experiment that is being tested is called the *experimental variable*.

? What is the experimental variable in our experiment? (the type of rice)

Have students record the experimental variable on page 1 of their journals.

Next have students turn to page 2 in the journals. Read the instructions together. Tell students that scientists always make sure their experiments are fair tests by keeping everything but the experimental variable the same. The conditions kept the same are called *controlled variables*.

? What are the controlled variables in our experiment? (size of cups, color of cups, amount of water, amount of seeds per cup, amount of sunlight, temperature)

Have students record the controlled variables on page 2 of their journals.

explore

Rice Experiment and Rice Journals

Review the information about growing rice from the Rice article by asking

? What conditions are necessary to grow rice? (a lot of water, temperature higher than 21°C, plenty of sunlight, soil)

Then have students set up their experiments according to instructions 1 through 3 (for germinating rice) in the "How to Grow Rice" section of the Rice article. Tell students to make sure to keep all variables controlled except the type of rice.

Setting Up the Rice Experiment

- Sprinkle 10 white rice grains in the bottom of a clear plastic cup and label the cup "White Rice."
- Sprinkle 10 brown rice grains in another cup and label the cup "Brown Rice."
- Sprinkle 10 grains of rice in the husk in a third cup and label the cup "Rice in the Husk."
- Fill each cup to the 5 cm level with clean water.
- Keep the temperature above 21°C (70°F).
- Observe the rice every few days.

After students have set up their experiments, ask

? Why do you think the article suggests sprinkling 10 rice seeds in the bottom of each cup instead of just one? (It gives you a better chance of getting some rice to grow.)

? Why not put different numbers of rice grains in each cup? (We need to control that variable to make it a fair test; each cup should have the same number of rice grains.)

Students use pages 3 and 4 of the Rice Journals to record observations of each type of rice every few days. Each day they should check to make sure the water level is at 5 cm and add more water as needed.

After four observations, students can fill in the "Results" section in the Rice Journal. Students should observe that only the rice in the husk actually germinates. Discuss the following questions:

? Why do you think the rice in the husk germinated and not the brown or white rice? What do you think might be missing from the brown and white rice?

If you would like to continue observing the rice plants as they grow, transfer the seedlings to a large plastic tub of soil and follow the directions in the Rice article.

MEASURING THE WATER LEVEL

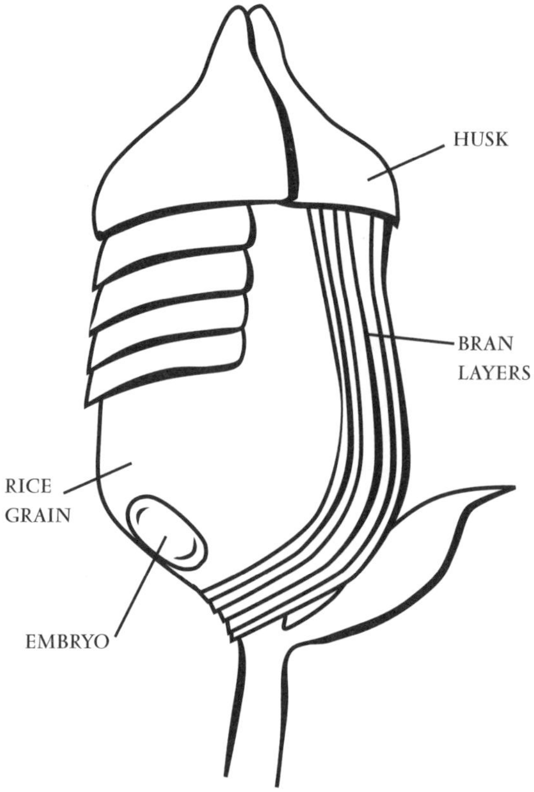

PARTS OF A RICE GRAIN

explain

Read Aloud

Using Features of Nonfiction

Tell students that they will learn about what's inside a grain of rice by looking at a nonfiction book called *Rice*. Introduce the nonfiction book *Rice* by Louise Spilsbury, and read pages 4 and 5, "What Is Rice?" Ask

? Is it necessary to finish reading the entire book to learn what's inside a grain of rice?

? What parts of a nonfiction book can help us look up specific information? (table of contents, index, glossary)

Show students the table of contents. Ask them to raise their hands when they think they hear a chapter title that might help them find out what a rice grain looks like inside. Then read aloud the table of contents. (The chapter titled "Looking at Rice" has the information they need.)

Read pages 12 and 13 of *Rice*, and point out the labels on the photo and diagram. Sketch a rice grain on the board and label the parts. Include the embryo, which is not mentioned in the reading.

Then write the following words and definitions on the board:

- Embryo—the part of the seed that develops into a rice plant
- Husk—the hard outer covering, or seed coat, of the rice grain, which protects the embryo
- Bran layers—the thin brown layers between the husk and the rice grain
- Rice grain—the food for the embryo as it develops

Ask students

? What are the differences among rice in the husk, brown rice, and white rice? (Rice in the husk is the rice grain still in its seed coat. Brown rice is the grain left after the outer husk has been removed. White rice is the same as brown rice, but with the outer bran layers removed.)

Show students the rice grain diagram again on page 13 of *Rice*, and refer to your diagram on the board. Then go back to the question generated by the rice experiment.

? Why do you think the rice in the husk germinated and not the brown or white rice? What do you think might be missing from the brown and white rice? (The milling process removes the husks as well as the embryos from the brown and white rice. They cannot germinate because the embryo is the part of the seed that develops into the plant.)

Students should now label the rice diagram on page 6 of their journals and fill in the explanation table on page 5. Then have them write their conclusions on the last page of their journals. Encourage them to use evidence from the experiment to write their conclusions.

elaborate

Journey Through a Rice Mill

Ask students

? How do you think rice gets from the field to your table?

Determining Importance

Tell students that the book *Rice* describes this process. As you read pages 14 through 21 in *Rice,* have students listen for the answers to the following questions:

? How are the rice grains removed from the stalks? (Farmers beat the stalks to shake off the grain. In some places they use a combine harvester to cut down the plants and separate the grain from the stalks.)

? How are the husks removed from the rice grains? (Some farmers crush the grains to loosen the hard husks, then toss the grains in the air to get the loose husks off. In some places, they use machines with big rollers to rub the grains off the husks. For white rice, the bran layer is also taken off by rubbing the grains together in a machine.)

Ask students to think about what happens to the rice after it is harvested. Pass out Journey Through a Rice Mill, sandpaper, and a few grains each of rice in the husk and instant white rice to each student. Have students complete the student page and discuss their answers to the questions.

1. Describe the way your rice grains have changed. (Students should observe that the husk has been removed and the grain is lighter in color.)
2. Why do you think the husk and embryos are removed before rice is sold for food? (The husks are not edible, and removing the embryos keeps the seeds from germinating.)
3. In what ways are the rice grains and the instant white rice different? (The instant white rice is very white, shriveled, and more brittle than the rice in the husk. The rice in the husk is darker, smoother, and harder.)
4. What might have been done to turn brown rice into instant white rice? Read the instant rice package for clues! (The bran layer has been removed, the rice has been enriched with vitamins and minerals, and it has been precooked.)

evaluate

Design a Plant Experiment

Tell students they will have an opportunity to design their own plant experiments. Pass out the Design a Plant Experiment student page. Allow time for students to complete number 1: "My questions about plant growth." Make a T-chart on the board labeled "testable" and "not testable." Tell students that some questions are testable questions that can be answered through experimentation. Then ask some of them to share a question from number 1 that might be testable. Write these questions on the left side of the T-chart.

Then explain that some questions can't be answered by experimentation. Often these questions can be answered through library or internet research. Ask some students to share a question from number 1 that is not testable. Write these questions on the right side of the T-chart. Then have students choose the testable question from their student page that they want to investigate by placing an * next to it.

Tell students they will receive two bean plants to use in their experiments. Then have them com-

Sample T-Chart

Testable	Not Testable
How does sunlight affect plant growth?	Why do plants make their own food?
Does fertilizer really help plants grow?	What is the largest plant in the world?
Can plants grow in substances other than soil?	Why do plants have green leaves?

plete the rest of the Design a Plant Experiment student page. Use the following rubric to assess student work.

After you finish assessing the Design a Plant Experiment student pages, pass them back to students. Allow students to correct any flaws in their experimental designs and give them the materials to complete their experiments.

Scoring Rubric for Design a Plant Experiment	
4 Point Response	The student selects a testable question, makes a prediction relating to the question, correctly identifies experimental and controlled variables, lists logical steps for performing the investigation, and lists materials needed for the investigation.
3 Point Response	The student demonstrates a flaw in understanding of the concepts of experimental design OR is missing one or two required elements.
2 Point Response	The student demonstrates a flaw in understanding of the concepts of experimental design AND is missing one or two required elements; OR is missing three or four required elements.
1 Point Response	The student demonstrates a flaw in understanding of the concepts of experimental design AND is missing three or more required elements; OR is missing four or more required elements.
0 Point Response	The student shows no understanding of the concepts of experimental design AND is missing all required elements.

evaluate

Experimental Design Quiz

Review experimental variables, controlled variables, and experimental design, and then administer the Experimental Design Quiz. The answers follow.

1. c
2. a
3. Responses may include any two of the following: type of bean, type of soil, amount of sunlight, size of containers, amount of soil, etc.
4. c
5. Brand of fertilizer
6. Responses may include any two of the following: The amount of water is different for each plant; the amount of sunlight is different for each plant; three different kinds of plants are used; three different sizes of container are used. Ashley could improve her experiment by making sure these variables are controlled.

Inquiry Place

Have students brainstorm questions about rice such as

? How does the amount of light affect the germination of rice seeds? Test it!

? How does temperature affect the germination of rice seeds? Test it!

? How do pollutants (bleach, salt, etc.) affect the germination of rice seeds? Test it!

? Why can rice plants be grown in flooded fields? Research it!

Have students select a question to investigate as a class, or have groups of students vote on the question they want to investigate as teams. After they make their predictions, they can design an experiment to test their predictions. Students can present their findings at a poster session.

Websites

California Rice Commission
www.calrice.org

USA Rice Federation
www.usarice.com

More Books to Read

Demi. 1997. *One grain of rice: A mathematical folktale.* New York: Scholastic.
Summary: This beautifully illustrated Indian folktale tells the story of a resourceful girl who outsmarts a greedy raja and saves her village. When offered a reward for a good deed, clever Rani asks for only one grain of rice, doubled every day for thirty days. The result is enough rice to feed her village for a long, long time.

Dooley, N. 1992. *Everybody cooks rice.* Minneapolis, MN: Carolrhoda Books.
Summary: A little girl travels the neighborhood trying to round up her younger brother for dinner. Each family invites her in for a taste of what they are cooking. She discovers that despite their divergent backgrounds, "everybody cooks rice."

Gibbons, G. 1993. *From seed to plant.* New York: Holiday House.
Summary: A simple introduction to plant reproduction, this picture book for lower elementary students discusses pollination, seed dispersal, parts of a seed, and growth from seed to plant. A simple project with step-by-step directions for growing a bean plant is also included.

Pascoe, E. 1996. *Seeds and seedlings: Nature close up.* Woodbridge, CT: Blackbirch Marketing.
Summary: This clearly written book of seed projects and experiments is enhanced by extraordinary close-up photographs.

References

California Foundation for Agriculture in the Classroom. 2003. *Rice activity sheet.* Sacramento, CA: California Foundation for Agriculture in the Classroom.
Journey Through a Rice Mill is adapted from an activity on this fact sheet.

Name: ______________________________

Let's Learn About Rice

Anticipation Guide

Before reading the article Rice, guess whether the following statements about rice are true (T) or false (F). Mark your guess in the left column. After reading the article, mark the statements (T or F) in the right column.

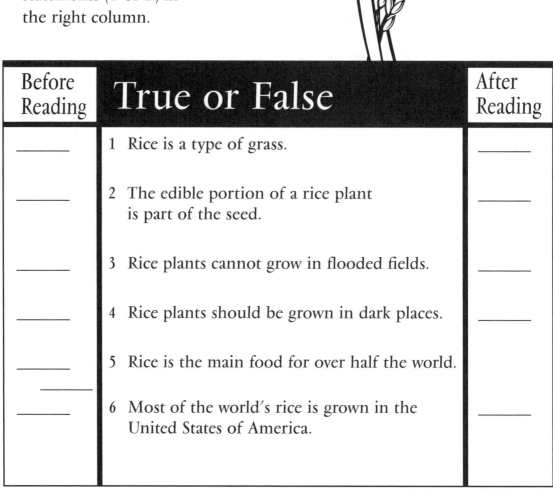

Before Reading	True or False	After Reading
______	1 Rice is a type of grass.	______
______	2 The edible portion of a rice plant is part of the seed.	______
______	3 Rice plants cannot grow in flooded fields.	______
______	4 Rice plants should be grown in dark places.	______
______	5 Rice is the main food for over half the world.	______
______	6 Most of the world's rice is grown in the United States of America.	______

Rice

The Rice Plant

Rice is a type of grass. It is usually grown in flooded fields because the water controls weeds and pests. The edible portion of the rice plant is part of the seed.

How to Grow Rice

You can grow rice by following this procedure:

1. Sprinkle 10 rice seeds in the bottom of a clear plastic cup.
2. Fill the cup to the 5 cm level with clean water.
3. Keep the temperature above 21°C (70°F).
4. After the seeds germinate, put them in a large plastic tub filled to the 5 cm mark with soil.
5. Fill the tub with water until the water is 5 cm above the soil level.
6. Keep the water level at 5 cm throughout the growth cycle.
7. Provide growing plants with plenty of sunlight.

Rice Is Important

Rice is the primary food for more than half of the world! Rice is packed with carbohydrates. This means it is a kind of food that gives you energy. In many countries, people eat rice for breakfast, lunch, and dinner. People in Asia have grown and eaten rice for more than 5,000 years.

Rice Around the World

About 90% of the world's rice is grown in Asia. China, India, and Indonesia are the top rice producers. There are a few states in the United States that grow rice, including California, Mississippi, Arkansas, Louisiana, and Texas.

Rice Journal

Scientist: ______________

Dates: from ____ to ____

Prediction

Which of the following do you predict will **germinate** and eventually grow into a rice plant: white rice, brown rice, or rice in the hull? Why do you think so?

Let's design an experiment to find out.

In this experiment, our **experimental** variable is

Let's make a list of **controlled variables**, in other words, conditions we should keep the same for each type of seed.

Controlled Variables

Conclusions

What conclusions can you make from the results of this experiment?

What is your evidence?

Label the following parts on the diagram below: husk, embryo, bran layer, rice grain

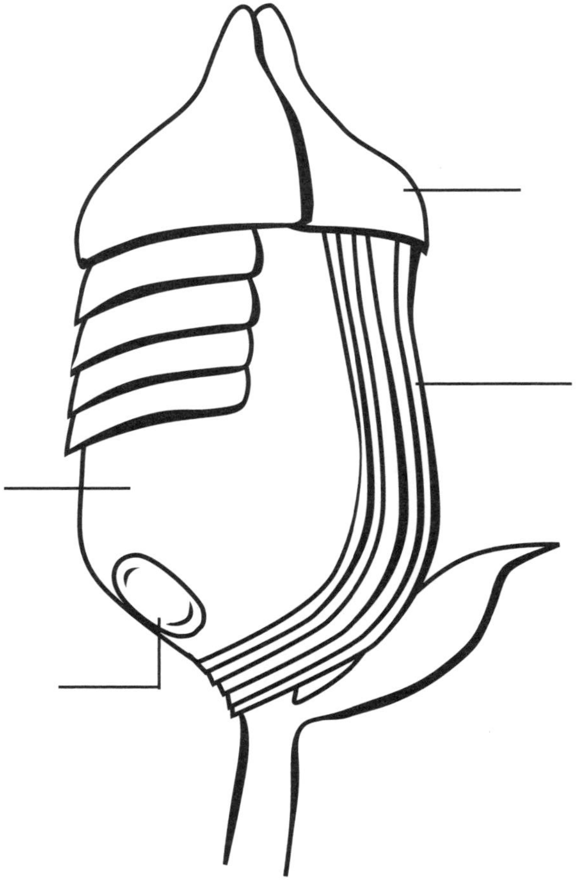

6

Observations

Observation #1 Date:

Type of Rice	Observations
White Rice	
Brown Rice	
Rice in the Husk	

Observation #2 Date:

Type of Rice	Observations
White Rice	
Brown Rice	
Rice in the Husk	

3

Observation #3 Date:

Type of Rice	Observations
White Rice	
Brown Rice	
Rice in the Husk	

Observation #4 Date:

Type of Rice	Observations
White Rice	
Brown Rice	
Rice in the Husk	

4

Results

Type of Rice	Results (How many seeds germinated?)
White Rice	
Brown Rice	
Rice in the Husk	

Label the parts of the rice seed on the diagram on the next page. Then write the function of each of the seed parts in the table below.

Seed Part	Function
Husk	
Bran Layer	
Embryo	
Rice Grain	

5

Name: ______________________________

Journey Through a Rice Mill

The following activity is a simulation of part of the rice milling process:

- Observe some grains of rice in the husk.
- Place a piece of sandpaper on the desk.
- Place several grains of rice in the husk on the sandpaper and place another piece of sandpaper on top.
- Gently rub the two pieces back and forth until you see a change in the grains.

1 Describe the way your rice grains have changed.

____

2 Why do you think the husk and embryos are removed before rice is sold for food?

____

- Take the sanded rice grains and put them next to some instant white rice from the grocery store.
- Compare the rice grains to the instant white rice.

3 In what ways are the rice grains and the instant white rice different?

____

4 What might have been done to turn brown rice into instant white rice? (Read the instant rice package for clues!)

____

Name: ________________________________

Design a Plant Experiment

1 My questions about plant growth:

____

____

2 Put an * next to the question you plan to investigate.

3 My prediction:

____

____

4 My experimental variable:

____

5 Variables I will control to keep the experiment fair:

____

6 Steps I will follow to investigate my question:

____

____

____

7 Materials I will need:

____

____

Checkpoint ☐

Name: ______________________________

Experimental Design

Quiz

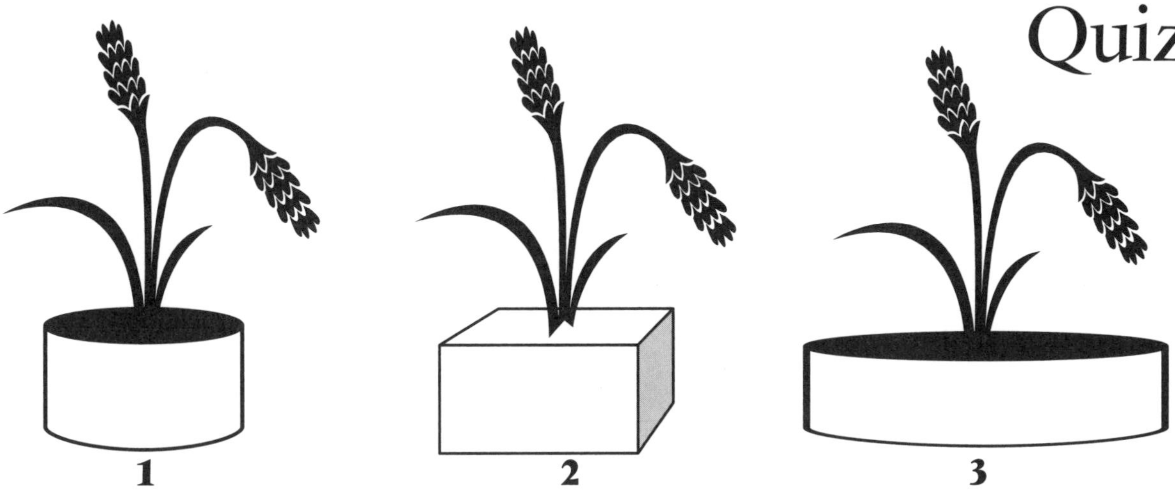

A researcher wants to learn which of three fields has the best soil for growing rice. The researcher fills each container with soil from a different field. The containers are placed next to one another in a sunny window. One rice plant is grown in each container, and each container receives the same amount of water.

1 What is wrong with the materials the researcher used in the experiment?

a The rice plant in container 1 will receive the most sunlight.

b The containers should each receive different amounts of water.

c The containers hold different amounts of soil in different shapes.

2 Jeff wants to find out how the amount of water affects the growth of bean plants. What is Jeff's experimental variable?

a amount of water

b type of bean

c type of soil

3 What are two things Jeff will need to control, or keep the same, to make his experiment fair?

_________________ and _________________

Name: ______________________________

Experimental Design Quiz cont.

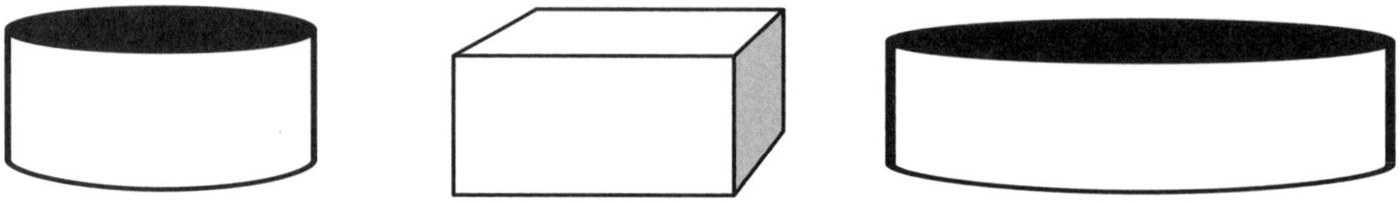

BLUEGRASS RYEGRASS BENT GRASS

Rani wants to find out which type of grass grows the tallest. She is testing three types of grass seed as shown above. She puts equal amounts of soil in each container.

4 How many grass seeds should Rani plant in each container?

- **a** Rani should plant only 1 grass seed in each container so that she will not have to measure as many grass plants.
- **b** Rani should plant 1 grass seed in the first container, 2 grass seeds in the second container, and 3 in the third container.
- **c** Rani should plant 10 grass seeds in each container in case some of them don't grow. She can measure all of the grass that grows in each container and average the measurements.

Experimental Design Quiz cont.

Ashley designed an experiment to find out which brand of fertilizer will make plants grow the tallest.

	Plant A	**Plant B**	**Plant C**
Brand of Fertilizer	Give Primo fertilizer.	Give K-Gro fertilizer.	Give Acme fertilizer.
Amount of Water	Water with 50 ml every day.	Water with 100 ml every day.	Water with 200 ml every day.
Amount of Sunlight	Place in bright sun.	Place in part sun.	Place in shade.
Data	Measure height daily.	Measure height daily.	Measure height daily.

5 What is Ashley's experimental variable?

____

6 There are several things wrong with Ashley's experimental design. Describe two things that are wrong. Then explain how she could improve her experiment so that it is a fair test.

____

____

____

____

What's Poppin'?

Description

Learners investigate what makes popcorn pop. They design a safe, fair, and repeatable experiment to test various popcorn brands and share their findings in a poster session.

Suggested Grade Levels: 5–6

Lesson Objectives Connecting to the *Framework*

Science and Engineering Practices
- Planning and carrying out investigations
- Analyzing and interpreting data

Crosscutting Concepts
- Cause and Effect

Featured Picture Book

Title	***Popcorn!***
Author	**Elaine Landau**
Illustrator	**Brian Lies**
Publisher	**Charlesbridge**
Year	**2003**
Genre	**Nonnarrative Information**
Summary	**Full of information about poporn, including where it comes from, its history, and what makes it pop.**

Time Needed

This lesson will take several class periods. Suggested scheduling is as follows:

Day 1: **Engage** with *Popcorn!* read aloud, and **Explore** with What's Poppin'? Checkpoint Lab, Part A

Day 2: **Explore** with What's Poppin'? Checkpoint Lab, Parts B–D; **Explain** with reading and relating to the checkpoint lab

Day 3: **Elaborate** with Popcorn Brand Test Checkpoint Lab

Day 4: **Evaluate** with Popcorn Poster Session

Materials

For Engage Activity

- Microwave popcorn (3 or 4 popped bags—enough for the whole class to eat)
- Bowls or napkins for popcorn (1 per student)
- Popcorn-shaped I Wonder/I Learned chart

For the What's Poppin'? Checkpoint Lab

Read safety note under "Explore."

- Fresh jar of popcorn
- Prepare ahead of time:
    - Write "A" on resealable plastic sandwich bags and divide 125 ml (about ½ cup) fresh popcorn kernels into the bags (1 bag per team of four).
    - Dry 125 ml (about ½ cup) of popcorn kernels by placing them in a single layer in a pan in an oven at 90° C (190° F) for at least 5 hours (or overnight). Write "B" on resealable plastic sandwich bags and divide the dried popcorn into the bags (1 bag per team).
- A red plastic cup and a green plastic cup with the bottoms taped together (1 per team)
- Hand lenses (1 per student)
- Safety goggles (1 per student)
- Glass test tubes (4 per team)
- Masking tape to label test tubes
- Wire test-tube holders (1 per team)
- Test-tube racks (1 per team)
- Large sturdy candles attached to a base made of a chunk of clay (1 per team)
- Aluminum pie plates to hold candles (1 per team)
- Safety matches (for teacher use only)
- 3 cm x 3 cm aluminum foil squares (4 per team)
- Pipettes or eye droppers (1 per team)
- Small plastic cups containing about 5 ml of cooking oil (1 per team)
- Stopwatches (1 per team) or clock with second hand for entire class to use

For Demonstration

- Brown paper bag
- White napkin or paper towel

For the Popcorn Brand Test Checkpoint Lab

Read safety note under "Elaborate."

- Three different brands of microwave popcorn to test: same size, same flavor (Use 1 of each brand per team. You can have students bring them in.)
- Microwave ovens (about 1 per every 3 teams)
- A red plastic cup and a green plastic cup with the bottoms taped together (1 per team)
- Poster board (1 per team)

Student Pages

- What's Poppin'? Checkpoint Lab
- Popcorn Brand Test Checkpoint Lab
- Popcorn Poster Session

Background

Each year Americans eat more than a million pounds of popcorn! Not only is popcorn a delicious and nutritious treat, it also provides an engaging way for students to be involved in scientific inquiry. This lesson addresses the question "What makes popcorn pop?" Through a series of observations, experiments, and readings, students find out that each kernel of popcorn contains a tiny bit of water, which is surrounded by soft starch and enclosed in the kernel's hard outer shell. When you heat the kernel, the water expands and turns into steam. Pressure from the steam builds up against the hard, airtight shell until ... *POP!* The shell gives way and the soft starch explodes outward, literally turning the kernel inside out.

But what about the kernels that don't pop? Either they have dried out, or the outer hull has been damaged so that the heated water can escape without building up the pressure it would take to explode. When you go to the grocery store, you probably see a dozen or so brands of popcorn on the shelf. How do you know which one pops the best? The fact is, it probably has less to do with the brand and more to do with the age of the popcorn. The brand with the expiration date that is farthest in the future is probably the one that will pop best. This is because fresher popcorn kernels generally contain more water. When the kernels dry out, they no longer pop.

In this lesson, students first investigate why popcorn pops. Then they design and conduct their own safe, fair, and repeatable experiment to test various microwave popcorn brands. Finally, they have the opportunity to communicate their explanations and procedures through a poster session.

engage

Read Aloud

I Wonder/I Learned Chart

Draw a large, whole-class I Wonder/I Learned chart titled "Popcorn." Make some microwave popcorn. Give each student a bowl of hot popped popcorn to eat as you fill out the chart together. Ask, "What are you wondering about popcorn?" and add to the "W" column of the chart. If students do not volunteer the question "What makes popcorn pop?" then add it to the chart as one of your own wonderings.

Show students the cover of *Popcorn!* Explain that authors and illustrators often will include a dedication in the front of their books. Point out that the author, Elaine Landau, dedicates the book to Michael, her son. She lives in Miami, Florida, with her husband and son. Many of her books have been written under a palm tree while drinking lemonade! The illustrator, Brian Lies (rhymes with "cheese"), dedicates the book to "the raccoon who raided my corn patch," which explains why a raccoon appears on almost every page of the book! He lives in a seaside town in Massachusetts with his wife and daughter and tends a big vegetable garden behind the house. Read pages 3 through 9 aloud, stopping to allow students to turn and talk about the questions on the "Pop Quiz on Popcorn" before revealing the answers.

Sample I Wonder/I Learned Chart

W	L
Where does popcorn grow? What makes popcorn pop? If you plant a popcorn kernel, will it grow?	Popcorn is the oldest of the three types of corn: field corn, sweet corn, and popcorn.

Have students add information they learned from the reading to the "L" column of the I Wonder/I Learned chart, as well as any more wonderings they have about popcorn as new understandings develop.

explore

What's Poppin'? Checkpoint Lab

In advance, prepare all of the materials necessary for the What's Poppin'? Checkpoint Lab. See "Teaching Science Through Inquiry," Chapter 3, for a list of tips for managing a checkpoint lab. Check your school policy for its rules on using an open flame in an elementary setting before using this activity.

Tell students they are going to investigate what makes popcorn pop. Divide students into teams of four. Have the following materials available for each team:

- A red plastic cup and a green plastic cup with the bottoms taped together
- 4 unpopped popcorn kernels
- 4 pieces of popped popcorn
- 1 sandwich bag of fresh popcorn (marked "A")
- 1 sandwich bag of oven-dried popcorn (marked "B")
- 4 hand lenses
- 4 glass test tubes
- 1 wire test-tube holder
- 1 large sturdy candle attached to a base made of a chunk of clay
- 1 aluminum pie plate to hold candles
- 1 test-tube rack
- 4 safety goggles (Safety goggles should be chemical splash safety goggles conforming to the ANSI Z87.1 standard. These are also impact goggles.)
- Masking tape to label test tubes
- 4 small squares of aluminum foil (large enough to cover openings of test tubes)

- 1 pipette or eye dropper
- About 5 ml of cooking oil in a small plastic cup labeled "oil"

Popcorn Testing

Distribute the What's Poppin? Checkpoint Lab. Assign one person to be the reader for each team. Readers will read the directions out loud for their teams. They will put the green cup on top if their team is working. They will put the red cup on top if their team has a question or if they are ready for a check mark. Each member of the group is responsible for recording data and writing responses.

Let teams begin and work at their own paces. Before you give a team a check mark or stamp so that they can move ahead in the lab, informally evaluate them by asking probing questions of each member of the team, such as

- What is your evidence?
- What observations support your conclusion?
- Could there be another explanation?

Be sure to check students' experimental setups and review the safety rules with each team before you light their candles in Part C of the checkpoint lab.

SAFETY

Tell students that in this experiment they will be popping popcorn by heating it in a test tube over a flame. Because they are working with flame, tell them they must follow the following safety rules.

1. Roll up your sleeves and tie back long hair.
2. Wear safety goggles over your eyes.
3. Use a wire holder to hold the test tube over the flame, but not directly in the flame.
4. When you heat anything in a test tube, point the open end away from yourself and others.
5. Keep your work area clean and clear of flammable materials.

In *Safety in the Elementary (K-6) Science Classroom: Second Edition,* the American Chemical Society (2001) gives the following safety rules for working with fire and heat sources:

1. Teachers should never leave the room while any flame is lighted or other heat source is in use.
2. Never heat flammable liquids. Heat only water or water solutions.
3. Use only glassware made from borosilicate glass (Kimax or Pyrex) for heating.
4. When working around a heat source, tie back long hair and secure loose clothing.
5. The area surrounding a heat source should be clean and have no combustible materials nearby.
6. When using a hot plate, locate it so that a child cannot pull it off the work top or trip over the power cord.

SAFETY

7. Never leave the room while the hot plate is plugged in, whether or not it is in use; never allow students near an in-use hot plate if the teacher is not immediately beside the students.
8. Be certain that hot plates have been unplugged and are cool before handling. Check for residual heat by placing a few drops of water on the hot plate surface.
9. Never use alcohol burners.
10. Students should use candles only under the strict supervision of the teacher. Candles should be placed in a "drip pan" such as an aluminum pie plate large enough to contain the candle if it is knocked over.
11. The teacher should wear safety goggles and use heat resistant mitts when working with hot materials. All students near hot liquids should wear safety goggles.*
12. The teacher should keep a fire extinguisher near the activity area and be trained in its use.
13. The teacher should know what to do in case of fire. If a school policy does not exist, check with local fire officials for information.

Before using this activity, check your school's policy on using an open flame. Some schools forbid it.

Tell students they should not eat popcorn from the test tubes.

**Investigating Safely: A Guide for High School Teachers* recommends that chemical splash safety goggles conforming to the ANSI Z87.1 standard be used for all activities that require goggles. These chemical splash safety goggles are also impact goggles (Texley, Kwan, and Summers 2004).

explain

Reading and Relating to the Checkpoint Lab

When all teams have completed the checkpoint lab, have students share their observations and conclusions in their own words. Then discuss the following questions:

? What did you observe inside the test tubes as they were being heated? (Students should have observed water condensing on the sides of the test tubes and on the foil.)

? Where can you infer the water came from? (from inside the popcorn kernels)

? What do you know about how water molecules behave as they are heated? Think about a pot of water heating on the stove. (The water molecules move faster and spread out as the water begins boiling. Then they spread out so much they rise into the air as steam.)

Determining Importance

Next tell students you are going to read more of *Popcorn!* Have them listen for an explanation of what makes popcorn pop. Read pages 10 through 13 aloud.

Then do the following demonstration: Place a white napkin or white paper towel inside a brown paper bag. Blow up the bag, and then pop it so that the napkin pops out. Ask students

- What does the bag represent? (the hull or outer covering of the popcorn)
- What does the white napkin represent? (the starchy stuff inside the popcorn)
- What makes the starch explode out of the hull in a real popcorn kernel? (The water inside boils and turns to steam. A little bit of water boils up into a lot of steam. There is much more steam than will fit inside the kernel. The steam builds up, and the kernel explodes.)

Finally, ask students what new information they have learned about popcorn and add it to the Popcorn I Wonder/I Learned chart.

elaborate

Popcorn Brand Test Checkpoint Lab

In advance, set up one or more microwave ovens in your classroom. You can provide the popcorn for this activity or, even better, have each student bring a bag from home, but make sure they bring in the same-size bags of the same flavor. See "Teaching Science Through Inquiry," Chapter 3, for a list of tips for managing a checkpoint lab.

Students can elaborate on what they have learned about popcorn by designing and carrying out their own experiments to find out which brand pops the most kernels. Ask the following questions to help students think about controlling variables and good experimental design:

- What were we testing in the checkpoint lab? (We compared fresh popcorn to dried popcorn to see which one would pop. We wanted to find out what makes popcorn pop.)
- What was the *experimental variable,* or the thing that we changed, in our test? (the type of popcorn: fresh or oven-dried)
- What were the *controlled variables,* or the things we kept the same, in our popcorn test? (same-size test tubes, same amount of oil, same number of kernels, same amount of heating time)
- Why did we keep all those things the same? (to keep the test "fair")

Pass out the Popcorn Brand Test student pages. Tell students they will design an experiment to find out which brand of popcorn pops the most kernels by counting the number of popped kernels. On these pages, students will determine that the experimental variable in this test is the brand of popcorn. They will also determine which of the following variables need to be controlled to make it a fair test, such as

SAFETY

Before using the Popcorn Brand Test Checkpoint Lab, check your school's policy on eating as part of a science lab activity. Some schools forbid it, and commercial labs can be fined for even the appearance of eating. Make sure your students know they should never taste anything in a lab activity. *Exploring Safely: A Guide for Elementary Teachers* recommends, "Nothing should be tasted or eaten as part of science lab work" (Kwan and Texley 2002). The best way to do this activity is as an experiment that does not include eating the popped popcorn, but if there is any chance your students will eat the popcorn, make sure your sanitary preparations have been adequate. Cleaning up a section of your room to do this activity in can be a teaching tool that helps students learn a way of doing science.

- size or weight of the popcorn bags,
- flavor of popcorn,
- microwave,
- power level of microwave,
- position of the bag in the microwave, and
- amount of time in the microwave.

Students will then write a procedure for their popcorn brand testing. Students should recognize the importance of formulating procedures and communicating data in a manner that allows others to understand and safely repeat an experiment. When each member of a team has completed "Part A: Designing a Popcorn Brand Test," that team can signal to you that they are ready to move on. Before signing off on their work, make sure their experimental design is safe, fair, and repeatable. Ask each member of the team a question about the experimental design as a quick assessment. Once each student gets a check mark, the team is ready to move ahead and perform the experiment.

Sample Procedure for Popcorn Brand Test

- Remove plastic covering from popcorn bag.
- Place 3-ounce bag of Brand A popcorn in center of microwave with correct side up.
- Cook for exactly 2 min. and 30 sec. at highest power and remove bag.
- Allow bag to cool for 3 min.
- Open bag carefully, and count popped kernels.
- Record data and graph results in a bar graph.
- Repeat with Brand B and Brand C.
- Compare results, and draw conclusions.

Students will use "Part B: Popcorn Data" to record the results of their experiments. Discuss the type of graph that is appropriate for displaying the data.

? Which type of graph is the best for displaying the data? (bar graph)

? Why? (We are comparing totals, not parts of a whole or changes over time.)

If all teams are using the same three brands of popcorn, you may want to record their data on a whole-class table and average results. You can then graph the averages on a whole-class graph. Discuss reasons for variations in the results—for example, different controls, different procedures, freshness of popcorn, and experimental error.

evaluate

Popcorn Poster Session

Students will present what they've learned about popcorn in a poster session. They will use the Popcorn Poster Session student page as a guide. Students should include the following in their poster presentations:

- Some important information they learned about popcorn
- A scientifically accurate diagram explaining how popcorn pops
- Their predictions for the popcorn brand testing
- The step-by-step procedures they followed in their experiments
- A graph showing the results of their experiments
- Their conclusions for the experiments
- An original advertisement, commercial, or jingle for the popcorn brand that popped the most kernels in their experiment

Use the following rubric to evaluate each team's work:

Scoring Rubric for Popcorn Poster Session

4 Point Response	The poster includes accurate facts about popcorn, a labeled and scientifically accurate diagram explaining how popcorn pops, a prediction, a logical and clearly communicated procedure, a labeled bar graph, an appropriate conclusion, and an original advertisement, commercial, or jingle for popcorn.
3 Point Response	The poster demonstrates a flaw in understanding of the concepts and procedures OR is missing one or two required elements.
2 Point Response	The poster demonstrates a flaw in understanding of the concepts and procedures AND is missing one or two required elements; OR the poster is missing three required elements.
1 Point Response	The poster demonstrates a flaw in understanding of the concepts and procedures AND is missing three required elements; OR the poster is missing more than three required elements.
0 Point Response	The poster shows no understanding of the concepts and procedures and is missing all required elements.

Inquiry Place

Have students brainstorm testable questions such as

- ? Does the color of the popcorn kernel affect the color of the popped corn?
- ? Which results in the most popped kernels: frozen, refrigerated, or room temperature kernels?
- ? Will other types of corn pop? Test field corn, sweet corn, and Indian corn.

Then have students select a question to investigate as a class, or groups of students can vote on the questions they want to investigate as teams. After they make their predictions, they can design an experiment to test their predictions. Students can present their findings at a poster session.

More Books to Read

de Paola, T. 1989. *The popcorn book.* New York: Holiday House.
Summary: This book is full of information on popcorn, including its history, varieties, and recipes.

Gibbons, G. 2009. *Corn.* New York: Holiday House.
Summary: This book offers up the history of popcorn as well as the details concerning planting, cultivating, and harvesting and its many uses.

Kudlinski, K. 1998. *Popcorn plants.* Minneapolis, MN: Lerner Publications Company.
Summary: This fact-filled chapter book describes the life cycle of the popcorn plant from the time the farmer plants the seed until the kernel explodes. Includes color photographs, a glossary, and ideas for sharing the book with children.

References

American Chemical Society (ACS). 2001. *Safety in the elementary (K–6) science classroom: Second edition.* Washington, DC: ACS.

Kwan, T., and J. Texley. 2002. *Exploring safely: A guide for elementary teachers.* Arlington, VA: NSTA Press.

Texley, J., T. Kwan, and J. Summers. 2004. *Investigating safely: A guide for high school teachers.* Arlington, VA: NSTA Press.

Name: ______________________________

What's Poppin'?

Checkpoint Lab

Follow the directions below. If your team is working, put the green cup on top. If you have a question, put the red cup on top. If you are finished with a part and you are ready for a check from your teacher, put the red cup on top.

Part A Popcorn Observations

Unpopped Popcorn	Popped Popcorn
Use a hand lens to observe an unpopped popcorn kernel and draw it in this box.	Use a hand lens to observe a popped popcorn kernel and draw it in this box.

Name: ______________________________

What's Poppin'?

Checkpoint Lab cont.

Part A Questions

1 What differences do you observe between unpopped and popped popcorn?

____

____

____

____

2 What do you think happened inside the popped popcorn kernel when it was heated?

____

____

____

____

Checkpoint A ☐

Name: ______________________________

What's Poppin'?
Checkpoint Lab cont.

Part B Setting Up the Popcorn

Investigation

☑ *Check the boxes as your team completes each step.*

- ☐ Attach the base of the candle firmly to the pie plate using a lump of clay.
- ☐ Place four test tubes in the test-tube rack.
- ☐ Put a small masking tape label near the top of each test tube. Use a pen or marker to label the test tubes A-1, A-2, B-1, and B-2.
- ☐ Use a pipette or eye dropper to place 2 drops of cooking oil into the bottom of each test tube. (The cooking oil will help the kernels heat evenly.)
- ☐ Place 4 kernels of **fresh** popcorn from the sandwich bag marked "A" into test tube A-1.
- ☐ Place 4 kernels of **fresh** popcorn from the sandwich bag marked "A" into test tube A-2.
- ☐ Place 4 kernels of **dried** popcorn from the sandwich bag marked "B" into test tube B-1.
- ☐ Place 4 kernels of **dried** popcorn from the sandwich bag marked "B" into test tube B-2.
- ☐ Cover each test tube with a square of aluminum foil and poke a tiny hole in the center of the foil with the tip of a pencil.

The popcorn in the test tubes labeled with an "A" is fresh popcorn straight from the jar. The popcorn in the test tubes labeled with a "B" has been dried in an oven overnight. Your task is to figure out what makes popcorn pop. You will make your conclusion based on evidence from this investigation. Before you begin, you will make some predictions.

Name: ______________________________

What's Poppin'?

Checkpoint Lab cont.

Part B Questions

1 What do you predict will happen when you heat the test tubes marked with an "A" over a flame?

____

____

____

____

2 What do you predict will happen when you heat the test tubes marked with a "B" over a flame?

____

____

____

____

Checkpoint B ☐

Name: ______________________________

What's Poppin'?
Checkpoint Lab cont.

Part C Setting Up the Investigation

SAFETY

THE FOLLOWING SAFETY RULES APPLY TO THIS ACTIVITY:

1 Roll up your sleeves and tie back long hair.
2 Wear safety goggles over your eyes.
3 Use a wire holder to hold the test tube over the flame.
4 When you heat anything in a test tube, point the open end away from yourself and others.
5 Keep your work area clean and clear of flammable materials.
6 Do not eat the popcorn!

SAFETY CHECK

Check the boxes as your team completes each step.

☐ 1 Are your sleeves rolled up and is long hair tied back?
☐ 2 Are your safety goggles protecting your eyes?
☐ 3 Do you have a wire test-tube holder?
☐ 4 Do you know where to point a test tube when heating it?
☐ 5 Is your work area clean and clear of flammable materials?

Name: ______________________________

What's Poppin'?

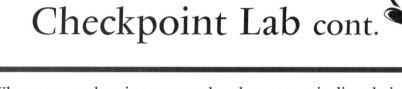

Checkpoint Lab cont.

SAFETY

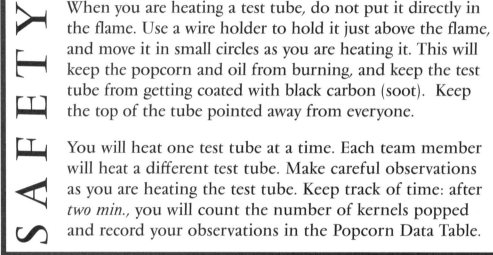

When you are heating a test tube, do not put it directly in the flame. Use a wire holder to hold it just above the flame, and move it in small circles as you are heating it. This will keep the popcorn and oil from burning, and keep the test tube from getting coated with black carbon (soot). Keep the top of the tube pointed away from everyone.

You will heat one test tube at a time. Each team member will heat a different test tube. Make careful observations as you are heating the test tube. Keep track of time: after *two min.*, you will count the number of kernels popped and record your observations in the Popcorn Data Table.

Part C Questions

1 How will you heat the test tube safely?

____

2 How long will you heat each test tube?

____

When you are ready to begin, signal your teacher by putting your red cup up. Your teacher will light the candle for you.

Checkpoint C ☐

Name: ______________________________

What's Poppin'?
Checkpoint Lab cont.

Part D What Makes Popcorn Pop?

POPCORN DATA TABLE		
Test Tube	# of Kernels Popped	Observations
A-1 Fresh Popcorn		
A-2 Fresh Popcorn		
B-1 Dried Popcorn		
B-2 Dried Popcorn		

Part D Questions

1 What did you observe on the sides and tops of the test tubes as you heated them?

____

2 Did you observe any differences between the A test tubes and the B test tubes as you heated them? If so, what was different?

____

Name: ____________________

What's Poppin'?

Checkpoint Lab cont.

3 What was the average number of fresh popcorn kernels that popped? (To find the average, add the number of kernels popped in A-1 and A-2 and divide by 2.)

Average = _____ kernels of fresh popcorn popped

4 What was the average number of dried popcorn kernels that popped? (To find the average, add the number of kernels popped in B-1 and B-2 and divide by 2.)

Average = _____ kernels of dried popcorn popped

5 How do your averages compare to other teams' averages?

____

____

6 What conclusion can you make from the data? What do you think makes popcorn pop? What is your evidence?

____

____

____

7 Why do you think one type of popcorn might pop more kernels than another type? What differences might there be between types?

____

____

Checkpoint D ☐

Name: ______________________________

Popcorn Brand Test
Checkpoint Lab

Which brand of popcorn does your family buy? Do you buy it because of the taste, the price, the advertising, or because it pops more kernels? Your team will design a test to find out which brand of popcorn pops the most kernels. You will test three different brands of popcorn. Design your experiment on the following pages.

Part A Designing a Popcorn Brand Test

1 When scientists design an experiment, they must determine what it is they want to test. This is called the **experimental variable**. It is the one thing in the experiment that is being changed. In this experiment, what is the experimental variable?

____

2 Scientists have to make sure their experiments are fair tests by keeping all other conditions the same. These conditions are called **controlled variables.** In this experiment, what variables should be controlled, or kept the same, to keep the test fair?

____

____

____

____

Name: ______________________________

Popcorn Brand Test
Checkpoint Lab cont.

3 Scientists must follow careful procedures to make sure their experiments are safe, fair, and easily repeated by other scientists. What step-by-step procedures will you follow to make sure that your popcorn brand test is safe, fair, and repeatable?

SAFETY

SAFETY CAUTION TO INCLUDE IN YOUR PROCEDURE:
Allow popcorn to cool for three min. before opening bags. Steam is hot!!!!

____
____
____
____
____
____
____
____
____
____

Checkpoint A ☐

Name: ______________________________

Popcorn Brand Test
Checkpoint Lab cont.

Part B Popcorn Data

Write the names of the popcorn brands you are testing in the data table below. Then examine the advertising on the packages.

Prediction: I predict that ______________________ will have the most popped kernels.
Brand

POPCORN DATA TABLE	
Brand of Popcorn	# of Popped Kernels

POPCORN BAR GRAPH

Number of Popped Kernels

Brands

Name: ______________________________

Popcorn Brand Test
Checkpoint Lab cont.

Part B Questions

1 What conclusion can you make from your data? Which brand of popcorn had the most popped kernels?

____

____

____

2 Was your prediction influenced by the advertising on the package? Was your prediction correct? How does advertising affect which brand of popcorn people buy?

____

____

____

3 Were you satisfied with your experimental design? What changes would you make if you were going to repeat the experiment? Why?

____

____

____

Checkpoint B ☐

Name: ______________________________

Popcorn Poster Session

Make a poster with your team displaying what you have learned about popcorn. Be ready to share it with the class and answer any questions they might have. Include the following in your poster session:

1. Some important information you learned about popcorn
2. A labeled diagram explaining how popcorn pops
3. Your prediction for the popcorn brand testing
4. The step-by-step procedure you followed in your experiment
5. A graph showing the results of your experiment
6. Your conclusion for the experiment
7. An advertisement, commercial, or jingle for the popcorn brand that popped the most kernels in your experiment

Decide who is going to explain each part of the poster. Everyone on your team should have a turn!

Posters will be presented on ____________________.
Date

Mystery Pellets

Description

Learners will explore food chains and webs by dissecting owl pellets, creating a food web poster, and describing the relationships among organisms in a pond food web.

Suggested Grade Levels: 3–6

Lesson Objectives Connecting to the *Framework*

Science and Engineering Practices

- Analyzing and interpreting data
- Constructing explanations (for science) and designing solutions (for engineering)
- Obtaining, evaluating, and communicating information

Disciplinary Core Ideas

LS2.A: Interdependent Relationships in Ecosystems
LS2.B: Cycles of Matter and Energy Transfer in Ecosystems

Crosscutting Concepts

- Systems and System Models

Featured Picture Books

Title	***White Owl, Barn Owl***
Author	**Nicola Davies**
Illustrator	**Michael Foreman**
Publisher	**Candlewick**
Year	**2009**
Genre	**Dual Purpose**
Summary	**A young girl and her grandfather look for a barn owl night after night.**

Title	***Butternut Hollow Pond***
Author	**Brian J. Heinz**
Illustrator	**Bob Marstall**
Publisher	**First Avenue Editions**
Year	**2000**
Genre	**Narrative Information**
Summary	**Presents the dramatic dynamics of survival and competition on a North American pond**

Time Needed

This lesson will take several class periods. Suggested scheduling is as follows:

Day 1: **Engage** with mystery pellets and read aloud of *White Owl, Barn Owl,* **Explore** with owl pellet dissection, and **Explain** with bone charts

Day 2: **Explain** with Owl Pellet Bar Graph, food webs, and food web poster

Day 3: **Elaborate** with *Butternut Hollow Pond*

Day 4: **Evaluate** with Food Web Posters and Food Web Quiz

Materials

- Unwrapped owl pellets (1 for every 2 students)
- Owl Pellet Bone Chart (1 for every 2 students) from Sheridan WorldWise or elsewhere (bone charts are included with owl pellet orders)
- Toothpicks
- Centimeter rulers and tape measures
- Hand lenses
- White card stock
- Balances (optional)
- White glue
- Owl Pellet Bar Graph (copied onto an overhead transparency)
- (Optional) Several copies of *Butternut Hollow Pond* for the Elaborate activity

Owl pellets are available from

Sheridan WorldWise Inc.
1-800-433-6259
www.classroomgoodies.com
and from
Carolina Biological Supply Co.
1-800-334-5551
www.carolina.com

Student Pages

- O-W-L Chart
- Owl Pellet Bar Graph
- *Butternut Hollow Pond* Word Sort Cards
- *Butternut Hollow Pond* article
- Food Web Quiz

Background

Barn owls are among the most widespread of all birds. They can be found on every continent except in the polar regions. They are the most distinctive looking type of owl, with pale, heart-shape faces and long legs. They live in open or lightly wooded countrysides, grasslands, and even cities and build their nests in barns, tree holes, and abandoned buildings. Barn owls prefer to keep out of sight, hunting by night and roosting in quiet places during the day. They are believed to mate for life and will raise between one and three broods per year. The young stay in the nest for about two months and are fed by both parents. Barn owls eat animals such as rodents and shrews and occasionally small birds. Many farmers encourage the presence of these excellent mousers in their barns.

When owls capture and kill their prey, they swallow it whole, passing bones and all through the esophagus into the *gizzard*. The gizzard acts as a trap, separating the indigestible parts from the soft, digestible parts of the prey. Parts that cannot be digested (bones, teeth, claws, insect exoskeletons, and fur and feathers) are formed into an elongated ball called a *pellet* that is regurgitated, or thrown up, by the bird. Interestingly, the bones are neatly packaged toward the middle of the pellet with soft fur or feathers on the outer layer, thus protecting the owl's esophagus. An owl pellet usually forms 6 to 10 hours after the prey is eaten and is regurgitated 10 to 16 hours after the meal. Pellet formation is typical of birds of prey, such as hawks, eagles, and owls.

Owl pellets give excellent clues as to what organisms are part of the owl's food chain. A *food chain* shows how living things get food and energy. The first organism in a food chain is a *producer*, or green plant. Producers take in energy from the Sun to make their own food. Animals cannot make their own food, so they must eat plants or other animals. Organisms that eat other living organisms are called consumers. *Consumers* can be classified as *herbivores*, which eat only plants; *carnivores*, which eat only other animals; or *omnivores*, which eat both plants and animals. Owls are carnivores because they eat only meat. *Scavengers*, such as vultures, are carnivores that specialize in eating dead animals. *Insectivores*, such as shrews, are carnivores that specialize in eating insects. Other organisms called *decomposers* play an important role in ecosystems by breaking down and recycling the nutrients in dead plant and animal materials. These organisms, primarily bacteria and fungi, release enzymes outside of their bodies that break apart the organic molecules in the dead organisms. (Organic molecules are those containing primarily carbon and hydrogen and are the building blocks of living organisms.) The inorganic material that results from this process is then recycled back into the soil and water, where producers can use it. Students are often taught that earthworms, millipedes, and certain insects are decomposers. However, these consumers of decaying organic material are more correctly termed *detritivores*. Detritivores must take their food into their bodies before digesting it, whereas decomposers break it down before it is taken in. Decomposers are the only organisms that can convert dead tissue back into inorganic elements. Although they are typically not represented in food chains, both decomposers and detritivores play a vital ecological role in recycling nutrients back into the soil.

When an animal from one food chain eats a member of another, the chains connect, forming a *food web*. Most consumers feed on multiple species and are, in turn, fed upon by multiple other species. So simple food chains do not typically exist alone in nature. It is important to teach students that food chains are almost always interconnected to form food webs. When drawing food chains and webs, the arrows should point in the direction that the energy is flowing. They can be described using the words *is eaten by* or *energy flows to*. For example, "Mouse → Owl" can be read as "the mouse is eaten by the owl," or "energy in the mouse flows to the owl." The "big idea" that you will want your students to understand is that in nature, all living things are connected. Every organism serves as a resource for other organisms, and the nutrients that make life possible are recycled again and again.

engage

Mystery Pellets and Read Aloud

Do not tell students that the "mystery pellets" are owl pellets at this point. Unwrap owl pellets prior to the lesson. Put students in pairs. Tell students you have a mystery for them to solve. Your friend has a farm in the country, and he keeps finding these things in his barn. He wants to know if the class can help him figure out the mystery of their origin. Pass out the mystery pellets. Do not tell students what they are at this point, as they will be discovering this through their observations and the information in the book.

Give a copy of the O-W-L Chart to each student. Have balances and tape measures available for measuring mass, length, and circumference. Have hand lenses available for examining the objects. Tell students to record their observations of the pellets in the first column. Give them a few minutes to observe and measure the mystery pellets without taking them apart. Encourage students to write quantitative as well as qualitative observations. Quantitative observations (numbers) involve counting and measuring ("the mystery pellet is 6.2 cm long"); qualitative observations (words) involve using the senses to describe the properties of the object ("the mystery pellet is grayish"). Then ask students to write their wonderings about the mystery pellets in the second column.

SAFETY

Check first with your school nurse to find out if any students have fur or feather allergies. Owl pellets are the undigested remains of food eaten by owls that instead of being excreted with other waste materials, are regurgitated as a compact mass of hair, bones teeth, claws, bird's beaks, and insect remains. Although each owl pellet has been sanitized and is safe to dissect without using gloves, students must still wash hands with soap and water when finished.

Inferring

Now that the students are curious and engaged, tell them you are going to read a book that might give them some clues about the mystery pellets. Introduce the author and illustrator of *White Owl, Barn Owl*. Ask students to listen for any clues on what the mystery pellets might be, and then read the book aloud. By merging clues from their mystery pellet observations and the text and illustrations on pages 8 through 11, students can infer that a mystery pellet is an owl pellet (the undigested fur, bones, and feathers from the animal[s] an owl ate). They can add this learning to the "L" column of the O-W-L chart.

EXPLORING THE "MYSTERY PELLETS"

explore

Owl Pellet Dissection

Tell students that they are each going to be a special kind of scientist who studies birds, an ornithologist. Their task is to determine as much information as they can about the diet of the owl that regurgitated (threw up) that particular pellet. Students may now take the pellets apart using toothpicks, separating the fur from the bones. Tell students the pellets have been sanitized by the vendor using high heat to kill germs, so they are safe to touch. Students should still wash hands with soap and water when they are finished with the pellet dissection.

explain

Bone Charts

Tell students that an owl pellet forms 6 to 10 hours after the meal is eaten and is regurgitated 10 to 16 hours after the meal. This is necessary to keep the bird healthy. Explain to students that because owls can't digest fur and bones, they spit these parts out in a compressed pellet.

- ? What can scientists learn by studying owl pellets? (Scientists can learn a great deal by studying the remains in an owl pellet. They can tell what species of animal the owl ate and how much it ate. Sometimes scientists even find a bird band—a small metal ring that has been placed around a bird's leg—in a pellet, giving them information about the movement and fate of the banded bird.)
- ? Why is this a good method of study? (It is a good way to study owls without handling or harming them.)

Owl pellet bone charts are included when ordering owl pellets from most vendors. They contain labeled drawings of the animal bones generally found in owl pellets. Students can use the charts to determine what animals their owl ate. They can then try to arrange the bones to assemble the skeleton of the prey (in the same manner that paleontologists assemble dinosaur bones). Alternately, you may want to have them glue the bones on the paper in groups—all the skulls together, all the legs together, and so forth. Students can use white glue on the end of a toothpick to attach the bones to a large piece of card stock and then label them with the name of the animal. Students can present these posters to other teams and share their findings.

Owl Pellet Bar Graph

After the students present their posters to other pairs, ask the following questions of the whole class:

- ? What bones would be the best to use to determine the different types of animals your owl ate? (The skulls would be best, because each type of animal the owl ate has a distinctly different skull. The other bones look similar from animal to animal and are much smaller.)
- ? How many of each animal did your owl eat? How can you tell? (Answers will vary; we can tell by counting the number of each type of skull.)

Have the students count how many skulls of each kind of animal were in their pellets. On the *x*-axis of the Owl Pellet Bar Graph transparency, write the names of the most common types of animals the students found, such as rodent, shrew, mole, and bird. Using the data from each pellet, make a whole-class bar graph. Then have students analyze the results and make inferences from the data.

- ? Why are we using a bar graph to display our owl pellet data? (A bar graph compares totals. Each bar represents the total number of each type of animal. We can easily compare the totals of each type by looking at the bars.)
- ? What animal was found most frequently in the owl pellets?
- ? Why do you think the owls ate more of these animals than any other?

Students may now add "learnings" to the "L" column of the O-W-L chart.

explain

Food Webs

Write an example of a simple food chain on the board:

SEED → MOUSE → OWL

Explain to students that when one animal eats another animal or plant, they both become part of a *food chain*. A food chain is the path that energy takes as one living thing eats another. The arrows represent the direction of the energy flow; in this case, the energy flows from the seed to the mouse to the owl. The Sun is the source of all the energy in a food chain. Plants use the Sun's energy to make food. Animals eat plants to get some of that energy, other animals eat those animals to get some of that energy, and so on.

There are some simple food chains in nature, but usually two or more food chains link to form a *food web*. A food web is made of many food chains put together. Write another simple food chain below the first. Ask students how you could link the two chains to make a food web. For example:

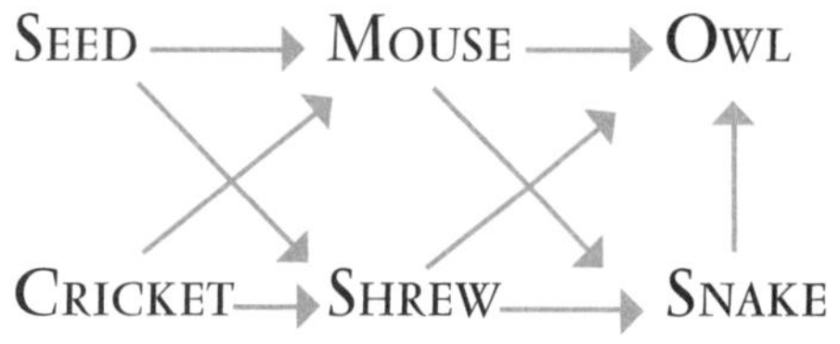

Then ask students

- ? What is missing from the food web on the board? (the Sun)

Draw a picture of the Sun on the food web with arrows pointing to the seed and the berry.

For more explanation of food webs, you can read excepts from *What Are Food Chains and Webs?* or *Who Eats What?* listed in the "More Books to Read" section.

Food Web Poster

Using the evidence from their owl pellets and their understanding of food chains and webs, have students work in pairs to create a labeled pictorial, "Owl Food Web Poster," including the owl, its prey, the food of the prey, the Sun, and energy flow arrows. Have students explain their posters to other teams. Use the following guiding questions as you encourage students to explain the food web posters in their own words:

- ? What do the arrows represent? (the direction of the energy flow)
- ? What did your owl eat? What is your evidence? (Answers will vary.)
- ? Why did your owl eat? (to get energy)
- ? Where did the animals the owl ate get their energy? (from eating plants or other animals)
- ? Why is the Sun an important part of your food web? (The Sun is the source of all the energy in a food web. Plants use the Sun's energy to make food.)

elaborate

Butternut Hollow Pond

Inferring

Hold open the front and back covers of *Butternut Hollow Pond,* which together give a panoramic view of a pond scene. Model the inferring strategy by making observations about the picture on the cover showing the hawk and the woodchuck and then inferring from your observations and your prior knowledge what the book might be about. For example, "I see a hawk flying close to the ground with its talons open. I also see a fat woodchuck running from the hawk. I think the hawk is hunting the woodchuck. I wonder if this book might be about food chains and webs."

Visualizing

Then model the visualizing strategy by closing your eyes and sharing what you might see, feel, smell, and hear if you were at the pond. For example, "I feel a light breeze blowing through my hair and the warm sun on my face. I hear the buzz of insects as they flit around the edge of the pond. I smell the wildflowers growing on the grassy bank. I see the shadow of a large bird as it passes overhead. I hear a rustling sound in the bushes as a woodchuck takes cover." Then ask students to close their eyes and visualize the scene.

This book is especially useful for having students practice the strategies of inferring and visualizing. After you have modeled these strategies, you may want to stop reading periodically to have students visualize, make predictions and inferences, or Sketch to Stretch by drawing a picture.

Determining Importance

Next ask students to listen for the different organisms in the pond food web as you read aloud *Butternut Hollow Pond.*

? What are some of the plants in the food web?

? What are some of the animals in the food web?

Word Sort

Word sorts help learners understand the relationships among key concepts and help teach classification. Classifying and then reclassifying helps students extend and refine their understanding of the concepts studied. Students can apply the scientific concepts they have learned about food webs from the owl pellet inquiry to a new situation through the following word sort activity.

Open Sort: Give pairs of students the *Butternut Hollow Pond* Word Sort Cards. Ask students to sort the words into different categories. At this point, it should be an open sort, in which students group words into categories of their choice and then create their own labels for each category (don't tell them the significance of the gray cards yet). As you move from pair to pair, ask students to explain how they categorized the words. This can help you become aware of students' prior knowledge and misconceptions about the relationships of organisms in a food web.

Closed Sort: Pass out a copy of the Butternut Hollow Pond article to each student and have them read it. In a closed sort, the teacher provides the categories into which students assign words. The closed sort categories can be found on the gray cards: *producer, consumer, omnivore, herbivore,* and *carnivore.*

Next discuss each term on the gray cards, and have pairs locate one example of that term from their word sort cards and hold it up. For example, when you discuss the term *producer,* they can hold up the green algae card. Have students explain why they chose that example, and redirect them if they have made incorrect choices. Students may need to refer back to *Butternut Hollow Pond* to find the role of some of the organisms in the pond food web.

Although students may classify raccoons and opossums as carnivores because in the book they are eating other animals, both are omnivores. The raccoon in the book eats crayfish, but tell students that raccoons also eat grubs, insects, fruits, and vegetables. The opossum in the book eats a tiger beetle, but tell students that opossums also eat insects, snails,

Closed Sort Key

Producer	Consumer		
	Herbivore	Carnivore	Omnivore
green algae	woodchuck	dragonfly	fisherman
wildflower	mallard duck	largemouth bass	raccoon
water shamrock	deer	pickerel frog	opossum
grass		snapping turtle	
		heron	
		brown bat	
		marsh hawk	

earthworms, fruit, nuts, seeds, and grasses. Try to have several copies of *Butternut Hollow Pond* available for students to use for reference. You may also want to give them additional resources to research the diet of some of the animals mentioned on the cards.

Next provide some time for students to sort the rest of their words into the five categories found on the gray cards. Informally assess their understanding of the terms as you move from pair to pair, and have them explain their reasoning. Ask clarifying questions such as

- ? What does that animal eat?
- ? Why did you place that organism in that category?
- ? Can that organism be placed in more than one category?

The relationship of the main categories on the gray cards to the rest of the cards is shown on the chart below:

After the word sort, tell students that every food web has some very important organisms that you haven't discussed yet. Ask

- ? What type of consumer is missing from the gray cards? Think back to the article you read. (decomposers)

Explain that *decomposers* are organisms that feed on the tissues of dead organisms and on the waste products of living organisms. They live in or on their food source. Decomposers cause things to rot or decay and eventually become part of the soil. Ask

- ? What would it be like if leaves never decayed after they fell from trees?
- ? What would it be like if dead animals never decomposed?
- ? What would it be like if apple cores, banana peels, and other garbage never rotted?

Tell students that decomposers play a major role in food webs because they recycle nutrients back into the soil. Some examples of decomposers are fungi, such as molds and mushrooms, and microscopic organisms, such as protozoans and bacteria. Other small animals, such as earthworms and some insects, also help break down the nutrients in food webs by eating decaying plant and animal materials.

Finally, have students complete the *Butternut Hollow Pond* Questions student page. Answers follow.

1. (b) the grasses
2. (c) The grasses are eaten by the woodchuck and the woodchuck is eaten by the hawk.

3 (b) consumer

4 (a) from the dragonfly, the moth, and the mosquito

5 The animals that eat insects would starve or leave the pond to find food elsewhere. Eventually, the animals that eat the insect eaters would starve or leave the pond to find food elsewhere. The entire food web would be affected by the elimination of the insects.

evaluate

Food Web Posters

Students can now place any of the appropriate key words—*producer, consumer, herbivore, omnivore,* or *carnivore*—on their owl food web posters, thereby attaching scientific terminology to concepts learned through exploration. Food web posters should demonstrate understanding of the relationships among producers, consumers, and the Sun and should include accurate use of terminology and proper placement of energy flow arrows.

evaluate

Food Web Quiz

As a final evaluation, give the Food Web Quiz. Answers follow.

1 (a) corn

2 (b) consumer

3 (a) Energy flows from the Sun to the corn to the mouse to the owl.

4 grasses and seeds

5 the Sun

6 Answers will vary.

7 The numbers of grasshoppers, sparrows, and mice will increase, because their consumers have been eliminated. The numbers of grasses and seeds will then decrease because they will be eaten by more grasshoppers, sparrows, and mice. (Students may also respond that the numbers of grasshoppers, sparrows, and mice will eventually decline because they will become overpopulated and have to compete for increasingly scarce grasses and seeds.)

Inquiry Place

Place several different types of bird feeders on the school grounds. Make daily observations of the numbers and types of birds that visit the feeders. Have students keep careful records of observations in an organized form. Have students brainstorm testable questions such as

- ? Which type of feeder do most birds prefer?
- ? Do birds feed more in the morning or afternoon?
- ? What is the effect on the numbers of birds if an artificial owl is placed near the feeders?
- ? How are other local organisms linked to the birds' food chain?

Then have students select a question to investigate as a class, or have groups of students vote on the question they want to investigate as teams. After they make their predictions, have them collect data to test their predictions. Students can present their findings at a poster session.

Project FeederWatch is a program sponsored by the Cornell Lab of Ornithology. Students can count the kinds and numbers of bird species that visit feeders placed in their school yard. Using web-based submittal and retrieval forms, they share their bird data with the lab and with other students doing the project. Their analyses help scientists and other student participants answer questions about changes in populations of bird species from month to month, year to year, and place to place. Go to *www.birds.cornell.edu/pfw* for information about signing up.

Websites

The Barn Owl Conservation Network
www.bocn.org

Owl Resource Guide (including bone charts)
www.carolina.com/owls/guide/owl_guide_intro.asp

More Books to Read

Johnston, T. 2000. *The barn owls.* Watertown, MA: Charlesbridge Publishing.
Summary: The poetic text describe the lives of barn owls who have slept, hunted, called, raised their young, and glided silently above the wheat fields around an old barn for many generations.

Kalman, B. 1998. *What are food chains and webs?* New York: Crabtree Publishing.
Summary: Clear photographs, illustrations, charts, and short chapters introduce children to food chains and webs.

Lauber, P. 1995. *Who eats what? Food chains and food webs.* New York: HarperCollins.
Summary: This book explains the concept of a food chain and how plants, animals, and humans are ecologically linked.

Tagholm, S. 2000. *Animal Lives: The Barn Owl.* New York: Kingfisher Books.
Summary: The author describes physical characteristics, hunting, feeding, nesting, mating, and molting of the barn owl.

Yolen, J. 1987. *Owl moon.* New York: Philomel Books.
Summary: The simple, melodious text and soft watercolors describe how a father and daughter hike the woods under a full moon to see the great horned owl.

Reference

Kaufman, D. G., and C. M. Franz. 2000. *Biosphere 2000: Protecting our global environment, 3rd edition.* Dubuque, IA: Kendall Hunt Publishing.

Name: ______________________________

O-W-L Chart

O	W	L
What do you **OBSERVE** about the object? (Don't forget to measure.)	What do you **WONDER** about the object?	What did you **LEARN** about the object?

Name: ______________________

Owl Pellet
Bar Graph

Number of Skulls

Types of Prey Found

Butternut Hollow Pond

Word Sort Cards

dragonfly	herbivore
largemouth bass	mallard duck
omnivore	heron
woodchuck	water shamrock
pickerel frog	green algae

Butternut Hollow Pond

Word Sort Cards cont.

deer	**producer**
wildflower	**snapping turtle**
brown bat	**fisherman**
consumer	**grass**
marsh hawk	**raccoon**
opossum	**carnivore**

Name: ______________________________

Butternut Hollow Pond

When one animal eats another living thing, they both become part of a food chain. A **food chain** is the path that energy takes as one organism eats another. There are some simple food chains in nature. But usually two or more food chains overlap and link, forming a food web. A **food web** is made of many food chains put together. All food webs include plants. Plants are **producers** and can make their own food. They get their energy from the Sun. Animals are **consumers**. They cannot make their own food so they must consume (eat) plants or other animals. The four main types of consumers are **herbivores** (plant eaters), **carnivores** (meat eaters), **omnivores** (plant and meat eaters), and **decomposers**. **Decomposers** are consumers that break down the tissues of dead organisms. They feed on everything that dies in a food web. Some examples of decomposers are bacteria and fungi (not shown on food web below).

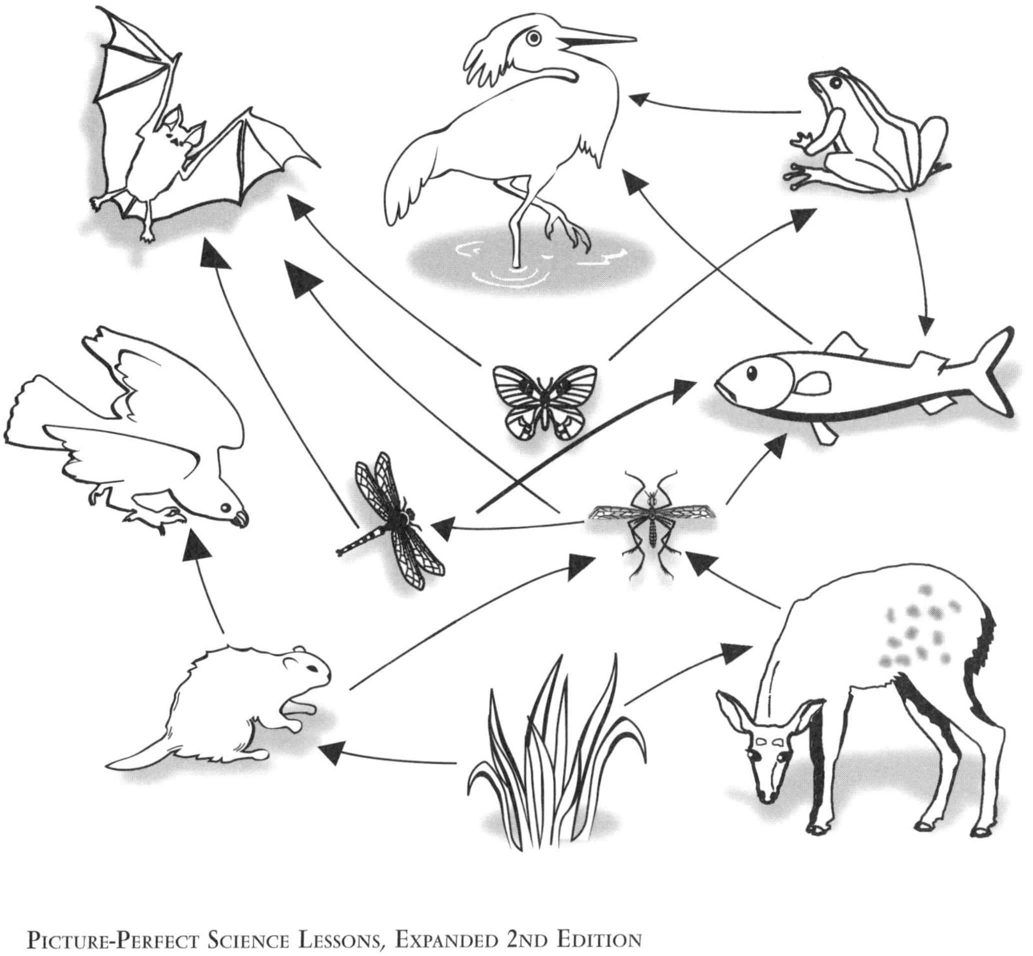

Chapter 10

Name: ______________________________

Butternut Hollow Pond Questions

Look through *Butternut Hollow Pond* to identify each organism in the food web. Then use the food web to answer the questions below.

1 What are the producers in the food web?
  a. the heron and the hawk
  b. the grasses
  c. the moth and the mosquito

2 Which food chain in the web is in the correct order?
  a. The moth is eaten by the deer and the deer is eaten by the grass.
  b. The heron is eaten by the fish and the fish is eaten by the mosquito.
  c. The grasses are eaten by the woodchuck and the woodchuck is eaten by the hawk.

3 In this food web, the fish is a
  a. producer
  b. consumer
  c. decomposer

4 Where does the bat in this food web get its energy?
  a. from the dragonfly, the moth, and the mosquito
  b. from the cattails and the grass
  c. from the hawk and the heron

5 How would the food web be affected if someone sprayed pesticide around the pond and all of the insects died? Explain your answer.

____

____

____

____

Name: ______________________________

CHAPTER 10

Food Web Quiz

Use the food chain diagram below to answer questions 1 to 3.

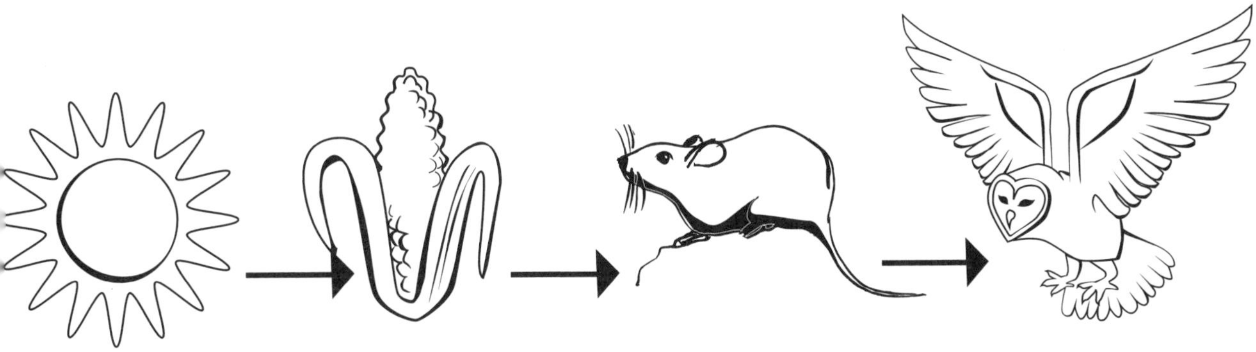

1 Which organism is the producer in this food chain?

a corn

b mouse

c owl

2 In this food chain, the owl is a

a producer

b consumer

c decomposer

3 Which statement describes the movement of energy in the diagram above?

a Energy flows from the Sun to the corn to the mouse to the owl.

b The owl gets its energy directly from the Sun.

c Energy flows from the owl to the mouse to the corn.

Name: ______________________________

Food Web
Quiz cont.

Use the food web diagram at the bottom of the page to answer questions 4 through 7.

4 What are the producers in the food web below? ______________

5 What is the source of all the energy in the food web? __________

6 Write down any food chain with three links in the food web:

____

7 What will happen to the other organisms in the food web if all of the snakes and owls are killed by someone? Explain your answer.

____

____

____

____

____

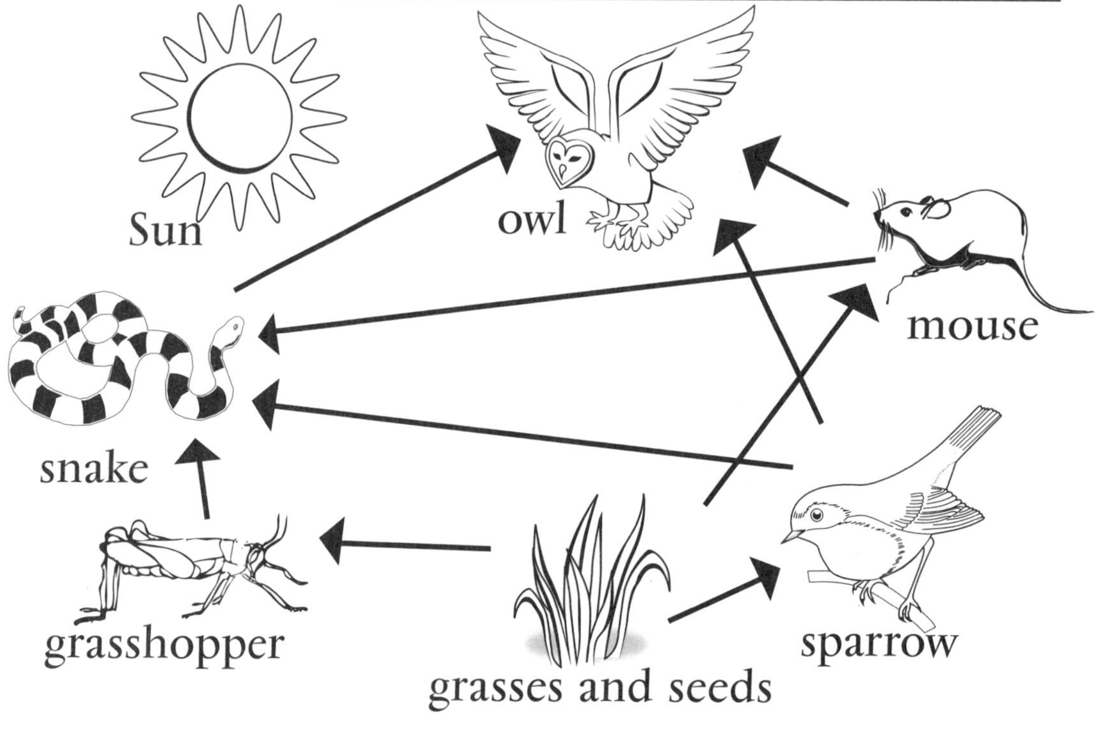

Chapter 11

Close Encounters
of the Symbiotic Kind

Description

Learners explore how some organisms interact with other organisms through symbiotic relationships by observing "mystery objects" (plant galls) collected from the local ecosystem.

Suggested Grade Levels: 3–6

Lesson Objectives **Connecting to the *Framework***

Science and Engineering Practices

- Constructing explanations (for science) and designing solutions (for engineering)
- Obtaining, evaluating, and communicating information

Disciplinary Core Ideas

LS2.A: Interdependent Relationships in Ecosystems

Crosscutting Concepts

- Systems and System Models

Featured Picture Books

Title	***What's Eating You? Parasites—The Inside Story***
Author	**Nicola Davies**
Illustrator	**Neal Layton**
Publisher	**Candlewick**
Year	**2009**
Genre	**Nonnarrative Information**
Summary	**Explores the weird and wonderful world of parasites, from tiny ticks to terrible tapeworms**

Title	***Weird Friends: Unlikely Allies in the Animal Kingdom***
Author	**Jose Aruego and Ariane Dewey**
Illustrator	**Jose Aruego and Ariane Dewey**
Publisher	**Harcourt**
Year	**2002**
Genre	**Nonnarrative Information**
Summary	**Details some of the amazing symbiotic relationships found in the animal kingdom**

Time Needed

This lesson will take several class periods. Suggested scheduling is as follows:

Day 1: **Engage** and **Explore** with mystery objects, and **Explain** with Close Encounters Dichotomous Key

Day 2: **Explore** and **Explain** with Word Sort, Close Encounters of the Symbiotic Kind article, and *What's Eating You? Parasites–The Inside Story*

Day 3: **Elaborate** with *Weird Friends*, and **Evaluate** with Symbiosis Quiz

Goldenrod Ball Gall

Materials

This lesson uses "mystery objects" to engage students and lead them into an inquiry on symbiotic relationships in nature. The mystery objects are plant galls. If goldenrod grows in your area, you can probably find galls on it. The spherical goldenrod gall is caused by a tiny fly. The spindle gall is caused by a kind of moth. The galls are often located about two-thirds of the way up the stem and can be seen easily, especially in the winter when the foliage has died. Another easy way to collect galls is to find them on trees. Oak trees in particular play host to hundreds of different gall-forming organisms. Keep the galls attached to the leaves or twigs if possible, to help with identification. See *www.cals.ncsu.edu/course/ent525/close/gallpix/index.htm* for color photographs of some common galls. (Safety note: Goldenrod is usually not responsible for allergies. The pollen is heavy and sticky, designed for insect pollination, not wind. Wind-blown ragweed pollen is the most common culprit for allergies.)

You will need to collect several specimens of at least two kinds of galls from the local ecosystem, such as the common galls pictured at right.

Goldenrod Spindle Gall

Other Materials

- Centimeter rulers and/or tape measures (1 per pair)
- Hand lenses (1 per student)
- Small knife or dissecting scalpel (for adult use only)
- Cutting board to use when cutting galls open (for adult use only)
- Symbiosis Quiz Key (for teacher use)

Oak Leaf Gall

Oak Apple Gall

Student Pages

- O-W-L Chart
- Close Encounters Dichotomous Key
- Close Encounters Sorting Cards
- Close Encounters of the Symbiotic Kind article
- *Weird Friends*
- Symbiosis Quiz

Background

Plant galls are actually abnormal outgrowths of the plant's own tissues. They can be caused by insects, mites, fungi, or bacteria. Because they are found in an astounding array of shapes, sizes, colors, and textures and can be easily spotted on trees and other plants, they make excellent specimens for inquiry in the elementary science classroom. By studying the gall and its location on the plant, you can usually determine what kind of organism caused it. Each gall-causing organism is adapted to only one type of host, and no other plant will do. Most galls are relatively harmless to their host plants, but all gall-causing organisms are considered parasites.

Parasitism is a form of symbiosis (close interaction between different species) in which one organism lives on or in a larger host organism and feeds on it while the host is still alive. In this lesson, students learn about both *ectoparasites* (parasites that live on the body, such as lice, mites, ticks, and fleas) and *endoparasites* (parasites that live inside the body, such as roundworms, hookworms, and tapeworms). Other types of symbiosis are *commensalism,* in which one of the organisms is helped while the other is not affected, and *mutualism,* in which both organisms benefit from their close encounter. Mutualism is a win-win relationship. The Elaborate portion of this lesson explores mutualism in depth.

Adaptations are structures or behaviors that help organisms survive in their environments. Symbiosis is the result of both *structural* and *behavioral* adaptations in organisms. For example, goldenrod gall fly larvae have special chewing mouthparts that help them eat the inside of the fibrous goldenrod gall. That is a structural adaptation. When the larvae go through metamorphosis inside the gall and become adult flies, their mouthparts change into sucking mouthparts. So how are they able to exit the gall and fly away if they no longer have chewing mouthparts? The secret is in a behavioral adaptation: The larvae chew an exit hole in the gall BEFORE they go through metamorphosis! This behavior helps them survive in their environment. They are able to leave the gall when the time is right to find a mate and lay their eggs.

Understanding adaptation can be challenging for students at this age. Many students think individual organisms adapt deliberately in response to their environments. However, organisms don't adapt because they "want to" or "try to." Furthermore, biological adaptation involves naturally occurring variations in populations, not individuals, and typically takes place over many thousands of years. This lesson focuses on how different types of adaptations help organisms exist in symbiotic relationships, rather than how those structures and behaviors have evolved over time.

Engage

Mystery Objects

Pass out a mystery object (goldenrod ball gall, oak apple gall, or other plant gall) to each student or pair of students. Do not tell them what the mystery objects are. Pass out an O-W-L chart to each student. Give students several minutes to carefully take measurements and write observations in the first column and then write their "wonderings" about the objects in the second column.

Ask several students to share their observations. Then ask whether the observations were truly *observations* based on measurements and the senses, or whether some of them were actually *inferences*. Explain that when you make an inference, you use past experiences to draw a conclusion based on your observations. So if any of the observations were guesses about the identity of the mystery objects, then those statements were actually inferences. Students who wrote inferences in the "Observations" column of the O-W-L chart can rewrite them into questions in the "Wonderings" column instead. For example, "I wonder if this is an insect living inside a plant?"

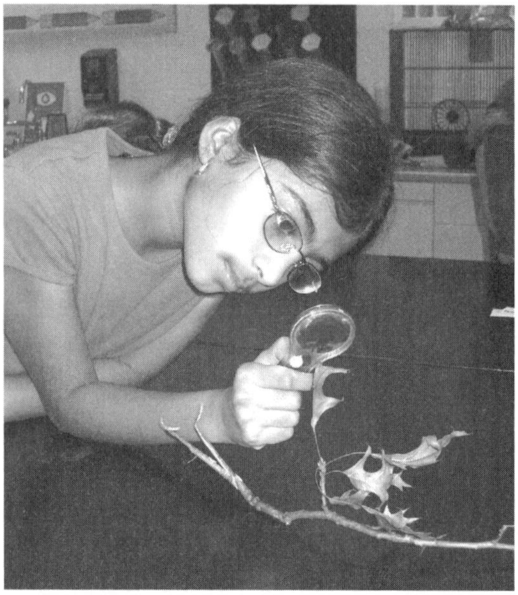

Observing oak leaf galls

Explore

Demonstrate how to safely cut open a gall. You will most likely want to open the galls for each student, especially the hardened goldenrod gall, because of safety concerns. Ask a parent volunteer to help. Use a sturdy cutting board and a small sharp knife or dissecting scalpel. Carefully insert the knife blade part way into a gall along its circumference. Twist the knife until the gall pops open. Galls can usually be opened this way without damaging the larvae inside.

Have students make observations of the opened objects and compare them with the observations of other students. Then have them add to the "Observations" and "Wonderings" columns of the O-W-L chart.

Explain

Close Encounters Dichotomous Key

Ask students if they are ready to develop some explanations about their mystery objects.

- ? Was anything inside your mystery object? Is it still there?
- ? How do you think it got inside? What do you think it was doing in there?
- ? What do you think it is?

Tell students they are going to do some research to clear up the mystery surrounding their objects. Pass out copies of the Close Encounters Dichotomous Key. Explain that the word *dichotomous* means dividing into two parts. A dichotomous key has two choices at every step. Discuss the different characteristics used in the key such as spherical, elliptical, encircling twig, and horns. Then tell students to start with number one, make a choice based on their observations, and follow the steps of the key until they have identified the object. They can find out more about their objects by reading the rest of the student page.

Oak galls can be difficult to identify because there are hundreds of varieties. It is sufficient for the students to identify them as "oak galls" if they cannot tell which type they have.

Students can now fill out the "Learnings" column of the O-W-L chart. Have students communicate their findings about their mystery objects by presenting their completed O-W-L charts in small groups to other students.

Discuss the following questions with the whole class:

- ? What is your mystery object?
- ? How did the insect get inside the plant?
- ? Is the insect helped or hurt by the plant? How?

Tell students the name for this type of "close encounter" between different organisms is called *symbiosis*. Explain that symbiotic relationships occur when one organism lives near, on, or, in some cases, inside another organism and when at least one organism benefits from the relationship.

- ? How does your mystery object show symbiosis? (An insect is living on or in a plant and getting food, shelter, and protection from the plant.)

Some students may have concerns about the survival of the organisms they are studying in this inquiry. To dispose of the insect larvae inside the galls, take the class outside to a natural area or bird feeder where students can gently return their organisms to the food chain. Make sure you are not introducing an organism into a habitat where it doesn't belong. You may want to keep some unopened galls that are still attached to a stem, twig, or leaf. Place them in a jar and cover the jar with fine mesh or cheesecloth. Mist the inside of the jar occasionally. Observe the jar every day—students will be amazed to see the insects that emerge from the galls!

explore

Symbiosis Word Sort and Article

Word Sort

Tell students they are going to do an activity to explore symbiosis further. Divide students into pairs. Pass out the Close Encounters Sorting Cards to each pair.

Open Sort: First, have students do an open sort of the cards. In an open sort, students group words into categories and create their own labels for each category. Have students explain their reasonings as they are sorting. An open sort helps students become familiar with the words, begin thinking about relationships among the words, and listen for the words in the reading. As you circulate, ask students to explain why they grouped the words the way they did. This can help you determine their prior knowledge about the meanings of the words on the cards.

Pairs Read

Pass out the Close Encounters of the Symbiotic Kind article. This article will give students the necessary information to do a closed sort with their cards. Have students take turns reading aloud from the article. While one student reads a paragraph, the other listens and makes comments ("I think ..."), asks questions ("I wonder ..."), or shares new learnings ("I didn't know ...).

Closed Sort: Next, have students perform a closed sort of the cards. In a closed sort, the teacher provides categories into which students assign the words. In this case, the article outlines three categories of symbiosis into which the organisms on the cards can be sorted: parasitism, commensalism, and mutualism.

Explain

Ask students to justify how they sorted their cards as you move around to each team. Students should recognize that there are three types of symbiosis and identify which organisms belong in each category. Discuss the following questions:

- ? Why is a goldenrod gall fly considered to be a parasite of the goldenrod plant? (It lives inside the much larger organism and feeds on it without killing the goldenrod plant.)
- ? Why is this relationship NOT considered to be an example of commensalism? (The goldenrod plant IS affected by the gall fly because it is made to produce abnormal growths. In commensalism, one of the organisms is helped but the other is not affected at all.)
- ? Could the goldenrod gall fly survive without the goldenrod plant? (No, it would not have a food source for its larvae. A goldenrod gall fly can live only on a goldenrod plant. No other kind of plant will do.)
- ? Why do you think it is beneficial for a parasite to *not* kill its host? (If the host died, the parasite would lose its food source.)
- ? Why is a flea considered to be a parasite of a dog? (It lives on the much larger dog and feeds on it without killing the dog.)

Next tell students you have a weird and wonderful book to share with them! This book will tell them everything they NEVER wanted to know about parasites. Introduce the author and illustrator of *What's Eating You? Parasites–The Inside Story*. Tell students that the author, Nicola Davies, is a zoologist whose father was

Relationship of Words in the Closed Sort

SYMBIOSIS		
Parasitism	**Commensalism**	**Mutualism**
Dog–Flea	Orchid–Kapok Tree	Clown Fish–Sea Anemone
Goldenrod–Gall Fly	Remora–Shark	Also correct: Human–Dog
Human–Mosquito		
Bark Beetle–Elm Tree		
Also correct: Dog–Mosquito		
Also correct: Human–Flea		

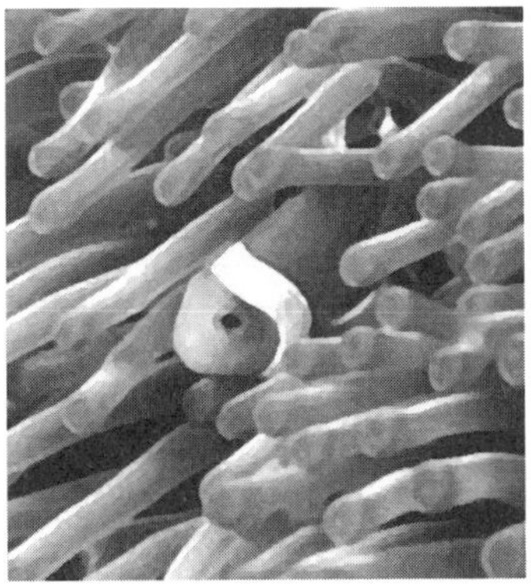

also a scientist. When she was young, her father would let her take apart dead animals so that she could learn about dissection! She was fascinated by the parasites that lived inside the animals. She writes, "I always wondered what their lives were like in that strange, warm, dark world that is inside all of us."

Turn and Talk

Ask

- ? Do humans have parasites? Turn and talk. (Students may be able to list parasites such as lice, ticks, or tapeworms.)

Determining Importance

Have the students listen for how many different kinds of parasites can live on the human body as you read pages 7 and 8 aloud (430 different kinds!). Next ask students to listen for the difference between ectoparasites and endoparasites as you read the interesting facts on pages 10 through 13 aloud. (Ectoparasites live on the body and endoparasites live inside the body.) Then ask

- ? What are some ectoparasites of dogs? (fleas, lice, mites, and ticks)
- ? What are some endoparasites of dogs? (roundworms, hookworms, and tapeworms)

Parasite Adaptations

Next explain that parasites have some remarkable adaptations that help them survive in or on their hosts. *Adaptations* are changes in body structures or behaviors that help organisms survive in their environments. For example, goldenrod gall fly larvae have special chewing mouthparts that help them eat the inside of the fibrous goldenrod gall. That is a *structural adaptation.* When the larvae go through metamorphosis inside the gall and become adult flies, their mouthparts change into sucking mouthparts. So how are they able to exit the gall and fly away if they no longer have chewing mouthparts? The secret is in a *behavioral adaptation:* The larvae chew an exit hole in the gall BEFORE they go through metamorphosis! This behavior helps them survive in their environment. They are able to leave the gall when the time is right to find a mate and lay their eggs.

Determining Importance

Tell students that you are going to read about some more fascinating parasite adaptations. As you read, have them raise their hands every time they hear about either a *structural* or a *behavioral* adaptation that helps the parasite survive in its environment. For example, as you read on page 15, "First, they need to be small: It's no good being the size of an elephant if your habitat is the fur of a mouse," students can raise their hands and say body size is a structural adaptation. Then have them explain how this adaptation helps the organism survive (it can hide in the fur of a much larger animal).

As you read on page 16, "They climb into grass and bushes, and when they smell an animal close by, they wave their legs to grab a ride," students can raise their hands and say that climbing grass and bushes is a behavioral adaptation. Then have them explain how this adaptation helps the organism survive in its environment (ticks get closer to their food source by climbing into the vegetation where the host animals can be easily reached).

Then read pages 15 through 24 aloud. If your students aren't too grossed out by this point, read on! However, they should be able to find plenty of examples of structural and behavioral adaptations in those pages, so you can stop after page 24 (about lice) if you wish.

elaborate

Weird Friends

After reading the suggested excerpts of *What's Eating You?* ask

? If the symbiotic relationship between a dog and a flea is parasitism, what kind of symbiosis is the relationship between a service dog or watch dog and its human owner? Explain. (The type of symbiosis is mutualism because the human is helped or protected by the dog, and the dog is fed and cared for by the human. They both benefit from the relationship.)

Then tell students they are going to learn more about the fascinating world of *mutualism,* a relationship that is beneficial to both partners. Mutualism can seem very strange because the most unlikely creatures do amazing things to help each other survive. Some act as bodyguards or booby traps, others as hairdressers or housekeepers. Ask students if they can think of other examples of mutualism in addition to the clown fish and the sea anemone featured in the symbiosis article.

Inferring/Making Connections

Show students the cover of *Weird Friends: Unlikely Allies in the Animal Kingdom.* Ask students to infer from the title what the book is about. Then ask them what they think it might have to do with the previous activity on plant galls. (Both the book and the activity are about symbiotic relationships.)

Determining Importance

Pass out the *Weird Friends* student page. Ask pairs of students to read through the examples listed and briefly discuss some predictions of how each partner might benefit from the relationship. Then tell students to listen for the relationships mentioned on the worksheet as you read the book aloud. Read aloud *Weird Friends,* and pause after each relationship is described to give students time to record their responses on the student page, listing the benefit for each partner.

evaluate

Symbiosis Quiz

Review the differences among the types of symbiosis, then administer the Symbiosis Quiz. Use the Symbiosis Quiz Key to grade the quiz.

Inquiry Place

Students can investigate goldenrod galls further by doing some field studies in a natural area containing many goldenrod plants or by doing further research. Have students brainstorm testable questions such as

- Can the gall fly larvae survive being frozen over the winter?
- Do gall fly larvae distinguish up from down? Do they make more exit tunnels in the upper or lower part of the gall, or are the tunnels randomly placed on the galls?
- At what height on the plant do most galls occur?
- What kinds of animals prey on gall fly larvae?
- Are goldenrods without galls on average taller than goldenrods with galls?

Students can select a question to investigate as a class, or groups of students may choose a question they want to investigate as teams. After they make their predictions, have them design an investigation and collect data to test their predictions. Students can present their findings at a poster session.

More Books to Read

Darling, K. 2000. *There's a zoo on you.* Brookfield, CT: Millbrook Press.
Summary: This fascinating introduction to the microorganisms that have symbiotic relationships with the human body explains that most of these microbes are harmless and may actually be helpful.

Hines, J. G. 2004. *Friendships in nature.* Chanhassen, MN: NorthWord Press.
Summary: Richly detailed paintings bring life to fascinating symbiotic relationships in nature.

Kalman, B. 2000. *How do animals adapt?* New York: Crabtree Publishing.
Summary: This fact-filled book describes how animals adapt to survive. It details camouflage, mimicry, poisons, and adaptations to climate, feeding, and mating. It also includes full-color photographs, informational insets, and words to know.

Parasites and Partners Series

Giles, B. 2003. *Parasites and partners: Lodgers and cleaners.* Chicago: Raintree.

Harman, A. 2003. *Parasites and partners: Farmers and slavers.* Chicago: Raintree.

Hoare, B. 2003. *Parasites and partners: Breeders.* Chicago: Raintree.

Houston, R. 2003. *Parasites and partners: Feeders.* Chicago: Raintree.

Martin, J. W. R. 2003. *Parasites and partners: Killers.* Chicago: Raintree.

Pitts, K. 2003. *Parasites and partners: Hitchers and thieves.* Chicago: Raintree.

Summary: This series introduces unique symbiotic relationships to readers in grades 5–7. Each book takes one broad relationship type and discusses it in an easy-to-understand way within a framework packed with full-color photographs and fascinating examples.

Parker, S. 2001. *Adaptation: Life processes series.* Chicago: Heinemann Library.
Summary: This informational book describes how living things develop habits and physical features that help them live where they do. It reveals how animals' bodies have adapted to help them live in their environments, and it explains what would happen to the animals if they continued to adapt.

Rhodes, M. J., and D. Hall. 2006. *Partners in the sea.* Danbury, CT: Children's Press.

Summary: From the Undersea Encounters series, this book explores various examples of marine symbiosis.

Name: ______________________________

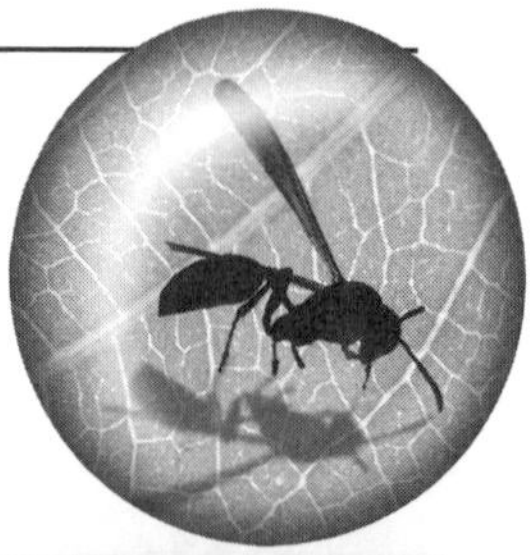

O-W-L Chart

O	W	L
What do you **OBSERVE** about the object? (Don't forget to measure.)	What do you **WONDER** about the object?	What did you **LEARN** about the object?

Close Encounters

Dichotomous Key

Directions: Use the dichotomous key below to identify your mystery object. Then read more about it!

1 Found along the goldenrod stem .... go to 2
Found on oak leaf or twig .... go to 3

2 Spherical (ball-shaped) growth .... GOLDENROD BALL GALL
Elliptical (oval-shaped) growth .... GOLDENROD SPINDLE GALL

3 Found on oak twig, leaf stem, or central vein .... go to 4
Found growing directly on oak leaf.......... (a type of) OAK LEAF GALL

4 Growth encircling twig .... go to 5
Growth hanging from twig or leaf stem .... go to 6

5 Hard, woody swelling with small "horns" .... HORNED OAK GALL
Hard, woody swelling with no "horns" .... GOUTY OAK GALL

6 Round, bumpy, and hard .... OAK BULLET GALL
Round with thin, papery shell and spongy center..... OAK APPLE GALL

Name: ____________________

Close Encounters

Dichotomous Key cont.

What Are Galls?

Imagine living inside a windowless, globelike room made out of your favorite food. The room gives you shelter, protection, and all the nutrition you need to grow into an adult. When the time is right to leave, you just eat your way out! That's what it would be like to trade places with a gall-making insect.

Galls are abnormal growths on a plant usually caused by insects, mites, bacteria, or fungi. Gall-making insects lay eggs on or in their host plant. The eggs hatch into larvae, and chemicals in the insects cause the plant to form protective growths around them. The larvae survive by eating the inside of the gall. Although the host plant is not killed by the formation of galls, it can be weakened. After metamorphosis, the adult insects crawl out, leave their host plant, and start the cycle all over again.

Types of Galls

Galls come in a wide variety of shapes and colors. By looking at the gall's shape, color, and location on the plant, you can determine what organism caused it. Each species of gall-making insect has a certain kind of plant for a host. No other kind of plant will do. For example, if you observe an oval-shaped gall growing in the stem of a goldenrod plant, then it was made by a kind of moth. If the gall is ball-shaped, it was made by a tiny goldenrod gall fly. Inside either kind of goldenrod gall you may find a tiny white insect larva.

Oak galls are usually caused by different species of gall wasps. The wasp lays an egg on the oak leaf, on the leaf stem or vein, or on a twig. When the larva hatches, it causes the leaf or twig to grow a swelling around it. The larva gets shelter and food inside the gall until it hatches into an adult wasp. Don't worry–these tiny wasps will not sting humans!

There are hundreds of different kinds of oak galls, so identification can be a real challenge. Your gall could be a hairy oak leaf gall, spiny vase oak gall, wooly fold oak gall, oak saucer gall, or oak spangle gall, to name a few.

My mystery object is most likely a ____________________

made by a ____________________ .

Name: ______________________________

Close Encounters

Sorting Cards

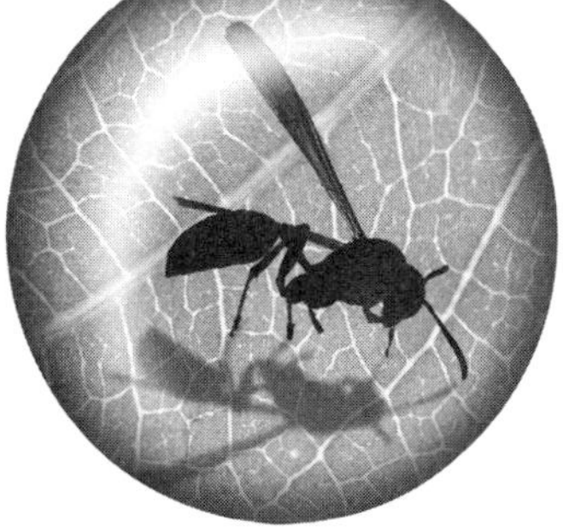

Directions: Cut out the cards below and sort them into different categories (choose any categories you want). Then read the article Close Encounters of the Symbiotic Kind and sort them a different way!

parasitism	commensalism
mutualism	symbiosis
gall fly	elm tree
sea anemone	dog

Name: ____________________

Close Encounters

Sorting Cards cont.

shark	bark beetle
remora	goldenrod
clown fish	flea
orchid	human
mosquito	kapok tree

Name: ________________________________

CHAPTER 11

Close Encounters
of the Symbiotic Kind

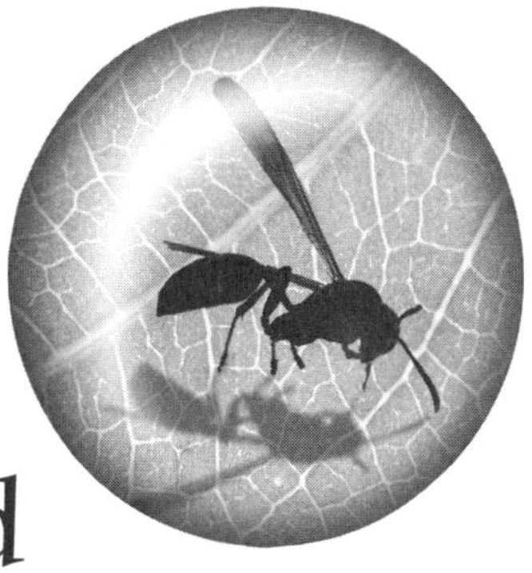

A bright little clown fish darts in and out of a deadly sea anemone's tentacles. A bark beetle bores into an elm tree to lay its eggs, which will hatch into hungry, wood-eating larvae. A beautiful flower called an orchid survives in the shadowy rain forest by growing high on the trunk of a giant kapok tree. What do these things have in common? They are all examples of **symbiosis**, a close relationship between two organisms in which one organism lives near, on, or even inside the other. In symbiosis, at least one organism benefits from the relationship. This article describes three types of symbiosis.

Has your dog had fleas? Have you ever been bitten by a mosquito? If so, you and your pet have been victims of parasites.

Parasitism is a type of symbiosis in which one organism (the **parasite**) lives on or in a much larger organism (the **host**) and feeds on it while the host is still alive. Parasites don't usually kill their host, but the host may be weakened by the relationship.

Commensalism is a type of symbiosis in which one of the organisms is helped while the other is not affected. For example, an orchid gets support and sunlight by living on the trunk or branches of a tall rain forest tree. The tree is neither helped nor harmed by the orchid. A remora is a hitchhiking fish that often attaches itself to the body of a shark. The remora gets a free ride, protection from predators, and food scraps left by the shark. The shark is not affected by the remora.

In **mutualism**, both organisms benefit from their close encounter. This is the "win-win" type of symbiosis. For example, the clown fish has a slimy coating that protects it from the stinging tentacles of the sea anemone. This colorful fish hides among the tentacles to gain protection from predators. The anemone benefits by eating leftovers from the fish's meals, and the fish helps keep it clean. The sea anemone gets one other benefit. Its enemy, the butterfly fish, is afraid of the little clown fish's nasty bite!

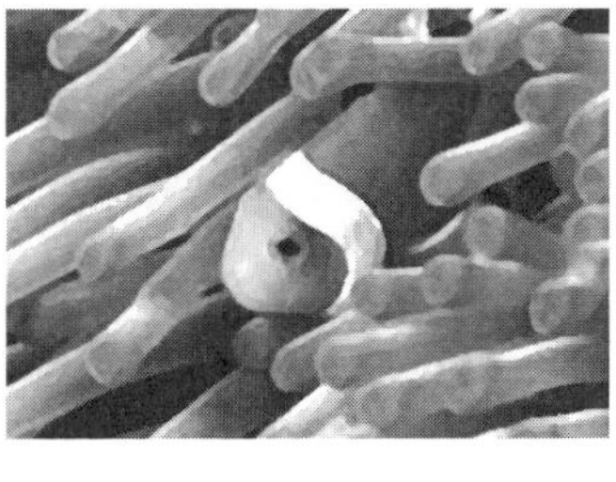

Name: ______________________________

Weird Friends

Unlikely Allies in the Animal Kingdom

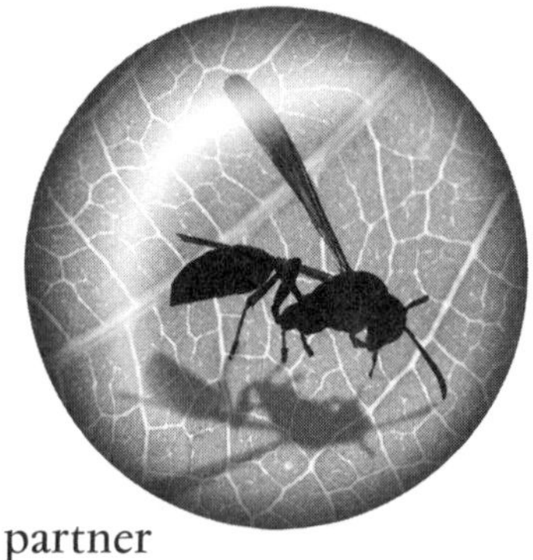

As your teacher reads the book *Weird Friends,* listen for how each partner benefits from the relationship. Beneath the name of each partner, list the benefit. The first one is done for you.

1	Clown fish Protection	Sea anemone Protection
2	Rhino	Cattle egret
3	Blind shrimp	Goby
4	Ostrich	Zebra
5	Red phalaropes	Sperm whale
6	Red ants	Large blue butterfly
7	Hermit crab	Sea anemones
8	Impalas	Baboons
9	Horse mackerel	Portuguese man-of-war
10	Forest mouse	Beetles
11	Hippo	Oxpeckers and Black labeo fish
12	Wrasse	Google-eye fish
13	Tuatara	Snooty shearwater

Name: ______________________________

Symbiosis Quiz

Three types of symbiosis are parasitism, mutualism, and commensalism. After reading each example, circle the type of symbiosis described (1 point) and explain how each organism is hurt, helped, or not affected by the relationship (2 points).

1 African tick birds can often be found sitting on the backs of large grazing animals such as Cape buffalo. The tick birds eat bloodsucking ticks found on the skin of the large animals. What type of symbiosis is shown by the tick birds and the Cape buffalo?

a parasitism

b mutualism

c commensalism

Explain ______________________________

____

2 A male golden weaver bird builds a hanging nest made of grass and straw high on the branches of a thorny acacia tree. The tree is not affected by the nest. What type of symbiosis is shown by the weaver bird and the acacia tree?

a parasitism

b mutualism

c commensalism

Explain ______________________________

____

Name: ______________________________

Symbiosis Quiz cont.

3 Aphids are tiny bugs that live on plants. They excrete a sugary liquid called honeydew from their abdomens. Ants find the honeydew both nutritious and delicious. Some kinds of ants protect herds of aphids from predators such as ladybugs. When danger threatens, the ants carry the aphids to safety on their backs or in their mouths! When the ants want to feed, they tickle the aphids into producing honeydew. What type of symbiosis is shown by the ants and the aphids?

a parasitism

b mutualism

c commensalism

Explain ______________________________

____

4 Tapeworms are long flatworms that live in the guts of animals, including humans. Tapeworms absorb nutrients through their skin. They stretch out their narrow bodies to reach the right kind of food, food that has been broken down by the host's digestive system. They dig their heads into the gut wall to avoid being swept away. Humans can lose many nutrients when infected by tapeworms, leading to disorders of the blood, brain, and nerves. What type of symbiosis is shown by the tapeworms and the humans?

a parasitism

b mutualism

c commensalism

Explain ______________________________

____

Name: ______________________________

Symbiosis
Quiz cont.

5 Flower mites are tiny animals that feed on the nectar and pollen of certain plants. They rely on hummingbirds to carry them from plant to plant. When a hummingbird stops to feed at a flower, the tiny mites run up the bird's beak and climb into its nostrils. The hummingbird doesn't even know the mites are there. When the hummingbird stops at the right kind of flower, the mites sense the flower's perfume and run back down the beak and into the flower. What type of symbiosis is shown by the mites and the hummingbird?

a parasitism

b mutualism

c commensalism

Explain ____

____

6 Some wasps lay their eggs inside living caterpillars. When the eggs hatch, the wasp larvae use their chewing mouthparts to feed on the bodies of the caterpillars. What type of symbiosis is shown by the wasps and the caterpillars?

a parasitism

b mutualism

c commensalism

Explain ____

____

Name: ______________________

Symbiosis Quiz cont.

7. Choose one of the organisms described in questions 1 through 6, and identify one of the *structural adaptations* the organism uses to survive within its symbiotic relationship (1 point). Then explain how the adaptation helps it survive (1 point).

For example, in question 6, the wasp larvae have chewing mouthparts. This is a structural adaptation that helps them get food from the bodies of the caterpillars.

____

____

____

____

____

8. Now choose one of the organisms described in questions 1 through 6, and identify one of the *behavioral adaptations* the organism uses to survive within its symbiotic relationship (1 point). Then explain how the adaptation helps it survive (1 point).

____

____

____

____

____

Symbiosis
Quiz Answer Key

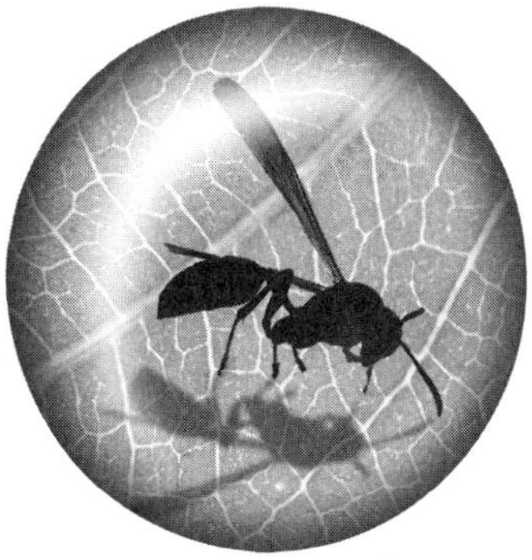

Three types of symbiosis are parasitism, mutualism, and commensalism. After reading each example, circle the type of symbiosis described (1 point) and explain how each organism is hurt, helped, or not affected by the relationship (2 points).

1 African tick birds can often be found sitting on the backs of large grazing animals such as Cape buffalo. The tick birds eat bloodsucking ticks found on the skin of the large animals. What type of symbiosis is shown by the tick birds and the Cape buffalo?

a parasitism

b mutualism

c commensalism

Explain: The tick birds are helped because they get food by eating the ticks, and the Cape buffalo are helped because the tick birds remove the bloodsucking parasites.

2 A male golden weaver bird builds a hanging nest made of grass and straw high on the branches of a thorny acacia tree. The tree is not affected by the nest. What type of symbiosis is shown by the weaver bird and the acacia tree?

a parasitism

b mutualism

c commensalism

Explain: The weaver bird is helped because it has a safe place to build its nest, but the tree is neither hurt nor helped.

Symbiosis
Quiz Answer Key cont.

3 Aphids are tiny bugs that live on plants. They excrete a sugary liquid called honeydew from their abdomens. Ants find the honeydew both nutritious and delicious. Some kinds of ants protect herds of aphids from predators such as ladybugs. When danger threatens, the ants carry the aphids to safety on their backs or in their mouths! When the ants want to feed, they tickle the aphids into producing honeydew. What type of symbiosis is shown by the ants and the aphids?

a parasitism

b mutualism

c commensalism

Explain: The ants are helped because they get food from the aphids, but the aphids are not harmed. Instead, they are helped because the ants protect them.

---

4 Tapeworms are long flatworms that live in the guts of animals, including humans. Tapeworms absorb nutrients through their skin. They stretch out their narrow bodies in order to reach the right kind of food, food that has been broken down by the host's digestive system. They dig their heads into the gut wall to avoid being swept away. Humans can lose many nutrients when infected by tapeworms, leading to disorders of the blood, brain, and nerves. What type of symbiosis is shown by the tapeworms and the humans?

a parasitism

b mutualism

c commensalism

Explain: The tapeworms are helped because they get food and a place to live. The humans are hurt because the tapeworms feed on them and can cause disorders.

Symbiosis Quiz Answer Key cont.

5 Flower mites are tiny animals that feed on the nectar and pollen of certain plants. When the plant stops flowering, the mites must move on. They rely on hummingbirds to carry them from plant to plant. When a hummingbird stops to feed at a flower, the tiny mites run up the bird's beak and climb into its nostrils. The hummingbird doesn't even know the mites are there. When the hummingbird stops at the right kind of flower, the mites sense the flower's perfume and run back down the beak and into the flower. What type of symbiosis is shown by the mites and the hummingbird?

a parasitism

b mutualism

c commensalism

Explain: The mites are helped because they get transportation from the hummingbirds. The hummingbirds are neither helped nor hurt.

---

6 Some wasps lay their eggs inside living caterpillars. When the eggs hatch, the wasp larvae use their chewing mouthparts to feed on the bodies of the caterpillars. What type of symbiosis is shown by the wasps and the caterpillars?

a parasitism

b mutualism

c commensalism

Explain: The wasp larvae are helped because they get food from the caterpillars' bodies. The caterpillars are hurt because the wasp larvae eat them and they probably die.

Symbiosis
Quiz Answer Key
cont.

7. Student should correctly identify an adaptation that is structural (1 point) and explain how it helps that animal survive within the symbiotic relationship described (1 point).

8 Student should correctly identify an adaptation that is behavioral (1 point) and explain how it helps that animal survive within the symbiotic relationship described (1 point).

Turtle Hurdles

Description

By taking part in a simulation, learners explore the many threats to sea turtles and the ways humans can help them survive. Learners identify which dangers result from human actions and which dangers are natural. Learners also explore the life cycles of sea turtles through literature.

Suggested Grade Levels: 3–5

Lesson Objectives Connecting to the *Framework*

Science and Engineering Practices

- Developing and using models
- Obtaining, evaluating, and communicating information

Disciplinary Core Ideas

LS4.D: Biodiversity and Humans

Crosscutting Concepts

- Cause and Effect

Featured Picture Books

Title	***Turtle Watch***
Author	**Saviour Pirotta**
Illustrator	**Nilesh Mistry**
Publisher	**Frances Lincoln Children's Books**
Year	**2009**
Genre	**Story**
Summary	**Taro is fascinated by old Jiro-San, who sweeps the beach while waiting for the arrival of sea turtles ready to lay their eggs.**

Title	***Turtle, Turtle, Watch Out!***
Author	**April Pulley Sayre**
Illustrator	**Annie Patterson**
Publisher	**Charlesbridge**
Year	**2010**
Genre	**Narrative Information**
Summary	**From before she hatches until she returns to the same beach to lay eggs of her own, a sea turtle escapes from danger with help from human hands.**

Time Needed

This lesson will take several class periods. Suggested scheduling is as follows:

Day 1: **Engage** with read aloud of *Turtle Watch* and I Wonder/I Learned chart

Day 2: **Explore** with *Turtle, Turtle, Watch Out!* read aloud and game, and **Explain** with Turtle T-Chart

Day 3: **Elaborate** and **Evaluate** with Write a Letter

Materials

- Think pads (pads of sticky notes—1 per student)
- Turtle-shaped I Wonder/I Learned chart
- Turtle Line Graph (copied onto an overhead transparency)
- Overhead projector
- Overhead markers of at least 3 different colors
- Dice chart
- 1 die
- Optional: CD of ocean sounds

Student Pages

- Optional: Sea Turtle Headband
- How to Make a Fortune-Teller
- Fortune-Teller Templates 1 and 2
- How to Play "Turtle, Turtle, Watch Out!"
- Turtle Line Graph
- Turtle T-Chart
- Write a Letter!

Background

Sea turtles are aquatic reptiles with streamlined bodies and large flippers. Although sea turtles are born on dry land and breathe air, they spend most of their lives swimming in the warm oceans, feeding on sea grass, crabs, and shrimp. There are seven different species worldwide, ranging in size from the 75-pound Kemp's ridley to the 1,300-pound, 8-foot-long leatherback. The turtles in the books *Turtle Watch* and *Turtle, Turtle, Watch Out!* are loggerhead turtles. All six species of sea turtles that live in U.S. waters are protected under the Endangered Species Act as either endangered or threatened. This designation makes it illegal to harm, harass, or kill any sea turtles, hatchlings, or their eggs. It is also illegal to import, sell, or transport turtles or their products. Other countries have their own conservation laws and regulations that apply to sea turtles.

Much of the research done on sea turtles has focused on nesting females and hatchlings emerging from the nest, because they are the easiest to find and study. Thousands of sea turtles around the world have been tagged to help collect information about their growth rates, reproductive cycles, and migration routes. Female turtles return to the same beach where they were born to lay their eggs. (Only the females come ashore; males very rarely return to land after crawling into the sea as hatchlings.) How they find the exact beach where they hatched is one of the greatest mysteries in the animal kingdom, and finding the answer has been the focus of generations of researchers. One current hypothesis about how sea turtles navigate suggests that they can detect the Earth's magnetic field.

Once ashore, each female digs a bucket-size pit with her flippers and lays a hundred or more eggs. The eggs have leathery shells, so they will not break as they plop into the nest. The turtle then covers her nest with sand to hide it from hungry creatures. After two months or so, the eggs hatch during the night, and the baby turtles scratch and dig their way up to the surface of the sand. As they scramble to the water, the hatchlings face many dangers, and once in the sea, there are even more threats. Scientists estimate that only one in 1,000 sea turtles survives to breeding age. Sea turtles grow slowly and take between 15 and 50 years to reach reproductive maturity, depending on the species. Scientists think some species can live more than 100 years.

There are many factors that can affect how long a sea turtle survives in the wild. This lesson focuses on those factors, some human and some natural, some helpful and some harmful. An example of a *natural factor* that can help sea turtles is the light of the Moon that guides the hatchlings into the sea. An example of a harmful factor in nature is predation by raccoons and birds. Some harmful *human factors* include poaching of turtles for meat, eggs, skin, and shells; destruction of feeding and nesting habitats; and pollution of the world's oceans. These factors all take a serious toll on remaining sea turtle populations. In an attempt to counteract some of these harmful actions, people have made efforts to help sea turtles, such as cleaning up beaches where turtles nest, setting up protective fences around turtle nests, moving the eggs to safer places, and requiring beachfront properties to turn out their outside lights so the turtles don't get confused when trying to follow the light of the Moon. In this lesson, students learn that humans change environments in ways that can be either beneficial or harmful for themselves or other organisms, and that natural factors can also have an impact on environments, some good, some bad, and some neither good nor bad.

SEA TURTLE I WONDER/I LEARNED CHART

engage

Read Aloud and I Wonder/I Learned Chart

Use paper to hide the cover of the book *Turtle Watch* in advance, and don't tell students the title of the book.

Tell them you have a very interesting book to share and you want them to make some inferences about the story without seeing the cover yet. Then begin reading aloud *Turtle Watch,* using the suggested reading strategies. Make sure each student has a sticky note "think pad" to write on.

Questioning

After reading page 5 (Jiro-San says his old friends are coming) and showing the pictures, model your students' thinking by asking aloud

? I wonder who Jiro-San's friends are?

Inferring

As you read pages 6 through 16 (Jiro-San and Taro are cleaning the beach and different animals are coming to the beach), periodically stop reading and have students get out their think pads to "stop and jot" their inferences about who Jiro-San's friends might be. Remind them to use clues from the text and the pictures.

Visualizing

Hide the illustrations as you read pages 23 through 25 (the sea turtles are hatching). Have students sketch to stretch. Have them visualize what the teacher is reading and draw a sketch of what they think it might look like. After reading the last page, "About Sea Turtles," ask students what they think would be a good title for the book. Then reveal the cover.

I Wonder/I Learned Chart

Then make a large I Wonder/I Learned chart on sea turtles, a turtle-shaped chart as pictured if you like. Ask students to turn and talk about what they learned about sea turtles from the book. Then have each student write one learning about sea turtles on a sticky note. Next have each student write a question about sea turtles on another sticky note and place it on the chart. Read and discuss some of the learnings and questions as a class. Tell students that you have another book to share that might answer some of their questions.

explore

Turtle, Turtle, Watch Out!

Determining Importance

Introduce the author and illustrator of *Turtle, Turtle, Watch Out!* Tell students that as you read the book, they should call out "Turtle, turtle, watch out!" in unison when that phrase

Making a fortune-teller. Read all eight steps on page 170.

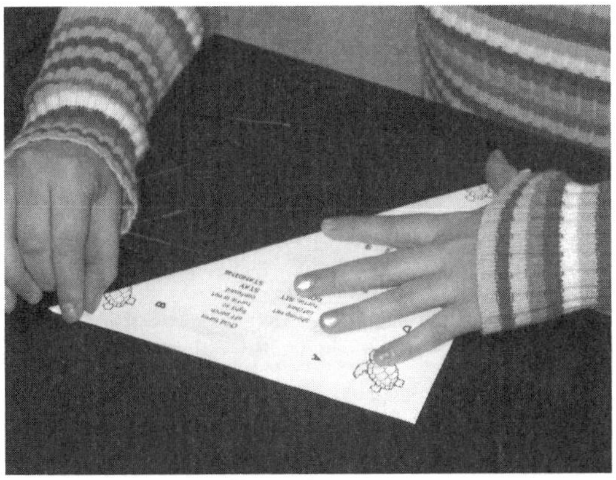

Step 2

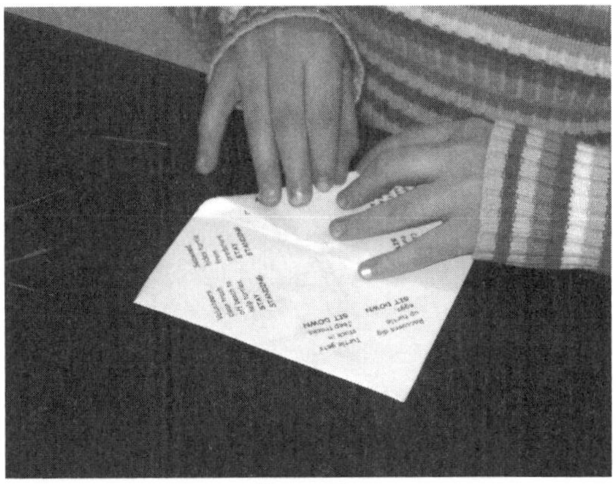

Step 5

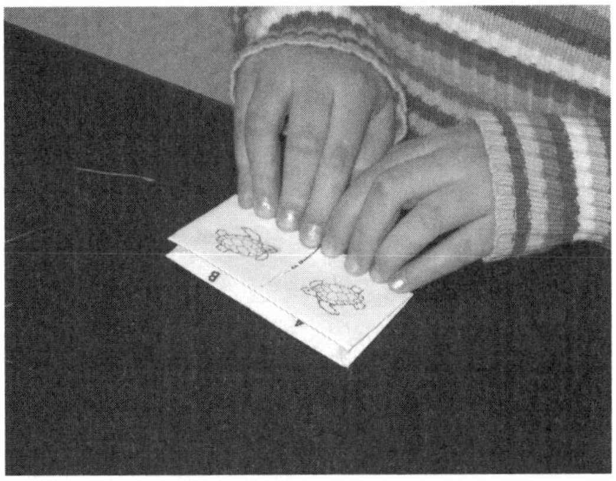

Step 6

Step 8

appears in the book. Also tell students to signal by touching their noses when they hear an example of a human changing the turtle's habitat. Read the book aloud, including "Helping Hands for Sea Turtles."

Next tell students they are getting ready to play a game in which they will pretend to be sea turtles. (Optional for younger students: Have them make a turtle headband to wear during the game using the Sea Turtle Headband student page.) Distribute the fortune-teller templates, randomly giving students either Template 1 or Template 2. To save time you can precut the fortune-teller templates on a paper cutter. Using the How to Make a Fortune-Teller sheet, have students cut and fold their fortune-tellers. You may want to read the directions together and model the steps.

Next place the Turtle Line Graph on the overhead projector and turn off the classroom lights to simulate nightfall on the beach. Play a CD of ocean sounds if you wish. Then set the stage for the students:

"Please stand to play a game called 'Turtle, Turtle, Watch Out!' You are now baby sea turtles. Your goal is to hatch safely, crawl across the beach to the ocean, and swim to deep water, all under the cover of darkness. You will face many hurdles. If your fortune-teller opens up to reveal that your turtle has been helped by a human or natural factor, stay standing for that turn. But if your fortune-teller opens up to reveal bad news for your turtle, sit down until the game is over. You may continue to follow along with your fortune-teller, but you must stay seated to represent the loss of that baby turtle. If you are still standing after five turns, you have made it to deep water. I will graph on the overhead how many turtles are left standing after each turn.

Be ready to reassure any student who becomes unusually discouraged if he or she is a turtle who gets bad news.

Directions for "Turtle, Turtle, Watch Out!" Game:

1. Have students stand up and spread out holding their assembled fortune-tellers.
2. Before each turn, call out "Turtle, turtle, watch out!" in unison.
3. Hold a die about 1 in. above the star on the dice chart and drop it.
4. Call out the number on the die. Have students open and close their fortune-tellers that number of times.
5. Call out the letter that the die landed on. Have students open the panel under the corresponding letter on their fortune-tellers and read their turtles' fate. If their turtle survives, they remain standing. If their turtle dies, they sit down. (Seated students can still follow along with their turtle fortune-tellers.)
6. Count the number of students standing after each turn and graph that number on the Turtle Line Graph.
7. The game ends after five turns or when no one is left standing.
8. Repeat game several times, using a different colored marker to graph results each time.

explain

Turtle T-Chart

Discuss the results of the game using the data from the Turtle Line Graph.

? Why did we use a line graph to display our turtle data? (A line graph shows changes over time. Each turn represented a point in time, and we used the line graph to show the change in the number of turtles as time passed.)

? What kinds of dangers did the turtles encounter?

? Why do you think sea turtles lay so many eggs?

? Based on the graph, what can you conclude about the number of baby sea turtles that survive to swim to deep water? How do you think this compares to real life?

? What things can people do to help sea turtles? Turn and talk.

Next have students open up their fortune-tellers to read all of the factors that could have affected them during the game. Give each student a Turtle T-Chart, and have them list all the natural factors that helped or harmed their turtles on one side and all the human factors that helped or harmed their turtles on the other.

After discussing the results of the game, have students answer the questions at the bottom of the Turtle T-Chart.

? Do human actions help or harm sea turtles? Explain. (Discuss the results of human actions on sea turtles. Students should realize that some human actions help sea turtles and others harm sea turtles. Students can debate whether human actions are mostly positive or mostly negative.)

? Do you think humans should interfere with nature by helping sea turtles? Why or why not? (Answers will vary. Some students may justify human interference by saying that it can help "un-do" some of the harm we have caused to the sea turtles and their habitat.)

I Wonder/I Learned Chart

Next ask students what they have learned about sea turtles from the book and the game and add to the "L" column of the I Wonder/I Learned chart. They may also want to add more wonderings to the chart to explore through further research.

elaborate & evaluate

Write a Letter!

Many students will be very concerned about the plight of sea turtles and will want to know what they can do to help them. Give students the Write a Letter! student page. Have each student write a letter to one of the organizations listed asking for information about helping endangered sea turtles. They should include the following in their letters:

- three facts about sea turtles
- three ways sea turtles are harmed by human actions
- one reason endangered sea turtles should be helped
- one question about sea turtles
- teacher's name and school address

When sending the letters to the various marine conservation organizations, be sure to use the teacher's name and school address for the return address so that responses come back to the school. Many marine conservation groups have limited budgets and may not be able to send each child a response. You can help them by sending all letters to an organization together with just one request for a reply. Include a self-addressed stamped envelope.

The information the students receive in response to their letters can be added to the I Wonder/I Learned chart and posted on a marine conservation bulletin board. Optional: Begin a class or schoolwide fundraiser for marine conservation efforts. Go to *www.cccturtle.org* for information on the Caribbean Conservation Corporation's Adopt-a-Turtle! program. Here, the students can track the migration of their adopted sea turtle in real time.

Scoring Rubric for Letter	
4 Point Response	The student's letter includes three important facts about sea turtles, clearly demonstrates understanding of three ways sea turtles are harmed by human actions, effectively communicates one reason sea turtles should be helped, and requests information about sea turtles.
3 Point Response	The student's letter demonstrates a flaw in the understanding of the concepts OR is missing one or two elements.
2 Point Response	The student's letter demonstrates a flaw in the understanding of the concepts and is missing one or two elements OR is missing three or four elements.
1 Point Response	The student's letter demonstrates a flaw in the understanding of the concepts and is missing three or four elements OR is missing five elements.
0 Point Response	The student shows no understanding of the concepts OR does not write a letter.

Inquiry Place

Some questions related to science cannot be answered by experimentation in the classroom. Students will have many questions about sea turtles, but it is not possible for them to observe or experiment with sea turtles in the classroom. The questions below are examples of research-type questions students can answer by doing internet or library research. Have students brainstorm researchable questions such as

- How do scientists track sea turtles? What are the advantages and disadvantages of their methods?
- Which sea turtle species travels the farthest in its migration?
- What are some theories on how sea turtles navigate? Which theory do you think is most probable? Why?

Students can select a question to research individually or as teams. They should collect and analyze information from a variety of sources. Students can present their findings at a poster session.

Websites

Sea Turtle Conservancy
www.conserveturtles.org

HEART (Helping Endangered Animals–Ridley Turtles)
www.ridleyturtles.org

Ocean Conservancy
www.oceanconservancy.org

Sea Turtle Rescue and Rehabilitation Center
www.seaturtlehospital.org

Sea Turtle Restoration Project
www.seaturtles.org

World Wildlife Fund
www.worldwildlife.org

More Books to Read

Davies, N. 2001. *One tiny turtle.* New York: Candlewick Press.
Summary: This introduction to the life cycle of the loggerhead turtle is written in poetic, informative text.

Gibbons, G. 1998. *Sea turtles.* New York: Holiday House.
Summary: This informative book describes the types, features, nesting, and protection of sea turtles.

Guiberson, B. Z. 1996. *Into the sea.* New York: Henry Holt.
Summary: The author takes the reader through the life cycle of a turtle, from hatching to migration to returning to the beach to lay her eggs.

Lasky, K. 2001. *Interrupted journey: Saving endangered sea turtles.* New York: Candlewick Press.
Summary: This photo essay depicts the efforts to save an endangered Kemp's ridley turtle rescued on a Cape Cod beach. Distinctive, full-color photographs carefully document each step of the extensive rescue procedure.

Monroe, M. A. 2007. *Turtle summer: A journal for my daughter.* Mt. Pleasant, SC: Sylvan Dell Publishing.
Summary: Organized as a scrapbook for the author's young daughter, this book describes how the mother turtles come ashore to lay their eggs, how the turtle team moves eggs in danger of washing away, and how the hatchlings head for the sea. Closing pages include more sea turtle information, short activities, and suggestions for constructing a nature scrapbook

Sea Turtle Headband

Directions for Making a Sea Turtle Headband

1. Color the sea turtle and cut it out.
2. Cut a strip of paper 5 cm wide and long enough to fit around your head.
3. Tape the turtle to the strip of paper and you have a turtle headband!
4. Wrap the headband around your head and tape it in the back.

Chapter 12

How to Make a Fortune-Teller

1 Cut the fortune-teller template at the dotted line to make a square.

2 Lay the paper square with the turtle side down. Fold the square in half to make a triangle, crease it, and then open it back up.

3 Lay the paper square with the turtle side down again. Fold the other corners into a triangle and crease again. Unfold so you are back to the square (turtle side down).

4 Next fold each corner point into the center of the creases.

5 Flip it over (turtle side down). Fold all four corner points into the center again.

6 Fold the square in half to make a rectangle with the turtles on the outside, and crease.

7 Open it back up to the square. Fold the other way to make a rectangle with the turtles on the outside, and crease.

8 Stick your two thumbs and two forefingers into each of the four turtle flap pockets. Fingers should press center creases so that all four flaps meet at a point in the center.

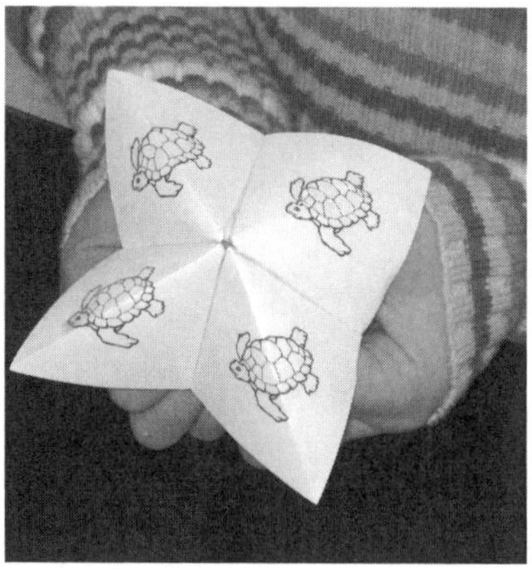

Now you are ready to play "Turtle, Turtle, Watch Out!"

Fortune-Teller

Template 1

A

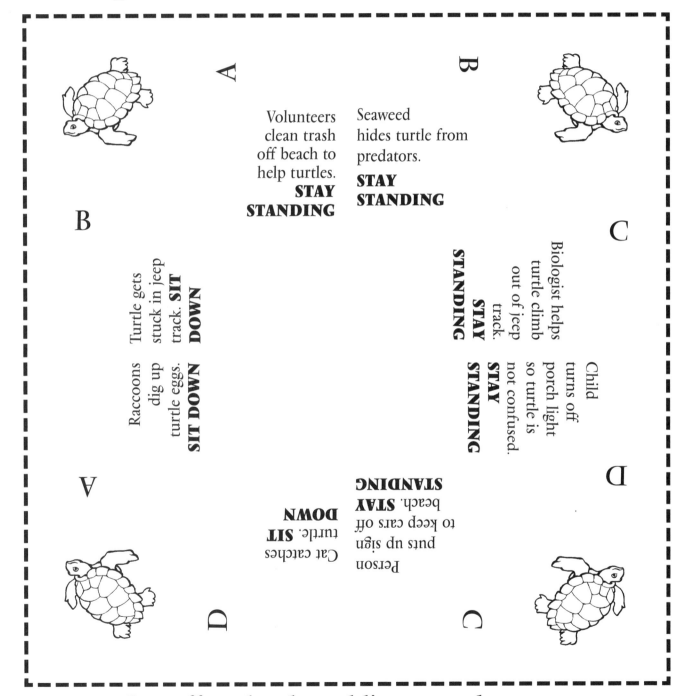

Volunteers clean trash off beach to help turtles. **STAY STANDING**

B

Seaweed hides turtle from predators. **STAY STANDING**

B

Turtle gets stuck in jeep track. **SIT DOWN**

Raccoons dig up turtle eggs. **SIT DOWN**

A

C

Biologist helps turtle climb out of jeep track. **STAY STANDING**

Child turns off porch light so turtle is not confused. **STAY STANDING**

D

Cat catches turtle. **SIT DOWN**

D

Person puts up sign to keep cars off beach. **STAY STANDING**

C

Cut off at the dotted line to make a square.

Fortune-Teller
Template 2

A

B

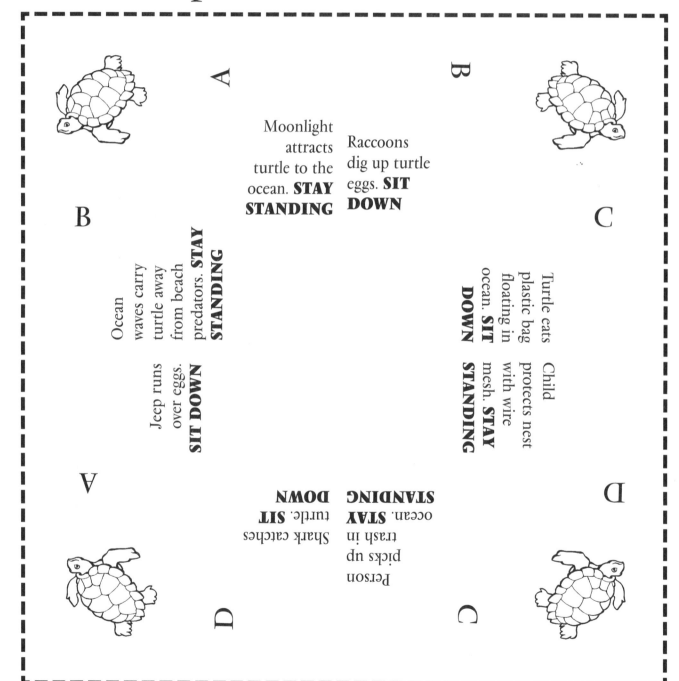

Moonlight attracts turtle to the ocean. **STAY STANDING**

Raccoons dig up turtle eggs. **SIT DOWN**

B

C

Ocean waves carry turtle away from beach predators. **STAY STANDING**

Jeep runs over eggs. **SIT DOWN**

Turtle eats plastic bag floating in ocean. **SIT DOWN**

Child protects nest with wire mesh. **STAY STANDING**

A

D

Shark catches turtle. **SIT DOWN**

Person picks up trash in ocean. **STAY STANDING**

D

C

Cut off at the dotted line to make a square.

How to Play "Turtle, Turtle, Watch Out!"

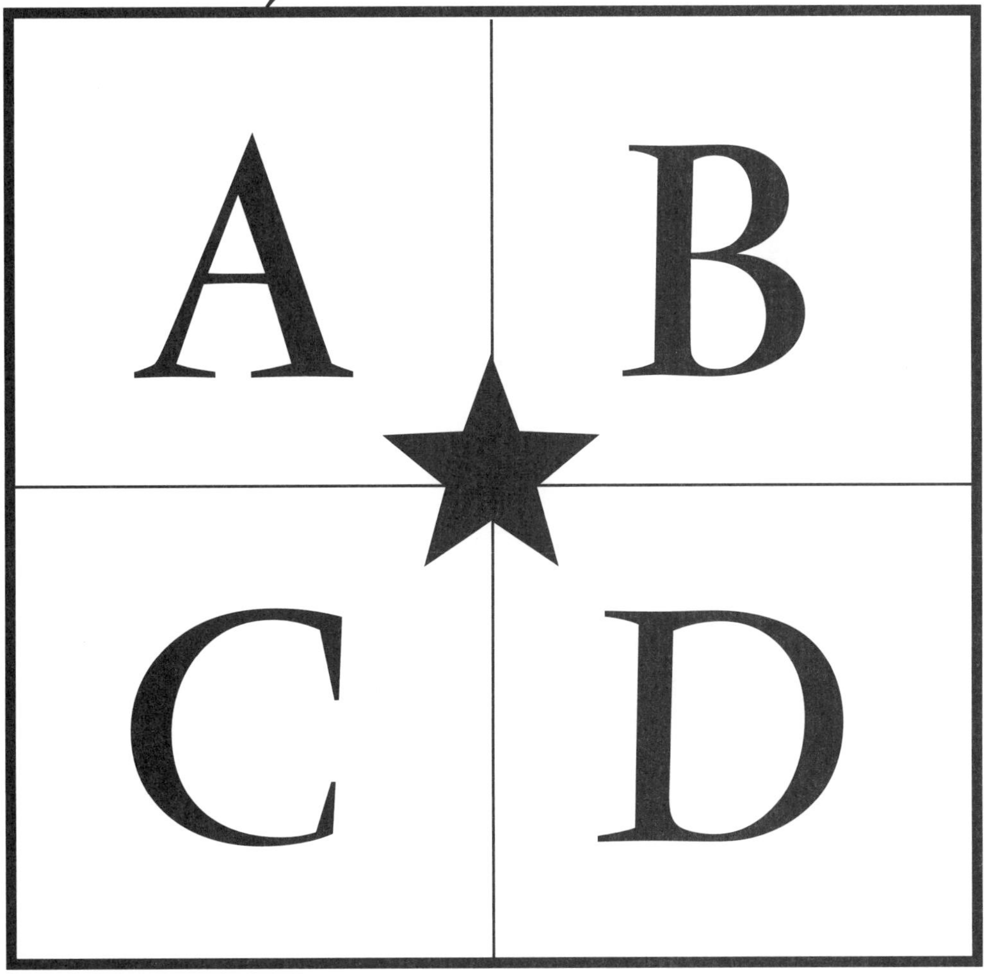

1. Have students stand up and spread out holding their assembled turtle fortune-tellers.
2. Before each turn, call out "Turtle, turtle, watch out!" in unison.
3. Hold a die about 1 in. above the star and drop it.
4. Call out the number on the die. Have students open and close their fortune-tellers that number of times.
5. Call out the letter that the die landed on. Have students open the panel under the letter and read their turtles' fate. If their turtle survives, they remain standing. If their turtle dies, they sit down. (Seated students can still follow along with their turtle fortune-tellers.)
6. Count the number of students standing after each turn and graph that number on the Turtle Line Graph.
7. The game ends after five turns or when no one is left standing.
8. Repeat game several times, using a different color to graph results each time.
9. Discuss results.

Turtle Line Graph

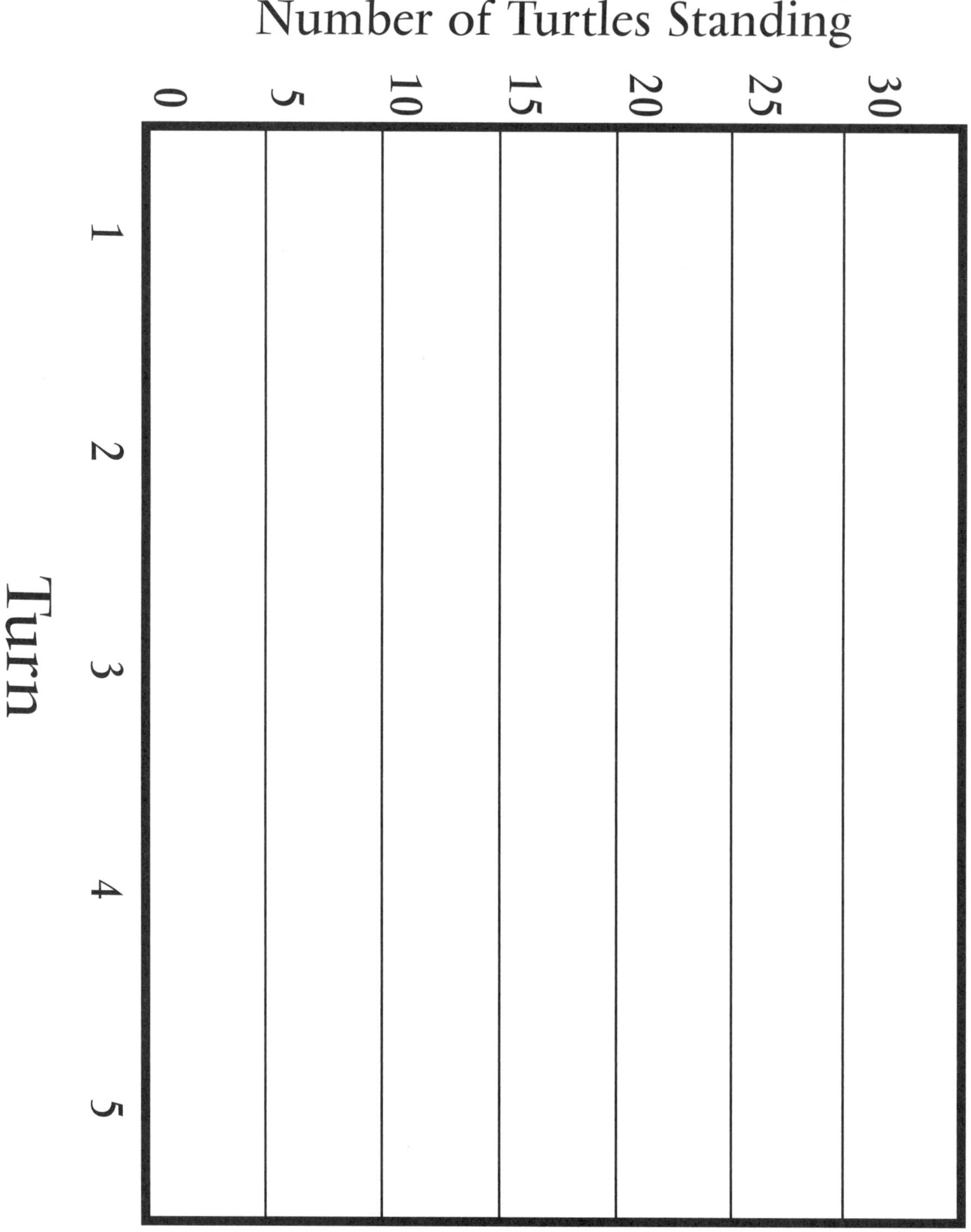

Name: ______________________________

Turtle T-Chart

After playing "Turtle, Turtle, Watch Out!" open your fortune-teller and read all the factors that could have affected your turtle during the game. Fill out the T-Chart, and answer the questions below.

Natural Factors	Human Factors
Helped the turtle:	Helped the turtle:
Harmed the turtle:	Harmed the turtle:

1 Do human actions help or harm sea turtles? Explain. ____________

____

____

2 Do you think humans should interfere with nature by helping sea turtles? Why or why not? ____________________

____

____

____

____

Name: ______________________________

Write a Letter!

Write a letter to one of the organizations listed below asking for information about helping endangered sea turtles. Include the following in your letter:

- three facts you learned about sea turtles
- three ways sea turtles are harmed by human actions
- one reason endangered sea turtles should be helped
- one question you have about sea turtles
- your teacher's name and school address (Ask the organization to send the information to your teacher at your school address.)

Marine Conservation Organizations

Sea Turtle Restoration Project
PO Box 370
Forest Knolls, CA 94933

HEART (Helping Endangered Animals–Ridley Turtles)
PO Box 681231
Houston, TX 77268-1231

Ocean Conservancy
1300 19th Street, NW, 8th Floor
Washington, DC 20036

Sea Turtle Conservancy
4424 NW 13th St., Suite B-11
Gainesville, FL 32609

Sea Turtle Rescue and Rehabilitation Center
PO Box 3012
822 Carolina Boulevard
Topsail Beach, NC 28445

World Wildlife Fund
1250 24th Street, NW
PO Box 97180
Washington, DC 20090

Oil Spill!

Description

Learners explore the effects of oil spills on plants, animals, and the environment and investigate cleanup methods through a simulated oil spill. Learners also use creative writing and letter writing to demonstrate their understandings about the effects of oil spills.

Suggested Grade Levels: 3–5

Lesson Objectives Connecting to the *Framework*

Science and Engineering Practices
- Developing and using models
- Planning and carrying out investigations
- Analyzing and interpreting data

Disciplinary Core Ideas
LS4.D: Biodiversity and Humans

Crosscutting Concepts
- Cause and Effect

Featured Picture Books

Title	***Prince William***
Author	**Gloria Rand**
Illustrator	**Ted Rand**
Publisher	**Henry Holt & Company**
Year	**1994**
Genre	**Story**
Summary	**On Prince William Sound in Alaska, Denny rescues a baby seal hurt by an oil spill and watches it recover in a nearby hospital.**

Title	***Oil Spill!***
Author	**Melvin Berger**
Illustrator	**Paul Mirocha**
Publisher	**HarperCollins**
Year	**1994**
Genre	**Narrative Information**
Summary	**Explains why oil spills occur and how they are cleaned up and suggests strategies for preventing oil spills in the future**

Time Needed

This lesson will take several class periods. Suggested scheduling is as follows:

Day 1: **Engage** with read aloud of *Prince William*

Day 2: **Explore** and **Explain** with read aloud of *Oil Spill!* and Oil Spill Cleanup Checkpoint Lab

Day 3: **Elaborate** with Animal Rescue

Day 4: **Evaluate** with Thank a Rescuer

Materials

- In advance, make black oil by adding 2 heaping tsp. of powdered black tempera paint to 750 ml of vegetable oil. With a lid tightly in place, shake to mix the powder with the vegetable oil. This will make enough oil for 10 teams.
- Newspaper
- Disposable aluminum pie pans (3 per team)
- Rocks, each no bigger than a deck of cards (3 per team)
- Leafy carrot or celery tops or plastic plants (3 per team)
- Pipe cleaners to represent animals
- Water
- 3 cups for collecting removed oil
- Metric measuring cups (1 per team)
- Red cup and green cup with the bottoms taped together (1 per team)
- Resealable plastic sandwich bags filled with these supplies (1 per team):
  - Spoon
  - Fork
  - 50 cm of yarn
  - 20 cm strip of nylon stocking
  - Large cotton ball
  - Disposable pipettes
  - Coffee filter
  - 5-cm-wide strip of paper towel

Student Pages

- Oil Spill Cleanup Checkpoint Lab
- Animal Rescue
- Thank a Rescuer

Background

Until the *Deepwater Horizon* oil spill in April 2010, the *Exxon Valdez* oil spill that occurred in Alaska in 1989 was the largest spill in the United States. An oil tanker ran ashore and released almost 11 million gallons of oil into Prince William Sound. Although oil in the ocean can originate from natural seepage from the ocean floor, it can also come from accidents involving tankers, barges, pipelines, refineries, and storage facilities, usually while the oil is being transported. Spills can also be caused accidently by leaking equipment or due to natural disasters such as hurricanes or deliberately by acts of war, terrorism, vandalism, or illegal dumping. Large oils spills such as the *Deepwater Horizon* and *Exxon Valdez* disasters make headlines, but much of the oil that pollutes aquatic environments actually comes from non-accidental sources such as drain disposal and road runoff. The spilled oil floats on the water and usually spreads out rapidly across the surface, forming a thin layer called a slick. Oil spills are very harmful to marine birds and mammals. Oil destroys the insulating ability of aquatic mammal fur and the water-repelling ability of seabird feathers, exposing these animals to the harsh elements. Many birds and mammals also swallow the oil, which can poison them, when trying to clean themselves. Oil can harm fish and shellfish as well. Affected wildlife populations tend to suffer an extremely high mortality rate, which is why it is important to clean up spilled oil as quickly and thoroughly as possible.

Once an oil spill has occurred, various local, state, and national agencies, as well as volunteer organizations, participate in the cleanup effort. Different cleanup methods work on different types of beaches and with different kinds of oil. Booms, or floating barriers, are used to keep the oil from spreading; skimmers can skim the spilled oil from the surface of the water; sorbents can absorb some of the oil; chemicals and even some microorganisms can break down the oil into other, less harmful chemicals; hoses and vacuums are used to clean beaches; and shovels and road equipment are sometimes used to pick up oil or move oiled beach sand and gravel.

Because oil is extremely difficult to clean up, the key to minimizing environmental damage from oil spills is keeping them from happening in the first place. There are several things that can be done to help. One important strategy is to avoid dumping oil into the sewer or garbage as it can end up in waterways. Another is to find ways to use less oil. The United States is the largest per capita consumer of oil in the world. The less we use, the lower the need for transporting it, the lower the risk of spills. In this lesson students explore how oil spills affect wildlife, learn about actual oil spill cleanup methods, and design investigations to test the effectiveness of various oil spill cleanup materials.

Engage

Read Aloud

Inferring

Show students the cover of the book *Prince William*. Then ask

- What do you think this book might be about?
- Who do you think Prince William is?

Questioning

Say, "As I read, I'm going to tell you what I'm wondering because good readers ask questions as they read."

Begin reading to the class. Stop periodically to model some questions that come to your mind as you read. For example:

- What would an oil-covered beach look and smell like?
- Why does Denny hear a baby crying on the beach?
- What would it be like to pick up a slippery baby seal?
- Will Prince William survive?

Be sure to read the author's note at the end of the book, which explains that *Prince William* is based on true events and that schoolchildren really did help with the seal recovery efforts.

Text-to-Self: Turn and Talk

After reading the story, model some text-to-self connections. For example, tell what you remember about the *Exxon Valdez* oil spill that occurred in 1989 or the *Deepwater Horizon* oil spill that happened in 2010. Ask students what they remember seeing in the news about the *Deepwater Horizon* oil spill. Give them a minute to think about it, then have them share their experiences with partners.

Explore & Explain

Read Aloud and Oil Spill Cleanup Checkpoint Lab

Determining Importance

Introduce the author and illustrator of *Oil Spill!* Have students jot down the methods and materials used by oil spill cleanup crews as you read *Oil Spill!* to the class.

- What methods and materials were described in the book? (using booms, skimmers, and pads; setting the oil on fire; spreading chemicals; spraying the shore; adding bacteria; taking no action)
- Which method do you think works the best? Why? (Answers will vary.)
- Are there any disadvantages to any of these methods? (Pads are difficult to dispose

CLEANING UP A SIMULATED OIL SPILL

of; fire sends smoke and gas into the air and leaves ash in the water; chemicals add poison to the water; hot spray pushes water farther into the rocks and sand; and using bacteria requires huge amounts of it.)

After discussing *Oil Spill!* tell students they are going to be members of an oil spill response team. An oil spill has just occurred in their region, and they must spring into action to find out which methods will work best to clean up the oil.

In advance, prepare the materials for the Oil Spill Cleanup Checkpoint Lab. See "Teaching Science Through Inquiry," Chapter 3, for a list of tips for managing a checkpoint lab.

Oil Spill Cleanup Checkpoint Lab

Divide students into four-person teams. Give each member of the team a copy of the Oil Spill Cleanup Checkpoint Lab. Explain that they will be following the directions on the student page. As they are working, they should keep their cups green side on top. If they need help or if they are at a checkpoint, they should put their cups red side on top. Each member of the group is responsible for recording data and writing responses. Before you give a team a check mark or stamp so they can move ahead in the lab, informally evaluate the students by asking probing questions to different members of the team. Redirect their investigations when necessary.

When all groups are finished with the checkpoint lab, discuss the following questions:

- ? What did you learn about designing an experiment?
- ? Would you make any changes in your experimental design?
- ? Can you propose any new methods for cleaning up oil spills?
- ? What do you think it would be like to clean up a real oil spill like the *Exxon Valdez* spill we have been reading about?

elaborate

Animal Rescue

Rereading

Reread pages 10 through 13 of *Oil Spill!* Then ask

- ? What types of animals were harmed by the oil spill in the book? (seabirds such as ducks and geese, fish, shrimp, crabs, sea otters, sea lions, harbor seals, and killer whales)
- ? How do oil spills harm birds? (The oil sticks to their feathers so they can't swim or fly.)
- ? How do oil spills harm fish, shrimp, and crabs? (Oil gets into their bodies and poisons them.)
- ? How do oil spills harm sea mammals? (They swallow oil and breathe poisonous fumes. The oil also coats their bodies.)

Reread the following pages in *Prince William*: pages 10 (about the doctor and volunteer), 19 (about the other animals being washed), and 20 (about Denny finding the empty incubator). Then ask

- ? Imagine you are cleaning a real, live animal that has been oiled. What things would you need to consider to keep you and the animal safe?
- ? What would your day be like if you were an animal rescuer?
- ? What would you enjoy about being a rescuer?
- ? What parts of the job would be difficult?

Pass out the Animal Rescue student page. Tell students to imagine they are animal rescuers. Have them write short stories describing their rescue experiences. They should each draw a picture to illustrate their stories and write a caption for the drawing.

evaluate

Thank a Rescuer

Pass out the Thank a Rescuer student page. Students will write letters to oil spill animal rescue organizations thanking the oil response team employees and volunteers. Use the rubric below to evaluate the letters.

When sending the letters, be sure to use the teacher's name and school address for the return address. Also, many conservation groups have limited budgets and may not be able to send each child a response. You can help them by sending all letters to an organization together with just one request for a reply. Include a self-addressed stamped envelope.

Scoring Rubric for Letter

4 Point Response	The student's letter includes a statement thanking the rescuer, clearly demonstrates understanding of the oil spill activity, lists two ways oil spills can affect the health and survival of organisms, effectively communicates his or her concern about oil spills, and requests information about how kids can support cleanup efforts or prevent oil spills.
3 Point Response	The student's letter demonstrates a flaw in the understanding of the concepts OR is missing one or two elements.
2 Point Response	The student's letter demonstrates a flaw in the understanding of the concepts and is missing one or two elements; OR is missing three or four elements.
1 Point Response	The student's letter demonstrates a flaw in the understanding of the concepts and is missing three or four elements; OR is missing five elements.
0 Point Response	The student shows no understanding of the concepts OR does not write a letter.

Inquiry Place

Have students brainstorm testable questions such as:

- ? Which cleaner is best for cleaning oiled material: dishwashing liquid, shampoo, vinegar, liquid hand soap, or baking soda and water?
- ? Which is best for insulating a marine animal: fur, feathers, or blubber?
- ? Do all types of oil float on water? Of the following types of oil—olive oil, corn oil, and baby oil—which is the most dense? The least dense?

Students can select a question to investigate as a class, or have groups of students vote on the question they want to investigate as teams. After they make their predictions, students can design an experiment to test their predictions. Students can present their findings at a poster session.

Websites

Clean the Oiled Sea Otter Activity
www.marinemammalcenter.org/learning/education/teacher_resources/cleanseaotter.asp

Effects of Oil on Wildlife
http://tristatebird.org/response/effects

Effects of Oil Spills on Wildlife and Habitat: Fact Sheet From U.S. Fish and Wildlife Service
http://alaska.fws.gov/media/unalaska/Oil%20Spill%20Fact%20Sheet.pdf

Exxon Valdez Photos: 20 Years On, Spilled Oil Remains
http://news.nationalgeographic.com/news/2009/03/photogalleries/exxon-valdez-anniversary

How Oil Affects Birds
www.ibrrc.org/oil_affects.html

National Oceanic and Atmospheric Administration (NOAA). 2008. What's the story on oil spills? *http://response.restoration.noaa.gov/topic_subtopic_entry.php?RECORD_KEY%28entry_subtopic_topic%29=entry_id,subtopic_id,topic_id&entry_id(entry_subtopic_topic)=184&subtopic_id(entry_subtopic_topic)=8&topic_id(entry_subtopic_topic)=1.*

Save a Wildlife
www.dawn-dish.com/en_US/savingwildlife/home.do

More Books to Read

D'Lacey, C. 2002. *A break in the chain.* New York: Crabtree Publishing Company.
Summary: This illustrated chapter book reveals how a terrible oil spill in the Arctic, a lesson about food chains, and a computer game featuring a polar bear turn into a magical adventure for Billy, whose class uses e-mail and a fund-raiser to help rescue the Arctic animals. A compelling story about environmental protection and how children can make their voices heard.

Goodman, S. 2001. *Animal rescue: The best job there is.* New York: Aladdin.
Summary: This riveting chapter book recounts the daring mission of real-life animal rescuer John Walsh, a member of the World Society for the Protection of Animals. Maps and full-color photographs enrich the informative and suspenseful text.

Hodgkins, F. 2000. *The orphan seal.* Camden, ME: Down East Books.
Summary: This beautifully illustrated picture book tells the true story of Howler, an abandoned harbor seal pup who was separated from his mother in a storm. Howler is rescued and rehabilitated by the New England Aquarium and eventually released back into the wild.

Landau, E. 2011. *Oil spill! Disaster in the Gulf of Mexico.* Minneapolis, MN: Millbrook Press.
Summary: This book details the largest oil spill in U.S. history, when the Deepwater Horizon drilling rig exploded and sank in the Gulf of Mexico.

Meeker, CH. 1999. *Lootas: Little wave eater.* Seattle: Sasquatch Books.
Summary: This fascinating photo essay describes how a young sea otter pup is rescued after its mother is accidentally killed by a motorboat. The pup, Lootas, is taken to a U.S. Fish and Wildlife Service office after her rescue and eventually finds a home in the Seattle Aquarium. The book includes insets with facts about sea otters.

Smith, R. 2003. *Sea otter rescue: The aftermath of an oil spill.* New York: Puffin.
Summary: When the *Exxon Valdez* struck the rocks in Prince William Sound, Alaska, nearly 11 million gal of crude oil spilled into the water. The result was an oil slick that threatened all of the area wildlife, especially the sea otters. This is the story of the animal rescue experts who went to Alaska to help out. Illustrated with the author's own photographs, this book is a fascinating first-hand account of the heroic measures taken to save the lives of hundreds of sea otters.

Chapter 13

Name: ______________________

Oil Spill Cleanup Checkpoint Lab

You are a member of an oil spill response team. An oil spill has just occurred in your region and you must spring into action to find out which methods will work best to clean up the oil! If your team is working, put the green cup on top. If you have a question, put the red cup on top. If you are finished with a part and you are ready for a check from your teacher, put the red cup on top.

Part A Setting Up an Oil Spill Simulation

☑ *Check the boxes as your team completes each step.*

☐ Cover your work area with newspaper.

☐ Get three aluminum pie pans from your teacher.

☐ Place one rock in each of the pans to represent the shore.

☐ Place a plant in each to represent shoreline plants.

☐ Make three models of animals out of pipe cleaners, and place the pipe cleaner animals on the edge of the rocks.

☐ Fill the pan with 250 ml of water.

☐ Get some simulated black oil from your teacher, and add 75 ml of the black oil mixture to each pan. Have one person from your group gently blow across the top of the pan to simulate wind and waves.

Note: The reason you are not using real petroleum oil is that it is toxic and should never be handled by children.

Describe what happens when someone blows across the water.

____

____

Checkpoint A ☐

Name: ______________________

Oil Spill Cleanup

Checkpoint Lab cont.

Part B Design an Experiment to Test Cleanup Materials

1 Your job is to find out which material will remove the most oil from the pan. Choose three materials to test from the list below. You will test one material per pan.

Circle your choices:

Disposable pipettes	Coffee filters	Spoon
Nylon stockings cut into strips	Cotton balls	Fork
Paper towels cut into strips	Yarn	

2 Make a prediction about which of the three materials will remove the most oil from the pan. Explain why you chose that material.

____

____

3 How will you decide which material removed the most oil?

____

____

4 Write a step-by-step procedure for your experiment.

____

____

____

____

Checkpoint B ☐

Name: ____________________

Oil Spill Cleanup
Checkpoint Lab cont.

Part C Data and Conclusions

1 You are now ready to test three cleanup materials. Collect your data and organize it in a table below.

2 What effects did the oil spill have on the simulated environment?

3 Conclusion: Which material was best for cleaning up the oil spill? What is your evidence?

4 If you were going to repeat this experiment, what would you do differently? Why?

Checkpoint C ☐

Author: ______________________________

Animal Rescue

Imagine you are an animal rescuer. Write a short story describing your rescue experiences. Draw a picture to illustrate your story, and write a caption for the picture.

Caption: ______________________________

____

____

Author: ______________________

Animal Rescue
cont.

Story: ______________________

CHAPTER 13

Thank a Rescuer

Write a letter thanking an oil spill animal rescue worker or volunteer involved in one of the organizations listed below. Include the following in your letter:

- A statement thanking the oil spill rescue worker
- A description of the activity you did to clean up an oil spill and what you learned
- Two ways oil spills affect the health and survival of organisms
- What concerns you most about oil spills
- A request for information on how kids can help support cleanup efforts or prevent oil spills (Ask them to send the information to your teacher at your school address.)

Oil Spill Animal Rescue Organizations

San Francisco Oiled Wildlife
Care and Education Center
(SFBOCEC)
4369 Cordelia Road
Fairfield, CA 94534
www.ibrrc.org

Marine Mammal Center
Marin Headlands
2000 Bunker Road
Fort Chronkite
Sausalito, CA 94965
www.marinemammalcenter.org

Oiled Wildlife Care Network
Wildlife Health Center
School of Veterinary Medicine
University of California, Davis
One Shields Avenue
Davis, CA 95616
www.owcn.org

Tri-State Bird Rescue and
Research
110 Possum Hollow Road
Newark, DE 19711
http://tristatebird.org

Sheep in a Jeep

Description

Learners investigate forces and motion using ramps, toy cars, and small plastic farm animals and share their findings in a poster session. Learners also design and evaluate a device to slow the motion of a falling object.

Suggested Grade Levels: 3–5

Lesson Objectives Connecting to the *Framework*

Science and Engineering Practices

- Planning and carrying out investigations
- Analyzing and interpreting data

Disciplinary Core Ideas

PS2.A: Forces and Motion

PS2.B: Types of Interactions

Crosscutting Concepts

- Cause and Effect

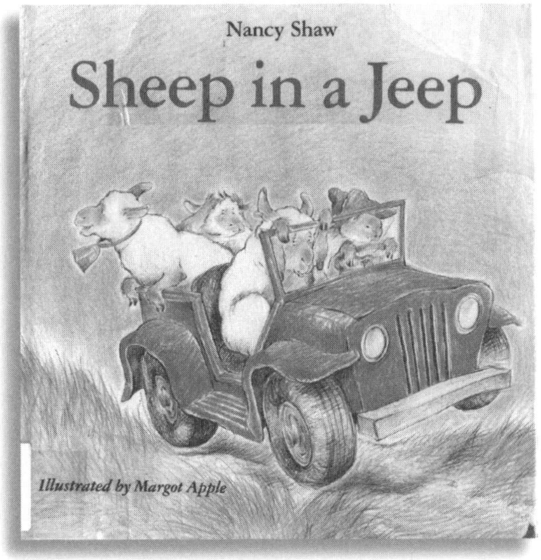

Featured Picture Book

Title	***Sheep in a Jeep***
Author	**Nancy Shaw**
Illustrator	**Margot Apple**
Publisher	**Sandpiper**
Year	**2006**
Genre	**Story**
Summary	**Records the misadventures of a group of sheep who go riding in a jeep**

Time Needed

This lesson will take several class periods. Suggested scheduling is as follows:

Day 1: **Engage** with read aloud of *Sheep in a Jeep*, and **Explore** with Checkpoint Lab, Part A and Part B

Day 2: **Explore** with Checkpoint Lab Part C and Part D, and **Explain** with Poster Session (from Checkpoint Lab, Part E)

Day 3: **Explore** and **Explain** with Motion and Forces Sentence Cards

Day 4: **Elaborate** with Sheep Leap, and **Explain** with Sheep Leap diagram

Day 5: **Evaluate** with Review and Motion Quiz

Materials

For the Sheep in a Jeep Checkpoint Lab

- Toy jeeps or toy die cast cars (1 per team)
- Small plastic animals (1 per team)
- Wooden ramps (1 per team)
- Books to build ramps and chutes (about 5 per team)
- Rough sandpaper (2 sheets per team)
- Tape (1 roll per team)
- Team task cards, precut
- Red cup and green cup with the bottoms taped together (1 per team)
- Calculators (1 per team)
- Poster-size paper (1 piece per team)
- Tape measure (1 per team)

Toy die cast jeeps and small plastic farm animals are available from
Oriental Trading Company
1-800-875-8480
www.orientaltrading.com

For the Sheep Leap Elaboration Activity (per pair)

- String
- Sandwich bag
- Scissors
- Sheet of copy paper
- Tape
- Paper lunch bag
- Sheet of tissue paper
- Styrofoam plate
- Small plastic trash bag

- Sheep Leap diagram (copied onto an overhead transparency, for teacher use)

Student Pages

- Sheep in a Jeep Team Task Cards
- Sheep in a Jeep Checkpoint Lab
- Motion and Forces Sentence Cards
- Motion and Forces article
- Sheep Leap
- Motion Quiz

The Sheep in a Jeep Checkpoint Lab is ideally done on tile floors. If your classroom floors are carpeted, try to find other areas in your school that have smooth-surfaced floors, such as in the hallways, gymnasium, or cafeteria.

Background

This lesson provides students with opportunities to observe and change the motion of an object and learn about the forces (pushes and pulls) that cause these changes, such as gravity, friction, and air resistance. *Gravity* is the force that pulls everything down. *Friction* is a force that slows motion by rubbing against moving objects. For example, when a toy car rolls from a tile floor to sandpaper, it slows down due to the increased friction provided by the rough surface of the sandpaper. *Air resistance,* or friction with the air, also slows the motion of objects. For example, when an airplane flies through the air, collisions with air molecules slow it down. This lesson also addresses Newton's first law of motion, which states that an object in motion will stay in motion unless acted upon by an outside force, and an object at rest will stay at rest unless acted upon by an outside force. This tendency to obey Newton's first law is called *inertia.* You experience inertia whenever your car stops suddenly. Your body keeps moving in the same direction until acted on by an unbalanced outside force. That force is provided by your seat belt.

In this lesson, students experiment with a toy car with a plastic farm animal attached to it. They change its motion by adjusting the height of a ramp and covering the floor with sandpaper. They observe inertia by crashing the car into a block with the plastic animal sitting on top unattached, then compare the results with the animal attached to the car with a "sheep belt." Finally, they investigate air resistance by designing and testing a device to slow the fall of a plastic farm animal. Through these activities, students learn how the position and motion of objects can be changed.

engage

Read Aloud

Determining Importance

Tell students that you will be reading a funny book called *Sheep in a Jeep* because it can help them learn about force and motion. Ask them to give a thumbs-up when they think they hear an example of a *force* or a *motion* in the book. The purpose of this is to determine students' prior knowledge about the meanings of the words *force* and *motion*. Then read *Sheep in a Jeep* aloud to the class.

Make a T-chart on the board. Label it "Force" on the left side and "Motion" on the right. Discuss students' ideas about force and motion using the guiding questions below:

- ? What is a force? (A force is a push or a pull on an object.)
- ? What can forces do? (They can make things move. They can make things speed up. They can make things slow down. They can make things change direction. They can make things move back and forth or around and around.)
- ? Is gravity a force? (yes)
- ? How do you know? (Gravity pulls all objects toward Earth.)
- ? What is motion? (Motion is a change in the position of an object. When you say that something has moved, you are describing its motion.)

Next ask students to name examples of force or motion from the book. List the examples on the T-chart. If students name a force, ask them to identify the resulting motion. If the students name a motion, ask them to identify what force caused the motion.

explore

Sheep in a Jeep Checkpoint Lab

In advance, prepare the supplies for the Sheep in a Jeep Checkpoint Lab. See "Teaching Science Through Inquiry," Chapter 3, for a list of tips for managing a checkpoint lab.

Tell students they will explore some things that affect motion. Divide students into four-person teams. Give each team member a copy of the Sheep in a Jeep Checkpoint Lab. Explain that they will follow the directions on the worksheet. Give each team member a Team Task Card. Assign tasks to each person on the team:

Reader—reads the directions as the group works and is in charge of the green and red cups

Sample Force and Motion T-Chart

Force	Motion
Sheep push on jeep	Jeep moves down hill
Gravity pulls on sheep	Sheep move down hill
Sheep tug on jeep	Jeep won't move
Pigs push on jeep	Jeep moves
Wheels push jeep forward	Jeep moves
Jeep runs into tree	Jeep stops moving

Releaser/Calculator—releases the jeep from the top of the ramp without pushing it and calculates average distances in Parts B and C using a calculator

Part B Measurer—measures the distance in centimeters the jeep travels from the end of the ramp in Part B

Part C Measurer—measures the distance in centimeters the jeep travels from the end of the ramp in Part C

Distribute the materials for the lab. Demonstrate how to release a jeep from the top of a ramp without pushing it. Before students begin working, discuss the following questions:

? How should you measure the distance the jeep rolls from the bottom of the ramp—from the front of the jeep or the back of the jeep? (It doesn't matter, as long as you measure in centimeters from the same point each time.)

? What will you do if the jeep falls off the ramp before it reaches the bottom, or if it gets stuck, or if it hits something? (We won't record that trial, and we will do it over.)

Discuss the concept of *variability*. Say, "Scientists do the same experiment over and over to make sure of their results. Your results probably won't be exactly the same for every trial— scientists call that variability. Your results will vary a little each time. That's why you are doing several trials and taking an *average* to find out about how far the jeep will usually roll. We're going to take the average of three trials for each setup. Scientists always repeat their experiments many, many times. We will repeat them only three times because of our time constraints."

? How do you calculate an average? (Add up the distances of all trials, and then divide by the number of trials.)

Have students begin the checkpoint lab. Observe and listen to the students as they interact. While they are working, they should keep the green side of their cups on top. If they need help, or if they are at a checkpoint, they should put the red side on top. Each member of the group is responsible for recording data and writing responses. Before you give a team a check mark or stamp so they can move ahead in the lab, informally evaluate the students by asking probing questions of each member of the team.

RELEASING THE JEEP DOWN THE RAMP

Explain

Poster Session

After each team has completed parts A through D of the checkpoint lab, it should begin its Poster Session assignments (Part E). At this point, students do not need to apply scientific terminology. Encourage students to use their own words, their recorded observations from the checkpoint lab, and their prior knowledge of motion as a basis for explaining concepts. Have students present their posters. Encourage the audience to listen carefully, ask thoughtful questions, examine the evidence, identify faulty reasoning, and suggest alternative explanations to presenters in a polite, respectful manner.

After the poster session, ask students if they have ever heard of a man named Isaac Newton. Explain that Newton was born in England about 360 years ago. When he was 23, as the story goes, he saw an apple fall to the ground, which led him to write a scientific law about gravity. Later he wrote the three famous laws describing motion that we call Newton's laws of motion. Tell students that they are going to do an activity to help them learn more about motion and forces.

Explore & Explain

Motion and Forces Sentence Cards

Word Sorts

Word sorts help learners understand the relationships among key concepts and help teach classification. Classifying and then reclassifying help students extend and refine their understanding of the concepts studied.

Open sort: Distribute a set of Motion and Forces Sentence Cards to each pair of students for an open sort. Instruct students to cut out the cards and see if they can make some sentences with them. As you move from pair to pair, ask students to explain the meaning of their sentences.

Pairs Read

Then pass out the Motion and Forces article. Have students take turns reading aloud from the article. While one person reads a paragraph, the other listens and then makes comments ("I think ..."), asks questions ("I wonder ..."), or shares new learnings ("I didn't know ...").

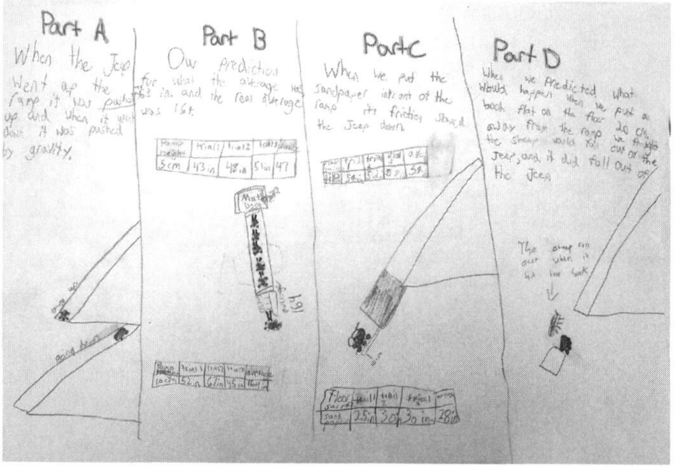

Sample sheep in a jeep posters

Closed sort: Provide the categories into which students are to assign words. In this case, the categories come from the meanings of the bold words in the article: *force, motion, inertia, gravity,* and *friction*. Students can now make new sentences based on the information they read in the article.

Ask students to justify their new sentences with evidence from the article as you move around to each team. Possible correct sentences include

- Sheep push jeep.
- Force causes motion.
- Inertia keeps sheep in motion.
- Gravity pulls sheep.
- Gravity pulls jeep.
- Friction slows jeep.

Discuss all the concepts the students have explored in each part of the checkpoint lab using the terminology they learned through the Motion and Forces article and the word sort. The following explanations of each part of the checkpoint lab are for you; modify as necessary to help students understand and apply the concepts.

Part A: The force that caused the jeep to move up the ramp was the push provided by the student's hand. The force that caused the jeep to move down the ramp was gravity. (Friction between the wheels and the ramp and between the jeep and the air played a part in slowing the motion of the jeep as it traveled down the ramp and when it reached the flat surface.)

Part B: As the jeep rolled down the lower ramp, its speed increased. As the jeep rolled down the higher ramp, its speed increased even more. The jeep rolled a longer distance from the bottom of the ramp when the ramp was raised because it was moving faster when it reached the bottom of the ramp. The faster the jeep was moving when it left the ramp, the more distance it could cover before friction slowed it.

Part C: Friction is a force that slows motion. It is caused by things rubbing against each other. In this case the jeep's wheels rubbed against the tile floor and then the sandpaper. The rough sandpaper caused more friction against the jeep's wheels than the smooth tile floor, so the jeep slowed down faster and thus rolled a shorter distance on the sandpaper.

Part D: As the jeep rolled down the ramp, its speed increased. The sheep had the same speed as the jeep. When the jeep hit the book, the force of impact stopped the jeep, but the unbelted sheep was free to continue moving until some force stopped it. The jeep and the sheep both had inertia, a resistance to a change in motion. Once started, both continued to move until outside forces acted against them, causing them to stop. The book stopped the jeep's motion, and air resistance slowed the sheep's forward motion as gravity pulled it down to the ground. Tell students everyone should always wear a seat belt because, if your vehicle stops and you are unbelted, your inertia will keep you moving until you hit something—the windshield or the ground!

After this discussion, send students back to their posters to add the following terminology where appropriate: *force, motion, inertia, gravity,* and *friction*.

Elaborate

Sheep Leap

Pass out the Sheep Leap student pages to each student. Provide materials for students to invent a device that slows the fall of a toy animal. Allow ample time for them to test their inventions. After testing is complete, have them redesign their invention by changing the materials used. They can compare the new invention to the original by dropping them at the same time from the same height.

TESTING AN INVENTION IN "SHEEP LEAP"

After students complete the Sheep Leap activity and the student page, use the questions below to help students apply the new labels, definitions, and explanations they learned in the Sheep in a Jeep activities to this new experience. This way, the students are beginning to provide formal definitions and labels to their work after they have constructed their own ideas about motion and forces through their hands-on experiences and class discussions. Ask

- ? What force pulls the plastic animals to the ground when they "leap"? (gravity)
- ? In the Sheep in a Jeep activity, we learned that friction (rubbing) slows objects down as they move. Is your plastic animal "rubbing" against anything as it falls? (Yes, the animals are rubbing against the air as they fall.)
- ? Does rubbing against the air slow an object down? (yes)
- ? How does your invention slow down the falling animal? (Answers will vary but should include friction with or "rubbing against" the air.)

Explain

Sheep Leap Diagram

Explain that friction with the air is called *air resistance*. Use the Sheep Leap diagram overhead transparency to explain how the force of gravity pulls all objects toward the center of the Earth and air resistance pushes up against objects in motion.

- ? In the Sheep Leap, which force was stronger, gravity or air resistance? (gravity)
- ? What is your evidence? (The sheep fell to the ground.)

Have students add arrows and the words *gravity* and *air resistance* to their drawings on the Sheep Leap student page.

Evaluate

Review and Motion Quiz

Use the team posters and the Sheep Leap student page to review the concepts and vocabulary of motion and forces. Then give students the Motion Quiz. Answers follow.

1. A push and a pull (or a person pushing and a person pulling)
2. Gravity
3. Smooth metal
4. Rough sandpaper
5. There is more friction between the car's wheels and the sandpaper than the other surfaces. Friction slows the car's motion.
6. The doll will fly off (or keep moving) when the car stops. The doll is in motion so it tends to stay in motion even though the car stops. (Or the doll's inertia keeps it in motion.)

Inquiry Place

Have students brainstorm testable questions such as

- Will adding weight make a difference in how far the jeep travels?
- Will the jeep travel farther on rough or fine sandpaper?
- What happens to the distance the jeep travels if you keep increasing the angle of the ramp?
- How does the weight of the load affect the motion of the parachute?

Then have students select a question to investigate as a class, or groups of students can vote on the question they want to investigate as teams. After they make their predictions, they can experiment to test their predictions. Students can present their findings at a poster session.

7 (b) Air resistance slows it down, and gravity pulls it to Earth.

More Books to Read

Branley, F. 2007. *Gravity is a mystery.* New York: Harper Collins.
Summary: With the help of an adventurous scientist and his fun-loving dog, students can read and learn about the mysterious force of gravity.

Cobb, V. 2004. *I fall down.* New York: Harper Collins.
Summary: Simple experiments introduce the concept of gravity and its relationship to weight.

Cole, J. 1998. *Magic school bus plays ball: A book about forces.* New York: Scholastic.
Summary: Ms. Frizzle and her class shrink to fit inside a physics book where they enter a page about a baseball field with no friction. The kids learn about how throwing, running, and catching would work in a world without friction.

Frazee, M. 2003. *Roller coaster.* New York: Harcourt, Inc.
Summary: The spare text and dynamic artwork of this picture book capture the anticipation and excitement a young girl experiences on her very first roller coaster ride. This book can be used as a delightful introduction to motion and forces.

Karpelenia, J. 2004. *Motion.* Logan, IA: Perfection Learning Corporation.
Summary: This informational chapter book on motion and forces includes a glossary, index, and several brief activities for readers to try.

Stille, D. 2004. *Motion: Push and pull, fast and slow.* Minneapolis, MN: Picture Window Books.
Summary: Lively cartoons illustrate this engaging nonfiction picture book about how things move and what makes them stop. Includes simple descriptions of inertia, gravity, friction, and relative motion. Fun facts, experiments, and a glossary are included.

Reference

Gertz, S. E., D. J. Portman, and M. Sarquis. 1996. *Teaching physical science through children's literature: 20 complete lessons for elementary grades.* Middletown, OH: Terrific Science Press. Sheep in a Jeep Checkpoint Lab adapted from "Ramps and Cars" on pages 189–196.

Sheep in a Jeep

Team Task Cards

Reader Read the directions out loud for your team. Put the green cup on top if your group is working. Put the red cup on top if you have a question or if you are ready for a check mark.	**Releaser/Calculator** Wait until you hear the directions from the Reader. Then release the jeep from the top of the ramp without pushing it. Calculate the average distance the jeep rolls in Parts B and C.
Part B Measurer Use a tape measure to measure the distance the jeep rolls from the end of the ramp in Part B. Measure to the nearest centimeter.	**Part C Measurer** Use a tape measure to measure the distance the jeep rolls from the end of the ramp in Part C. Measure to the nearest centimeter.

Name: ______________________________

CHAPTER 14

Sheep in a Jeep

Checkpoint Lab

Follow the directions below. If your team is working, put the green cup on top. If you have a question, put the red cup on top. If you are finished with a part and you are ready for a check from your teacher, put the red cup on top.

Part A Motion and Forces

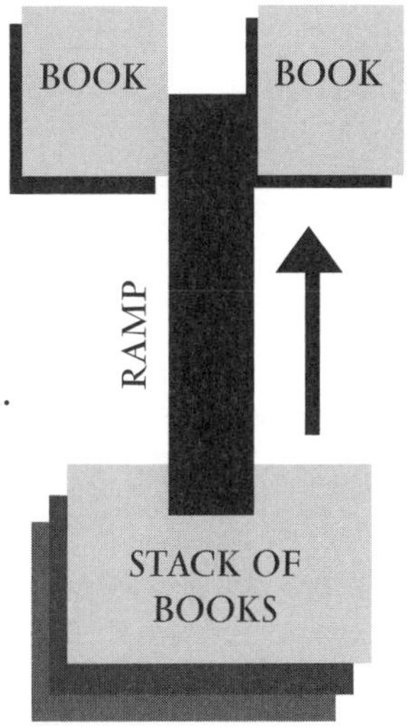

- Tape the sheep (or other animal) into the jeep with one piece of tape.
- Stack some books until they are about **5 cm** high.
- Raise one end of the ramp and place it on the books.
- Make a chute with some books at the end of the ramp.
- Push the jeep *up* the ramp to the top.

1 What force caused the jeep to move *up* the ramp?

____

- Now let the jeep roll *down* the ramp without pushing it.

2 What force caused the jeep to move *down* the ramp?

____

Checkpoint A ☐

Name: ______________________________

Sheep in a Jeep
Checkpoint Lab cont.

Part B Changing the Height of the Ramp

- Release the jeep without pushing from the top of the **5 cm** high ramp.
- Measure in centimeters how far it rolls from the end of the ramp and record under Trial 1 Distance. (If it falls off before reaching the bottom, do over!)
- Repeat for Trial 2 and Trial 3.
- Find the average distance the jeep rolled by adding the three distances and dividing by 3.

Ramp Height	Trial 1 Distance	Trial 2 Distance	Trial 3 Distance	Average Distance
5 cm				

Make a prediction: If you raise the ramp to **10 cm** high, will the jeep roll a longer distance or a shorter distance from the end of the ramp?

____

- Now raise the ramp to **10 cm** high and release the jeep without pushing.
- Measure in centimeters how far it rolls from the end of the ramp and record under Trial 1 Distance. (If it falls off before reaching the bottom, do it over!)
- Repeat for Trial 2 and Trial 3.
- Find the average distance the jeep rolled by adding the three distances and dividing by 3.

Ramp Height	Trial 1 Distance	Trial 2 Distance	Trial 3 Distance	Average Distance
10 cm				

Name: ______________________________

Sheep in a Jeep
Checkpoint Lab cont.

Part B Questions

1 Were there any trials that your team didn't record? Why or why not?

____

2 What was the average distance the jeep rolled with a **5 cm** high ramp?

____

3 What was the average distance the jeep rolled with a **10 cm** high ramp?

____

4 Did the jeep roll a shorter or longer distance when you raised the ramp?

____

5 Write a conclusion: How does the height of the ramp affect the distance the jeep rolls? What is your evidence?

____

____

____

Checkpoint B ☐

Name: ______________________

Sheep in a Jeep

Checkpoint Lab cont.

Part C Changing the Surface

- Change the ramp back to **5 cm high**. Release the jeep from the top of the ramp without pushing.
- Measure in centimeters how far it rolls from the end of the ramp and record under Trial 1 Distance. Repeat for Trial 2 and Trial 3.
- Find the average distance the jeep rolled by adding the three distances and dividing by 3.

Floor Surface	Trial 1 Distance	Trial 2 Distance	Trial 3 Distance	Average Distance
Tile				

Make a prediction: If you cover the tile floor at the end of the ramp with sandpaper, will the jeep roll a longer distance or a shorter distance from the end of the ramp?

____

- Now cover the floor at the end of the ramp with two sheets of sandpaper taped together and release the jeep without pushing.
- Measure in centimeters how far it rolls from the end of the ramp and record under Trial 1 Distance. Repeat for Trial 2 and Trial 3.
- Find the average distance the jeep rolled by adding the three distances and dividing by 3.

Floor Surface	Trial 1 Distance	Trial 2 Distance	Trial 3 Distance	Average Distance
Sandpaper				

Name: ______________________________

Sheep in a Jeep
Checkpoint Lab cont.

Part C Questions

1 Did the jeep roll a shorter or longer distance when you covered the tile floor with sandpaper? ______________________________

2 Write a conclusion: How does the surface of the floor affect the distance the jeep rolls? What is your evidence? ____________________

____

____

____

____

____

____

____

____

____

____

____

Checkpoint C ☐

Name: ______________________________

Sheep in a Jeep

Checkpoint Lab cont.

Part D "Sheep-Belts"

- Remove the tape from the sheep and place the sheep back in the jeep.
- Change the ramp to **10 cm** high.
- Place a book flat on the floor **20 cm** from the end of the ramp.

Make a prediction: What will happen to the sheep when the jeep hits the book?

____

____

____

- Release the jeep from the top of the **10 cm** high ramp without pushing it. Let it hit the book.

Part D Questions

1 What happened to the sheep when the jeep hit the book? Why?

____

____

2 Why is it important to always wear a seat belt in a moving vehicle?

____

____

Checkpoint D ☐

Name: ______________________________

Sheep in a Jeep

Checkpoint Lab cont.

Part E Poster Session

Make a poster with your team displaying what you learned about forces and motion from the Sheep in a Jeep lab. Label your poster with **Part A, Part B, Part C,** and **Part D**. Some things to think about for your poster:

- What is the most important information to share from each part of the checkpoint lab activity?
- What data tables or graphs will you include?
- What pictures will you draw?
- Who is going to draw each part of the poster?
- Who is going to explain each part of the poster? (Everyone on your team should have a turn!)

Be ready to share your poster with the class and answer any questions they might have.

Checkpoint E ☐

Chapter 14

Motion and Forces

Sentence Cards

Directions: Cut out the cards below and make sentences with them. Then read the article Motion and Forces and make new sentences with them.

force	motion
inertia	friction
gravity	causes
keeps	sheep
in	motion

Motion and Forces

Sentence Cards cont.

jeep	slows
pulls	jeep
push	sheep
jeep	sheep
pulls	gravity

Chapter 14

Motion and Forces

What is a force?

A **force** is a push or a pull. In *Sheep in a Jeep,* the sheep push the jeep. The push is a force. The sheep also tug, or pull, on the jeep. The pull is a force.

What is motion?

We consider an object to be in **motion** when it is not standing still. For an object to move or to stop moving, a **force** must be applied to it. The sheep apply a force as they push the jeep and the force causes motion. When the jeep hits the tree, the tree applies a force to the jeep and the jeep stops moving.

What is inertia?

Inertia is a resistance to change in motion. For example, when the jeep gets stuck, its inertia keeps it from moving easily. It is at rest and tends to stay at rest. When the jeep full of sheep hits the tree, the inertia of the sheep keeps them in motion. Because the sheep are not wearing seat belts to stop them, they tend to stay in motion.

What is gravity?

Gravity is a force that we encounter all the time. It is the force that pulls all things toward Earth. When the sheep push the jeep to the top of the hill, gravity pulls the jeep down the hill. Gravity also pulls the sheep down the hill after the jeep.

What is friction?

The jeep's tires rub against the road as it rolls. The rubbing is called **friction**. Friction is a force that slows things down as a result of the rubbing. Friction between the road and the jeep's tires slows the jeep. A rough road causes more friction than a smooth road.

Name: ______________________________

Sheep Leap

1 Hold two plastic sheep or other animals in your hands and then let go of them. What happens? What causes this to happen?

2 Use any of the following supplies to invent something that will slow the fall of one of your animals. When testing your invention, drop both animals from the same height at the same time to see which one falls more slowly.

String	Tape	Sheet of tissue paper
Sheet of copy paper	Scissors	Styrofoam plate
Sandwich bag	Paper lunch bag	Small plastic trash bag

3 How well did your invention work? How can you tell?

4 Try it again, using a different material. Which one works better? How can you tell?

5 Draw and label a picture of your best invention falling through the air in the box at right.

Chapter 14

Sheep Leap

Name: ______________________________

Chapter 14

Motion Quiz

1 Look at the picture above. What two forces are causing the wagon to move?____________________ and ____________________________

2 Look at the picture above. What force is causing the ball to roll down the ramp?

____

Name: ______________________________

Motion Quiz cont.

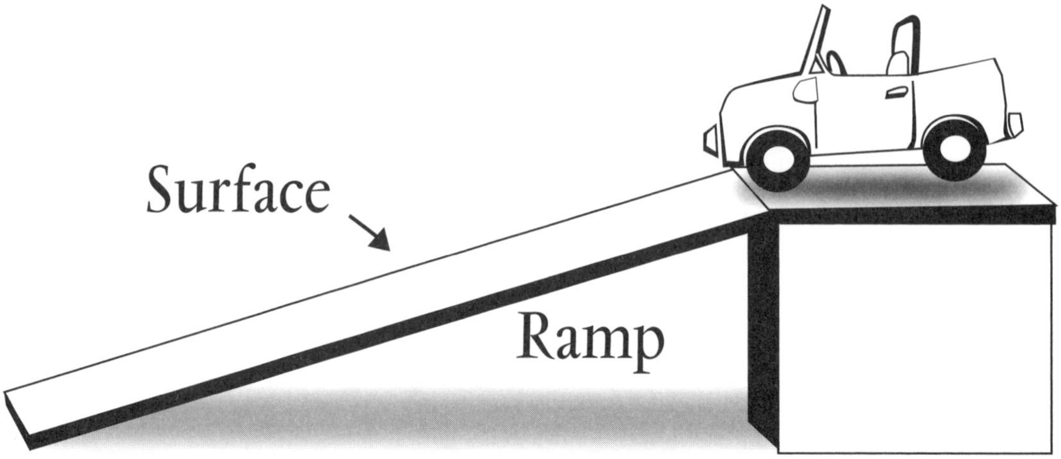

Ramp Surface	Trial 1 Distance	Trial 2 Distance	Trial 3 Distance	Average Distance
Smooth Metal	85 cm	125 cm	90 cm	100 cm
Smooth Wood	90 cm	70 cm	65 cm	75 cm
Rough Sandpaper	18 cm	24 cm	18 cm	20 cm

Jamie is testing to see how the surface will affect the distance a toy car travels. He is using a small car and a long ramp that is 10 cm high. Jamie puts different surfaces on the ramp, and then lets the car roll down the ramp. He measures how far the car travels from the bottom of the ramp.

3 On which surface does the car roll the longest distance?

____

4 On which surface does the car roll the shortest distance?

____

Name: ______________________________

Motion Quiz cont.

5 What do you think causes the car to roll the shortest distance on that surface?

____

6 If a doll is sitting on the hood of Jamie's car, and the car hits a brick at the bottom of the ramp, how will the doll's motion be affected? What causes that to happen?

____

____

____

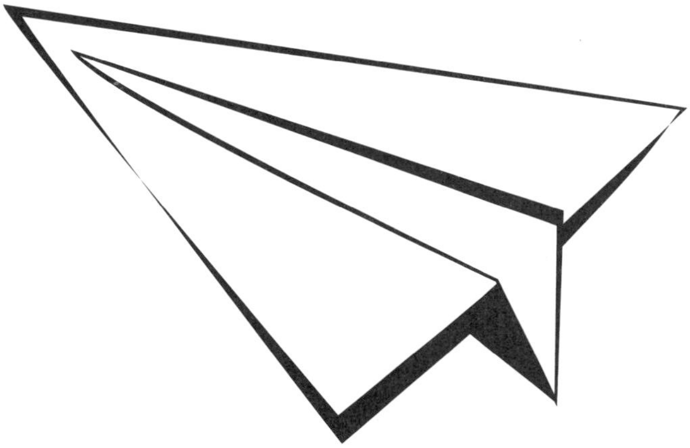

7 Marla throws a paper airplane. The airplane flies for several meters, then slows down and begins to fall to the ground. What two forces cause the airplane to slow down and fall to the ground?

a Friction from Marla's hand makes it slow down, and a magnetic force pulls it to Earth.

b Air resistance slows it down, and gravity pulls it to Earth.

c Gravity makes it slow down, and the pull of the Moon makes it fall to Earth.

Chapter 15

Sounds of Science

Description

Learners explore how sound is produced by vibrations. They make a straw instrument and investigate how to vary its pitch. Learners also design and build an instrument that produces a high pitch and a low pitch and explain how it works.

Suggested Grade Levels: 3–6

Lesson Objectives Connecting to the *Framework*

Science and Engineering Practices

- Developing and using models
- Constructing explanations (for science) and designing solutions (for engineering)

Disciplinary Core Ideas

PS3.A: Definitions of Energy
PS4.A: Wave Properties

Crosscutting Concepts

- Energy and Matter

Featured Picture Books

Title	***Sound (Energy Works! series)***
Author	**Jenny Karpelenia**
Publisher	**Perfection Learning**
Year	**2004**
Genre	**Nonnarrative Information**
Summary	**Explains that vibrations create sound, how high and low pitches are made, how the ear works, and how musical instruments make sound**

Title	***The Remarkable Farkle McBride***
Author	**John Lithgow**
Illustrator	**C. F. Payne**
Publisher	**Simon & Schuster**
Year	**2003**
Genre	**Story**
Summary	**The musical prodigy Farkle McBride tries a number of instruments before discovering that conducting the orchestra makes him happy.**

Time Needed

This lesson will take several class periods. Suggested scheduling is as follows:

Day 1: **Engage** with straw instrument demonstration, **Explore** with playing straw instruments, and **Explain** with read aloud from *Sound*

Day 2: **Explore** with making high and low sounds, and **Explain** with read aloud from *Sound*

Day 3: **Elaborate** with Making Music and *The Remarkable Farkle McBride*

Day 4: **Evaluate** with Make an Instrument (project due after one week)

Materials

- Straws (nonflexible, plastic, several per student)
- Wooden rulers (1 per team)
- Scissors
- Making Music Answer Key (for teacher use)
- Optional: Recordings of various instruments

Student Pages

- Making Music
- Make an Instrument

Background

Sound is a form of energy caused by *vibrations*. If you hum and hold your fingers on the front of your neck, you can feel your vocal cords rapidly moving back and forth. These vibrations also cause particles of air around them to vibrate. Sounds need a *medium* to travel through. Most of the sounds we hear are traveling through air, but sound can also travel through solids and liquids. Although science-fiction movies often include sound effects in outer-space scenes, sound cannot travel through empty space because there is no medium in which to vibrate.

The speed of sound differs for each medium. Some materials are better at carrying sounds than others. Sound travels fastest through solids, slower through liquids, and slowest through gases. Sounds pass through steel at about 13,300 miles per hour and through air at about 750 miles per hour. *Volume* is the measure of how loud or soft a sound is. Volume is measured in decibels (dB). *Pitch* is the measure of how high or low a sound is and is determined by the rate of vibrations: The higher the rate of vibration, or frequency, the higher the pitch. Students sometimes confuse volume and pitch, so it is important to give them examples of each and challenge them to distinguish between the two.

Music is defined as the ordering of sounds to produce a composition having unity and continuity. Music can be created by voices or instruments, each producing sound in different ways. *Wind instruments* produce sound when they are blown, causing the air inside the instrument to vibrate. Wind instruments can be classified into two groups: *woodwinds* (flute, clarinet, saxophone, etc.) and *brass* (trumpets, trombones, tubas, etc.). To play a wind instrument, the musician presses keys, closes valves, or moves a slide to create different pitches. Generally, the larger the instrument, the lower the pitch. For example, a tuba produces lower pitches than a trumpet. *Stringed instruments* (violins, guitars, etc.) produce sound when the strings are plucked or strummed. The pitches produced depend on the thickness, tightness, and length of the strings. Thinner, tighter, shorter strings create higher pitches; thicker, looser, or longer strings create lower pitches. The musician shortens and lengthens the strings by pressing down on them. *Percussion instruments* (drums, cymbals, xylophones, etc.) create sound when they are hit or shaken so they vibrate. Drums are covered with a thin skin, and turning keys on the sides of the drum can loosen or tighten that skin. The tighter the skin, the higher the pitch. Xylophones are made of wooden or metal bars of different sizes that vibrate when hit with a mallet. The shorter the bars, the higher the pitch.

engage

Straw Instrument Demonstration

In advance, make a straw instrument by cutting one end of a straw into a triangular shape. Insert the cut end into your mouth forming a soft seal in your mouth so that no air leaks out. Blow into the straw to make the flaps vibrate like reeds, and you will hear a buzzing sound. You may need to chew the flaps to flatten them out a little bit. Then play the straw instrument for your students.

"FLAPS" OF STRAW INSTRUMENT

explore

Playing Straw Instruments

Give students one straw each and have them try to make it sound the same as your straw instrument. Let students try for a few minutes. Have students consider the following questions as they experiment with their straws:

- ? What is sound?
- ? What causes sound?

explain

Read Aloud

Using Features of Nonfiction

Tell students you have a nonfiction book, *Sound*, that might be able to help them answer their questions about sound. Model how to use the index of a nonfiction book by looking up the answer to the question "What is sound?" Flip to the index and demonstrate how to look up a word; point out "sound, definition of, 8"; and turn to that page. Tell students that many nonfiction books include an index that can save the reader a lot of time when looking for a specific piece of information. The definition of sound on page 8 reads, "Sound is a form of energy caused by vibrations." Write this definition on the board.

Determining Importance

Continue reading pages 8 and 9 ("Sound Energy") in *Sound* and have students listen for

Playing straw instruments

any clues that might help them get their straws to make a sound.

- ? What causes sound? (vibrations)
- ? What does *vibration* mean? (Vibration is a very fast back and forth motion.)
- ? How do you think you can get the straw to vibrate? (Answers will vary.)

Have students try different ways to get their straws to vibrate. Then show them how you cut a triangular shape into the end of the straw that goes in your mouth. Students can now cut the ends of their straws into triangular shapes and try to produce a buzzing sound. They can try chewing on the triangular flaps a little bit if they can't produce a sound. Tell them that when they blow just right, the flaps vibrate. The vibrating plastic causes the air inside the straw to vibrate, making a humming sound. Give students time to explore their straw instruments.

If you have students who are unsuccessful in producing sound after many attempts at playing the straw instrument, you may want to provide them with an instrument that is easier to play, such as a slide whistle, kazoo, or recorder.

explore

Making High and Low Sounds

After everyone has successfully made a straw instrument, have students brainstorm ideas to make their straw instruments produce a high sound and a low sound. Provide extra straws, and give them time to try their ideas.

After a few minutes of exploration, tell students this next activity will give them a hint about how to make high and low sounds with their straws. Give each team of four students a wooden ruler. Have them hold the ruler flat on the desk with about 25 cm of the ruler hanging over the edge of the desk. Have them flick the part of the ruler hanging over the edge so that it vibrates against the desk. Students should observe a low-pitched sound. Next have them pull the ruler back so only 20 cm of it is hanging over the edge and flick the end again. Students should observe a higher-pitched sound. They can repeat the activity, varying the length of the ruler each time.

- ? How does the length of the ruler hanging over the edge of the desk affect the pitch? (The longer the part hanging over the edge, the lower the pitch. The shorter the part hanging over the edge, the higher the pitch.)

explain

Read Aloud

Tell students that the scientific term *pitch* is used to describe how high or low a sound is.

Determining Importance

Have students listen for clues on how to make their straw instruments produce high and low pitches as you read about wind instruments on pages 28 and 29 of the book *Sound*.

- ? What kind of instrument is the straw instrument? (wind instrument)
- ? How do people who play wind instruments change pitch? (opening and closing holes on the instrument)
- ? How does the size of a wind instrument affect its pitch? (the larger the instrument, the lower the pitch)
- ? The pitch of a note depends on the length of the column of vibrating air. How can you change the length of the column of vibrating air on your straw instrument? (cut it off or make holes in it to use as keys)

Using scissors, students can snip three small holes into their straw instruments to be used as keys. They should space the holes so that one of their fingers can cover each hole. Some students may need help cutting the holes. They can test how opening and closing the holes can change the pitch. First have them cover all of the holes with their fingers and blow into the straw. Then have them uncover one key at a time and notice the change in pitch. Ask

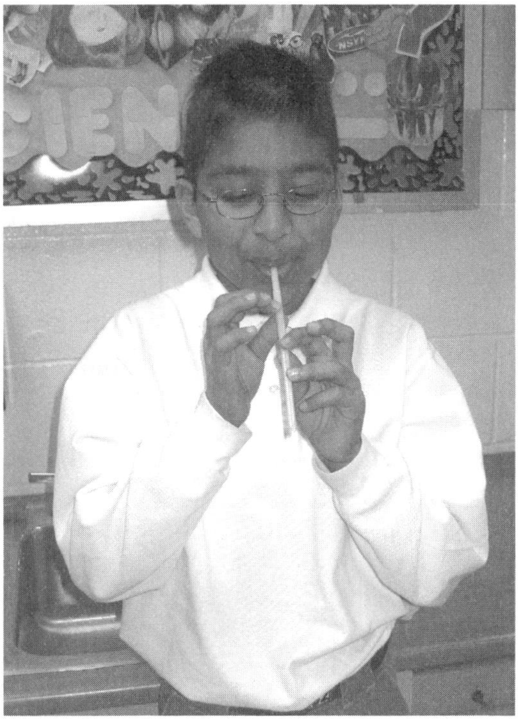

Using the "keys" on a straw instrument

- ? Why does the pitch sound lower when you cover one of the holes? (A longer column of air is created.)
- ? Why does the pitch sound higher when you uncover one of the holes? (A shorter column of air is created.)

elaborate

Making Music and *The Remarkable Farkle McBride*

Determining Importance

Give students the Making Music student page. Read pages 28 through 32 in *Sound* about how wind, stringed, and percussion instruments create high and low pitches. After each section, have students summarize what you read by filling in the corresponding row on the student page.

Synthesizing

Introduce the author and illustrator of *The Remarkable Farkle McBride* and then read the book aloud, having students identify each instrument that Farkle plays as a wind instrument, stringed instrument, or percussion instrument. Discuss how each instrument in the book makes sound and changes pitch.

If you like, ask your school's music teacher for recordings of the instruments played in the book so students can hear what each instrument sounds like. Compare the sizes of the instruments to their pitches. Smaller instruments, such as the flute, produce higher-pitched sounds. Larger instruments, such as the trombone, produce lower-pitched sounds.

evaluate

Make an Instrument

Tell students they are going to use what they have learned about sound and pitch to make their own instruments. Pass out the Make an Instrument student page, and discuss the requirements for the presentation. Students should include

- the name of the instrument;
- the type of instrument (wind, percussion, or stringed);
- an explanation of how they made the instrument;
- an explanation and demonstration of how the instrument makes sound; and
- an explanation and demonstration of how the instrument changes pitch.

Tell students that they must get a check mark or stamp from you at the checkpoint before they can begin making their instruments. Make sure they are able to answer the following questions before you give them a check or stamp:

? How will your instrument make sound?

? How will your instrument change pitch?

You can either provide materials for students to make their instruments at school or assign the project as homework.

Use the following rubric to assess student instrument presentations:

Scoring Rubric for Instrument Presentations

4 Point Response	The student states the name of the instrument, identifies the materials used and clearly explains how the instrument was built, correctly identifies the type of instrument, demonstrates and accurately describes how the sound is produced, and demonstrates and accurately describes how the pitch is changed.
3 Point Response	The student demonstrates a flaw in understanding of the concepts and is missing one required element OR demonstrates understanding but is missing two required elements of the presentation.
2 Point Response	The student demonstrates a flaw in understanding of the concepts AND is missing two required elements of the presentation.
1 Point Response	The student demonstrates a flaw in understanding of the concepts AND is missing three or more required elements of the presentation.
0 Point Response	The student does not make an instrument.

Inquiry Place

Have students brainstorm testable questions such as

- ? Does sound travel through water?
- ? Through which solids does sound travel best?
- ? What are the best materials for sending sound through a toy "telephone"?
- ? What materials muffle sound best?

Then have students select a question to investigate as a class, or groups of students can vote on the questions they want to investigate as teams. After they make their predictions, they can design an experiment to test their predictions. Students can present their findings at a poster session.

More Books to Read

Beech, L. 1995. *The Magic School Bus in the haunted museum: A book about sound.* New York: Scholastic.
Summary: On the way to a concert at the Sound Museum, the Magic School Bus breaks down in front of a haunted house. Ms. Frizzle's class hears some weird sounds coming from the spooky house. When they go inside to investigate, they learn about sound and how it is produced.

Hayes, A. 1995. *Meet the orchestra.* New York: Voyager Books.
Summary: This lyrical introduction to the orchestra begins with animal musicians slowly gathering for the evening performance. Each instrument of the orchestra is explained, with clear definitions as well as information on how each one sounds.

Hunter, R. 2001. *Discovering science: Sound.* Austin, TX: Steck-Vaughn.
Summary: This volume provides information and activities exploring sound; it also includes information on sound waves, hearing, volume, musical instruments, and uses of sound.

Moss, L. 1995. *Zin! Zin! Zin! A violin.* New York: Simon and Schuster Books for Young Readers.
Summary: Written in elegant and rhythmic verse and illustrated with playful and flowing artwork, this unique counting book is the perfect introduction to musical groups.

Pfeffer, W. 1999. *Sounds all around.* New York: HarperCollins.
Summary: The author provides simple explanations of sound and hearing for younger readers. Activities listed at the end of the book would be fun for home or school.

Rosinsky, N. 2004. *Sound: Loud, soft, high, and low.* Mankato, MN: Picture Window Books.
Summary: This book describes how sound is created through vibrations that vary in pitch and volume.

Reference

Karpelenia, J. *Sound.* Energy Works! Series. 2004. Logan, IA: Perfection Learning. Straw instrument adapted from an activity on page 29. Ruler activity adapted from page 17.

Name: ______________________________

Making Music

Fill out the chart below as your teacher reads about each type of instrument.

Type of Instrument	Picture	How the Sound Is Made	How the Pitch Is Changed
Wind	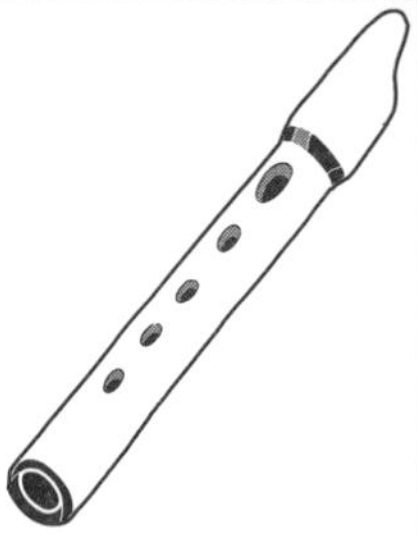		
Stringed			
Percussion			

Making Music
Answer Key

Type of Instrument	Picture	How the Sound Is Made	How the Pitch Is Changed
Wind	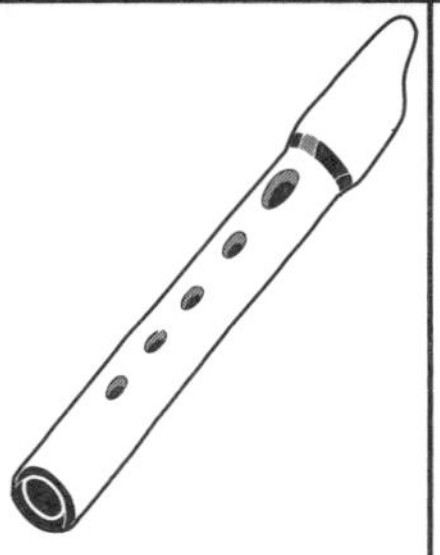	Blowing into it makes the wood, plastic, or brass vibrate, causing the air inside the instrument to vibrate.	Pushing keys changes the length of the column of vibrating air, which changes the pitch.
Stringed		Plucking or strumming strings causes them to vibrate. The air inside the instrument vibrates too.	Placing fingers on the strings creates different string lengths.
Percussion		Hitting or shaking materials causes them to vibrate.	Hitting different-size instruments or different-size parts of the instrument creates different pitches.

Name: ______________________

Make an Instrument

Design and make an instrument that produces a high pitch and a low pitch. You will be presenting your instrument to the class and playing a high pitch and a low pitch with it.

Include the following in your presentation:

1 The name of your instrument
2 The type of instrument (wind, percussion, or stringed)
3 An explanation of how you made the instrument and what materials you used
4 An explanation and demonstration of how your instrument makes sound
5 An explanation and demonstration of how your instrument changes pitch

Think about how your instrument will make sound and change pitch. Design your instrument in the space below, and label the materials you will use to build it.

Sketch

Checkpoint ☐

Chemical Change Café

Description

Learners explore the differences between chemical and physical changes by observing a variety of changes in matter. Learners observe the chemical change of cooking pancakes and identify new menu items for the Chemical Change Café.

Suggested Grade Levels: 3–5

Lesson Objectives Connecting to the ***Framework***

Science and Engineering Practices

- Constructing explanations (for science) and designing solutions (for engineering)

Disciplinary Core Ideas

PS1.B: Chemical Reactions

Crosscutting Concepts

- Cause and Effect

Featured Picture Book

Title	***Pancakes, Pancakes!***
Author	**Eric Carle**
Illustrator	**Eric Carle**
Publisher	**Aladdin**
Year	**2005**
Genre	**Story**
Summary	**By cutting and grinding the wheat for flour, Jack starts from scratch to help make his breakfast pancake.**

Time Needed

This lesson will take several class periods. Suggested scheduling is as follows:

Day 1: **Engage** with changing paper, and **Explore** with Observing Changes in Matter lab stations

Day 2: **Explain** with Chemical Changes article, Frayer Model, and *Pancakes, Pancakes!* read aloud

Day 3: **Elaborate** with Chemical Change Café

Day 4: **Evaluate** with New Menu Items

Materials

For Changing Paper Demonstration

- Piece of paper
- Glass jar
- Matches (for teacher use only)

For Observing Changes in Matter Lab Stations

SAFETY

Station 1: Before this activity, check with your school nurse to see if any students have latex allergies. Students who are allergic to latex should not do the activity at Station 1.

Station 3: Before this activity, demonstrate for students the safe way to smell any chemical by "wafting."

- A red plastic cup and a green plastic cup with the bottoms taped together (1 per team)
- Station 1
  - 7 pieces of bubble wrap
- Station 2
  - Small cup of vinegar
  - Small cup of baking soda
  - Wax paper (1 piece per group)
  - Spoon
  - Pipette
- Station 3
  - Cup of fresh milk covered with foil (labeled "fresh")
  - Cup of sour milk covered with foil (labeled "sour")
- Station 4
  - Lump of clay
- Station 5
  - New steel wool
  - Rusted steel wool in water (leave in water for at least 24 hours)
- Station 6
  - Resealable plastic sandwich bags (1 per team)
  - 2 teaspoons
  - 25 ml graduated cylinder
  - Small cup of cream of tartar
  - Small cup of baking soda
  - Room temperature water
  - 3 thermometers (labeled "1," "2," and "3")
- Station 7
  - Two 25 ml graduated cylinders
  - Clear plastic cups (1 per group)
  - Cup of whole milk
  - Cup of vinegar

For Chemical Change Café

> **SAFETY** Before using this activity, check your school's policy on eating as part of a science lab activity. Some schools forbid it, and commercial labs can be fined for even the appearance of eating. Make sure your students know they should never taste anything in a lab activity. *Exploring Safely: A Guide for Elementary Teachers* recommends, "Nothing should be tasted or eaten as part of science lab work" (Kwan and Texley 2002). Also check with your school nurse to see if any students have dietary restrictions.

- Box of "just add water" pancake mix (1 per group)
- Metric measuring cups for food preparation (1 per group)
- Water
- Wire whisks or spoons (1 per group)
- Mixing bowls (1 per group)
- Electric griddle or hot plate with a pancake pan (for teacher use only)
- Spatula
- Paper plates
- Forks
- Bottles of pancake syrup

Student Pages

- Observing Changes in Matter
- Chemical Changes article
- Chemical Change Frayer Model
- Chemical Change Café Menu
- New Menu Items

Background

A *chemical change* occurs when a substance changes into a new substance with new properties. For example, when you add baking soda to vinegar, a gas bubbles up. The gas, carbon dioxide, has different properties from the baking soda and the vinegar. This is a chemical reaction, which is just another way of saying chemical change. The opposite of a chemical change is a *physical change*. A physical change is a change in matter that might change the form or appearance of a substance but does not produce any new substances. For example, when you chop a piece of wood, its appearance changes, but it is not a new substance. It is still wood. When you put water in the freezer, it turns to ice, but it is still water, just in a different form. Observing any of the following when you combine two or more substances can give you clues that a chemical change has occurred:

- Gas is produced (bubbles).
- Temperature changes.

- Odor changes.
- Color changes.
- A solid forms when two liquids are combined (precipitate).
- Light is emitted.

Although any of these phenomena may be evidence of a chemical change after combining substances, sometimes a physical change can have similar results. For example, boiling water causes bubbles to appear. The bubbles contain water vapor–liquid water that has physically changed into a gas–so no *new* substance is produced. Another example is mixing paint. Although the resulting color may be different from the original colors, the chemical properties of the paint are the same. No new substance has been produced–it's still paint!

A common misconception about distinguishing between physical and chemical changes is that with a physical change, you can "change it back." That is not always true. For example, after you tear a piece of paper into a thousand pieces, you can't return it to its original form. But tearing paper is a physical change because the small pieces are still the same substance as the whole piece of paper was. And in fact, there are some chemical changes that can be reversed. So the best defining characteristic of a chemical change is the presence of a new substance or substances that are entirely different from the starting substances. Sometimes it is really difficult to distinguish between a chemical change and a physical change (in some cases scientists don't even agree!), but the important idea is that matter can be changed in different ways.

engage

Changing Paper

Show students a piece of blank paper. Ask

? What can I do to change this piece of paper?

Students may suggest folding it, rolling it up, cutting it, tearing it, writing on it, and crumpling it up into a ball. Try all of the students' suggestions, and after each one, ask

? Is it still paper? (yes)

Then roll up the piece of paper, and put it in a large glass jar. Strike a match, light the paper on fire, and let the students watch it burn. After the paper has finished burning, ask students

? Is it still paper? How do you know? (No, it is a different substance with new properties.)

explore

Observing Changes in Matter Lab Stations

In advance, set up seven separate locations in the room as lab stations. Number each station, and supply all of the necessary materials for the Observing Changes in Matter activity to be done at that station. Put students in groups of two to four, and give each student the Observing Changes in Matter student page. Tell students they will have a red-green cup to signal the teacher. While they are working, they should keep the green side on top. If they need help, or if they are finished and ready to move to the next station, they should put the red side on top.

Each team will begin at a different station and will visit all seven stations during the lab. Students will complete the activities at each station and record their observations on the student page. They will learn what "P" and "C" mean later. Each member of the group is responsible for writing responses. When all teams are finished (all red cups are up), students may rotate to the next numbered station.

"WAFTING" FRESH AND SOUR MILK IN THE LAB

SAFETY

Demonstrate for students the safe way to smell any chemical by "wafting" (Station 3). Remind students that they should never taste anything during a laboratory activity.

explain

Chemical Changes Article

Pairs Read

Pass out the Chemical Changes article. Tell students this article will help them learn more about the changes they observed. Have students take turns reading aloud from the article. While one person reads a paragraph, the other listens and makes comments ("I think ..."), asks questions ("I wonder ..."), or shares new learnings ("I didn't know ..."). Students can use the information they learn from this article on the Chemical Change Frayer Model student page.

Frayer Model

The Frayer Model is a tool to help students develop their vocabularies by studying concepts in a relational manner. Students write a particular word in the middle of a box and proceed to list characteristics, examples, nonexamples, and a definition in other quadrants of the box. They can proceed by using the examples and characteristics to help them formulate a definition or, conversely, by using the definition to determine examples and nonexamples.

In this case, have students use the preceding article to formulate a definition for "chemical change" in their own words in the top left box of the Chemical Change Frayer Model. Then have students write some characteristics of chemical changes in the top right box. Have students work in pairs to come up with exam-

Physical and Chemical Changes in *Pancakes, Pancakes!*

Physical Changes	Chemical Changes
Cutting wheat	Burning wood for a fire
Separating grain from chaff	Cooking the pancake
Grinding wheat	
Squirting milk in the pail	
Churning butter	
Melting butter	
Chopping wood	
Breaking an egg	
Stirring the batter	

ples and nonexamples from their own lives. As you observe students working, encourage them to use their previous experiences as a basis for their chemical change examples. Students can then present and explain their models to other groups. As they present to each other, informally assess their understanding of the concept and clarify as necessary.

After the reading and the Frayer Model activity, point out that with a chemical change, the change happens without any external assistance. For example, water can get hot in a physical change if there is an external source of heat. Materials can change color in a physical change if there is an external source of color—paint, for example.

Refer back to the paper you used in the Engage phase. Ask students

? Which of the changes that I made to the paper demonstrated a chemical change? Why? (Burning the paper was a chemical change because when the change was complete, there was a new substance formed: black ash.)

With this new information students have learned from the article, have them go back to the Observing Changes in Matter student page they completed in the Explore phase and identify each change as physical or chemical by circling "P" or "C."

Answers

The physical changes in the Observing Changes in Matter exploration were

Station 1: Popping the bubble wrap

Station 4: Forming clay into different shapes

The chemical changes in the Observing Changes in Matter exploration were

Station 2: Vinegar and baking soda reaction (gas bubbles produced)

Station 3: Souring milk (change in odor)

Station 5: Rusted steel wool (change in color and odor)

Station 6: Cream of tartar, baking soda, and water reaction (change in temperature)

Station 7: Vinegar and milk reaction (precipitate formed)

SAFETY

In *Safety in the Elementary (K-6) Science Classroom: Second Edition,* the American Chemical Society (2001) gives the following safety rules for working with hot plates:

1. When working around a heat source, tie back long hair and secure loose clothing.
2. The area surrounding a heat source should be clean and have no combustible materials nearby.
3. When using a hot plate, locate it so that a child cannot pull it off the worktop or trip over the power cord.
4. Never leave the room while the hot plate is plugged in, whether or not it is in use; never allow students near an in-use hot plate if the teacher is not immediately beside the students.
5. Be certain that hot plates have been unplugged and are cool before handling. Check for residual heat by placing a few drops of water on the hot plate surface.

In addition, read the safety box included in the Materials List for the Chemical Change Café.

explain

Pancakes, Pancakes!

Introduce the author and illustrator of *Pancakes, Pancakes!* Ask students if they have read any other books by Eric Carle (information about him can be found at *www.eric-carle.com*).

Determining Importance

Tell students that as you read the story aloud, they should listen for examples of chemical and physical changes that occur in the story. Have students signal (raise their hands) when they hear examples. Have them classify the change as chemical or physical and provide justification.

PICTURES FROM THE CHEMICAL CHANGE CAFÉ

elaborate

Chemical Change Café

The day after reading *Pancakes, Pancakes!* convert your classroom into the Chemical Change Café. Set up a hot plate with a pancake pan or an electric griddle for your use only. Locate the cooking area away from any high traffic areas in your classroom. Provide a box of "just add water" pancake mix, metric measuring cup, spoon or whisk, and container of water for each table of students.

Greet students at the door, divide them into groups, and distribute the menus. All supplies should be on the desks, and students

will follow directions on the menu to make the batter. Invite groups to bring their prepared batter to the cooking area, and they can observe changes as you cook the pancakes according to the package directions. On the menus, students should draw and describe the pancakes before and after they are cooked and explain why cooking pancakes is a chemical change.

Student Procedure for Chemical Change Café (Making Pancakes)

- Please mix 250 ml of pancake mix with 175 ml of water and stir until smooth.
- Please raise your hand to notify the chef that you are ready to have your batter cooked.
- Watch as the batter is changed into a light and fluffy pancake.
- Add a little syrup.
- Enjoy!

Evaluate

New Menu Items

As a final evaluation of student understanding of chemical versus physical changes, have students complete the New Menu Items student page.

The following items can be added to the Chemical Change Café menu because they are turned into new substances with new properties:

1 Toast
3 Scrambled eggs
6 Buttermilk biscuits
8 Cottage cheese
10 Toasted marshmallows

The other items cannot be served at the Chemical Change Café because they undergo only physical changes in their preparation.

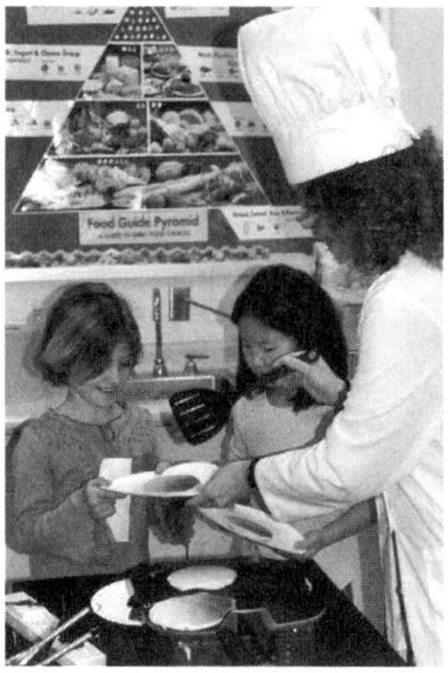

Inquiry Place

Have students brainstorm testable questions such as

- ? How does temperature affect the rate of a chemical change?
- ? Will steel wool rust faster in water, salt water, or vinegar?
- ? How can you make a sugar cube undergo a physical change? A chemical change?

Have students select a question to investigate as a class, or groups of students can vote on the question they want to investigate as teams. After they make their predictions, they can design an experiment to test their predictions. Students can present their findings at a poster session.

More Books to Read

Cole, J. 1995. *The Magic School Bus gets baked in a cake: A book about kitchen chemistry.* New York: Scholastic Books.
Summary: Ms. Frizzle's class takes the Magic School Bus to the local bakery to find out about the chemistry of baking.

Stille, D. 2006. *Chemical change: From fireworks to rust.* Mankato, MN: Compass Point Books.
Summary: This book for grades 5–7 describes chemical changes and highlights some of the commercial and consumer products that result from chemical changes, such as plastics and dyes.

Stille, D. 2006. *Physical change: Reshaping matter.* Mankato, MN: Compass Point Books.
Summary: This book for grades 5–7 describes the physical changes of matter, including melting, freezing, suspensions, boiling, and condensing.

References

American Chemical Society (ACS). 2001. *Safety in the elementary (K-6) science classroom: Second edition.* Washington, DC: ACS.

Kwan, T., and J. Texley. 2002. *Exploring safely: A guide for elementary teachers.* Arlington, VA: NSTA Press

Name: ______________________________

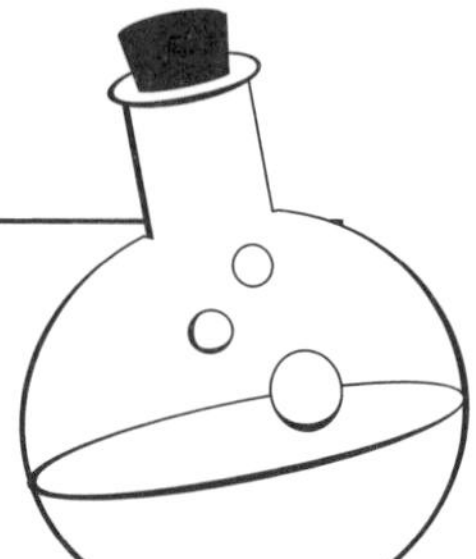

Observing Changes in Matter

Follow the directions below and record your observations at each station. Use all of your senses, except taste, to make your observations. You will decide whether each change is *physical* (P) or *chemical* (C) later in this lesson.

Station 1 P or C

- Observe the bubble wrap. Record your observations.

____

____

- Pop the bubbles with your fingers.
- Observe the bubble wrap again. How has it changed?

____

____

Station 2 P or C

- Observe the cup of baking soda and the cup of vinegar, and record your observations.

____

____

- Put a small spoonful of baking soda on the wax paper.
- Put 5 drops of vinegar on the baking soda.
- Observe what is on the wax paper. How has it changed?

____

____

Name: ______________________________

Observing Changes in Matter cont.

Station 3 P or C

- Take the foil off the fresh milk and observe.
- Smell the fresh milk by "wafting." Put the foil back on.

____

____

- Take the foil off the sour milk and observe.
- Smell the sour milk by "wafting." Put the foil back on.
- How has the milk changed?

____

____

Station 4 P or C

- Observe the clay, and record your observations.

____

____

- Form the clay into a different shape.
- Observe the clay again. How has it changed?

____

____

Name: ______________________________

Observing Changes in Matter cont

Station 5 P or C

- Observe the new steel wool, and record your observations.

____

____

- Observe the steel wool that has been in water.
- Describe the differences between the new steel wool and the wet steel wool.

____

____

Station 6 P or C

- Put 1 teaspoon of cream of tartar and 1 teaspoon of baking soda in a sandwich bag.
- Observe the cream of tartar and baking soda.
- Record the temperature of the mixture with thermometer 1.

____

- Observe the water in the cup.
- Record its temperature with thermometer 2.

____

- Add 10 ml of water to the cream of tartar and baking soda mixture in the sandwich bag.
- Feel the outside of the bag.

Name: ______________________________

Observing Changes in Matter cont.

- Record the temperature of the "stuff" inside the bag with thermometer 3.

____

- How have the water and cream of tartar and baking soda changed?

____

____

Station 7 P or C

- Observe the milk, and record your observations.

____

____

- Observe the vinegar, and record your observations.

____

____

- Pour 20 ml of milk into a clear plastic cup.
- Pour 10 ml of vinegar into the milk, stir once, and let it sit for 1 min.
- Observe the "stuff" in the cup. How have the milk and vinegar changed?

____

____

____

Name: ______________________________

Chemical Changes

Changing Matter

Every day we see changes in the matter around us. Sometimes there is a change in the appearance of matter and other times the change results in an entirely new substance.

Chemical Changes

A **chemical change** is a change in matter that produces new substances. For example, when a piece of wood is burned, it is no longer wood. It is changed into an entirely new substance with new properties. The wood changes from a hard solid into various gases, smoke, and a pile of ash. When cake batter is cooked, the ingredients form a new substance with a different smell, color, texture, and taste.

Physical Changes

The opposite of a chemical change is a **physical change**. A physical change is a change in matter that might change the form or appearance of a substance, but does not produce any new substances. For example, when you tear a piece of paper, its appearance changes, but it is not a new substance. It is still paper. When you put water in the freezer, it turns to ice, but it is still water, just in a different form.

Evidence of a Chemical Change

You can use your senses to detect chemical changes. Here are some characteristics that can help you determine if a chemical change has occurred:

- Gas produced (bubbles)
- Change in temperature
- Change in odor
- Change in color
- A solid formed when combining two liquids (precipitate)
- Light emitted

Any one of these characteristics is evidence that a chemical change has occurred. But sometimes a physical change can have similar results. The key characteristic of a chemical change is the presence of a new substance or substances that are entirely different from the starting substances.

Name: ______________________________

Chapter 16

Chemical Change

Frayer Model

Definition	Characteristics

Chemical Change

Examples	Nonexamples

Is cooking pancakes a physical or chemical change? What is your evidence?

Chemical Change Café

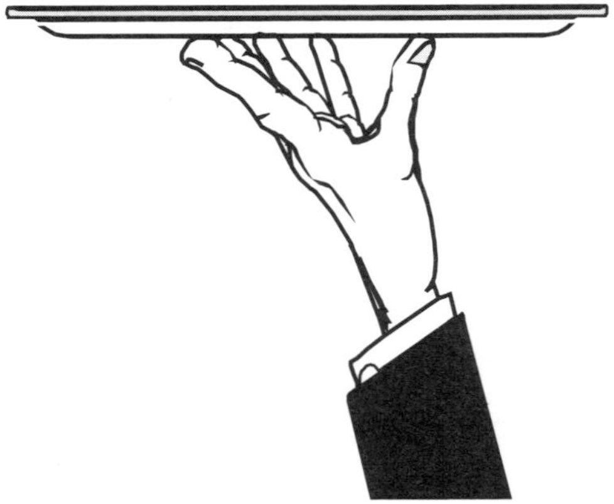

Menu

Today's Special

Pancakes

- Please mix **250 ml of pancake mix** with **175 ml of water** and stir until smooth.
- Please raise your hand to notify the chef that you are ready to have your batter cooked.
- Watch as the batter is changed into a light and fluffy pancake.
- Add a little syrup.
- Enjoy!

Draw and describe the pancakes before cooking.

Draw and describe the pancakes after cooking.

Name: ______________________________

New Menu Items

The Chemical Change Café would like to add some new items to the menu. Only food that has been prepared through a chemical change can be featured on our menu. Put a check mark next to each item that can be added to the menu at the Chemical Change Café.

❑ **1** Toast

We begin with a plain white piece of bread and heat it until it turns brown and produces a delightful smell.

Is making toast a chemical change? Why or why not?

____

____

❑ **2** Orange Juice

Lovely fresh oranges are hand squeezed until the delicious juice drips into your glass.

Is making orange juice a chemical change? Why or why not?

____

____

❑ **3** Scrambled Eggs

Grade A eggs are cooked until they are light, fluffy, and yellow.

Is making scrambled eggs a chemical change? Why or why not?

____

____

Name: ______________________________

New Menu Items cont.

❑ **4** Strawberry Smoothie

We begin with strawberries, ice, sugar, and milk. We blend them together to make a thick, delicious drink.

Is making a strawberry smoothie a chemical change? Why or why not?

❑ **5** Trail Mix

We mix together the finest fresh nuts and dried fruits to create this tasty blend.

Is making trail mix a chemical change? Why or why not?

❑ **6** Buttermilk Biscuits

Creamy buttermilk, baking powder, flour, butter, and salt are mixed together and baked until gas bubbles cause them to rise. The batter turns into flaky, golden brown biscuits. The aroma of the baked biscuits is delightful.

Is making buttermilk biscuits a chemical change? Why or why not?

Name: ______________________________

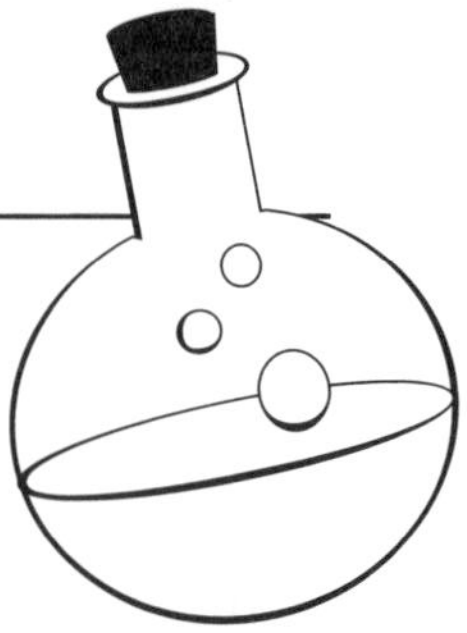

New Menu Items cont.

☐ **7** Orange-sicles

We freeze our finest fresh orange juice until the orange liquid becomes a tasty, frozen solid.

Is making orange-sicles a chemical change? Why or why not?

☐ **8** Cottage Cheese

Fresh milk is combined with special enzymes until the milk becomes thick and clumpy with a completely new taste and smell.

Is making cottage cheese a chemical change? Why or why not?

☐ **9** Fruit Salad

Fresh pineapple, strawberries, kiwi, and blueberries are sliced and mixed together to make this sweet treat.

Is making fruit salad a chemical change? Why or why not?

☐ **10** Toasted Marshmallows

Fluffy white marshmallows are toasted over an open flame until they begin to turn golden brown and smell heavenly.

Is making toasted marshmallows a chemical change? Why or why not?

The Changing Moon

Description

Learners make observations of the Moon each night for a month, model how the Moon changes shape, and illustrate a picture book with scientifically accurate Moon phases.

Suggested Grade Levels: 3–5

Lesson Objectives Connecting to the *Framework*

Science and Engineering Practices
- Asking questions (for science) and defining problems (for engineering)
- Developing and using models
- Analyzing and interpreting data

Disciplinary Core Ideas

ESS1.B: Earth and the Solar System

Crosscutting Concepts
- Patterns

Featured Picture Books

Title	***Next Time You See the Moon***
Author	**Emily Morgan**
Publisher	**NSTA Kids**
Year	**2014**
Genre	**Nonnarrative Information**
Summary	**Explains how the Moon's orbit around Earth causes the Moon phases.**

Title	***Papa, Please Get the Moon for Me***
Author	**Eric Carle**
Illustrator	**Eric Carle**
Publisher	**Simon and Schuster Books for Young Readers**
Year	**1991**
Genre	**Story**
Summary	**Monica's father gets the Moon for her after it is small enough to carry, but it continues to change in size.**

Time Needed

This lesson will take several class periods. Suggested scheduling:

One month before Day 1: **Engage** with Moon Journals

Day 1: **Explore** with Moon Survey and Moon Modeling and **Explain** with Model Discussion and *Next Time You See the Moon* read aloud

Day 2: **Elaborate** with *Papa, Please Get the Moon for Me* retelling

Day 3: **Evaluate** with Phases of the Moon cards and Moon Phases Quiz

Materials

- 2½ in. diameter smooth white foam balls (1 per student). *Note:* Regular Styrofoam balls do not work as well.
- Pencils (1 per student)
- Lamp (lamp shade removed so light is given off in all directions)

> **Foam balls are available from**
>
> ezMolecule (called "polystyrene balls")
> *www.ezMolecule.com*
>
> Walmart (called "smooth foam balls")
> *www.walmart.com*

Student Pages

- Moon Journal
- Moon Survey
- *Next Time You See the Moon* Extended Anticipation Guide
- Phases of the Moon cards
- *Papa, Please Get the Moon for Me* Retelling Book
- Moon Phases Quiz

Background

From the time they are very young, children are naturally curious about the Moon. Some planets have many moons, but the Moon we see is Earth's only natural satellite. It is about one-fourth the size of Earth and is made of rock. There is no air on the Moon and no signs of life (though evidence of frozen water has recently been discovered). The Moon reflects the Sun's light; it has no light of its own. It takes 27.3 days for the Moon to *revolve* around, or *orbit,* Earth. It takes that same amount of time to *rotate,* or spin, on its axis. This causes the same side of the Moon to be facing Earth at all times. The side of the Moon facing away from Earth has been photographed only from spacecraft.

Half of the Moon is always illuminated by the Sun and half is dark, but the *shape* of the Moon appears to change throughout the month when viewed from Earth. The stages in this predictable, repeating cycle are known as *Moon phases.* These phases occur because you see different parts of the lighted side of the Moon from Earth at different times during its orbit. When the Moon is almost directly between the Sun and Earth, you can't see any of the lighted side.

This is called *new Moon*. In a few days, you start to see a tiny sliver of the lighted side, a *crescent Moon*. When the Moon is a quarter of its way around Earth, you see half of the lighted half, or a *quarter Moon*. When you can observe almost the whole lighted half, it is called a *gibbous Moon*. Next you see the whole lighted half, or a *full Moon*. After a full Moon, you see less of the lighted half, another *gibbous Moon*. Then you see half of the lighted half, another *quarter Moon*. Next you see a tiny sliver of the lighted side, another *crescent Moon*. And finally, you can't see any of the lighted half, and it's the new Moon phase again. As you begin to see more and more of the lighted side of the Moon, it is said to be *waxing*. When the right side of the Moon looks bright, then the Moon is in its waxing phase. ("Light on the right, the Moon is getting bright.") After a full Moon, you start to see less and less of the lighted side, so the Moon is said to be *waning*.

A *lunar eclipse* occurs when the Earth comes between the Sun and the Moon and blocks the sunlight that illuminates the Moon. A lunar eclipse is visible only at night and can occur only during the full Moon phase. A *solar eclipse* occurs when the Moon comes between the Earth and the Sun and blocks the Sun's light on a certain location on Earth. Solar eclipses are visible only during the day and can be viewed only from a specific location on Earth. A solar eclipse can occur only during a new Moon. The reason we do not experience lunar and solar eclipses each month is because the Moon's orbit around Earth is slightly tilted. It is only in rare instances that the three bodies line up just right, creating eclipses.

Earth's *gravity* keeps the Moon in orbit. The Moon has a gravitational pull on Earth as well. This pull is the main cause of ocean *tides* on Earth. There are typically two high tides and two low tides each day at a given location on the ocean shore.

Research reveals that students have many misconceptions about the Moon. One of the most common misconceptions is that Moon phases are caused by Earth's shadow falling on the Moon. This idea is challenged during the Moon modeling activity in the Explain phase of this lesson. Other misconceptions include clouds covering the Moon cause the Moon's phases, the Moon has a face, the Moon can be seen only at night, and there is no gravity on the Moon. This lesson addresses many of these misconceptions. *Note:* The order of the Moon phases and explanations shared apply to Earth's Northern Hemisphere.

Engage

Moon Journal and *Next Time You See the Moon* Introduction

Read pages 6–9 of *Next Time You See the Moon*. Ask students what they have noticed about the Moon through their own observations, then invite them to tell you what they are wondering about the Moon. Ask students how they might find the answers to some of their questions. Discuss how scientists find answers by such means as making careful observations of things, doing experiments over and over, and communicating with other scientists.

Tell students that they are going to find out more about the Moon by observing it for a month. Give each student a copy of the Moon Journal. Ask them to look for the Moon each day and draw what it looks like (if it can be seen). You can also keep a daily bulletin board of the Moon phases for that month. Check *www.stardate.org* or *www.moonconnection.com* for monthly Moon calendars.

Modeling the moon phases

Students often have the misconception that the Moon gets larger and smaller. Empty circles on the Moon Journal student page are provided so that students can darken the areas of the Moon that are not lit. This method of recording moon phases takes into account that the entire Moon is present, even if some of its surface cannot be seen.

Discuss students' observations throughout the month using some of the questions that follow.

- ? Was the Moon the same shape each time you saw it?
- ? Was the Moon the same color each time you saw it?
- ? Did you see the Moon every time you looked for it?
- ? Was the Moon in the same place in the sky each time you saw it?
- ? On a cloudy night, how can you tell if the Moon is still there?
- ? What did the Moon look like on the first night of your journal? What did the Moon look like on the last night of your journal?
- ? When you look at your journal, do you see any patterns?

Explore

Moon Survey and Moon Modeling

The day before this activity, assign the Moon Survey student page to students as homework. In this assignment, they record the responses of three people to the question "What causes the Moon to look different each night?"

Have students take out their completed Moon Survey student page and discuss the results of their surveys before they begin the next activity. Ask the following questions as you discuss the surveys:

- ? How did people feel about answering the question on the survey?
- ? What are some of the answers you received?
- ? Are there any answers that you think aren't correct?
- ? What do *you* think causes the Moon phases?

Moon Modeling

Now that students have heard a lot of different ideas people have about why the Moon looks different throughout the month, tell them that they can find the answer to the question using a model.

Darken the room—the darker, the better. Give each student a pencil and a foam ball. Explain that the foam ball, stuck on the end of a pencil, is a model of the Moon; the lamp is a model of the Sun; and their heads represent Earth. Before the guided activity below, give students time to explore the model and test different ideas about what causes Moon phases.

Next guide students through the following activity to model how the Moon appears to change shape.

1. With their faces toward the lamp, students hold the balls slightly above their heads so that they have to look up a little to see them. In this position, students cannot see the lit side of the ball. This is called a *new Moon*.
2. Tell students to turn their bodies slightly to the left while still looking at the ball and holding it a little above their heads. They should turn until they see a *crescent Moon*.

Ask

- ? Where does the Moon's light come from? (The light is coming from the Sun and is reflected off the Moon.)
- ? Some people think the Moon phases are caused by the Earth's shadow. How does this model disprove that theory? (The shadow of my head, which represents the Earth, is nowhere near the Moon in this position. It is behind me.)

3. Instruct the students to keep turning to the left and soon they will see more of the lit half of the ball. This is called a *quarter Moon*.
4. Have them turn a little more and almost all of the ball will be lit. This is called a *gibbous Moon*.
5. Students can keep turning until they see all the lit half of the ball. This is a *full Moon*.
6. As students continue to turn in the same direction, they will see less and less of the lit part of the ball. First they will see a gibbous Moon, then a quarter Moon, then a thin crescent Moon, and finally they will be back to the new Moon.
7. Tell students that the shapes they have observed in this activity are called the *Moon phases*.
8. Have students go through the rotation several times. Ask them to chorally respond with the name of each phase as it is modeled.
9. Point out that no matter where they are in the Moon's orbit, half of the Moon is always lit by the Sun. Sometimes we see the whole lit half from Earth (full Moon);

sometimes we see almost all of the lit half (gibbous Moon); sometimes we see half of the lit half (quarter Moon); sometimes we see only see a tiny sliver of the lit side (crescent Moon); and sometimes we can't see any of the lit half (new Moon). The portion we see from Earth depends on where the Moon is in its orbit around the Earth. Be sure to explain that the order of the phases applies only to Earth's Northern Hemisphere. You can compare how the Moon looks in the Northern Hemisphere to the Southern Hemisphere on the Moon phases calendar feature on *www.moonconnection.com*.

You may want to challenge students to use the foam ball and lamp model to develop an explanation for how lunar and solar eclipses occur.

Note: For a video showing how to do this Moon phases modeling activity with your students, go to *www.nsta.org/nexttime-moon*.

explain

Model Discussion and *Next Time You See the Moon* Read Aloud

After the activity, ask students these questions:

? How does the pattern of the phases you observed in your Moon Journal compare to the pattern of the phases you observed in the model? (The patterns observed in one month with the journal are the same as the pattern observed in one orbit of the Moon in the model.)

Tell students that scientists often use their observations in combination with models to develop explanations of scientific events. Ask

? What explanations can we develop from our month of Moon observations and the Moon modeling activity we just did? (The Moon phases occur in a regular pattern. The orbit of the Moon around the Earth causes the phases.)

Next have students go back to their Moon Survey to see if anyone they surveyed had the correct explanation for the cause of Moon phases. Encourage them to use the Moon phases model to show the people they surveyed how the Moon appears to change shape.

Extended Anticipation Guide

Have students complete the "Before Reading" section of the *Next Time You See the Moon* Extended Anticipation Guide. Then take students to a reading corner (or have them put their papers away). Tell them you will be reading a nonfiction book, *Next Time You See the Moon,* to find the answers to the questions on the anticipation guide. Have students signal (raise their hands) when they hear an answer to one of the questions from the anticipation guide. After you read, they can fill in the "After Reading" section of the anticipation guide. When students finish, go over each question and ask students to share their answers and record their explanation for each answer on the lines at the bottom of the page.

Answers and explanations from the reading:

1 False—page 11
2 True—page 12
3 False—page 21
4 True—page 25
5 False—page 26
6 True—page 27

1 The Moon's different shapes, or phases, have to do with its particular location in its orbit around Earth.
2 The Moon makes no light of its own. It reflects the light of the Sun.
3 It takes about a month for the Moon to orbit Earth.

4 The Moon always orbits in the same direction and takes the same amount of time to circle Earth, so the phases of the Moon are regular and predictable.
5 You can see the Moon during the day quite often.
6 The Moon rises in the eastern sky and sets in the western sky, just like the Sun and stars, because Earth always turns in the same direction.

elaborate

Papa, Please Get the Moon for Me Retelling

Determining Importance

Introduce the author and illustrator of *Papa, Please Get the Moon for Me,* and read the book once just for fun. Then tell the students that you are going to read it again for a different purpose. Explain that this book was not written as a science book, but you would like them to listen for anything that might be scientifically incorrect. Ask them to think back to the things they have learned about the Moon, and if they see a picture or hear something in the book they think is incorrect, they should raise their hands and explain their reasoning. Responses might include

- A ladder could not reach the Moon.
- The Moon cannot talk.
- The Moon phases don't change the way they are pictured in the book.
- The Moon is too big to carry.

Tell students that Eric Carle didn't write *Papa, Please Get the Moon for Me* as a science book, so it's all right if isn't scientifically accurate. Tell students they are going to use his ideas as a basis for a book that *is* scientifically accurate. Pass out copies of the *Papa, Please Get the Moon for Me* Retelling Book and have students illustrate the story and label the correct Moon phases in their drawings. When students are finished illustrating and labeling, they should cut out each page separately and staple the pages together in order.

evaluate

Phases of the Moon Cards

Give students the Phases of the Moon student page. Have students cut out the cards and use the information they learned from the Moon phases model and *Next Time You See the Moon* to place the cards in a circle in the correct order. Then have them label the cards with the names of the Moon phases. The correct sequence for Moon phases is as follows: new Moon, waxing crescent Moon, first quarter Moon, waxing gibbous Moon, full Moon, waning gibbous Moon, last quarter Moon, waning crescent Moon.

Moon Phases Quiz

Give students the Moon Phases Quiz. The answers follow.

1. A. Sun
   B. Moon
   C. Earth
2. c. The Moon revolves around the Earth.
3. c. gibbous Moon
4. a.
5. b. new Moon, crescent Moon, first quarter Moon, gibbous Moon, full Moon

Inquiry Place

See "Teaching Science Through Inquiry," Chapter 3, for an example of how one teacher chose to use this Inquiry Place in her classroom.

Choose one of the following questions to investigate or have students brainstorm other testable questions about the Moon:

- Does the speed of a meteorite affect the size of the crater it makes?
- Does the size of a meteorite affect the size of the crater it makes?
- Does the weight of a meteorite affect the size of the crater it makes?
- Does the shape of the meteorite affect the shape of the crater it makes?
- How do the Moon phases look in the Northern Hemisphere compared with the Southern Hemisphere?

You can choose one of these questions for a whole-class investigation, students can select a question to investigate as a class, or groups of students can vote on the questions they want to investigate as teams. After students make their predictions, they can design experiments to test their predictions. Students can present their findings at a poster session.

More Books to Read

Branley, F. M. 1987. *The Moon seems to change.* New York: HarperTrophy,
Summary: Easy-to-read text and simple diagrams explain how the Moon seems to change and show how to model the changing Moon phases using a pencil, an orange, and a flashlight.

Branley, F. M. 2000. *What the Moon is like.* New York: HarperTrophy.
Summary: Photos and information gathered by the Apollo space missions are used to describe how the Moon's composition, terrain, and atmosphere differ from Earth's. Apollo landing sites are identified and operation of a future Moon colony is depicted.

Crelin, B. 2009. *Faces of the Moon.* New York: Charlesbridge.
Summary: Innovative die-cuts and playful verse track the Moon's phases as seen in the Northern Hemisphere.

Pollock, P. 2001. *When the Moon is full: A lunar year.* New York: Little, Brown, and Company.
Summary: This lunar guide describes the 12 moons according to Native American tradition in short verse and beautifully detailed hand-colored wood cuts. A question-and-answer section includes information about the Moon's surface, an explanation of a lunar eclipse, and the true meaning of a blue moon.

Ray, D. M. 2006. *Night light: A book about the moon.* Minneapolis, MN: Picture Window Books.
Summary: Simple text and cartoonish illustrations provide an introduction to Moon phases, tides, and physical characteristics of the Moon.

Simon, S. 2003. *The Moon.* New York: Simon & Schuster.
Summary: From Apollo 11's first landing to the mystery of moonquakes and the genesis of craters, this introduction to our nearest neighbor in space describes the Moon and its relationship to Earth. Full-color photography and an informative text are included.

Name: ______________________________

Moon Journal

Dates of Observation ______________

Saturday

Friday

Thursday

Wednesday

Tuesday

Monday

Sunday

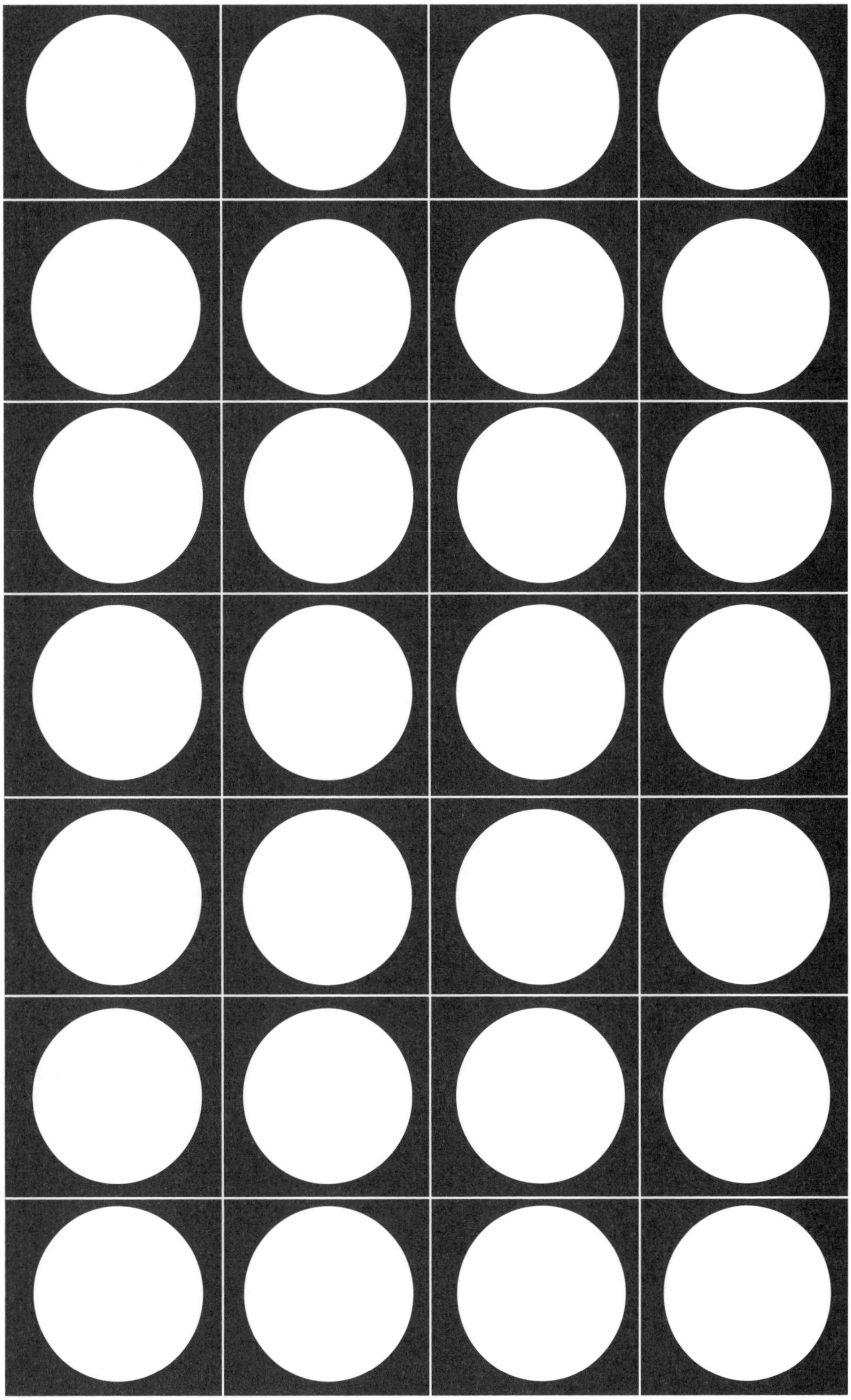

Name: ______________________________

Moon Survey

Ask three people the following question and record their answers on the lines below.

What causes the Moon to look different throughout a month?

Person 1

____

____

____

____

Person 2

____

____

____

____

Person 3

____

____

____

____

Name: ______________________________

Anticipation Guide

Before Reading **True or False**			***After Reading*** **True or False**
____	**1**	The Moon changes shape because of Earth's shadow.	____
____	**2**	The Moon reflects the light of the Sun.	____
____	**3**	It takes about a year for the Moon to orbit Earth.	____
____	**4**	Scientists can predict the Moon phase on any given date thousands of years in the future.	____
____	**5**	The Moon is only visible at night.	____
____	**6**	The Moon rises in the east and sets in the west just like the Sun.	____

Explanations from the reading:

1 ____

____

2 ____

____

3 ____

____

4 ____

____

5 ____

____

6 ____

____

Name: ______________________

Phases of the Moon

Directions: Cut out the Phases of the Moon cards and place them in a circle in the correct order. Then, write the name of the Moon phase under each picture.

New Moon
First Quarter Moon
Full Moon
Waxing Gibbous Moon
Waxing Crescent Moon
Waning Gibbous Moon
Waning Crescent Moon
Last Quarter Moon

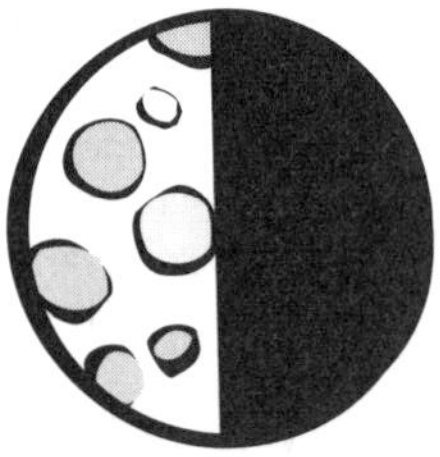

Moon Phase: ______________

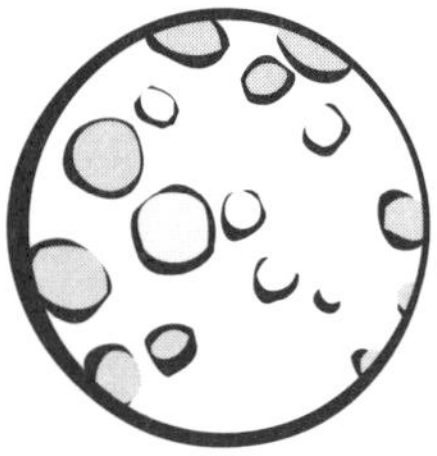

Moon Phase: ______________

Moon Phase: ______________

Moon Phase: ______________

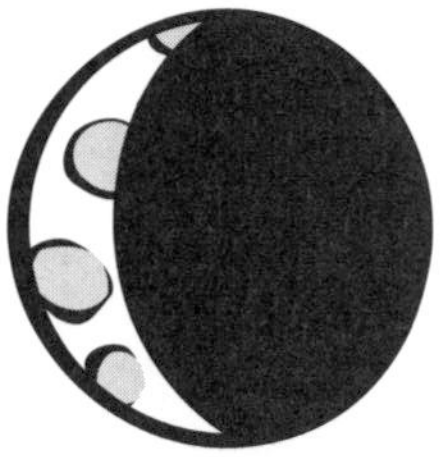

Moon Phase: ______________

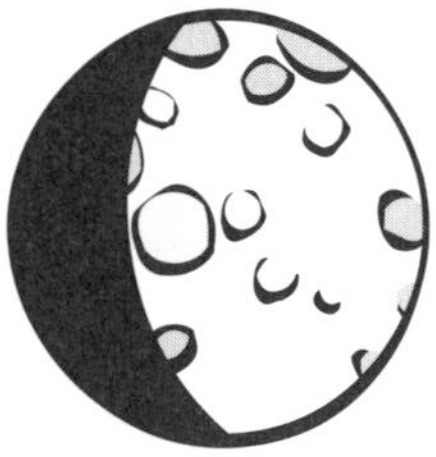

Moon Phase: ______________

Moon Phase: ______________

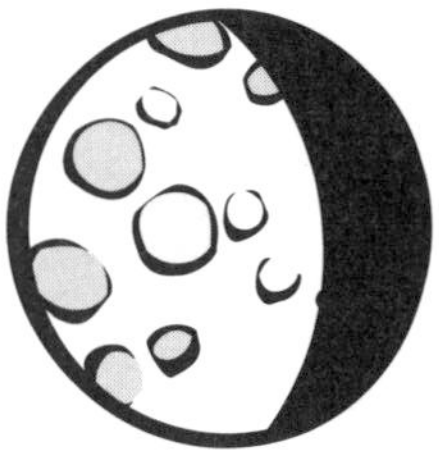

Moon Phase: ______________

Name: ______________________________

CHAPTER 17

Papa, Please Get the Moon for Me Retelling Book

By Eric Carle

Retold by

____

1

Before Monica went to bed she looked out of her window and saw the full moon. The moon looked so near. "I wish I could play with the moon," said Monica to her Papa. But no matter how much she stretched, she could not touch the moon.

2

"The moon is much too big and too far away to play with," said her Papa. "But you can play in the light reflected off the moon." So every night before she went to bed Monica jumped and danced in the moonlight.

3

But the moon seemed to get smaller and smaller each night, until finally it disappeared altogether.

Name: ______________________

Papa, Please Get the Moon for Me

Retelling Book cont.

4

Then, one night, Monica saw a thin sliver of the moon reappear.

5

Each night the moon seemed to grow ...

6

and grow ...

7

... until it was full again.

Name: ______________________________

Moon Phases Quiz

1 Look at the picture below. Label each object using the words *Earth, Moon,* or *Sun*. (Picture is not to scale.)

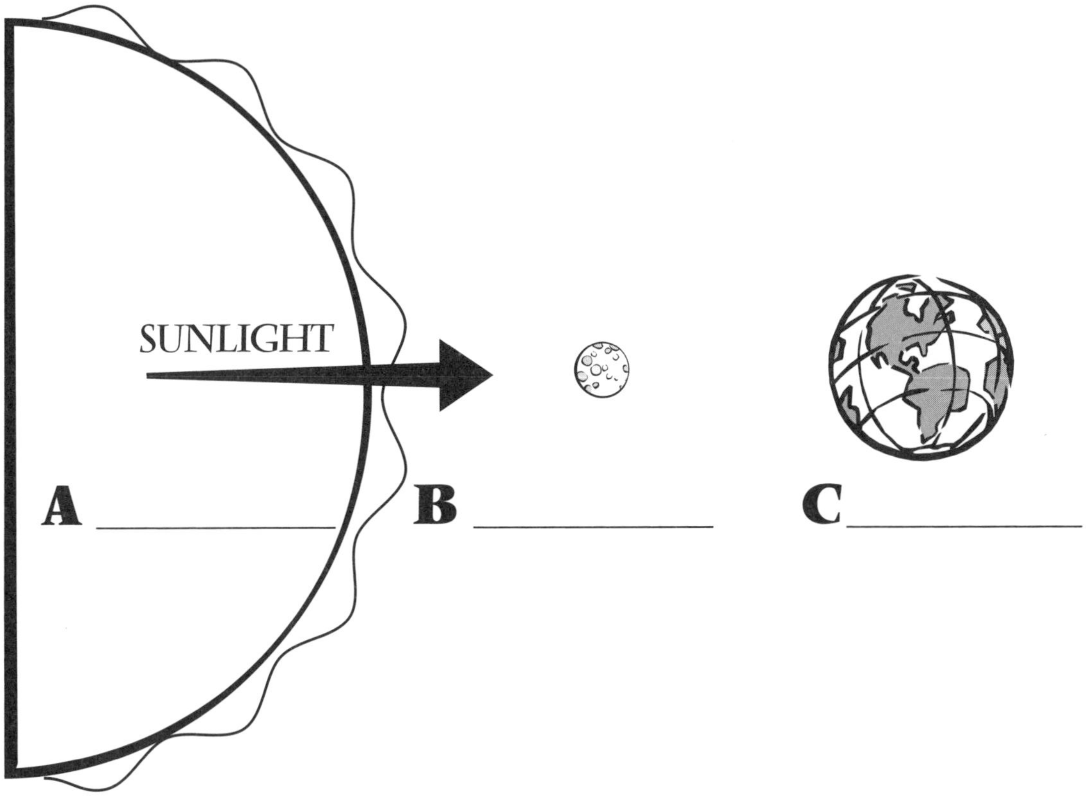

2 The phases of the Moon occur because:

a Clouds cover part of the Moon.

b The Earth's shadow falls on the Moon.

c The Moon orbits the Earth.

Name: ____________________

Moon Phases

Quiz cont.

3 Vonda keeps a journal of the Moon phases she sees each night. Tonight she observes a gibbous Moon. What Moon phase can Vonda expect to see in about one month?

a full Moon

b crescent Moon

c gibbous Moon

4 The pictures above show phases of the Moon, taken four nights apart. Which of the pictures below shows the Moon four nights later?

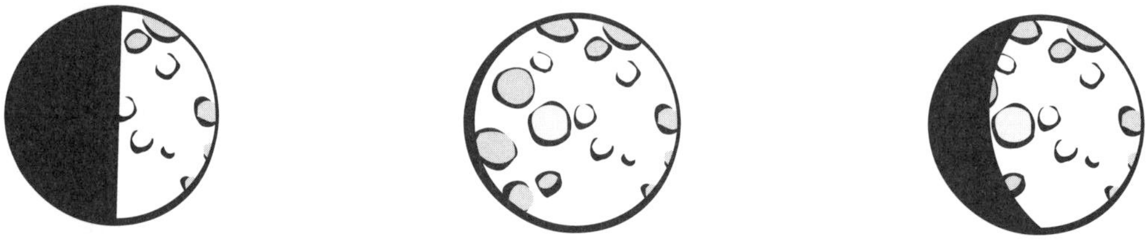

a **b** **c**

5 Which of the following states the correct order of the Moon phases from new Moon to full Moon?

a new Moon, first quarter Moon, gibbous Moon, crescent Moon, full Moon

b new Moon, crescent Moon, first quarter Moon, gibbous Moon, full Moon

c new Moon, full Moon, first quarter Moon, crescent Moon, gibbous Moon

Day and Night

Description

Using a model, learners explore time zones and what causes day and night and how time zones change. Learners observe the position of the Sun in the sky at different times of day and relate those positions to the rotation of the Earth.

Suggested Grade Levels: 3–5

Lesson Objectives Connecting to the *Framework*

Science and Engineering Practices

- Asking questions (for science) and defining problems (for engineering)
- Developing and using models
- Analyzing and interpreting data

Disciplinary Core Ideas

ESS1.B: Earth and the Solar System

Crosscutting Concepts

- Patterns

Featured Picture Book

Title	***Somewhere in the World Right Now***
Author	**Stacey Schuett**
Illustrator	**Stacey Schuett**
Publisher	**Dragonfly Books**
Year	**1997**
Genre	**Story**
Summary	**Describes what is happening in different places around the world at a particular time**

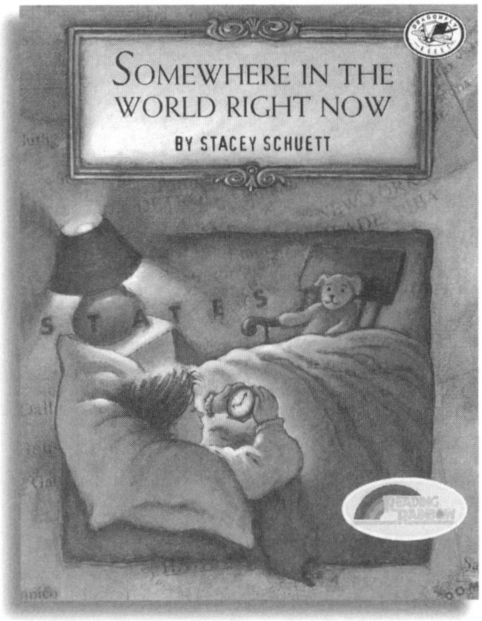

Time Needed

This lesson will take several class periods. Suggested scheduling is as follows:

Day 1: **Engage** with read aloud of *Somewhere in the World Right Now*

Day 2: **Explore** and **Explain** with modeling with lamps and globes

Days 3–5: **Elaborate** with Where Is the Sun?

Day 6: **Evaluate** with Make a Picture Book

Materials

- Several clocks set at different times labeled with city and country
- Globes (1 per group)
- Lamps (1 per group)

Student Pages

- Somewhere in the World Right Now
- Where Is the Sun?
- Make a Picture Book

Background

The next time you watch the Sun rise, take a minute to think about what's really going on. You are standing on a giant ball of rock that is hurtling through space, and the spot where you are standing is rotating toward a star located 93 million miles away! It makes a beautiful sunrise seem even more amazing.

This lesson focuses on the phenomena of day and night, which is caused by Earth's *rotation,* or spin. Earth makes a full rotation every 24 hours. When your location on Earth spins toward the Sun, you see the Sun "rising," and when your location is turning away from the Sun, you see the Sun "setting." As Earth continues to rotate, the Sun appears to move across the sky. Long ago people measured time by looking at the apparent position of the Sun in the sky. When the Sun appeared at its highest point overhead, it was noon. But this method meant that neighboring cities had different clock times at the same instant. This became inconvenient as people began to travel and communicate more, so in 1884 an international agreement was made to adopt a system of standard times. The Earth was divided into 24 equal parts, called *time zones.* At each location in a specific time zone, the time is exactly the same. When a person moves from one time zone to the next, however, he or she experiences a change in time of one hour—one hour behind if you move west, and one hour ahead if you move east. One important feature of this system is the international date line, an imaginary line drawn through the Pacific Ocean where a new date begins. The line is not completely straight—there are a few zigzags around some inhabited islands. To the east of the international date line it is one date and to the west it is another. So no matter where you are in the world, somewhere else it is a different day!

In this lesson, daily observations of the Sun's position in the sky provide the basis from which students can construct a model explaining the reason why we have day and night.

Engage

Before class, bring in several clocks set at different times around the world and label them with the city and country. You can find times of many cities around the world at *www.timeanddate.com/worldclock.*

Questioning

Point out the clocks and ask why they are set for different times. Explain that you have a book to read that might answer that question. Introduce the author and illustrator of *Somewhere in the World Right Now*. Skip "A Note to the Reader" in the front of the book (this section will be used later to provide the scientific explanation for the students), and read the book aloud to students. Model the questioning skills of a good reader by asking the following types of questions as you read.

- ? Is it true that somewhere in the world it is already tomorrow?
- ? How can the Sun be rising and setting at the same time?
- ? How can all of these things be happening in the world right now?

Making Connections: Text-to-Self

Ask students

- ? Do you know someone who lives in a different part of the country or world, where it is a different time than it is here?
- ? Have you ever been to a place where you had to set your watch differently?

Have students examine the clocks set for different times for different places in the world. Determine students' prior knowledge and misconceptions about Earth-Sun relationships by asking them to share ideas about how it can be so many different times at the same moment.

Explore & Explain

Modeling With Lamps and Globes

Provide each group of students with a lamp and a globe. Tell them they are going to use the lamp as a model of the Sun and the globe as a model of the Earth.

Before they begin the activity, ask students

- ? How does the Earth move? (It rotates on its axis and revolves around the Sun.)
- ? What do the movements of the Earth have to do with how we keep time? (One rotation is one day, and one revolution is one year.)
- ? Which movement do you think causes day and night? (Earth's rotation)

STUDENTS MODELING DAY AND NIGHT WITH LAMPS AND GLOBES

Then give students a few minutes to explore the following question with the model:

? How can it be different times in different places on the Earth?

After students have had time to explore the model, pass out the Somewhere in the World Right Now student pages. Tell students to use the lamp and globe to answer the questions on the student pages.

Discuss the students' responses on the Somewhere in the World Right Now student pages. Have students share any observations, answers, and questions.

The correct answers for the student pages follow.

1 List three locations that are experiencing night when it is daytime in your city. (Answers will vary but should be locations on the opposite side of the globe.)

2 Can the Sun be rising and setting at the same time? Explain. (Yes, it is always rising somewhere on the Earth and setting on the opposite side of the Earth at the same time.)

3 Where on the globe is the international date line? (It runs through the middle of the Pacific Ocean in a north-south direction.)

4 Why do you think the international community agreed to place the international date line in that location? (To have a date change in the middle of a country would cause too many problems for people living there. There aren't very many people living in the middle of the Pacific Ocean,

so few people are affected by the change of date there.)

5 Which locations are first to begin the new day? (Places west of the international date line move into the new date first. Those locations include New Zealand, Russia, and Japan.)

6 Which locations are last to see the sunrise on that day? (Locations just east of the international date line are last to see the sunrise on a particular day. Those locations include Hawaii, Marquesas, and the Aleutian Islands.)

7 Which part of the United States is the first to see the sunrise, the East Coast or the West Coast? (the East Coast)

8 Think back to the book *Somewhere in the World Right Now*. On the lines below, explain how all of the events in the book could be taking place in the same moment. (All of those events were happening at the same moment because different places have different times based on location. Somewhere right now it is day and somewhere else right now it is night because the Sun lights up half of Earth at all times. As Earth rotates, different locations enter the sunlight at different times.)

Looking for the location of the Sun in the sky

Determining Importance

Tell students you will be reading an informational page titled "A Note to the Reader" from the front of *Somewhere in the World Right Now*. Have students listen for answers to any questions they might still have about time zones, the international date line, and Earth's rotation.

elaborate

Where Is the Sun?

Distribute the Where is the Sun? student pages. Have students choose a location where they can face south and observe the Sun in the morning, at noon, and in the afternoon. Students will record the position of the Sun relative to a landmark at each of these times for three days.

After the third day, students can answer the questions on the Where Is the Sun? student pages. Have them revisit the lamp and globe

SAFETY

Never look directly at the Sun! Looking at the Sun can damage your eyes!

model to reinforce their understanding of the abstract concepts they are learning with a concrete representation. Then discuss the questions from the student pages together.

1. Did you notice any patterns in where you saw the Sun in the sky each day? (Students should notice that the Sun is always lowest in the eastern sky in the morning, highest in the sky at noon, and lowest in the western sky in the afternoon.)
2. At what time of day did the Sun seem highest in the sky? (noon)
3. Think back to the globe and lamp you used to model day and night. Does the Sun really move across the sky during the day? Explain. (No, in our model, the Sun stayed in the same place and the globe was rotating.)
4. How does the rotation of the Earth affect the appearance of the Sun in the sky in the morning, at noon, and in the afternoon? (In the morning, my location is turning toward the Sun. It appears in the east because of the direction the Earth turns. At noon, my location is turned all the way toward the Sun, so it appears to be right above me. In the afternoon, my location is turning away from the Sun. It appears in the west because of the direction the Earth turns.)

Evaluate

Make a Picture Book

Pass out the Make a Picture Book student page. Tell students they will write and illustrate a children's picture book that can be used to explain what causes day and night, and what causes the Sun to appear to move across the sky each day. Their finished products should

Scoring Rubric for Make a Picture Book

4 Point Response	The picture book includes an accurate explanation of what causes day and night, a clearly labeled diagram showing what causes day and night, an accurate explanation of what causes the Sun to appear to move across the sky each day, a clearly labeled diagram of what causes the Sun to appear to move across the sky each day, simple text, and colorful, scientifically accurate illustrations.
3 Point Response	The student demonstrates a flaw in understanding of the concepts OR the book is missing one or two required elements.
2 Point Response	The student demonstrates a flaw in understanding of the concepts AND the book is missing one or two required elements; OR the student demonstrates understanding, but the book is missing three required elements.
1 Point Response	The student demonstrates a flaw in understanding of the concepts AND the book is missing three or more required elements; OR the student demonstrates understanding, but the book is missing four or more required elements.
0 Point Response	The book shows no understanding of the concepts AND is missing all required elements; OR the student did not make a book.

include simple text, colorful illustrations, and clearly labeled diagrams.

Have available some picture books about astronomy written for young children, such as *The Sun Is My Favorite Star* by Frank Asch and *The Moon Book* by Gail Gibbons. Share some examples of simple text, colorful illustrations, and clearly labeled diagrams.

Inquiry Place

Have students brainstorm questions such as

- ? How does the length of daylight in summer compare to the length of daylight in winter where you live? Research it!
- ? How does the length of daylight in summer compare to the length of daylight in winter at the North Pole? How can you use a model to explain this difference? Test it!
- ? How do the direction and length of your shadow in the morning compare to its direction and length at noon or in late afternoon? Test it!
- ? Where and when on Earth is the longest day? Research it!

Students can select a question to investigate as a class, or groups of students can vote on questions they want to investigate as teams. Students can present their findings at a poster session.

Websites

Virtual Globe: Areas of Sunlight and Darkness Updated Every Five Minutes

www.anutime.com/globe/3Den.html

World Clock

www.timeanddate.com/worldclock

More Books to Read

Branley, F. M. 1986. *What makes day and night?* New York: HarperTrophy.
Summary: A simple explanation of how the rotation of the Earth causes day and night.

Fletcher, R. 1997. *Twilight comes twice.* Boston: Houghton Mifflin.
Summary: Free-verse text describes the transition from day to night and from night to day, revealing the magic in these everyday moments.

Singer, M. 1993. *Nine o'clock lullaby.* New York: HarperCollins.
Summary: While Mama reads a story at 9 p.m. in Brooklyn, people have a snack in the pantry at 2 a.m. in England, the cat knocks over the samovar at 5 a.m. in Moscow, a family has a barbecue in Australia, and the Sun is setting in Los Angeles.

References

Asch, F. 2000. *The Sun is my favorite star.* New York: Harcourt.

Gibbons, G. 1997. *The Moon book.* New York: Holiday House.

Name: ______________________________

Somewhere in the World Right Now

Place your lamp and globe about 50 cm apart with the lamp shining toward the globe. Use the lamp to represent the Sun and the globe to represent Earth.

- Find the arrow near the equator that shows the direction the Earth turns. Be sure to always turn your globe in that direction.
- Model daytime in your city.

1 List three locations that are experiencing night when it is daytime in your city.

____

- Model sunrise in your city by turning the globe so that your city is just entering the lamp's light.

2 Can the Sun be rising and setting at the same time? Explain.

____

____

- Find the international date line on your globe. This is where one day changes to the next.

3 Where on the globe is the international date line?

____

4 Why do you think the international community agreed to place the international date line in that location?

____

____

____

Name: ______________________________

Somewhere in the World Right Now cont.

- Turn your globe so that the international date line is just entering the lamp's light (sunrise).

5 Which locations are first to begin the new day?

____

- Slowly turn your globe and notice each location turning toward the lamp.

6 Which locations are last to see the sunrise on that day?

____

- Model sunrise in the United States. Be sure you are turning the globe in the direction the Earth turns.

7 Which part of the United States is the first to see the sunrise, the East Coast or the West Coast?

____

8 Think back to the book *Somewhere in the World Right Now.* On the lines below, explain how all of the events in the book could be taking place at the same moment.

____

____

____

____

____

____

Name: ______________________________

Where Is the Sun?

1 Choose a spot to observe the position of the Sun and face south.

2 Locate a landmark (tree, flagpole, building, etc.) and draw it in each box. Be sure to use the same landmark all three days.

3 Draw the position of the Sun relative to the landmark in the morning, at noon, and in the afternoon for three days. Be sure to stand in the **exact same location**, facing south each time.

4 Write the time of day inside each picture of the Sun.

SAFETY

Never look directly at the Sun!

Looking at the Sun can damage your eyes!

Example

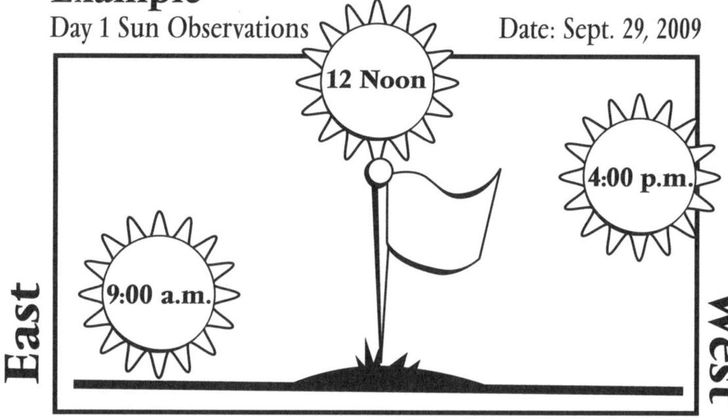

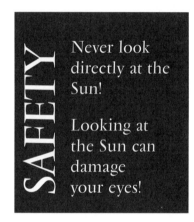

Day 1 Sun Observations

Date: ______________

East

West

Name: ____________________

Where Is the Sun? cont.

Day 2 Sun Observations

Date: ____________

East

West

Day 3 Sun Observations

Date: ____________

East

West

Name: ______________________________

Where Is the Sun? cont.

Questions

1 Did you notice any patterns in where you saw the Sun in the sky each day?

____

____

2 At what time of day did the Sun seem highest in the sky?

____

____

3 Think back to the globe and lamp you used to model day and night. Does the Sun really move across the sky during the day? Explain.

____

____

____

4 How does the rotation of the Earth affect the appearance of the Sun in the sky in the morning, at noon, and in the afternoon?

____

____

____

____

Name: ______________________________

CHAPTER 18

Make a Picture Book

Write and illustrate a children's picture book that can be used to explain what causes day and night, and to explain what causes the Sun to *appear* to move across the sky each day.

Books should include

1 An accurate explanation and clearly labeled diagram showing what causes day and night.

2 An accurate explanation and clearly labeled diagram of what causes the Sun to *appear* to move across the sky each day.

3 Simple text a young child could understand.

4 Colorful, scientifically accurate illustrations.

Be creative! Have fun!

Grand Canyon

Description

Learners explore through a checkpoint lab simulation how weathering and erosion have contributed to the formation of the Grand Canyon. They will create a travel brochure for the Grand Canyon demonstrating their understandings about weathering and erosion.

Suggested Grade Levels: 3–6

Lesson Objectives Connecting to the *Framework*

Science and Engineering Practices
- Developing and using models
- Constructing explanations (for science) and designing solutions (for engineering)
- Obtaining, evaluating, and communicating information

Disciplinary Core Ideas

ESS2.A: Earth Materials and Systems

Crosscutting Concepts
- Stability and Change

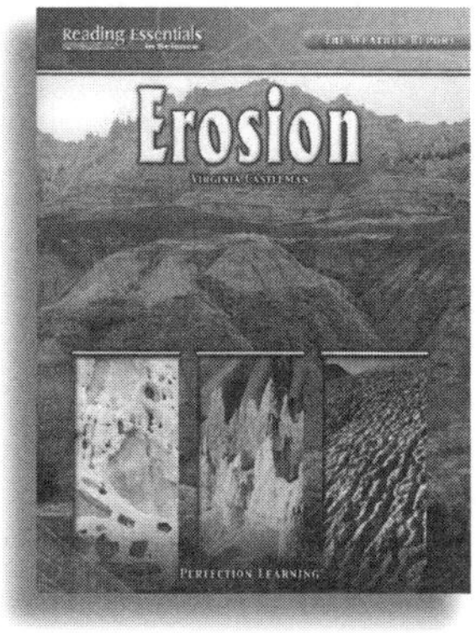

Featured Picture Books

Title	***Erosion*** **(The Weather Report series)**
Author	**Virginia Castleman**
Publisher	**Perfection Learning**
Year	**2004**
Genre	**Nonnarrative Information**
Summary	**Tells how water, wind, and ice change the surface of the Earth through erosion**

Title	***Grand Canyon: A Trail Through Time***
Author	**Linda Vieira**
Illustrator	**Christopher Canyon**
Publisher	**Walker and Company**
Year	**2000**
Genre	**Narrative Information**
Summary	**Describes the deep trench known as the Grand Canyon and activities of visitors to the national park**

Time Needed

This lesson will take several class periods. Suggested scheduling is as follows:

Day 1: **Engage** with thinking about the Grand Canyon, and **Explore** with Wind and Water Checkpoint Lab

Day 2: **Explain** with reading and relating to the Checkpoint Lab

Day 3: **Elaborate** and **Evaluate** with Grand Canyon Brochure

Materials

- A variety of travel brochures from different places
- Pictures of the Grand Canyon (e.g., photos, prints, books)

For the Wind and Water Checkpoint Lab

- A red plastic cup and a green plastic cup with the bottoms taped together (1 per team)
- Jug of water or a water source
- Safety goggles (1 per student)

For Part A (per team)

- Large plastic jar with a screw-top lid
- Small cup of soil
- Small cup of sand
- Small cup of large gravel
- Small cup of small gravel

For Part B (per team)

- Cup of unwashed rocks
- Large plastic jar with a screw-top lid
- Wire strainer
- Paper coffee filter
- 2 large plastic containers for collecting the dirty water
- Paper plate

For Part C (per team)

- Sheet of newspaper
- Paper box lid
- Cup of sand

For Part D (per team)

- Plastic or metal paint tray

Student Pages

- Grand Canyon
- Wind and Water Checkpoint Lab
- New Vocabulary List
- Grand Canyon Brochure

Background

The Grand Canyon is one of the most spectacular natural features on our planet. Millions of people from all over the world visit the canyon each year. Located in northwestern Arizona, it is the largest and deepest canyon in North America. The Grand Canyon is a breathtaking example of the power of water in shaping the land. A widely accepted scientific theory about the canyon holds that the Colorado River began forming it about 6 million years ago. The weathering and erosion caused by this river is mainly responsible for the depth of the Grand Canyon, but wind and rain pounding on the sides of the canyon are responsible for its width. *Weathering* refers to the breakdown of rock and can be put into two categories: mechanical weathering and chemical weathering. *Mechanical weathering* is the physical breakdown of rock that can be caused by water, wind, or ice moving past rock; changes in temperature (especially changes that lead to freezing and thawing); and plant growth. *Chemical weathering* occurs when the chemical composition of rock is broken down into new substances. Substances such as water and acids (acid rain) react with the minerals that make up rock, which cause the rock to break down. *Erosion* occurs when weathered rock and soil fragments are transported to another place. *Deposition* occurs when the materials are dropped in another place.

Scientists have evidence that Earth is about 4.6 billion years old! During this long span of time, Earth's surface has been in a state of constant change. Both constructive and destructive forces of nature have changed Earth's surface throughout its history. *Constructive forces,* such as volcanic eruptions, crustal deformation, and deposition, build up mountains and landmasses. *Destructive forces,* such as weathering and erosion, break down or slowly wear away mountains and other landforms.

engage

Thinking About the Grand Canyon

Pass out the Grand Canyon student page and have students make inferences from the picture. Providing students with additional color photographs of the canyon before they answer the following questions would be helpful.

? How do you think the Grand Canyon formed?

? Why do you think it has gotten wider and deeper over time?

? How long do you think it took for the Grand Canyon to form?

explore

Wind and Water Checkpoint Lab

In advance, prepare all of the materials necessary for the Wind and Water Checkpoint Lab. See "Teaching Science Through Inquiry," Chapter 3, for tips on managing a checkpoint lab.

Using Features of Nonfiction

Tell students you have a nonfiction book that might help them find out how the Grand Canyon formed. Show them the cover of *Erosion*. Tell students that a unique feature of nonfiction is that the reader can enter the text at any point to get information. Turn to page 15, and read the inset about the Grand Canyon.

Tell students that they will do activities in a checkpoint lab to help them understand how wind and water can cause changes on the surface of the Earth.

Checkpoint Lab

Distribute the Wind and Water Checkpoint Lab student pages. Tell students to take turns being the reader for their teams. The reader's job involves reading the directions out loud for the team, putting the green cup on top if

SHAKING THE JAR OF ROCKS IN THE CHECKPOINT LAB

the team is working, and putting the red cup on top if the team has a question or if it is ready for a check mark. Each member of the group is responsible for recording data and writing responses.

Have the students complete the checkpoint lab, working at their own paces. While they are working, observe and listen to them interact. Before you give a team a check mark or stamp so they can move ahead in the lab, informally evaluate them by asking probing questions of each member of the team, such as

- ? How do you know?
- ? What is your evidence?
- ? Are you surprised by the results? Why or why not?
- ? What does this remind you of?
- ? What do you think will happen next?

Explain

Reading and Relating to the Checkpoint Lab

New Vocabulary List

Ask students if they have ever heard the words *weathering* and *erosion,* and discuss their prior knowledge of the terms. Pass out the New Vocabulary List student page. A new vocabulary list is a "guess and check" type of visual representation. Students develop vocabulary as they draw and write predictions about a new word's meaning, read the word in context, and draw and write their new definitions of the word. Have students write the words *weathering* and *erosion* in the top two boxes of the first column. Then have them draw and write what they think each word means in the next column. Tell students they will use this sheet to keep track of new words as they learn about the Grand Canyon. Let them know that they will get to find out if their predictions about the meanings of the words *weathering* and *erosion* are correct by comparing their observations from the checkpoint lab to the information in *Erosion*.

Chunking

Read pages 4 through 7 and page 11 in *Erosion*. (Skip the inset "Know Your Rocks" about the three types of rocks.) Then ask the students

- ? What is weathering? (Weathering is the natural breakdown of rocks into particles.)
- ? In which part of the checkpoint lab did you observe weathering? (Part B, in which we shook up the jar of rocks and water and observed that some particles broke off.)

Provide time for students to fill in the "What It Means" column of the New Vocabulary List student page.

Then ask the students

? What is erosion? (Erosion is the process by which weathered rock and soil on Earth's surface are picked up in one location and moved to another.)

? In which part of the checkpoint lab did you observe erosion? (Part C, in which we observed small particles of sand carried to the end of the box by wind, and Part D, in which we observed small particles being carried to the bottom of the pan by water)

Provide time for students to complete the "What It Means" column of the New Vocabulary List student page.

Ask students to add the words *water erosion* and *wind erosion* to the "Word" column of the New Vocabulary List student page. Provide time for them to fill in the second column, "What I Think It Means," based on what they have learned so far. Then read pages 12 through 14 about water erosion in *Erosion*.

? What is water erosion? (Water erosion occurs when water flows over the ground and takes other loose weathered material with it.)

? In which part of the checkpoint lab did you observe water erosion? (Part D in which we observed small particles being carried to the bottom of the pan by water.)

Provide time for students to complete the "What It Means" column of the New Vocabulary List student page.

Then read pages 21 and 22 in *Erosion* about wind erosion, including the inset about the dust bowl. (See *Children of the Dust Days* in the "More Books to Read" section for more information.) Then ask students

? What is wind erosion? (Wind erosion is the movement of very small particles by wind.)

? In which part of the checkpoint lab did you observe wind erosion? (Part C in which wind [or breath] carried some of the sand, and we felt it hitting our hands.)

Provide time for students to complete the "What It Means" column of the New Vocabulary List student page.

Next explain that scientists have evidence that Earth is about 4.6 billion years old! During this long span of time, Earth's surface has been in state of constant change. Both constructive and destructive forces have changed Earth's surface throughout its history. Constructive forces build up mountains and landmasses. Destructive forces break down, or slowly wear away, mountains and other landforms. Ask

? Is weathering an example of a constructive or a destructive force? Why? (a destructive force, because weathering breaks down rock into smaller particles)

? Is erosion an example of a constructive or a destructive force? Why? (a destructive force, because erosion carries away pieces of rock)

? Can you think of an example of a constructive force ... something in nature that would build up the Earth's surface? (a volcanic eruption, because it covers part of the Earth's surface in lava, building it up with new rock)

Determining Importance

Go back to the original questions asked on the Grand Canyon student page:

? How do you think the Grand Canyon formed?

? How do you think it has gotten wider and deeper over time?

? How long do you think it took for the Grand Canyon to form?

Introduce the author and the illustrator of the book *Grand Canyon: A Trail Through Time*. Tell students they can find out if their inferences about the Grand Canyon were correct by listening as you read the book. Have students signal (raise their hands) if they hear any clues from the reading and invite discussion about them.

? How do you think the Grand Canyon formed? (The Grand Canyon was formed by weathering and erosion. The Colorado River flowed through it over a long period of time and weathered away the rock, and the rock was carried away by the water, page 11.)

? How do you think it has gotten wider and deeper over time? It has gotten wider and deeper as the rushing Colorado River continues to flow through it, deepening the canyon by eroding away rocks and soil. Blustering wind and pounding rain continue to weather away the rocky sides of the canyon (page 28).

? How long do you think it took for the Grand Canyon to form? (The Colorado River took almost six million years to carve the canyon, page 11.)

Elaborate & Evaluate

Grand Canyon Brochure

Distribute a variety of travel brochures from different places. Have students examine them and pass them around. Then ask

? What are some common features of travel brochures? (photographs, maps, sketches, reasons to visit, catchy slogans, etc.)

Next pass out the Grand Canyon Brochure assignment. Use the following rubric to assess student work.

Scoring Rubric for Grand Canyon Brochure

4 Point Response	The brochure includes a creative slogan, a drawing or photograph of the Grand Canyon, a map showing the correct location of the Grand Canyon, complete definitions of weathering and erosion with clear descriptions of how each contributed to the formation of the canyon, an accurate explanation of the changes still occurring at the Grand Canyon, and three reasons tourists should visit the Grand Canyon.
3 Point Response	The student demonstrates a flaw in understanding of the concepts of weathering and erosion OR the brochure is missing one or two required elements.
2 Point Response	The student demonstrates a flaw in understanding of the concepts of weathering and erosion AND the brochure is missing one or two required elements; OR the student demonstrates understanding, but the brochure is missing three required elements.
1 Point Response	The student demonstrates a flaw in understanding of the concepts of weathering and erosion AND the brochure is missing three or more required elements; OR the student demonstrates understanding, but the brochure is missing four or more required elements.
0 Point Response	The brochure shows no understanding of the concepts of weathering and erosion AND is missing all required elements.

Inquiry Place

Have students brainstorm testable questions such as

- ? How will a mound of dirt in the school yard change in width and height over a one-week period? Two weeks? Four weeks? Twelve weeks?
- ? Which type of rock will react the most to chemical weathering (acid): limestone, sandstone, or granite?

Have students select a question to investigate as a class, or groups of students can vote on the questions they want to investigate as teams. After they make their predictions, they can design an experiment to test their predictions. Students can present their findings at a poster session.

More Books to Read

Anderson, P. 1997. *A Grand Canyon journey: Tracing time in stone.* Danbury, CT: Franklin Watts.
Summary: Color photographs and informative text take readers on a guided tour from the rim of the Grand Canyon down to the valley floor, describing the geological history that created the canyon along the way.

Bailey, J. 2006. *Cracking up: A story about erosion.* Mankato, MN: Picture Window Books.
Summary: This book describes the process of erosion and how water, ice, and wind wear away at Earth's surface.

Coombs, K. M. 2000. *Children of the dust days.* Minneapolis, MN: Carolrhoda Books.
Summary: This informative book brings the dust days of the 1930s to life through simple, straightforward text and period photographs. Explains how poor farming techniques and drought led to massive erosion.

Koontz, R. 2007. *Erosion: Changing Earth's surface.* Mankato, MN: Picture Window Books.
Summary: The author describes how rain, waves, wind, snow, and ice can shape the land.

Minor, W. 2000. *Grand Canyon: Exploring a natural wonder.* New York: Blue Sky Press.
Summary: Retraces the steps of 19th-century artist-explorer Thomas Moran, whose paintings helped convince Congress to preserve the Grand Canyon as a national park. Lyrical text and stunning watercolors describe both the scenery of the Grand Canyon and the emotions it stirs in the visitor.

Stewart, M. 2002. *Sedimentary rocks.* Chicago: Heinemann Library.
Summary: This informational book answers questions about the three kinds of rock, how sedimentary rock forms, how rocks are changed by erosion and weathering, how the Grand Canyon formed, and how the Great Sphinx lost its nose. Full-color photographs, diagrams, bold-print vocabulary words, table of contents, glossary, and index are also included.

Reference

Castleman, V. *Erosion.* The Weather Report Series. 2004. Logan, IA: Perfection Learning. "How can water cause changes in rocks?" activity adapted from the activity on page 10. "How can wind cause changes in rocks?" adapted from the activity on page 23.

Name: ______________________________

Grand Canyon

Look carefully at the photograph of the Grand Canyon.

U.S. NATIONAL PARK SERVICE

1 How do you think the Grand Canyon formed?

____

____

____

____

____

____

____

____

____

2 How do you think it has gotten wider and deeper over time?

____

____

____

____

3 How long do you think it took for the Grand Canyon to form?

____

____

____

____

Chapter 19

Name: ______________________________

Wind and Water Checkpoint Lab

Follow the directions below. If your team is working, put the green cup on top. If you have a question, put the red cup on top. If you are finished with a part and you are ready for a check from your teacher, put the red cup on top.

Part A How does water carry rocks and soil?

- Fill a large plastic jar halfway with equal amounts of large and small gravel, sand, and soil.
- Add water to fill up the jar.
- Close the jar, and then take turns shaking the jar for a total of 1 min.
- Set the jar aside for at least 20 min. (you will observe it in Part D).

Part B How can water cause changes in rocks?

- Divide a cup of rocks into two equal piles.
- Put one pile of rocks into a plastic jar, and fill the jar halfway with clear water.
- Close the lid, and take turns shaking the jar for a total of 10 min.
- Pour the mixture through a strainer into a clear container.
- Dump the rocks onto a paper plate.

1 How do the rocks that were shaken in the water compare to the other pile of rocks?

____

2 Examine the water. Is it still clear?

3 Place a coffee filter in the strainer, then *very slowly* pour the water through the coffee filter into another container.

4 Examine the coffee filter. What do you see on it? How does it feel?

____

Checkpoints A and B ☐

Chapter 19

Name: ______________________________

Wind and Water Checkpoint Lab cont.

Part C How can wind cause changes in rocks?

- All team members must have safety goggles covering their eyes before continuing!
- Open a sheet of newspaper in the center of your table.
- Place a paper box lid in the center of the newspaper.
- Pour a cup of sand into one end of the lid.
- Have one student put his or her hand inside the other end of the lid, open palm facing the pile of sand.
- Have someone blow *gently* on the sand and then blow harder until the sand hits the other student's hand.
- Repeat until all team members have felt the sand hitting their hands.

1 How did the sand feel blowing against your hand?

____

- Observe the sand that was blown to the other end of the box and rub it between your fingers.
- Do the same to the sand left in the original pile.

2 Do the textures of the sand feel different? If so, why?

____

____

Checkpoint C ☐

Name: ______________________________

CHAPTER 19

Wind and Water Checkpoint Lab cont.

Part D How does water carry rocks and soil?

1 In the box below, sketch and label materials in the jar from Part A.

2 Now imagine that the water in the jar is flowing down a river. Which type of material would be carried for the longest distance?

____

3 Which type of material would settle to the bottom of the river?

____

- *Very, very slowly* pour the contents of the jar into the high end of the paint tray and observe.

4 What happened to each of the materials in the jar when you poured them out into the paint tray? Which materials were carried with the water?

____

Checkpoint D ☐

Name: ____________________

New Vocabulary List

Word (Draw and Write)	What I Think It Means (Draw and Write)	What It Means (Draw and Write

Name: ________________________________

Grand Canyon
Brochure

Create a travel brochure advertising the Grand Canyon to tourists. Include the following in your brochure:

1 A catchy slogan to grab the attention of the reader.

2 A drawing or photograph of the Grand Canyon.

3 A map showing the location of the Grand Canyon.

4 A definition of weathering, and a description of how weathering contributed to the formation of the Grand Canyon.

5 A definition of erosion, and a description of how erosion contributed to the formation of the Grand Canyon.

6 An explanation of the changes that still occur every day in the Grand Canyon as a result of weathering and erosion.

7 Three reasons tourists should visit the Grand Canyon.

Be creative! Have fun!

Brainstorms:
From Idea to Invention

Description

Learners explore the design process by improving an existing invention; designing and building a drink holder for an airplane seat and communicating their design process; and designing an investigation to evaluate Scotchgard.

Suggested Grade Level: 5–6

Lesson Objectives Connecting to the ***Framework***

Science and Engineering Practices

- Asking questions (for science) and defining problems (for engineering)
- Planning and carrying out investigations
- Constructing explanations (for science) and designing solutions (for engineering)

Disciplinary Core Ideas

ETS1.A: Defining and Delimiting Engineering Problems
ETS1.B: Developing Possible Solutions
ETS1.C: Optimizing the Design Solution

Crosscutting Concepts

- Structure and Function

Featured Picture Books

Title	***Imaginative Inventions***
Author	**Charise Mericle Harper**
Illustrator	**Charise Mericle Harper**
Publisher	**Little, Brown**
Year	**2001**
Genre	**Dual Purpose**
Summary	**The who, what, when, where, and why of roller skates, potato chips, marbles, and pie told in whimsical verse**

Title	***Girls Think of Everything: Stories of Ingenious Inventions by Women***
Author	**Catherine Thimmesh**
Illustrator	**Melissa Sweet**
Publisher	**Sandpiper**
Year	**2002**
Genre	**Narrative Information**
Summary	**How women throughout the ages have responded to situations by inventing various items**

Time Needed

This lesson will take several class periods. Suggested scheduling is as follows:

Day 1: **Engage** with Draw an Inventor and read aloud of *Girls Think of Everything*

Day 2: **Explore** and **Explain** with *Imaginative Inventions* read aloud and Improve an Invention

Day 3: **Explore** and **Explain** with Design a Drink Holder

Day 4: **Elaborate** and **Evaluate** with Evaluate an Invention Checkpoint Lab, and **Evaluate** with Draw an Inventor

Materials

- Optional: Chocolate chip cookies (1 per student)
- Optional: Examples of inventions from *Imaginative Inventions* (Frisbee, eyeglasses, high-heeled shoes, paper bag, piggy bank, etc.)
- Colored pencils
- "Think pads" (sticky notes)

For the Design a Drink Holder Activity

- Bags or trays with the following supplies (1 per pair):
  - 1 m of masking tape
  - 40 plastic straws (not the flexible kind)
  - Scissors
  - Full can of soda
  - Small Styrofoam or plastic bowl
- Timer or clock

For the Evaluate an Invention Checkpoint Lab

- 1 can Scotchgard fabric protector (It takes 24 hours for Scotchgard to dry; for teacher use only)
- Index cards (5 per team)
- A red plastic cup and a green plastic cup with the bottoms taped together (1 per pair)
- White cotton or poly-cotton fabric pretreated by teacher with Scotchgard (5 swatches per pair)
- White cotton or poly-cotton fabric not pretreated with Scotchgard (5 swatches per pair)
- Various substances for staining fabric, such as
  - Mustard
  - Spaghetti sauce
  - Grape juice
  - Tomato juice
- Pipette and cup for each staining substance
- Roll of paper towels

Student Pages

- Draw an Inventor (2 copies per student)
- Imaginative Inventions
- Improve an Invention
- Straighten Up and Fly Right Airline letter
- Design a Drink Holder
- Questions About Your Product Design
- Evaluate an Invention Checkpoint Lab

Background

In today's fast-growing, highly competitive global marketplace, innovative thinking is more important than ever. Teachers must encourage our students' creativity, imagination, and problem-solving skills. Technology involves, among other things, using science to solve problems or meet needs, and students' understanding of technology can be developed by challenging them to design a solution to a problem or invent something to meet a need.

The *design process* in technology is the parallel to inquiry in science. In scientific inquiry, students explore ideas and propose explanations about the natural world, whereas in technological design students identify a problem or need, design a solution, implement a solution, evaluate a product or design, and communicate the design process. In grades 3–5, students can begin to differentiate between science and technology by complementing their scientific investigations with activities that are meant to meet a human need, solve a problem, or develop a product.

In this lesson students design an investigation to evaluate how well a product called Scotchgard works. They also apply the technological design process to the invention of a drink holder for an airplane. Design challenges at this level should include consideration of *constraints*. It is important for students to understand that all technological designs involve constraints, or restrictions. Some constraints are unavoidable, such as the properties of materials, and others limit choices in the design, such as cost, environmental protection, human safety, and aesthetics. Decisions about technological designs almost always involve trade-offs, choices that help in some ways and hurt in others. For example, a choice might be made to use environmentally friendly materials to manufacture a product, but the trade-off might be that the product is more expensive to make. In this lesson students are challenged to build drink holders given the following constraints: a 40-minute time limit, size requirements, and limited materials. They are also asked to identify the constraints faced by the inventors they read about. After learning about technological design and many different inventors and inventions, students should understand that women and men of various backgrounds and with diverse talents, qualities, and motivations contribute to science and technology.

Engage

Draw an Inventor

To determine student preconceptions of gender, social and ethnic backgrounds, talents, and qualities of inventors, ask students to draw what they think an inventor looks like and describe some characteristics of the inventor on the Draw an Inventor student page. Provide colored pencils.

Engage

Read Aloud

Inferring

Show the cover of *Girls Think of Everything,* and introduce the author and illustrator. Ask students to predict what the book is about by looking at the cover. Read pages 8 through 10 of *Girls Think of Everything* about inventor Ruth Wakefield, but instead of the words *chocolate chip cookie,* use *this invention*. Have students use clues from the reading to guess the name of the invention. Students can write down their inferences on sticky note "think pads" while you are reading. Pause periodically to allow students time to write and revise their inferences as they get more clues from the reading.

Then read pages 19 through 22 in *Girls Think of Everything* about Bette Nesmith Graham, but instead of the words *Liquid Paper correction fluid,* use *this invention*. Have students use clues from the text to guess the name of this invention. Again pause periodically to allow students time to write and revise their inferences as they get more clues from the reading.

Finally, read pages 27 through 30 in *Girls Think of Everything* about Ann Moore, leaving out the name of her invention (the Snugli baby pouch). Have students use clues from the text to guess the name of this invention. Again pause periodically to allow students time to write and revise their inferences as they get more clues from the reading.

Discuss the following questions:

? What do all of these inventors have in common? (They are all women, creative people, problem-solvers, etc.)

? Who are some other inventors?

? What is the difference between an invention and a discovery? (An invention is something that is created; a discovery is something that is found for the first time. For example, Ben Franklin *discovered* that lightning is electrical current and *invented* the lightening rod.)

? Have you ever had an idea for an invention?

? What qualities do you think are necessary for a person to be an inventor?

? Do you think inventing a new product would be an easy process? Why or why not?

Explore & Explain

Imaginative Inventions and Improve an Invention

Determining Importance

Introduce the author and illustrator of *Imaginative Inventions.* Tell students to listen for the problem, solution, and name of the invention for each story. Pass out the Imaginative Inventions student page to students, and have them complete it as you read aloud the book to the class. Pause periodically to give them time to complete the student page as you read.

Next pass out the Improve an Invention student page to each student. Explain that instead of coming up with completely new inventions, inventors often think of ways to make old ones better. Have pairs of students choose an invention from the book that they would like to improve on. Then have them complete the Improve an Invention student page. If you like, have samples of some of the inventions in the book—such as a Frisbee, eyeglasses, or a paper bag—available for students to look at while they are completing the student page. Then have students present their advertisements for their improved inventions, explain their improvement process, and tell why the improvement would make the invention more useful and/or more fun.

Explore & Explain

Design a Drink Holder

Tell students you have been contacted by the CEO of a major airline. She would like the students to design a device to help solve a problem for the airline. Give each team of students a copy of the letter from Straighten Up and Fly Right Airline, and read it aloud to the class.

Ask each team to design and build an imaginary product—a drink holder—given three constraints: time, materials, and size. Tell them they will have only 40 min. to design and build the product. Pass out the Design a Drink Holder student page and the following materials to each pair, but don't let them begin yet.

- 1 m of masking tape
- 40 plastic straws (not the flexible kind)
- Scissors
- Full can of soda
- Small Styrofoam or plastic bowl

Tell students that they must complete the Design a Drink Holder student page before they can begin building. As soon as everyone has the student page and materials, set the timer for 40 min. and announce that it is time to begin. Circulate as teams work, asking questions and informally assessing their progress toward the goal.

When the 40 min. are up, instruct students to stop building and fill out the Questions About Your Product Design student page. Discuss the following questions from the student page.

? Was your product effective? How do you know?

? What challenges did you face during the design process?

? What improvements would you make if you had more time and more materials?

Explain to students that perfectly designed solutions do not exist. All technological solu-

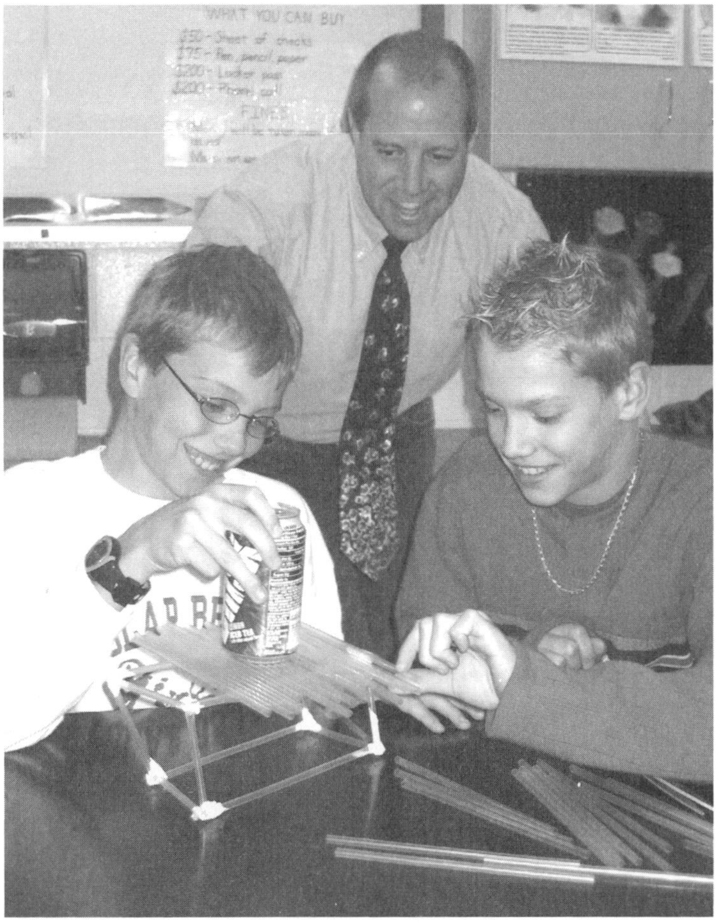

Students in Mr. Wintz's class build a drink holder for an airline tray tions have trade-offs, such as safety, cost, efficiency, and appearance. Inventors almost always have *constraints*. Constraints limit choices in technological design, for example, cost, time, and materials needed. Ask

- ? What were the trade-offs you were forced to make while designing the drink holder? (The materials were cheap, but the trade-off was a weak and unattractive product. We worked quickly, but the trade-off was a shoddy product.)
- ? What were the constraints you dealt with while designing the drink holder? (40 min. time limit, size requirements, and limited materials)

Elaborate & Evaluate

Evaluate an Invention Checkpoint Lab

In advance, prepare all of the materials necessary for the Evaluate an Invention Checkpoint Lab. See "Teaching Science Through Inquiry," Chapter 3, for a list of tips for managing a checkpoint lab.

Determining Importance

Ask students to listen for the constraints that inventor Patsy O. Sherman faced when developing Scotchgard as you read pages 23 through 26 in *Girls Think of Everything*.

- ? What constraints did Patsy O. Sherman have to deal with when inventing Scotchgard? (She was not allowed in the textile mills because she was a woman. She had to figure out a way to make it economical so people would be willing to pay for it. She had to come up with a protector for new permanent press fabrics, something that would repel stains *and* release them when they are washed.)

In advance, set out the materials students will need to test fabrics treated with Scotchgard. Then tell students they are going to have a chance to try out and evaluate Patsy O. Sherman's invention. Pass out the Evaluate an Invention Checkpoint Lab. Have students work in pairs. They put the green cup on top if their team is working. They put the red cup on top if their team has a question or if they are ready for a check mark. Both members of the group are responsible for recording data and writing responses.

Have the students complete the checkpoint lab, working at their own paces. While they are working, observe and listen to them interact. Before you give a team a check mark or stamp so they can move ahead in the lab, evaluate their work by asking probing questions of both members of the team. As a final evaluation, you can assess each student's checkpoint lab.

Evaluate

Draw an Inventor

To determine whether student preconceptions of gender, talents, qualities, and social and ethnic backgrounds of inventors have changed, ask students to again draw what they think an inventor looks like. Have them describe some characteristics of the inventor on another Draw an Inventor student page. Provide colored pencils.

Engage students in a discussion of how their first drawings compare to their second drawings. Survey students to find out how many drew women, men, or minorities. (See *Brainstorm!* and *Great Black Heroes: Five Notable Inventors* in the "More Books to Read" section at the end of this lesson for more stories about child inventors of many backgrounds.)

Inquiry Place

Have students keep an Inventor's Journal for one week. They should keep their journals with them at all times to record any ideas and designs that come to them during the week. Remind students that every time they write in their journals, they should initial, date, and have a witness sign it. A witness can be a parent or a friend. Tell students the witness signatures provide proof that their ideas are original. Guide students with the following questions:

- ? What problems do you observe other people having around their homes, jobs, or neighborhoods that could be solved by an invention?
- ? If you could invent something to make your life easier, what would you invent?
- ? What are your constraints?

Students can present their new product ideas and designs at a poster session.

Some other inquiries for students to try include

- ? Which brand of paper towel is the strongest? The most absorbent?
- ? Which brand of diaper holds the most liquid?
- ? Which detergent cleans stains the best?

Have students select a question to investigate as a class, or groups of students can vote on the questions they want to investigate as teams. After they make their predictions, they can design an experiment to test their predictions. Students can present their findings at a poster session.

More Books to Read

Barretta, G. 2008. *Now & Ben: The modern inventions of Benjamin Franklin.* New York: Square Fish.
Summary: Each left-hand page in this clever book describes one of Franklin's inventions as we know it today; the opposite page goes back in time to reveal how Franklin conceived of and developed it.

Crowther, R. 2009. *Robert Crowther's pop-up house of inventions: Hundreds of fabulous facts about your home.* Somerville, MA: Candlewick Press.
Summary: From this elaborate pop-up book, readers learn hundreds of fun facts about everyday inventions.

Foltz Jones, C. 1994. *Mistakes that worked.* New York: Doubleday.
Summary: Cartoons illustrate the stories behind serendipitous inventions such as Silly Putty, Coca-Cola, Popsicles, penicillin, and bricks.

Hudson, W. 1995. *Great black heroes: Five notable inventors.* New York: Cartwheel Press.
Summary: The author describes the achievements of five African American inventors: Elijah McCoy (machinery oiling equipment), Madame C. J. Walker (hair products), Granville Woods (train signal system), Garrett Morgan (traffic signals), and Jan Matzeliger (shoe lasting machine).

Perry, A. 2003. *Here's what you do when you can't find your shoe (Ingenius inventions for pesky problems).* New York: Atheneum.
Summary: This collection of clever poems introduces imaginary inventions to make life easier, such as "The Sure-Footed Shoe Finder," a device with a "powerful Foot-Odor-Sensitive Vent" that "tracks down your sneaker by matching its scent." Humorous pen-and-ink cartoons accompany each selection.

Tucker, T. 1998. *Brainstorm! The stories of twenty American kid inventors.* New York: Sunburst.
Summary: This inspiring book features young inventors from colonial to modern times. Black-and-white photographs and pen-and-ink drawings accompany the stories describing the invention of earmuffs, the Popsicle, the resealable cereal box, and many more.

Name: ______________________________

Draw an Inventor

Draw what you think an inventor looks like in the box below:

Describe some characteristics of the inventor:

____

____

____

Name: ______________________________

Imaginative Inventions

Problem or Need	Solution	Name of Invention
Fried potatoes too thick	Cut fries up super thin	Potato chips

Name: ______________________________

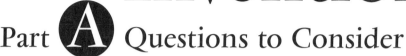

Improve an Invention

Part A Questions to Consider

1 Choose an invention from the book *Imaginative Inventions* that you would like to improve upon.

____

2 What was the original purpose for this invention?

____

3 What could you do to make this invention more useful or more fun?

____

____

4 What parts of the original invention will you keep?

____

____

5 How could you test the product to make sure it works?

____

____

6 What will you call your new product?

____

Part B Advertise Your Idea

Create an advertisement for your new product. Be sure to include a drawing of it and how it will be more useful and/or more fun than the original.

Straighten Up and Fly Right Airline

Dear Inventors,

We really need your help. Straighten Up and Fly Right Airline is downsizing the cabin areas on its airplanes. We are trying to accommodate four passengers in a row instead of two. This will result in a size reduction of the pull-down serving trays fastened to seat backs. The reduced tray size has become problematic because passengers will no longer have space for the signature in-flight meal, Sloppy Joe Soup and 7-Upchuck Cola. To solve this problem, Straighten Up and Fly Right Airline would like to provide passengers with a drink holder to go on each serving tray.

These are the product specifications:

1. The device must support a full 12 oz. can of soda above a 30 cm × 30 cm tray.
2. You must be able to slide a soup bowl underneath the drink holder.
3. The device must be assembled by your design team in 40 min. or less.

We have enclosed the supplies you can use to create your version of the drink holder. Please use only these supplies. We cannot afford any additional supplies at this time. Send your drink holder invention to us as soon as possible. Please also send the "Design a Drink Holder" sheet and the "Questions About Your Product Design" page along with your finished drink holder.

Sincerely,

Ms. Penny Pincher

Ms. Penny Pincher, CEO

Straighten Up and Fly Right Airline

Design a Drink Holder

Names of Inventors:

____

Name of Product:

____

Diagram of the Product:
(Please label with dimensions in centimeters and identify where the soda can will fit.)

Straighten Up and Fly Right Airline

Questions About Your Product Design

Names of Inventors: ____

____

Name of Product: ____

____

1 Was your product effective? How do you know? ____________________

____

2 What challenges did you face during the design process? __________

____

____

____

____

3 What improvements would you make if you had more time and more materials? ____

____

____

____

____

Name: ______________________________

Evaluate an Invention
Checkpoint Lab

You just heard about how Patsy Sherman invented Scotchgard. Let's find out if it works!

Part A Prepare the Product for Testing

1 Get five index cards and label each one with "No Scotchgard" on one half and "Scotchgard" on the other half.

2 Ask your teacher for five swatches of fabric *not* treated with Scotchgard. Staple one piece of untreated fabric onto the "No Scotchgard" half of each index card.

3 Ask your teacher for five swatches of fabric treated with Scotchgard. Staple one piece of treated fabric onto the "Scotchgard" half of each index card.

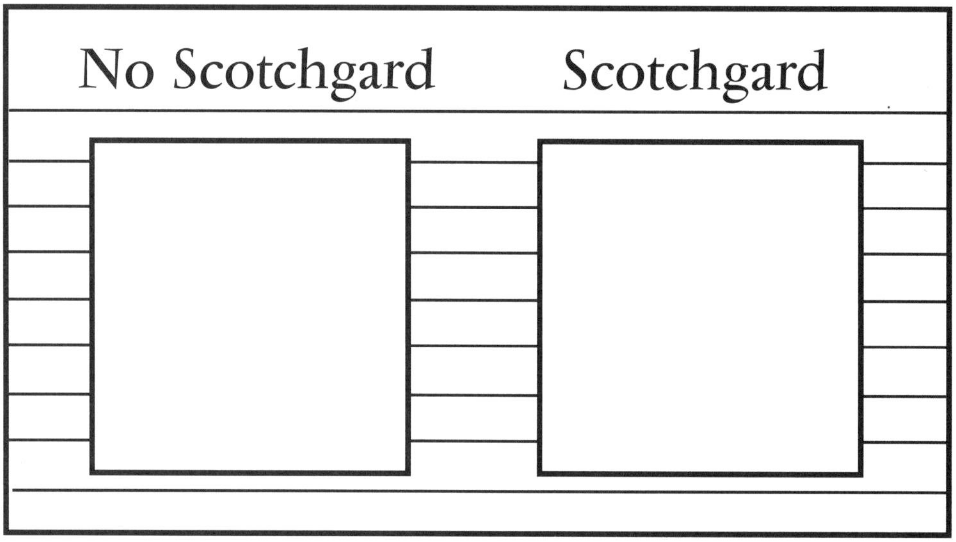

Now you are ready to design your experiment!

Checkpoint A ☐

Name: ______________________________

Evaluate an Invention

Checkpoint Lab cont.

Part B Design a Procedure

1 How will you keep the test fair? (What things will you need to keep the same?)

____

____

2 What procedure will you use to determine if Scotchgard is an effective product? List the steps of your procedure below.

____

____

____

____

3 Draw a data table below to help you organize your observations.

Checkpoint B ☐

Name: ______________________________

Evaluate an Invention

Checkpoint Lab cont.

Part C Evaluate the Invention

When evaluating the overall effectiveness of an invention, there are many things to consider. Write a summary of your product test, and give your evaluation of Scotchgard. Continue on the back of this page if you need more room to write. Use the following questions to guide you:

- How did you keep the test "fair"?
- How well did the product work? How do you know? (Use the data from your experiment to answer this one.)
- How does it fulfill a consumer's needs or desires?
- What is the price? Is it affordable?
- Is it safe for the consumer and the environment? (Read the label.)
- What would you do differently if you were going to repeat your experiment? Why?

____

____

____

____

____

____

____

____

Checkpoint C ☐

Bugs!

Description

Learners collect invertebrates for observation, determine which invertebrates are insects and which are noninsects, explore insect structures and functions, ask questions about insects, learn the differences between bugs and other insects, and use a key to identify a variety of invertebrates.

Suggested Grade Levels: 3–5

Lesson Objectives Connecting to the *Framework*

Science and Engineering Practices

- Constructing explanations (for science) and designing solutions (for engineering)
- Obtaining, evaluating, and communicating information

Disciplinary Core Ideas

LS1.A: Structure and Function

Crosscutting Concepts

- Structure and Function

Featured Picture Books

Title	***The Perfect Pet***	***Bugs Are Insects***	***Ant, Ant, Ant! (An Insect Chant)***
Author	**Margie Palatini**	**Anne Rockwell**	**April Pulley Sayre**
Illustrator	**Bruce Whatley**	**Steve Jenkins**	**Trip Park**
Publisher	**Katherine Tegen Books**	**HarperCollins**	**NorthWord Books for Young Readers**
Year	**2009**	**2001**	**2005**
Genre	**Story**	**Nonnarrative Information**	**Poetry**
Summary	**Elizabeth really wants a pet, but her parents do not. After all of her suggestions are vetoed, she finds just the right one: an insect.**	**The main differences between insects and arachnids are explained, as well as what makes a bug a bug.**	**An ant and 59 other American insects appear in a catchy chant. Although the bright, digitally produced caricatures are not always scientifically accurate, this book is a fun survey of insect names.**

Time Needed

This lesson will take several class periods. Suggested scheduling is as follows:

Day 1: **Engage** with *The Perfect Pet* read aloud and *The Perfect Pet* Anticipation Guide

Day 2: **Explore** with Collect a "Pet" Invertebrate

Day 3: **Explain** with Card Sort and *Bugs Are Insects*

Day 4: **Elaborate** with Invertebrate Dichotomous Key

Day 5: **Evaluate** with *The Perfect Pet* Anticipation Guide (post), *Ant, Ant, Ant! (An Insect Chant!),* and Entomology Convention poster project

Day 6 and beyond: Continue insect research and hold Entomology Convention

Materials
(per pair)

- Aquarium nets for collecting small invertebrates (2 in. to 6 in. size)
- Clear Lucite magnifying "Bug Box" (1 in. or 1.5 in. cubes) or petri dishes with lids
- Hand lenses
- Large insect sweep net (optional)
- Centimeter rulers
- Poster board
- Markers
- Safety glasses or goggles

Bug Boxes available from

www.Acornnaturalists.com
www.insectlore.com
www.Nature-Watch.com

Student Pages

- *The Perfect Pet* Anticipation Guide
- My "Pet" Invertebrate
- Invertebrate Sorting Cards
- Invertebrate Dichotomous Key
- Insect Poster Rubric

Background

Insects are a remarkable group of animals and a source of delight (and sometimes apprehension) for many children. Not only do insects make interesting specimens to use for exploring animal structures and functions, but collecting, observing, sharing discoveries, and asking questions about insects can help students develop an understanding of what science is and how scientists do their jobs. Learning to treat insects gently during collection and observation can also help students develop a sense of responsibility toward living things.

Animals are living things that eat other living or once-living things and digest food inside their bodies. Most animals are motile, meaning they can move spontaneously. The animal kingdom can be divided into two broad categories: *vertebrates,* which are animals with backbones, and *invertebrates,* which are animals without backbones. Invertebrates make up more than 95% of all animal species on Earth! Some main groups, or *phyla,* of invertebrates (generally classified by their body plans) are mollusks, sponges, segmented worms, and arthropods. *Arthropods* have exoskeletons, segmented bodies, and at least three pairs of legs. This group includes arachnids (e.g., spiders and scorpions), crustaceans (e.g., crabs and lobsters), and insects.

Insects can be classified into about 28 main subdivisions, called *orders.* This number varies depending on whom you ask because some insect taxonomists organize the insects according to physical traits, while others use evolutionary links. The largest insect order by far is Coleoptera—the *beetles.* Beetles have a distinctive line down the middle of their backs where their hard outer wings meet. Some people call all insects "bugs," but this label is not correct. True bugs belong to their own insect order, Hemiptera. They are characterized by beaklike mouths that are designed for piercing and sucking. Many of the true bugs also have triangular shapes on their backs made by their overlapping wings. See Figure 21.1.

Some examples of true bugs are stinkbugs, bedbugs, and water striders. Ladybugs and lightning bugs are actually beetles. *Entomologists* (scientists who study insects) have identified more than one million different *species,* or distinct groups, of insects, which is more than twice the number of all other animals combined! Some entomologists believe there may be millions more yet to be discovered.

In this lesson, students go on a hike to collect and observe live invertebrate specimens. They find out how to tell if an invertebrate is an insect or not after learning that all insects share the following structures (see Figure 21.2): *exoskeletons,* three main body parts (*head, thorax, abdomen*), three pairs of *legs* (attached to the thorax), usually two pairs of *wings,* and usually one pair of *antennae.* The common misconception that insects are not animals is addressed, and students learn to treat all animals, no matter how small, with respect. They find out that a bug is a special type of insect, and they learn how to use a dichotomous key to identify a variety of invertebrates. Finally, they share their research about an insect of their choice with other student entomologists at an Entomology Convention, similar to gatherings that real-world scientists hold.

Here is an example of how one insect, the Convergent Ladybird Beetle (a type of ladybug), is classified:

Kingdom: Animalia (animal)
Phylum: Arthropoda (arthropods)
Class: Insecta (insects)
Order: Coleoptera (beetles)
Family: Coccinellidae
Genus: *Hippodamia*
Species: *convergens*

Figure 21.1. Stinkbug

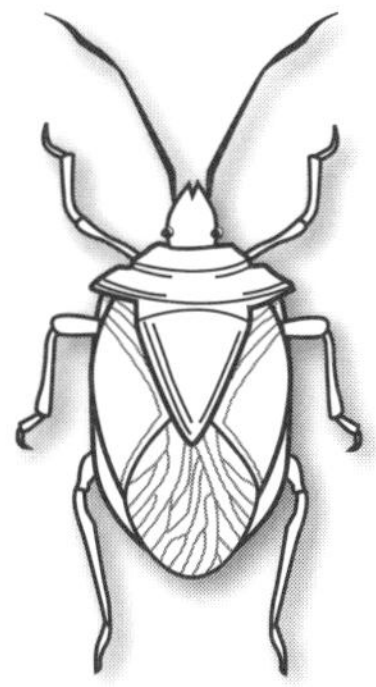

Figure 21.2. Insect anatomy

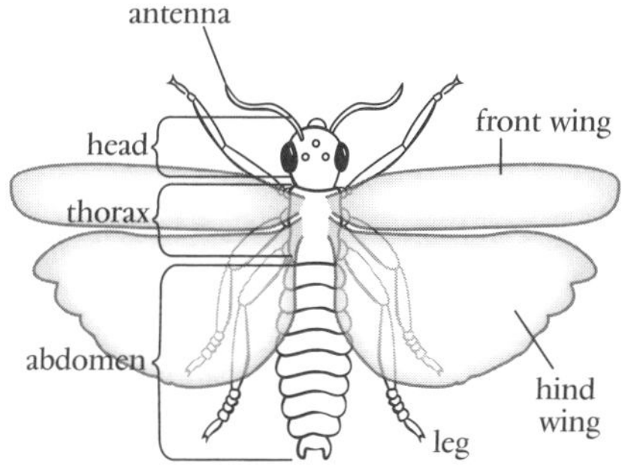

engage

Making Connections

Turn and Talk

Show the cover of the book *The Perfect Pet,* and introduce the author and illustrator. Ask students to turn and talk with a partner about what they think the perfect pet would be and why. Then read the book aloud. After reading, ask

- ? Is this book fiction or nonfiction? How do you know? (The illustrations look like cartoons; the bug has a human face; it has none of the features of nonfiction, etc.)
- ? Why does Elizabeth think Doug is the perfect pet? (He's not big or loud; he doesn't jump on furniture, scratch, or shed; and he doesn't eat much.)
- ? What is Doug? (a bug)
- ? What's a bug? (Answers will vary, but some students will say a bug is an insect.)

The Perfect Pet Anticipation Guide

Pass out *The Perfect Pet* Anticipation Guide. This set of pre- and post-questions can be used to activate and assess students' prior knowledge about bugs and other insects and uncover any misconceptions they may have. It can also motivate students to explore and read about insects to find out the answers to the questions. Have each student make their "best guess" to answer the before questions, then conduct a class discussion about the students' responses. Tell them that they will be learning the answers to those questions and more over the next several class periods. Collect the anticipation guides to find out what the students know or misunderstand about insects, and keep them until the Evaluate portion of the lesson. Students will fill out the after portion at that time.

Next tell students that they will be going on an expedition the following day to collect some real live "perfect pets." They will be looking for invertebrates—small animals without backbones. Explain that a backbone is a column of bones along the center of an animal's back, also called a spine. Have students feel their own backbones. Explain that scientists sort all animals into two groups, those with backbones (vertebrates) and those without backbones (invertebrates). Insects, snails, pill bugs, spiders, and millipedes are examples of invertebrates.

Tell students they will be collecting only invertebrates that are small enough to fit in a clear Lucite "bug box" (show them a bug box). They will keep their pets long enough to draw pictures and make observations, then release the pets where they were found. Explain that although many people keep invertebrates as pets, it is important to know the needs and requirements of any animal before keeping it as a pet. That is why they will be letting the animals go instead of keeping them. They will be only temporary "pets"—kept just long enough to observe in the classroom.

explore

Collect a "Pet" Invertebrate

In advance, locate a spot on the school grounds where students are likely to find a variety of invertebrates. Before going outside, discuss why it is important to treat all animals humanely, no matter how small they are. (See *Hey Little Ant* in More Books to Read for more on this topic.) Give each pair of students an aquarium net and a clear Lucite bug box. (You may want to pair up students who are apprehensive about catching invertebrates with those who aren't.)

Model how to use an aquarium net to gently capture an animal and then transfer it to a bug box without hurting it. You may want to take a large insect sweep net with you on the walk in case some students have trouble catching their pets. A sweep net is used either by sweeping the net back and forth rapidly in

SAFETY

1. Students should wear closed-toe shoes or sneakers, long pants, long-sleeve shirts, hats, sunglasses, sunscreen, and safety glasses or goggles.
2. Caution students against collecting ticks, mosquitoes, stinging insects, and other potentially hazardous insects.
3. Check with the school nurse regarding student medical issues (e.g., allergies to bee stings) and how to deal with them.
4. Find out whether outdoor areas have been treated with pesticides, fungicides, or any other toxins and avoid any such areas.
5. Caution students against poisonous plants such as poison ivy or poison sumac.
6. Bring some form of communication, such as a cell phone or two-way radio, in case of emergencies.
7. Inform parents, in writing, of the planned field trip, any potential hazards, and the safety precautions being taken.
8. Have students wash their hands with soap and water upon completing the activity.

the grass or by pulling the net through the grass while running. When finished, you can shake the invertebrates down to the bottom of the net so students can transfer them to their bug boxes. Caution students against trying to capture stinging or biting invertebrates, such as ticks, bees, or spiders, or animals that might be too large to fit safely into the box.

Remind students that after the animals are gently collected and carefully observed, they will be released where they were found and all rocks or logs will be returned to their original position. Then take the class outside to find their temporary "pets." During the expedition, instruct students to walk quietly so they can listen for animal sounds: buzzing bees, chirping crickets, singing cicadas, and so on.

After each pair of students has collected a specimen, check to be sure the specimens are safe to work with (e.g., no ticks or bees). Then return to the classroom and have them place the bug boxes on their desks. Pass out the My "Pet" Invertebrate student page and have students begin observing, drawing, and describing their pets. Encourage students to add labels to their drawings. To get the best close-up view of an invertebrate, hold a hand lens close to one eye and bring the animal in the bug box into focus. Students can use centimeter rulers to make approximate measurements of length.

OBSERVING AN INVERTEBRATE

Next have them write an inference about what they think their animal is and a list of questions they have about it. After they finish, have them look at some of the other specimens that were collected and make comparisons.

Finally, go back outside and have students gently release the animals where they were found. Return to the classroom and discuss the drawings, observations, and questions on the My "Pet" Invertebrate page. Tell them that on the following day, they will learn more about some of the "pets" they have just observed.

Sorting the cards

explain

Open Sort

Make several sets of the Invertebrate Sorting Cards. Place each set in an envelope. Have pairs or teams of students sort the cards into groups, any way they like (things that fly/don't fly, legs/no legs, and so on). Walk around the room and ask students to justify how they sorted their cards. Tell them that they will get another chance to sort them after you read a nonfiction book aloud.

Determining Importance

Read the title, author, and illustrator and show the cover of *Bugs Are Insects*. Tell students that the information in this book might help them sort their cards, as well as answer some of the questions from *The Perfect Pet* Anticipation Guide. As you read the book, ask students to signal ("touch your ear") when they hear an answer to the questions below, then stop to discuss each one:

- ? How many legs does an insect have? (six, page 7)
- ? An insect's body is divided into three main parts. What are they? (head, thorax, and abdomen, page 14)
- ? Is a bug an insect? (Yes, explain that many people tend to call all insects bugs, but technically speaking, a "true bug" is a special kind of insect with a mouth like a beak and a head that forms a triangle, page 19.)
- ? Is an insect an animal? (yes, page 30)

Explain that an insect is an animal because it can move on its own and gets food by eating other living or once-living things. Note that there are a few animals that can't move from place to place, such as sponges and barnacles, but all animals need to eat other things for food. In contrast, a plant can't move from place to place and makes its own food using sunlight. Sometimes people think only vertebrates (animals with backbones, such as mammals, fish, birds, reptiles, and amphibians) are animals, but invertebrates (animals without backbones) are animals too. Insects are invertebrates.

Then ask

- ? Are humans animals? Why? (Yes, they can move and they eat other living things.)
- ? Are humans vertebrates? Why? (Yes, they have backbones; have students feel their backbones.)

Closed Sort

Tell students that if they were to go just about anywhere on Earth and look for animals, most of the animals they would find would be insects. There are more kinds of insects than any other animal in the world! The study of insects is called *entomology*. Have each pair or team re-sort their cards into two groups: insect and noninsect. Remind students to count the legs! Tell them that later they will learn how to use a key to identify all of the animals on the sorting cards. Answers are below:

INSECTS	NONINSECTS
B	A
C	D
E	H
F	I
G	L
J	
K	

After collecting the sorting cards for later use, generate a list on the board of the characteristics that adult insects have in common:

- Hard external skeleton (exoskeleton)
- Three main body parts (head, thorax, and abdomen)
- Six legs (attached to the thorax)
- Two pairs of wings, often
- One pair of antennae, often

Ask the following questions:

- Do all baby insects have these characteristics too? (not always)
- Can you think of a baby insect that doesn't share all of these characteristics? (e.g., caterpillars, mealworm larvae, etc.)

Explain that baby insects sometimes look very different from their parents, sometimes don't have three distinct body parts (caterpillars, for example), and sometimes have more than six legs. However, all adult insects have an exoskeleton, head, thorax, abdomen, and at least six legs. Note that some insects, such as

LABELING INSECT STRUCTURES

fleas and ants, have no wings; flies have only one pair of wings.

Then describe a "structure" as a body part and how all animals have specialized structures to help them survive in their environment. Make a simple drawing of an insect on the board, and have the class help label the structures (see Figure 21.2, p. 309). With input from the class, make a T-chart like the one below and discuss the various functions of insect structures.

Next ask the students

? Why do you think the book we read is called *Bugs Are Insects*? (Bugs are a type of insect.)

Sample T-Chart

Insect Structures	Functions
Exoskeleton	Support, protection, camouflage, warning coloration
Legs	Jumping, paddling, carrying pollen, making sound, grooming, catching prey
Mouth	Sucking, piercing, biting, chewing
Antennae	Sensing
Wings	Flying

- Could it be called "Insects Are Bugs"? (No, not all insects are bugs.)
- What makes a bug a bug? (A "true bug" is an insect with a mouth like a beak and a head that forms a triangle.)

Add that many true bugs also have wings that overlap and fold flat over their bodies, forming a triangle shape on their backs. Beetles, on the other hand, have wings that make a straight line down their backs when closed.

Elaborate

Invertebrate Dichotomous Key

Tell students there are millions of different kinds of invertebrates in the world. They may wonder how scientists keep track of them all. Introduce a dichotomous key as a special tool that scientists use to identify things in nature. These keys are most often used for identifying things in nature, such as trees, flowers, seashells, or animals. Pass out the Invertebrate Dichotomous Key. Explain that the word *dichotomous* means to divide into two parts. A dichotomous key is a series of statements about an organism's characteristics. It has two choices at every step. You keep following the key, deciding between the two choices at each step, until you can identify the organism being studied.

Tell students they will use the key to identify the animals on the invertebrate cards that they sorted earlier. Pass out the envelopes containing the Invertebrate Sorting Cards. Groups of students can share card sets, but students should work in pairs or on their own. Tell students that this key will work only for the animals pictured on the cards. Direct students to the diagram of the insect at the top of the page, and tell them that they can refer to the diagram to help them use the key. Then model how to use the key using Invertebrate A (the easiest one to identify!). Tell them to always start at number 1 and always read both choices at each step (even if the first choice seems to be a logical answer). Talk through each step of the key together, until they are able to identify Invertebrate A as an earthworm. Then have students use the key to identify the remaining invertebrates and write their answers at the bottom of the key. Correct answers are below:

A. Earthworm	G. True bug
B. True fly	H. Scorpion
C. Dragonfly	I. Centipede
D. Spider	J. Wasp
E. Silverfish	K. Earwig
F. Beetle	L. Tick

Next show the class some pictures of Doug the "bug" from *The Perfect Pet.* Ask

- Do you think Doug is really a bug? Why or why not? (No, he is a beetle, because it looks like his wings meet in the center of his back, forming a straight line.)

Evaluate

My "Pet" Invertebrate

Next have students revisit their My "Pet" Invertebrate student pages and think about the animals they collected for observation. Ask

- Was it an insect? (Answers will vary.)
- Why or why not? (All insects have six legs.)
- If it was an insect, was it a beetle? Was it a bug? How do you know? (Beetles have a straight line down their backs where their wings meet. Bugs have a triangular shape on their backs where their wings overlap.)

Anticipation Guide (After)

Then have students fill out the after column on *The Perfect Pet* Anticipation Guide. Collect the anticipation guides to assess your students' progress and determine if they have any remaining misconceptions about insects. Answers are

1 six
2 head, thorax, abdomen labeled correctly
3 yes
4 yes, because they can move and they eat other living things

Ant, Ant, Ant! (An Insect Chant)

Before reading this book aloud, you may want to practice! Introduce the author and illustrator of *Ant, Ant, Ant! (An Insect Chant)*. Tell students that April Pulley Sayre wrote the book because she likes learning about all kinds of animals, and she really likes to make up chants. A chant is a rhythmic speaking or singing of words or sounds. The artist, Trip Park, wanted to make the illustrations interesting and humorous. As a result, the pictures in the book may not be quite true to life. As you read, have students look for any insect structures or behaviors that are not drawn accurately. Read the book a little slowly the first time through, so students have a chance to study the illustrations. After reading, ask

? Did you notice any insect structures that are not scientifically accurate? (The two-spotted stinkbug has a nose; the cockroach and slug caterpillar have teeth and tongues; the dragonfly has lips; the chrysalis has a zipper; and so on.)
? Did you notice any insect behaviors that were not scientifically accurate? (The ant is changing the firefly's bulb; the conehead is holding toilet paper for the dung beetle who is reading a book; the thrip is water-skiing; and so on.)
? What things in the book ARE scientifically accurate? (All of the adult insects have six legs; all of the insect names are real insect names; the insects have antennae; the earwig has pincers; the butterflies' wings look realistic; and so on.)

Author April Pulley Sayre reading aloud

Finally, ask students to recall their favorite insects from the book as you read it aloud a second time (only faster!). The faster you read it, the more fun it is. More information about each insect is located at the back of the book. Tell students that they are going to have a chance to learn a lot more about their favorite insects!

Entomology Convention

Announce to the class that you are going to have an "Entomology Convention," where the students will present poster projects on insects. Explain that entomologists really do meet this way to share poster projects. For example, each year the Entomological Society of America has a four-day event when thousands of entomologists and professionals from related fields gather from around the world

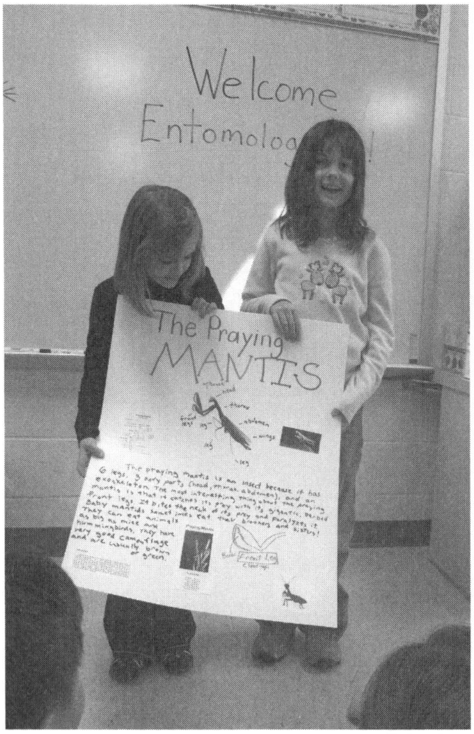

PRESENTING AT AN ENTOMOLOGY CONVENTION

to exchange scientific information and ideas through poster presentations, workshops, and discussions (see *www.entsoc.org*). Entomologists also gather every four years to share scientific posters at the International Congress of Entomology (see *www.ice2008.org.za*). Tell students they may choose any insect they wish for their poster. They may want to research an insect they found during the Collect a "Pet" Invertebrate walk, an insect featured in *Ant! Ant! Ant! (An Insect Chant)*, or any other insect that interests them. Remind students that there are more kinds of insects on Earth than kinds of any other animal, so they have a lot of choices!

Provide a variety of resources for students to use in their research, such as nonfiction books, insect guides such as the *Peterson First Guide to Insects of North America* (see More Books to Read), and websites. You may want to invite experts such as entomologists, biologists, agriculturalists, park naturalists, beekeepers, hobbyists, or even exterminators to talk to your class about insects. Once students have chosen their insects for study, have them use the Insect Poster Rubric as a guide for their projects. Some students may choose to build three-dimensional models of their insects instead of drawing them. When the projects are finished, invite other classrooms to the convention. Have students stationed at their posters to discuss them with visitors. You may want to have visiting students jot down questions or comments on cards or sticky notes to leave at each poster. Evaluate the projects using the Insect Poster Rubric.

Inquiry Place

Have students brainstorm questions about insects, such as

- ? Which invertebrates are more common in your school yard, insects or noninsects? Count and compare!
- ? Do pill bugs prefer light or dark? Damp or dry? Test it!
- ? Does your state have an official state insect? Research it!
- ? How do honeybees, ants, or other insects communicate with one another? Research it!

Then have students select a question to investigate, or have groups of students vote on the question they want to investigate as a team. Students can present their findings at a poster session or gallery walk.

Websites

The Bug Club
www.amentsoc.org/bug-club
The Amateur Entomologists' Society is the UK's leading organization for people interested in insects. The AES website includes the Bug Club for kids, which offers caresheets for keeping insects as well as a fun and games section.

Bugbios
www.insects.org
This website dedicated to the "shameless promotion of insect appreciation" includes a collection of stunning insect photography combined with informative descriptions.

Bugwise: All About Invertebrates
www.bugwise.net/invertebrates
This website from the Australian Museum includes an excellent guide to invertebrates.

University of Kentucky Entomology for Kids and Teachers
www.ca.uky.edu/entomology/dept/youth.asp
This website includes information on common insects, as well as a section on edible insects and links to the "Wee Beasties" entomology newsletter.

More Books to Read

Aloian, M., and B. Kalman. 2005. *Insect life cycles*. New York: Crabtree.
Summary: This nonfiction book explores the life cycles of a variety of insects in an engaging, fact-filled format. It includes full-color photographs, table of contents, bold-print words, captions, and a glossary.

Florian, D. 2002. *Insectlopedia*. Orlando, FL: Voyager Books.
Summary: Contains 21 delightful poems about insects such as crickets, termites, and mayflies. Watercolor collage illustrations are the perfect complements to Florian's whimsical poems.

Froman, N. 2009. *What's that bug? Everyday insects and their really cool cousins*. Toronto: Madison Press Books.
Summary: Large, bright, detailed paintings will attract readers to this overview of nine selected insect orders. Within each order, several common and exotic species are highlighted, including scientific names and a brief overview of major characteristics.

Hoose, P., and H. Hoose. *Hey little ant*. 2004. Berkeley, CA: Tricycle Press.
Summary: In 1992, Phillip Hoose and his daughter Hannah, then nine, wrote a musical conversation between an ant about to get flattened and the child about to squish it. It ended with the question "What do you think that kid should do?" Their popular recording of the song "Hey Little Ant" led to the story's publication as a children's picture book. Illustrated with brightly colored cartoons by Debbie Tilley, the book's message is clear: Respect all creatures and their right to live.

Leahy, C. 1998. *Peterson first guide to insects of North America*. New York: Houghton Mifflin Harcourt.
Summary: This condensed version of the famous *Peterson Field Guide* makes insect identification simple for beginning naturalists.

Parker, N. W., and J. R. Wright. 1988. *Bugs*. New York: Greenwillow Books.
Summary: Twelve insects and four other invertebrates are described in lively couplets, illustrations, and diagrams. Although the term "bug" is loosely applied to all invertebrates in the couplets, the diagrams and descriptions on the right-hand pages are detailed and scientifically accurate.

Chapter 21

Name: ______________________________

The Perfect Pet

Anticipation Guide

In the book *The Perfect Pet,* Elizabeth thinks "Doug the bug" is the perfect pet. Show what you know about bugs by filling in the BEFORE chart below. Later, you will fill out the AFTER chart.

Before

1 How many legs does an insect have? ____

2 Draw an insect and label its three main body parts in the space below.

3 Is a bug an insect? __________

4 Is an insect an animal? Why or why not?

____

____

____

After

1 How many legs does an insect have? ____

2 Draw an insect and label its three main body parts in the space below.

3 Is a bug an insect? __________

4 Is an insect an animal? Why or why not?

____

____

____

Name: ______________________________

My "Pet" Invertebrate

1 Drawing

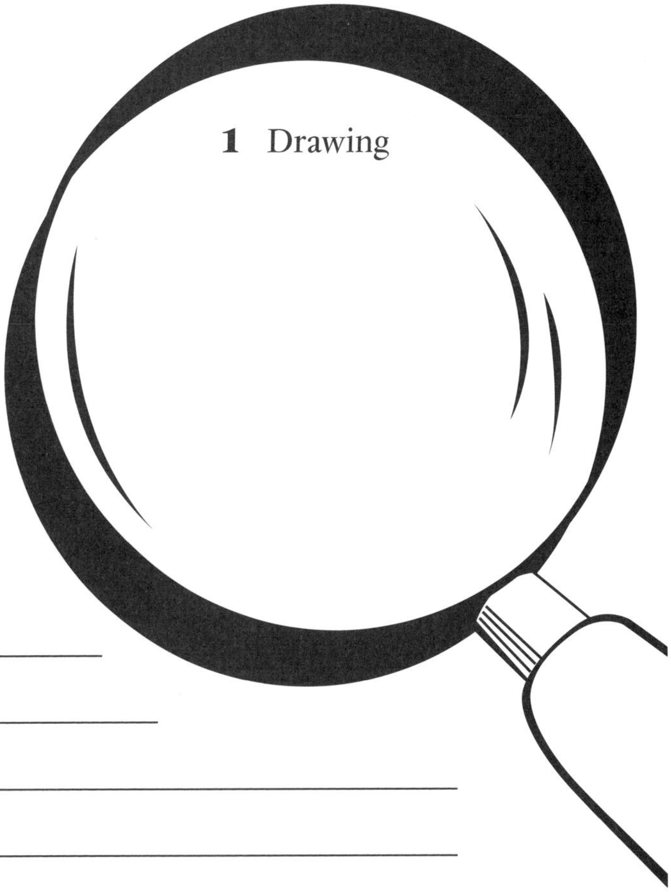

2 This is what my pet looks like: ___________

____

____

____

3 This is where I found my pet: ______________________________

4 My pet has ________ legs.

5 My pet has ________ wings.

6 My pet is about ________ cm long.

7 I think my pet is a ______________________________.

8 This is what I am wondering about my pet: ____________________

____

____

____

CHAPTER 21

Invertebrate
Sorting Cards

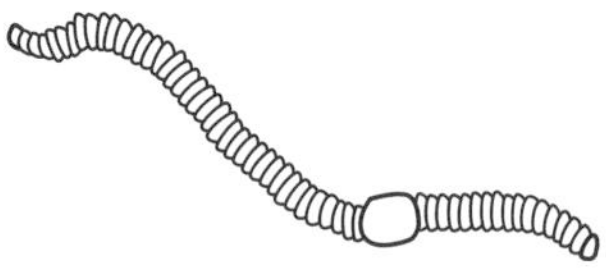
A

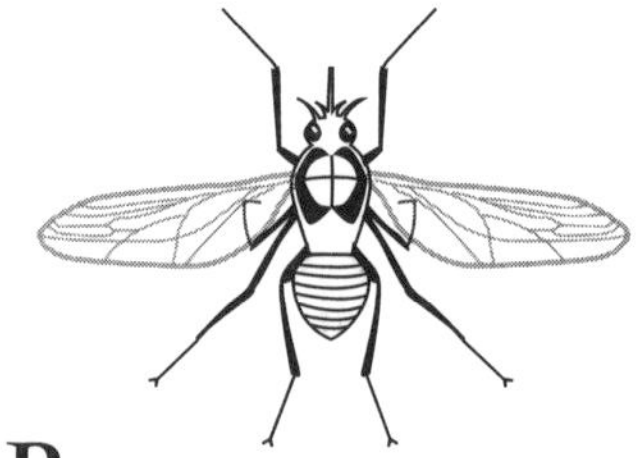
B

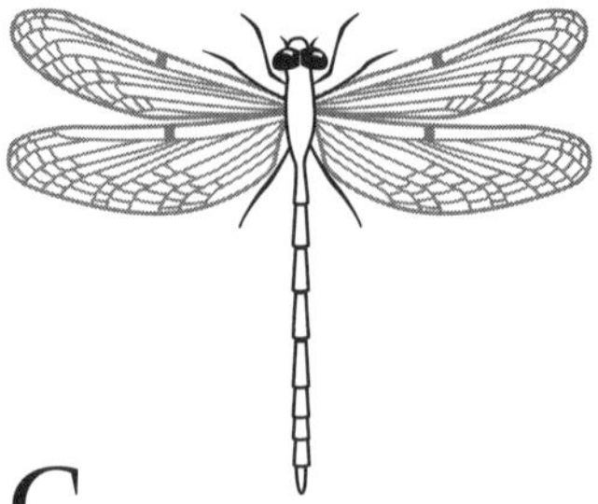
C

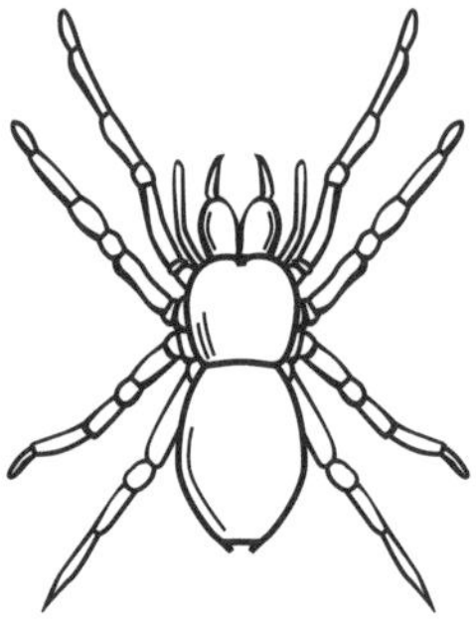
D

E

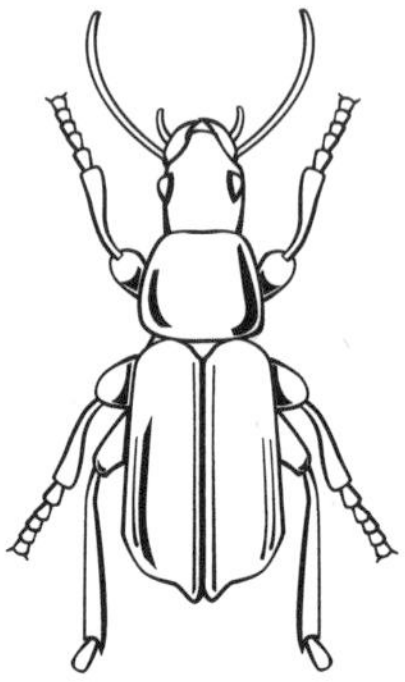
F

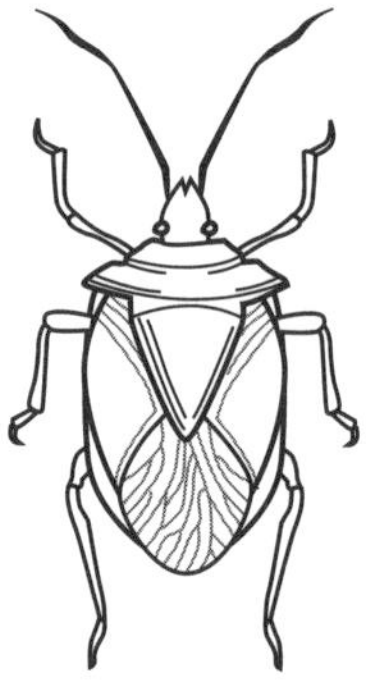
G

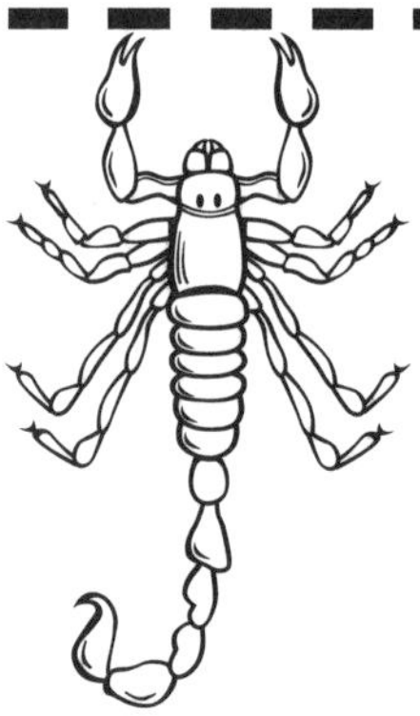
H

I

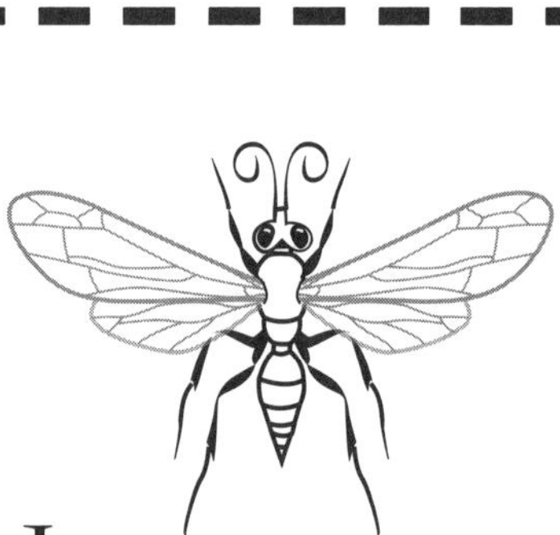
J

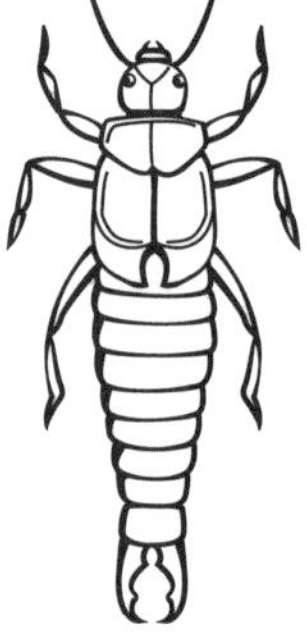
K

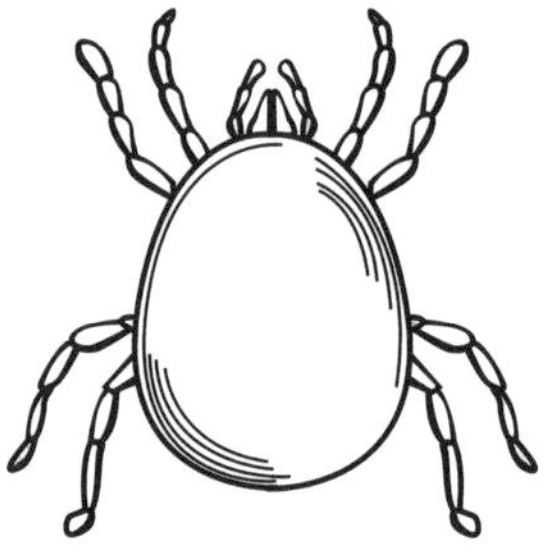
L

ILLUSTRATIONS BY LINDA OLLIVER

Name: ______________________________

Invertebrate
Dichotomous Key

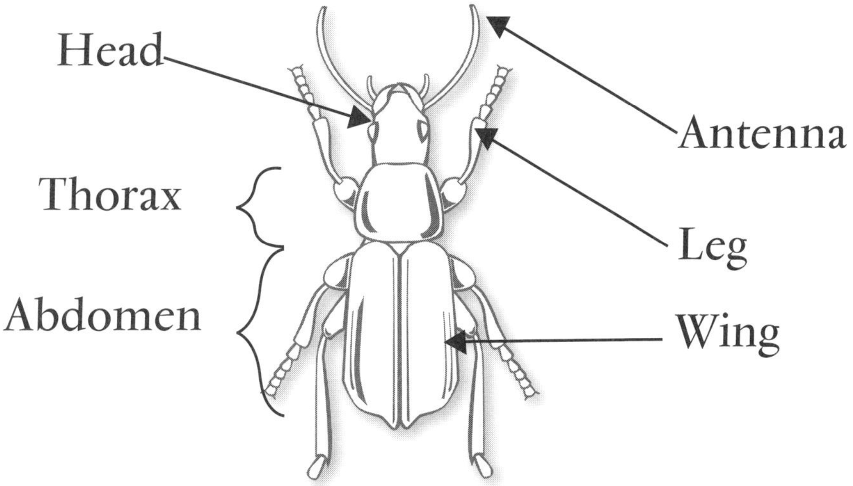

Insect

Directions: Starting with the picture of Invertebrate A, use the key below to identify each invertebrate. Write the name of each invertebrate on the answer sheet. *Remember to go back to #1 on the key each time you start with a new invertebrate!*

1	Insect (6 legs)	go to 2
	Noninsect (more or less than 6 legs)	go to 8
2	Wings are held out from body	go to 3
	Wings are absent or held close to body	go to 5
3	One pair of wings	TRUE FLY
	Two pairs of wings	go to 4
4	Front and hind wings similar in shape and size	DRAGONFLY
	Front and hind wings not similar in shape and size	WASP
5	Wings cover abdomen	go to 6
	Wings are absent or do not cover abdomen	go to 7

Name: ______________________________

Invertebrate
Dichotomous Key cont.

6 Wings meet to form straight line down back .... BEETLE
Wings overlap to form triangle shape on back .... TRUE BUG

7 Sharp pincers at tip of abdomen .... EARWIG
Three threadlike tails at tip of abdomen .... SILVERFISH

8 No legs .... EARTHWORM
Legs .... go to 9

9 Eight legs .... go to 10
More than eight legs .... CENTIPEDE

10 Tail .... SCORPION
No tail .... go to 11

11 Body looks like it is separated into two parts .... SPIDER
Body looks like it is one part .... TICK

Answers

A.	G.
B.	H.
C.	I.
D.	J.
E.	K.
F.	L.

Name: ______________________________

Insect Poster
Rubric

Common Name of Insect: ______________________________

4 Points: At least four fascinating facts about your insect

4 3 2 1 0

3 Points: A large, detailed, full-color drawing or 3-D model of your insect, with the head, thorax, and abdomen labeled

3 2 1 0

2 Points: A close-up photo or drawing of one of your insect's most interesting structures and a description of what the structure does

2 1 0

1 Point: An explanation of why your insect is classified as an insect

1 0

Extra Credit: A poem, song, rap, cheer, or chant about your insect

1 0

Total Points ____ /10

Comments: ______________________________

Chapter 22

Batteries Included

Description

Learners make drawings of what they think might be inside "energy balls," small plastic spheres that light up and buzz. After investigating simple circuits using batteries, bulbs, and wires, they learn that electricity needs a complete loop to flow. Learners then revise their drawings and find out what makes the energy balls work. They also take apart simple, battery-operated children's toys to find out how they work.

Suggested Grade Levels: 3–5

Lesson Objectives Connecting to the *Framework*

Science and Engineering Practices

- Asking questions (for science) and defining problems (for engineering)
- Constructing explanations (for science) and designing solutions (for engineering)

Disciplinary Core Ideas

PS3.A: Definitions of Energy

PS3.B: Conservation of Energy and Energy Transfer

Crosscutting Concepts

- Energy and Matter

Featured Picture Books

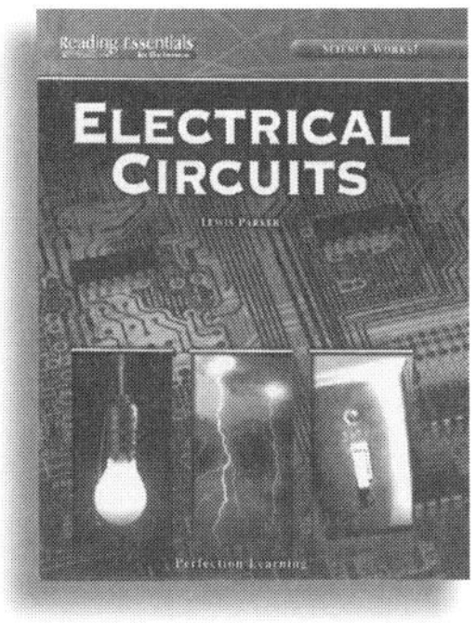

Title	***Electrical Circuits***
Author	**Lewis Parker**
Publisher	**Perfection Learning**
Year	**2005**
Genre	**Nonnarrative Information**
Summary	**This overview of electricity includes electricity in nature, current electricity, battery power, and how various types of electric circuits work.**

Title	***Too Many Toys***
Author	**David Shannon**
Publisher	**Scholastic**
Year	**2008**
Genre	**Story**
Summary	**Spencer has too many toys. The house is overflowing with them. Finally, Spencer's mom has had enough, and she helps him pack a box of toys to give away. In the end, Spencer decides the one toy he can't part with is the box.**

Time Needed

This lesson will take several class periods. Suggested scheduling is as follows:

Day 1: **Engage** with Energy Balls and **Explore/Explain** with Can You Light a Bulb?

Day 2: **Explain** with *Electrical Circuits* read aloud and cloze paragraph

Day 3 & 4: **Elaborate/Evaluate** with *Too Many Toys* read aloud and Toy Take-Apart Checkpoint Lab

Day 5: **Evaluate** with Batteries and Bulbs Quiz

Materials

- Wire strippers (for teacher use)
- Vise (for teacher use)
- Coping saw (for teacher use)

For Engage Activity (per pair)

- Energy ball

> **Energy Balls can be found at**
>
> *www.onlinesciencemall.com,* where they are called Touch-N-Glow Circuit Balls

For Explore/Explain Activity

- D battery
- 2 insulated copper wires (about 20 cm long) with the ends stripped
- Flashlight bulb
- Roll of masking tape

For the Explain Activity (per class)

- Battery and Bulb Cutouts (Cut out with a loop of tape or a magnet on the back of each.)
- Energy ball opened by the teacher to show the battery and wires

(Note: To open the energy ball, put it in a vise tight enough to keep it from rotating, but not so tight that it would break. Use a small coping saw to gently saw through the plastic, rotating a quarter turn and gently sawing until it comes apart into two pieces.)

(per pair)

- D battery
- 2 insulated copper wires (about 20 cm long) with the ends stripped
- Flashlight bulb
- Roll of masking tape
- Metal paper clip
- Safety glasses or goggles

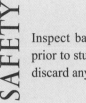

For the Elaborate Activity (per pair)

- Simple battery-operated toy (buy at garage sales or thrift stores, or have students bring them in)
- Phillips screwdriver
- Small zipper baggies
- Small sticky notes
- Red and green cups with the bottoms taped together

SAFETY

Inspect batteries for chemical leaks prior to student use and appropriately discard any leaking batteries.

Student Pages

- Energy Ball
- Electrical Circuits
- Letter Home
- Toy Take-Apart Checkpoint Lab
- Batteries and Bulbs Quiz

Background

Batteries power many of the devices we use each day, from flashlights to MP3 players, from cell phones to wristwatches, and so on. You can think of a battery as a small power plant that converts a chemical reaction into electrical energy. If you look at any battery, you'll notice that it has **two** *terminals*. One terminal is marked +, or positive, while the other is marked –, or negative. Batteries store chemical energy. When connected to a complete circuit, a chemical reaction in the battery drives electrons (the negatively charged particles in atoms) from the negative terminal, through the external circuit, to the positive terminal. These moving electrons can light a lightbulb or operate other devices placed in the external circuit. Because electrons move only when the circuit is complete, a battery can sit on a shelf for a year and still have plenty of energy. One common misconception is that the electrons flow through an "empty" wire from one end of the battery to the other, but actually, the wire itself contains electrons that are pushed along the wire when the circuit is closed.

A circuit is the pathway along which an electric current flows. A *closed circuit* is where conductors, such as copper, connect all the parts of the circuit and electricity flows freely. An *open circuit* has an opening in the pathway or a nonconductive material that prevents electrons in the wires from moving in a current. Metals are good *conductors* because electrons can easily flow through them. Plastic and rubber are good *insulators* because they don't allow electrons to move freely. Often a switch is used to open and close a circuit. For example, when you click the switch on your flashlight, you close the circuit and the bulb lights. If you click it again, a gap is created in the circuit and the light goes out.

An energy ball is a great device to use when describing open and closed circuits. The plastic ball contains a light, a buzzer, wires, and two batteries. On the outside are two small metal electrodes that when touched simultaneously by one person or by two people holding hands create

Figure 22.1. Lighting a bulb

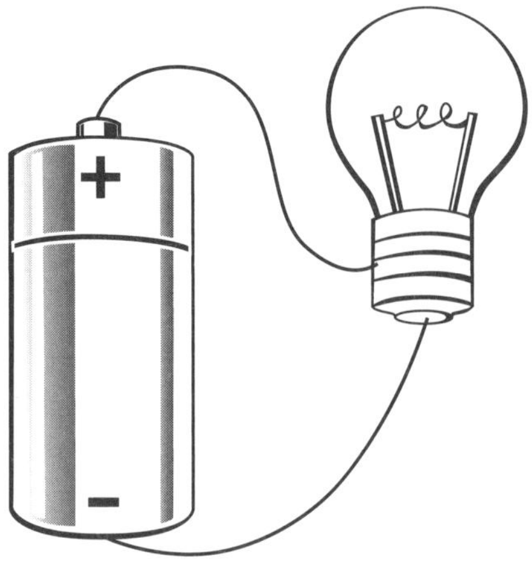

Figure 22.2. Lighting a bulb with one wire

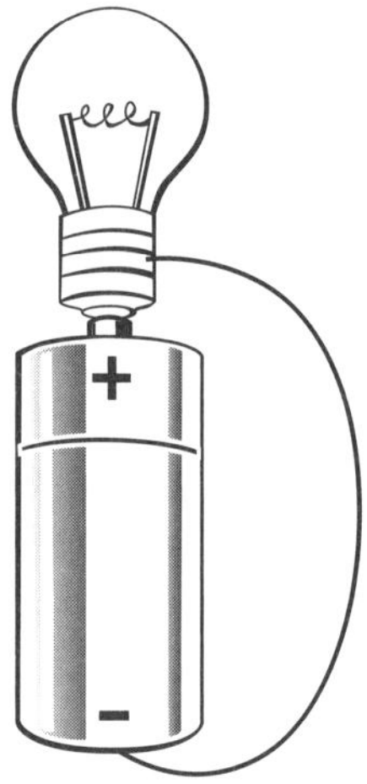

Figure 22.3. Inside a lightbulb

a closed circuit. The closed circuit results in the flashing light and buzzing sound. A person's skin serves as the conductor that completes the circuit in an energy ball.

Many students have the misconception that electricity begins at a source and goes to a target. This misconception can be seen in students' first attempts to light a bulb by attaching a wire from one end of the battery to the bulb. The activities in this lesson are designed to help students understand that a complete loop is required for electricity to flow through a circuit. In the Explore phase, students try different arrangements of battery, wires, and a lightbulb to get a bulb to light. Not only do the wires need to touch each end of the battery, but they must also touch both the *side* and *bottom* metal parts of the bulb. See Figure 22.1.

It is also possible to light the bulb with only one wire by using the configuration in Figure 22.2. The batteries may be reversed in any of these configurations.

The metal contacts on the bottom and side of the bulb are connected to two wires that hold up a thin metal filament. When the bulb is hooked up to a battery, an electric current flows from one contact to the other, through the wires and the filament. As the electrons flow along the filament, it begins to glow. See Figure 22.3.

SAFETY

Be sure to tell students that even though the energy ball toy is safe to play with, electricity can be very dangerous.

Engage

Energy Ball

Give each pair of students an energy ball and time to examine it. Students eventually will discover that if they touch both of the metal pieces, the ball will light up and make a buzzing sound. Have them try the following activities with their partners, making sure each person gets a turn:

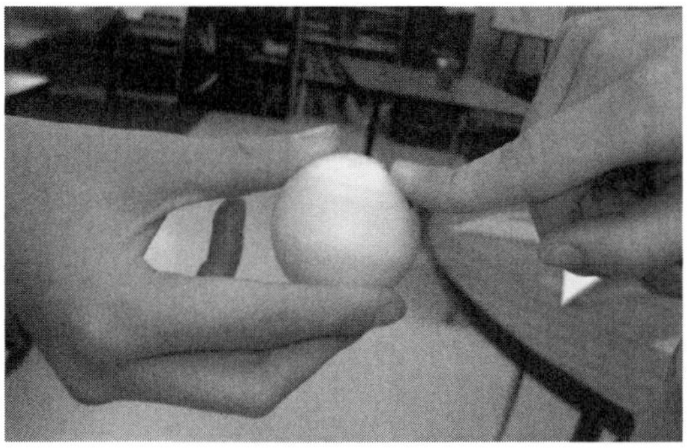

ENERGY BALL

1. Touch one of the metal pieces with one finger. What happens? (nothing)
2. Touch both metal pieces with the same hand. What happens? (It lights up and makes a sound.) Why do you think so? (Answers will vary.)
3. Put one finger on one of the metal pieces and another finger on the plastic. What happens? (nothing)
4. Touch both metal pieces with your index fingers. What happens? (It lights up and makes a sound.) Why do you think so? (Answers will vary.)
5. Touch one finger to one of the metal pieces and have your partner touch the other one. What happens? (nothing)
6. Now join hands with that person while keeping your fingers on the metal pieces. What happens? (It lights up and makes a sound.) Why do you think so? (Answers will vary.)
7. Try adding people to your circle. What happens? (It lights up and makes a sound.) Why do you think so? (Answers will vary.)
8. Predict whether or not the energy ball will light if the whole class holds hands. Try it. (If everyone is touching, it still lights up and makes a sound.) Why do you think so? (Answers will vary.)

EXPLORING WITH THE ENERGY BALL

Hand out the Energy Ball student page. Have students draw a picture of what they think is inside the energy ball. Then ask them to explain their drawings to their partners. Next ask them to share their ideas with the whole class so that you can uncover any misconceptions or preconceptions about electrical circuits. (Students may guess that there is a lightbulb, wires, battery, etc. inside.) Tell students to keep thinking about what might be inside the energy ball. Later, they will find out.

Explore & Explain

Batteries, Bulbs, and Wires

Show students a flashlight bulb and two wires. Ask

? Is it possible to light a bulb with just wires? (Answers will vary.)

EXPLORING WITH A BATTERY, BULB, AND WIRES

SAFETY

Students should wear safety goggles or glasses and use caution while working. The ends of wires are sharp and could cut or puncture skin. Glass bulbs can break and cut skin.

Give each pair of students a bulb and two wires. Students will soon discover that the bulb does not light. Then ask

? Why is the bulb not lighting? What is missing? (power source)

Show students a D battery and ask

? Is it possible to light a bulb with just a battery and two wires? (Answers will vary.)

Give each pair a D battery and some masking tape. Challenge students to light the bulb using only these materials. Small pieces of masking tape will help hold the wires in place. Through experimenting with different configurations, some pairs will begin to discover that they can light a bulb with just a battery and two wires. The key is to attach one wire to the + end of the battery and the other to the – end of the battery. Then touch one of the wires to the bottom of the bulb and the other on the side of the bulb. See Figure 22.1 (p. 328).

After all pairs have had plenty of time to experiment with different configurations, invite a duo that was able to make the bulb light to come to the board. Have them use the battery and bulb cutouts and a marker or chalk to draw the wires and show the rest of the class exactly where they placed the wires. Then give the rest of the class a chance to try that arrangement.

Next ask if anyone had a different set up that worked. Invite them to use the cutouts and a marker or chalk to show how they were able to light the bulb. Continue until all configurations have been shared. Next ask

? Is it possible to light the bulb with just one wire? Why or why not? (Answers will vary.)

Give all pairs plenty of time to try their ideas. Then invite a pair that was successful to share their setup with the cutouts and a marker or chalk. See Figure 22.2 (p. 328).

Next, invite some pairs up to show some attempts at lighting the bulb that didn't work, and ask them to explain why they think those arrangements didn't work.

Ask

? What are all the things that must happen for the bulb to light up? Turn and talk. (Possible answers include the following: You have to be touching the positive and negative ends of the battery with the wire or bulb; you have to put one wire on the side of the bulb and the other on the bottom; and so on.)

Ask

? What do you think would happen if we added a second battery? (Answers will vary. The bulb will burn more brightly, which students will discover in the following activity.)

Have pairs join together to make teams of four and then try to light up one bulb with two batteries. Students will find that the light becomes brighter with two batteries. Ask

? Does the bulb light when the two positive ends of the batteries are touching? (no)

? Does the bulb light when the two negative ends of the batteries are touching? (no)

? Does the bulb light when the negative end of one battery is touching the positive end of the other battery? (yes)

explain

Electrical Circuits Read Aloud

Cloze Paragraph

Cloze is an activity to help readers infer the meanings of unfamiliar words. In this cloze paragraph, key words about electricity are deleted in the passage. Students fill in the blanks with the words that make sense and sound right before reading, then make changes as necessary after reading. Give each student the Electrical Circuits student page. Have them cut out the words and place them where they think they belong in the cloze paragraph. Have them turn and talk with a partner to explain why they placed the words where they did. Then show students the cover of *Electrical Circuits*. Read pages 10–16 and page 20 of the book aloud (including the "switches" inset). After the read aloud, ask students to move the cards if necessary and tape or glue them in the correct place. The paragraph should read as follows:

Electrical Circuits

A **circuit** is the pathway along which current electricity flows. Metals are good **conductors** because electricity can easily flow through them. Plastic and rubber are good **insulators** because they don't conduct electricity. In **closed circuits**, conductors connect all the parts of the circuit. In **open circuits**, there is an opening that prevents electricity from moving in a current. A circuit uses a **switch** to open and close it. A **battery** stores **chemical** energy and changes it into electrical energy.

Next ask students to use their batteries, bulbs, wires, and metal paper clips to show their understanding of the words from the cloze:

1 Show a closed circuit.

2 Show an open circuit.

3 Add a switch using a paper clip, then close the circuit using the switch.

4 What parts of your circuit are conductors? (wires, metal on bulb and battery, switch)

5 What parts of your circuit are insulators? (plastic coating on wires, masking tape)

6 What part of your circuit stores chemical energy? (battery)

Then ask

? Have your ideas changed about what you think might be inside the energy ball? (Answers will vary.)

Have students draw pictures of what they think is in the energy ball. Then ask them to record how their ideas have changed at the

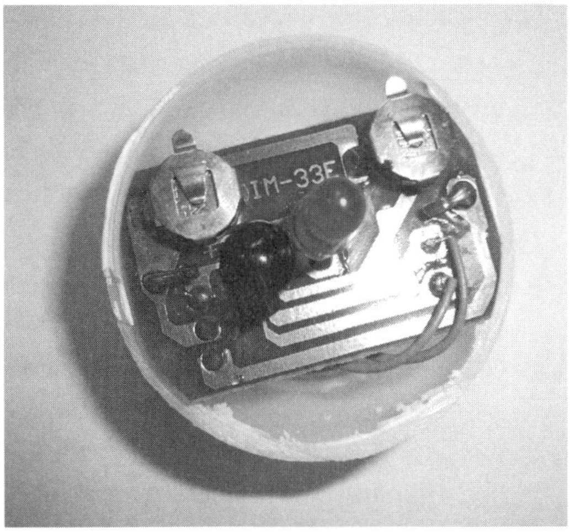

THE INSIDE OF THE ENERGY BALL

bottom of that page. Show them the inside of the energy ball and trace the flow of electricity through all of the components (batteries, wires, lightbulb, buzzer, and back to the batteries). See the Materials section for directions on how you can open the energy ball.

Elaborate & Evaluate

Too Many Toys Read Aloud and Toy Take-Apart Checkpoint Lab

Making Connections

Tell students that you are going to share a book by author-illustrator David Shannon. He made his first book when he was only five years old. He drew pictures of himself doing the things that got him into trouble, such as sneaking into the cookie jar, jumping on the bed, and making too much noise. The only two words in the book are *no* and *David*—two words he heard often and knew how to spell. Ask

- ? Has anyone ever read the book *No, David!* or any other book by David Shannon?

Tell students that he is best known for his David books, but you are going to share another book by David Shannon about a boy named Spencer. Spencer has a problem. He has too many toys! Show students the cover of *Too Many Toys*. Read the book aloud, then ask

- ? What were some favorite toys you played with when you were little?
- ? Did you have any toys that had lights, sounds, or moved?
- ? Did Spencer have any toys that had lights, sounds, or moved? (robotic dog, talking books, and video games)
- ? How do you think those kinds of toys are powered? (batteries)
- ? Have you ever thought about what might be inside those kinds of toys?
- ? Wouldn't it be fun to find out?

Tell students that soon they will be taking apart some simple battery-operated children's toys to see what's inside and how they work. Give students a copy of the Letter Home and explain that you will have some extra toys if they are not able to bring one.

SAFETY

1. Students should wear safety glasses or goggles.
2. Demonstrate for students the correct and safe use of screwdrivers in advance of the activity. Direct adult supervision of students working with screwdrivers is strongly recommended.
3. Remind students that sharp objects, including metal and plastic objects, can cut skin.

The following day, give each pair of students a battery-operated toy and a screwdriver. Give each student a copy of the Toy Take-Apart Checkpoint Lab. (For tips on managing a checkpoint lab, see Chapter 3.) In Part A of the Checkpoint Lab, they will describe the toy and predict what the inside of the toy looks like. In Part B, they will open the toy, label the parts, and draw what the inside looks like. In Part C, they will explain how their toy works and prepare to display their labeled toy and tell others how it works. When students are finished with Part C, divide the class in half and have one group stay at their desks to explain what their toys do and how they work as the other students visit the displays. Then have the groups switch roles.

Evaluate

Batteries and Bulbs Quiz

Review the concepts that have been explored in this lesson, then give students the Batteries and Bulbs Quiz. Answers follow:

1 b, e, and f, because these are complete circuits; all parts of the circuit are connected; and so on.

2 a and c, because these are complete circuits; all parts of the circuit are connected; and so on.

3 Copper is a conductor; electricity can flow through copper; and so on.

4 Plastic is an insulator; plastic keeps the electricity in the cord; and so on.

5 The bulb doesn't light because the positive ends are touching. Electricity will not flow from the positive end of one battery to the positive end of another battery.

6 Responses will vary but should include two acceptable reasons why the bulb does not light and a corresponding way each could be tested. For example, the bulb is burned out (replace with another bulb); the battery is dead (replace the battery); a connection is not made (check all the connections to make sure metal is touching metal); the wire is broken inside the insulation (replace with another wire); the switch is defective (replace with another paper clip); and so on.

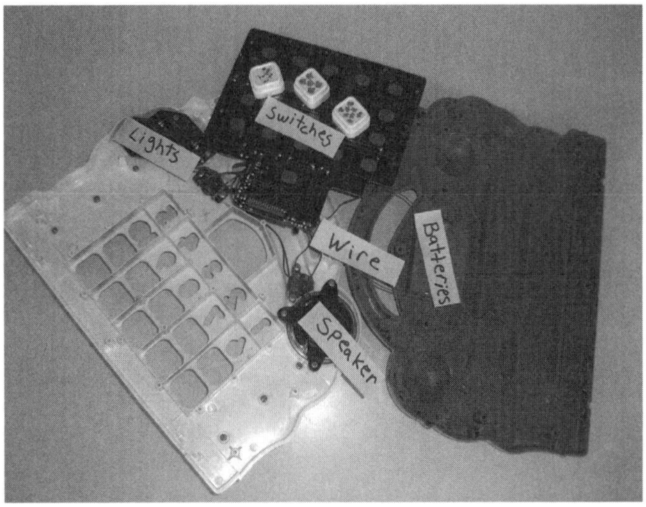

TOY TAKE-APART

Inquiry Place

Have students brainstorm questions about electricity, such as

? What materials make good conductors? What materials make good insulators? Build a circuit and test it!

? How does electricity get to your home? Research it!

? Can you light every room in a dollhouse using batteries, insulated wires, and flashlight bulbs? Try it!

? Can you invent a burglar alarm using a battery, insulated wires, a 1.5-volt mini-buzzer, and any other materials you need? Try it!

Website

How Batteries Work
www.howstuffworks.com/battery.htm

More Books to Read

Bailey, J., and M. Lilly. 2003. *Charged up: The story of electricity.* Minneapolis, MN: Picture Window Books.
Summary: Children learn how electrical energy is generated in power stations and how it travels

through pylons, power cables, and wires into people's homes.

Sueling, B. 2003. *Flick a switch: How electricity gets to your home.* New York: Holiday House.
Summary: Informative text and cartoon illustrations describe how electricity was discovered, how early devices were invented to make use of it, how it is generated in power plants, and how it is distributed for many different uses.

Suen, A., and P. Carrick. 2007. *Wired.* Watertown, MA: Charlesbridge.
Summary: This book describes how electricity is conducted and follows its route from a power plant into the home. Includes glossary.

Name: ______________________________

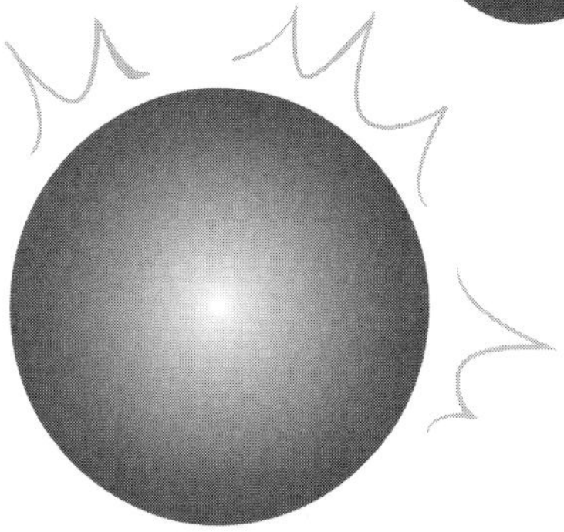

Energy Ball

Before

Draw a picture of what you think is inside the energy ball.
Be sure to label your drawing.

After

Draw a picture of what you think is inside the energy ball.
Be sure to label your drawing.

How have your ideas changed? ______________________________

____

____

Battery and Bulb Cutouts

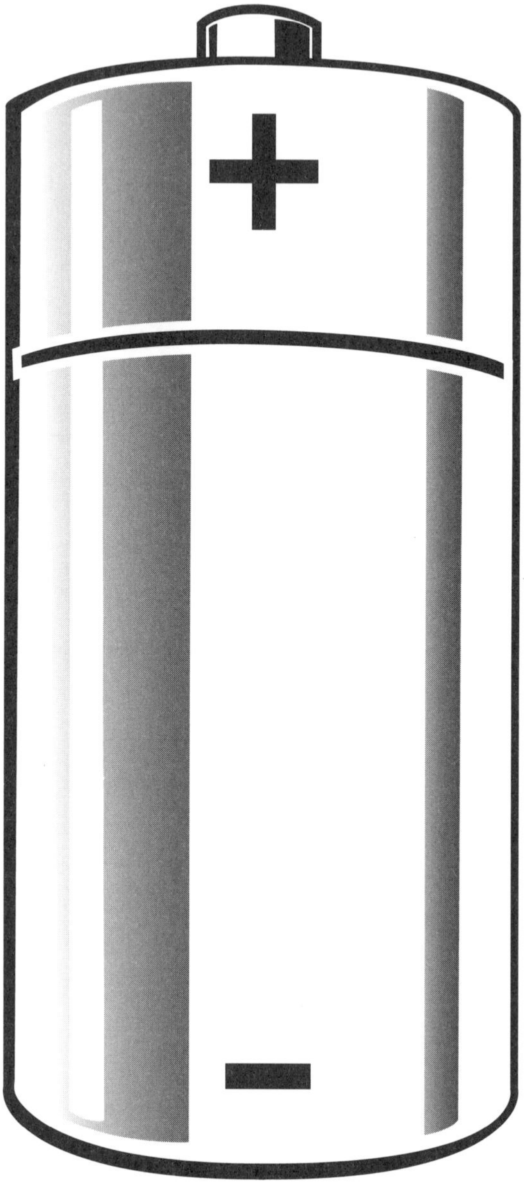

Name: ________________________________

Electrical Circuits

Directions

1. Cut out the cards in the boxes below.
2. Read the cloze paragraph and place the cards where you think they belong on the blanks.
3. Listen carefully while your teacher reads *Electrical Circuits*.
4. After reading, move the cards if necessary and glue or tape them on the page.

chemical	open circuits
insulators	closed circuits
switch	conductors
battery	circuit

Name: ______________________________

Electrical Circuits

A ______________________ is the pathway along which current electricity flows.

Metals are good _________________ because electricity can easily flow through

them. Plastic and rubber are good __________________ because they don't conduct

electricity. In ______________________, conductors connect all the parts of the

circuit. In _____________________, there is an opening that prevents electricity from

moving in a current. A circuit uses a _____________________________ to open and

close it. A ______________________ stores __________________________ energy

and changes it into electrical energy.

Dear Parents,

We are learning about electrical circuits in class. We will do an activity called Toy Take-Apart, during which the students will take apart simple battery-operated children's toys. If you have any toys that you can donate for this project, it would be greatly appreciated. The toys will be disassembled and may not be usable after the project, so please send only toys that your family does not want anymore.

Please send any old, battery-operated toys in by ____________________.

If you are not able to send any toys, that's okay. Toys will be provided for those who do not bring them from home.

SAFETY

PLEASE MAKE SURE THE TOYS ARE FREE OF BATTERY CORROSION.

Thank you,

Name: ______________________________

Toy Take-Apart
Checkpoint Lab

Follow the directions below. If your team is working, put the green cup on top. If you have a question, put the red cup on top. If you are finished with a part and you are ready for a check from your teacher, put the red cup on top.

Part A Describe Your Toy

1 Name of toy: ______________________________

2 Explain how to play with the toy and what it does: ______________________________

____

3 Open the battery compartment. How many batteries does your toy require?

____

4 What size batteries does your toy require? ______________________________

5 Look closely at where the batteries are held in the toy. Do you see + or – signs in the battery compartment? __________ If so, why do you think they are there?

____

6 Draw and label what you think the toy looks like inside.

Checkpoint A ☐

Toy Take-Apart

Checkpoint Lab cont.

Part B Take It Apart

SAFETY

Wear safety goggles or glasses. Sharp objects, including metal and plastic objects, can cut skin. Be sure to use the screwdriver carefully, as demonstrated by your teacher.

1 Unscrew all of the screws that are holding the toy together and place them in a baggie.

2 Open the toy very carefully so that you do not disconnect any of the wires inside.

3 Using sticky notes, label the following parts of your toy:

- **a** Battery
- **b** Wires
- **c** Switch
- **d** Speaker/buzzer/bulb/etc.

4 Draw and label a picture of the inside of your toy.

Checkpoint B ☐

Name: ______________________________

Toy Take-Apart
Checkpoint Lab cont.

Part C How Does It Work?

1 Explain how your toy works. In other words, what has to happen for the toy to make sound or light or to move? What is the path of the electricity inside the toy? Use the following words in your explanation: *battery, conductor, insulator, open circuit, closed circuit, switch.*

Be prepared to display your labeled toy and your drawing and explain how the toy works to other students.

Checkpoint C ☐

Name: ____________________

Batteries and Bulbs Quiz

1 Circle all of the setups below in which the bulb will light.

a

b

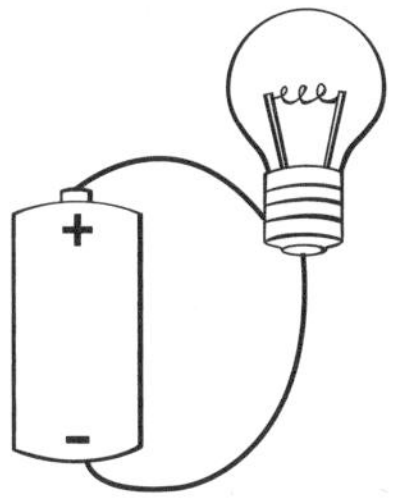

c

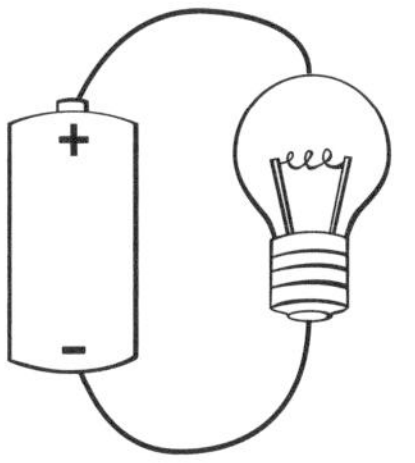

d

e

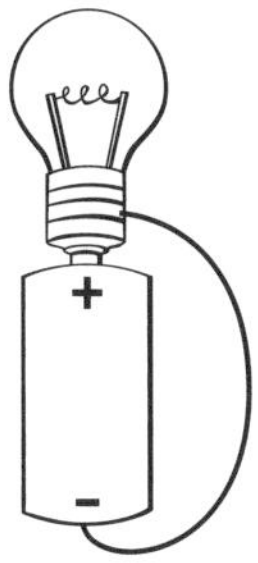

f

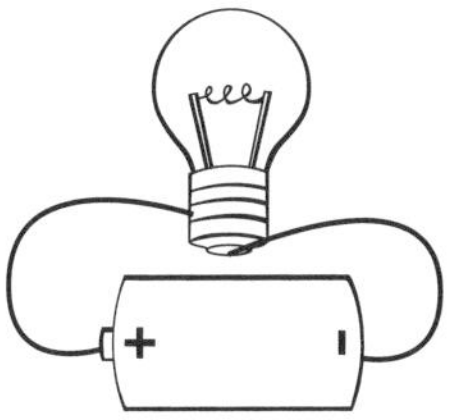

2 Katie and David each put one finger on one of the metal parts of an energy ball. In which two pictures below would the energy ball light up and buzz?

a

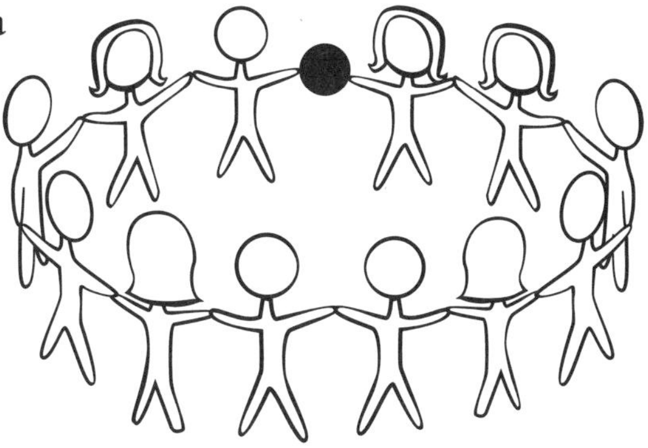

b

c

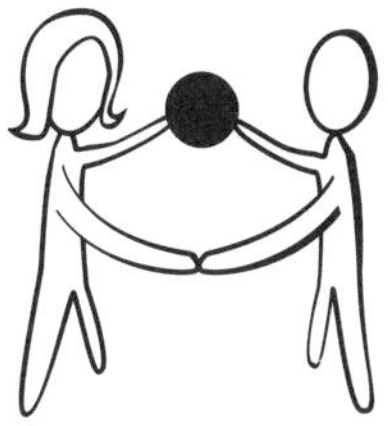

Explain why you think so.

____

____

____

3 Explain why many of the electrical wires in your home are made of copper.

____

____

Name: ______________________________

Batteries and Bulbs Quiz cont.

4 Explain why lamp cords are coated with plastic.

____

____

5 One group of students wants to add another battery to a circuit to make the bulb brighter. They add a battery, but the bulb does not light. See their setup below. Explain why the bulb doesn't light.

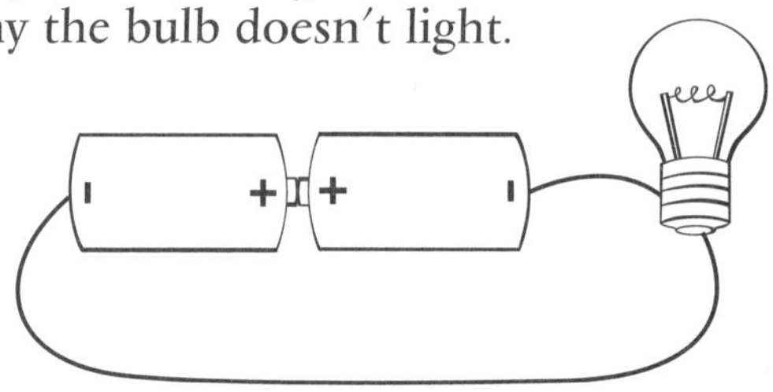

____

____

6 Kevin and Juanita build the complete circuit below to light a bulb. They use a metal paper clip as a switch.

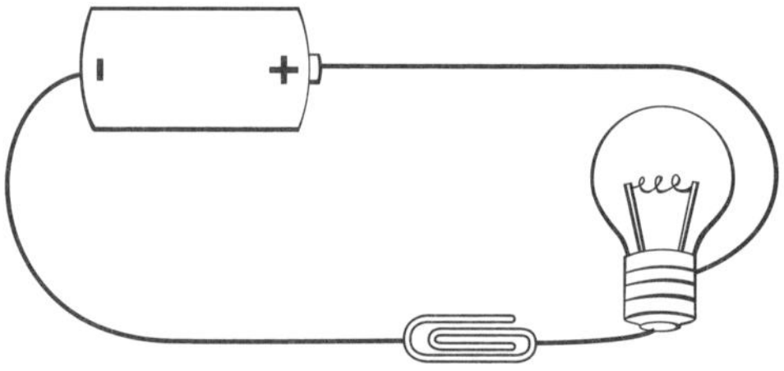

After building the circuit, they close the switch, but the bulb does not light. Identify two possible reasons why the bulb does not light. For each possible reason, describe a way the students could test whether the suggested reason is the cause of the bulb not lighting.

____

____

____

____

The Secrets of Flight

Description

Students explore the forces of flight and use the design process to improve the flight times of paper airplanes.

Suggested Grade Levels: 3–6

Lesson Objectives Connecting to the *Framework*

Science and Engineering Practices

- Asking questions (for science) and defining problems (for engineering)
- Constructing explanations (for science) and designing solutions (for engineering)

Disciplinary Core Ideas

PS2.A: Forces and Motion
PS2.B: Types of Interactions
ETS1.A: Defining and Delimiting Engineering Problems
ETS1.B: Developing Possible Solutions
ETS1.C: Optimizing the Design Solution

Crosscutting Concepts

- Cause and Effect

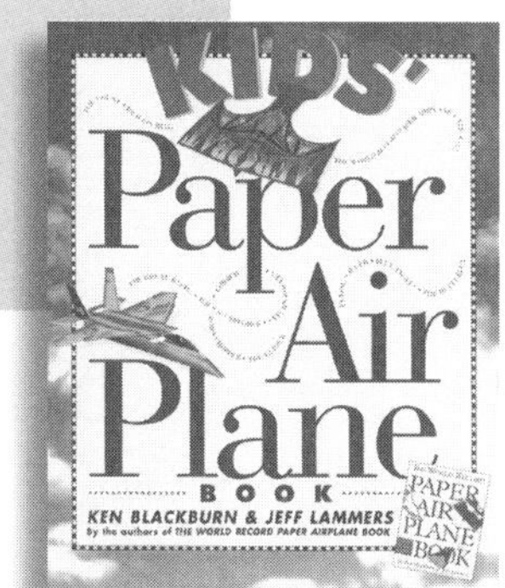

Featured Picture Books

Title	***How People Learned to Fly***
Author	**Fran Hodgkins**
Illustrator	**True Kelley**
Publisher	**HarperCollins**
Year	**2007**
Genre	**Nonnarrative Information**
Summary	**Reveals the many obstacles that have been overcome in the history of human flight and explains the four forces of flight with simple text and illustrations**

Title	***Kids' Paper Airplane Book***
Authors	**Ken Blackburn and Jeff Lammers**
Publisher	**Workman**
Year	**1996**
Genre	**Nonnarrative Information**
Summary	**This activity book provides information on the principles of aerodynamics, suggestions for designing airplanes, and instructions for folding paper planes and doing stunts.**

Time Needed

This lesson will take several class periods. Suggested scheduling is as follows:

Day 1: **Engage** with Flight Semantic Map and **Explore** with Flight Data Sheet

Day 2: **Explain** with *How People Learned to Fly* and Forces of Flight diagram

Day 3: **Elaborate** with *Kids' Paper Airplane Book* and introduction of the Paper Airplane Contest and rules

Day 4: Test flights and modifications

Day 5: **Evaluate** with Paper Airplane Contest and Our Best Airplane

Materials
(per pair)

- Scotch tape
- Glue stick
- Scissors
- Paper clips
- Several sheets of 8 ½ in. × 11 in. copier paper
- MyChron silent student timer or a stopwatch
- Safety glasses or goggles
- Paper Airplane Contest Announcement (for teacher use)

MyChron timers are available from

www.onlinesciencemall.com

www.teachersource.com

SAFETY

Use glue sticks with low or no volatile organic compounds (VOCs).

Student Pages

- Flight Data Sheet
- Simple Paper Airplane Instructions
- Forces of Flight
- Test Flight Log
- Our Best Airplane

Background

The date was December 17, 1903. The place was a windswept beach near Kitty Hawk, North Carolina. With Orville Wright at the controls and his brother, Wilbur, running alongside, the small airplane took off. This event lasted for only 12 sec., but it made history as the first successful, sustained flight by a human-piloted aircraft. The Wright brothers had uncovered the secrets of flight. In this lesson, students use the technological design process to build simple gliders, test them, and make changes to improve them.

They learn that the flight of a paper airplane, bird, jet, or any other flying object involves four forces: gravity, lift, drag, and thrust. *Gravity* pulls objects to the Earth. *Lift* is the force pushing up on the weight of a flying object and is created primarily by air molecules hitting the underside of the plane. For flight, the force of lift must be equal to or greater than the force of gravity. When anything flies through the air, it collides with air molecules that slow it down. This force is called *drag*. *Thrust* is the push that keeps the object from slowing down. In a real airplane, this force is created by an engine. When an airplane is flying level and thrust is greater than drag, the plane speeds up. If there is less thrust than drag, the airplane slows down. The initial thrust for a paper airplane is created by throwing it.

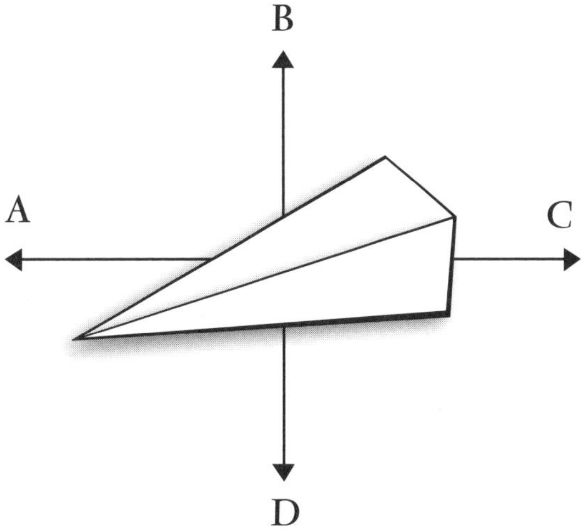

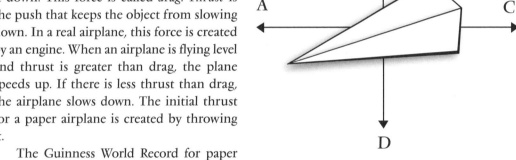

The Guinness World Record for paper airplane time aloft, 27.6 sec., was held by Ken Blackburn until 2009. He has an engaging and informative website at *www.paperplane.org*, where you can see a video of this record-making flight and download free paper airplane templates and a teachers guide for the *Kids' Paper Airplane Book*.

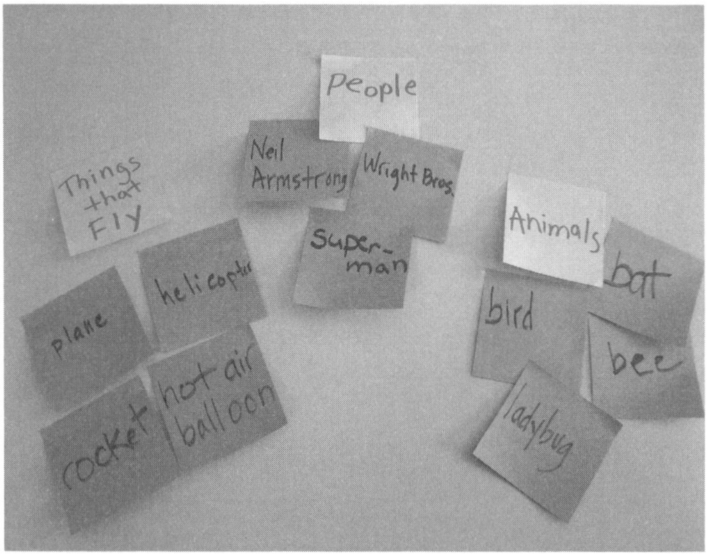

CREATING CATEGORIES

Engage

Flight Semantic Map

A semantic map is a tool that helps activate prior knowledge, determine misconceptions, and show relationships among concepts. Discussion of a semantic map helps students become aware of new words, create new meanings for terms, and recognize the relationships among numerous words related to the science content. Before making the semantic map, throw a paper airplane and ask students

? What are some terms you think of when you hear the word *flight*?

Give groups of 2 to 3 students some sticky notes and ask them to write one word about flight on each sticky note. Give them time to generate a dozen or so sticky note words per group. Then ask them to sort the sticky notes into categories. They can label each category with another sticky note. For example, the category "Things That Fly" might include the words *airplane, helicopter, hot air balloon,* etc.

Write the word *flight* in the center of a sheet of chart paper or on the board, and circle it. Have students share their words and how they categorized them. Discuss the categories and terms, choose several main categories to write on the map, and have students place their sticky notes on the board or chart paper under the corresponding categories. Display the map throughout the lesson, adding new categories and terms as students learn more about flight.

Explore

(The following activity is adapted from the last page of *How People Learned to Fly*.) Tell students the Wright brothers, who invented the first successful airplanes, began by building gliders. Explain that a paper airplane is actually a glider because it doesn't have an engine. Ask

- How does a paper airplane get the push it needs to fly? (from your hand)

Give each pair of students the Flight Data Sheet, a MyChron timer or stopwatch, a sheet of copier paper, and the Simple Paper Airplane Instructions. Allow time for each pair to create a paper airplane. Next find a large open space inside your school (e.g., cafeteria, gym, hallway, etc.) to be used as a designated flying area. After reviewing safety procedures (do not throw paper airplanes toward people!), have students go to the designated flying area and test their models a few times. Then students should take turns throwing their airplanes while their partners use a stopwatch to determine how long the planes are in the air. They can use the Flight Data Sheet to record their times. Students should wear safety goggles or glasses during this activity.

Next tell students they will be comparing how their airplane flies outside compared to how it flew inside. Ask

? What do we need to do to make a fair comparison between inside flight and outside flight? (Use the same plane design with no adjustments; throw it with the same amount of force; use the same stopwatch; etc.)

Sample Semantic Map for Flight

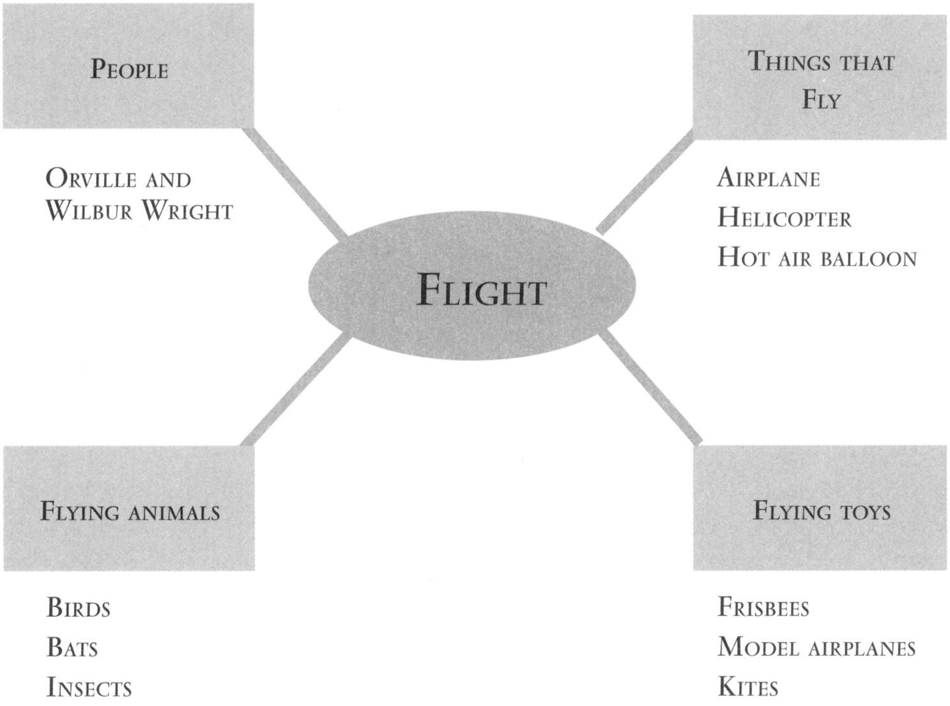

Now have students go outdoors, record the weather conditions, repeat the timing procedure, and answer the remaining questions on the Flight Data Sheet.

explain

Discuss the answers to the questions on the Flight Data Sheet:

- ? Were all of your plane's flight times indoors the same? Why or why not? (Times will vary. Students should understand that this is due to the person throwing it, how hard they threw it, the person timing it, etc.)
- ? Describe the weather conditions. (Students should describe the wind conditions, precipitation, temperature, etc.)
- ? Were all of your planes' flight times outdoors the same? Why or why not?

TESTING PAPER AIRPLANES OUTDOORS

- ? Did your paper airplane glide longer inside or outside? Why do you think that happened? (Depending on weather conditions, the paper airplanes may fly shorter or longer times outside than inside. The important thing is that students identify conditions that affect the flight time.)

- How do you think weather conditions affect a real airplane's flight? (It is harder for planes to fly against the wind and easier to fly in the direction of the wind; aircraft icing can make flying dangerous; etc.)
- Why doesn't your paper airplane keep flying like a real airplane? (The paper airplane does not have an engine to keep it moving through the air, so gravity pulls it down; it is not really flying but gliding; etc.)

Next give each student a copy of the Forces of Flight student page. Explain that a force is a "push" or a "pull" on an object. Read the names of the four forces in the word bank.

Tell students that as you read *How People Learned to Fly,* you would like them to listen for each of the four forces. Read the book aloud, stopping to discuss how each force affects flight.

After reading, have students place the words in the correct places on the student page. Answers are A–thrust, B–lift, C–drag, and D–gravity.

Ask

- What force pulls your paper airplane to the ground? (gravity, page 12)
- What creates drag on your paper airplane? (air resistance, page 16)
- What creates lift on your paper airplane? (the wings, page 22)
- What creates thrust with your paper airplane? (the force we throw it with, page 27)

Next brainstorm ways to solve the following problem:

- How could you make your paper airplane fly longer? (add or remove paper clips, add tape or glue, bend the wings up, etc.)

Point out that the scientists and inventors who have contributed to human flight over the years have had to continually design, test, evaluate, modify, and communicate with others. The Wright brothers' first flight was the culmination of years of research, design, experimentation, and even frustration. Orville and Wilbur Wright were never completely satisfied with their airplane designs. They were always trying to improve their safety, flight time, distance traveled, and so on.

elaborate

Tell students that the Guinness World Record for the longest hand-launched paper airplane flight is held by Ken Blackburn. His plane flew for 27.4 sec.! Show them the cover of *Kids' Paper Airplane Book* and tell them that one of the authors is Ken Blackburn. Read aloud from pages 9–10 about how he set the Guinness World Record. He set a new world record on October 8, 1998, of 27.6 sec. For more information about Ken Blackburn and to view a video of his record flight, go to *www.paperplane.org/record.html.*

Next announce that you are going to have a paper airplane flight contest to see whose paper airplane can stay aloft (in the air) the longest. Post the paper airplane contest announcement and explain the rules. These rules have been modified from official Guinness rules (the official Guinness guidelines can be found on page 10 of *Kids' Paper Airplane Book*):

1. The plane must be made of a single sheet of 8 ½ in. × 11 in. copy paper. It may be cut smaller, but it cannot be larger.
2. You may use tape, glue, or paper clips.
3. The plane must be thrown from level ground.
4. The timer must start when you release the plane and end when the plane touches ANYTHING (the floor, a wall, a chair, etc.).

Determining Importance

Tell students that you are going to read a section of the book called "World Record Throw." Have them listen for the description of the world record throw as you read pages 14–15 of the *Kids' Paper Airplane Book*. After reading, ask a student volunteer to act out the throw described and pictured on page 14. Next set a date for the contest and allow students time to create and test various airplane designs.

Provide each pair of students with several sheets of paper, paper clips, a glue stick, scissors, a MyChron timer or stopwatch, and a copy of the Test Flight Log. Explain that a test flight log is a convenient way for students to keep track of their designs, modifications (changes to their designs), and flight times. Ken Blackburn used a log similar to this when testing planes for his world record attempt. Set up both a design area and a testing area in your school. A gymnasium works well because of the high ceilings. Indoors is best, but if you are unable to find a space indoors, students can test their planes outside. Be sure to explain that to see if a certain change helps a paper airplane stay in the air longer, students should change only one thing at a time. Have students repeat this problem-solving process until they are satisfied with their paper airplane designs or until you run out of time. Explain that the Wright brothers were successful because they didn't give up; they kept trying different designs until they solved the problems they were working on.

Students should wear safety glasses or goggles during this activity. Also remind them to work carefully when using scissors.

KEEPING A TEST FLIGHT LOG

evaluate

On the day of the contest, have each pair choose its best airplane, name it, write the name on the plane with marker, and decorate it if they wish. Choose one student in the class to be the timer and another to be the judge (you may want to ask another staff member to be the judge to add excitement).

The timer's role is to use the stopwatch to time each flight and call out the time. The judge's role is to write down each team's name and the flight time of its airplane. The timer should start the stopwatch as soon as the thrower lets go of the plane and stop it as soon as the plane lands or hits something. The judge tells each person when he or she can make a throw. Have each pair make one official throw. The duo with the longest-lasting flight wins the contest. You may want to give pairs several opportunities to throw and enter their best flight time in the contest. (Note: Guinness allows six attempts.) After the contest, have students create a poster featuring their pair's best airplane. Give each pair a copy of the Our Best Airplane student page. Here they will draw a picture of their team's most successful design, including the plane's name and any

PAPER AIRPLANE MOBILE

special features. They will label the four forces of flight, using arrows to show the direction of each force. They also will list their best flight time and explain why they think that design worked better than the others they tried.

You may want to have students display the paper airplanes in your classroom by making paper airplane mobiles as described on page 25 of *Kids' Paper Airplane Book*. Teams can write the longest time aloft on their planes with a marker before hanging them on the mobiles.

Inquiry Place

Have students brainstorm questions about airplane design, such as

- ? Which type of paper makes a better paper airplane: notebook paper, construction paper, or card stock? Test it!
- ? Do paper airplanes with longer wings fly longer or farther than paper airplanes with shorter wings? Test it!
- ? What is "aircraft icing" and how can it be prevented? Research it!
- ? What is the world's fastest aircraft? Research it!
- ? What is the world's largest aircraft? Research it!

Then have students select a question to investigate, or have groups of students vote on the question they want to investigate as a team. Students can present their findings at a poster session or gallery walk.

Websites

Ken Blackburn's Paper Airplanes
www.paperplane.org

National Paper Airplane Contest
http://teacher.scholastic.com/paperairplane/index.htm

What Makes Paper Airplanes Fly?
http://teacher.scholastic.com/paperairplane/airplane.htm

NASA's Ultra Efficient Engine Technology (UEET) Kid's Site
www.ueet.nasa.gov/StudentSite

More Books to Read

Adler, D. 1999. *A picture book of Amelia Earhart.* New York: Holiday House.
Summary: This book recounts the life of the famous pilot, from her days as a tomboyish schoolgirl to her career as a courageous and determined pilot to the mystery surrounding her doomed flight around the world. Realistic, double-page watercolor illustrations complement the text.

Burleigh, R. 1997. *Flight.* New York: Putnam Juvenile.
Summary: Relive the historic and dramatic story of Charles Lindbergh and his flight across the ocean, the first solo Atlantic crossing ever, which brought him from the United States to Paris with only two compasses and the stars as his guides. Lush, impressionist paintings accompany the brief text.

Crowther, R. 2007. *Flight: A pop-up book of aircraft.* Somerville, MA: Candlewick Press.
Summary: From an acclaimed 3-D master comes a jam-packed, interactive book on flying machines that will send readers soaring. Loaded with flaps, pull tabs, and pop-ups to manipulate, this fact-filled exploration of flying machines from balloons to Boeings builds up to two big finales—an intricate pop-up cockpit that puts readers at the controls and a bustling airport runway that zooms into the future of flight.

Hunter, R. A. 2003. *Into the air: An illustrated timeline of flight.* Des Moines, IA: National Geographic Children's Books.
Summary: From flying prehistoric creatures through hot air balloons and the first manned flights to today's space travel and envisioned future wonders, this lavishly illustrated picture book traces the entire history of flight in a colorful and innovative way that will strongly appeal to young children. An accompanying fact-filled time line running throughout the pages features whimsical spot illustrations that complement the text and provide another layer of information for young flight enthusiasts.

Old, W. C., and R. A. Parker. 2002. *To fly: The story of the Wright brothers.* New York: Clarion Books.
Summary: This detailed picture book traces the work of the two Wright brothers to develop the first machine-powered aircraft. The story begins with two young brothers who dreamed of flying; describes their printing business, bicycle shop, glider tests, and modifications; and ends with that first flight on December 17, 1903.

Name: ______________________________

Flight Data Sheet

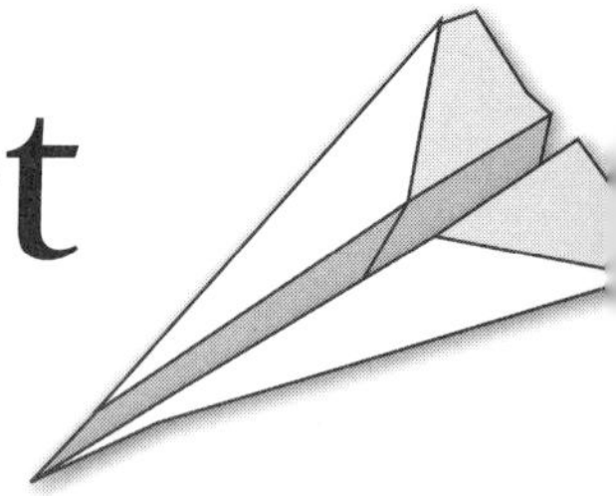

Indoor Flight

1 Find an open space in your classroom or hallway. Safety warning: DO NOT THROW PAPER AIRPLANES TOWARD OTHERS. One person should throw the paper airplane while the other measures the amount of time the paper airplane stays in the air. Record the time in the table below. Discuss and record any flight observations. Then switch jobs.

FLIGHT DATA: Indoors

Trial	Flight Time (sec.)	Flight Observations
1		
2		
3		
4		

2 Were all of your plane's flight times the same? Why or why not?

____

____

____

Outdoor Flight

3 With your teacher, go outdoors. Describe the weather conditions.

____

____

____

4 Repeat the procedure above with your airplane outdoors, and record your data on the following page.

Name: ______________________________

Flight Data Sheet cont.

FLIGHT DATA: Outdoors

Trial	Flight Time (sec.)	Flight Observations
1		
2		
3		
4		

5 Were all of your plane's flight times outdoors the same? Why or why not?

____

____

____

6 Did your paper airplane glide longer inside or outside? Why do you think that happened?

____

____

____

7 How do you think weather conditions affect a real airplane's flight?

____

____

____

8 Why doesn't your paper airplane keep flying like a real airplane?

____

____

____

Name: ______________________________

Simple Paper Airplane Instructions

(Adapted from "Build a Simple Paper Airplane" at *www.paperplane.org*)

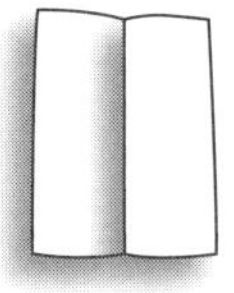

1 Fold a piece of copy paper in half lengthwise.

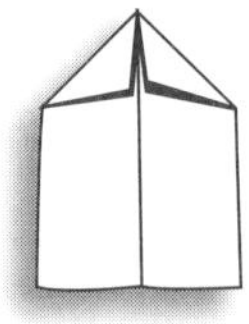

2 Fold both top corners into the center crease.

3 Fold the paper in half with the flaps on the outside.

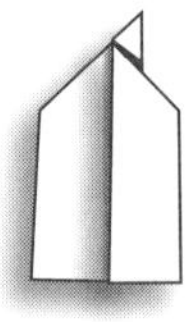

4 Fold one wing down.

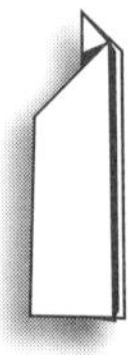

5 Fold the other wing down.

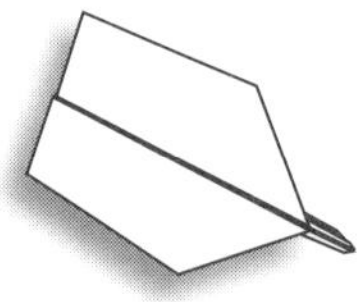

6 Fold the wings out.

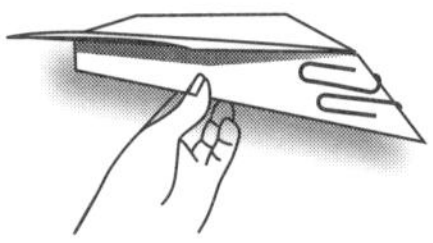

7 Add paper clips to the nose (3 small or 2 large).

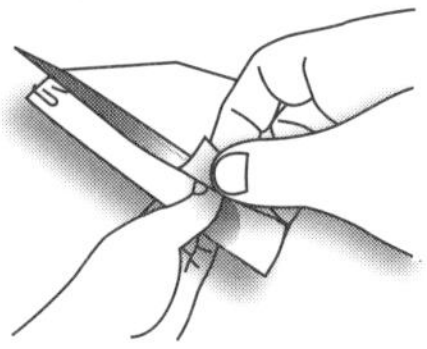

8 Bend the back of each wing up a little bit.

Name: ______________________________

Forces of Flight

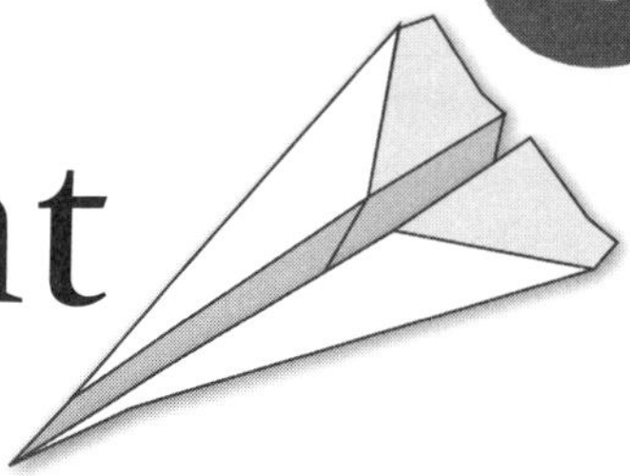

WORD BANK
Lift Thrust Drag Gravity

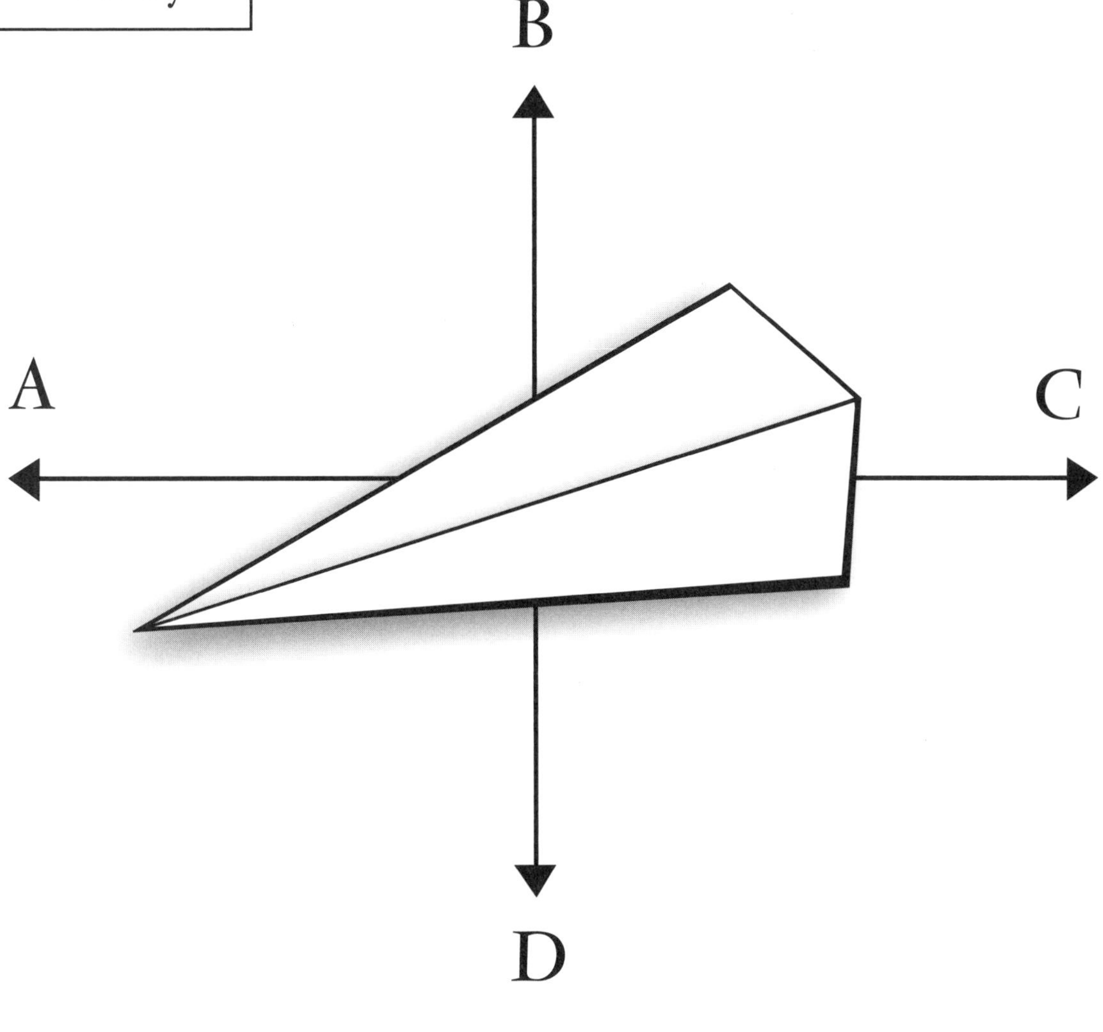

Name: ______________________________

ANNOUNCING!

Our class will be holding a

PAPER AIRPLANE CONTEST

on ____________________
(date)

RULES

1 The plane must be made of a single sheet of 8 1/2 in. × 11 in. copy paper. It may be cut smaller, but it cannot be larger.

2 You may use tape, glue, or paper clips.

3 The plane must be thrown from level ground.

4 Timing will begin when you release the plane and end when the plane touches ANYTHING (the floor, a wall, a chair, etc.).

GOOD LUCK!

Name: ______________________________

Test Flight Log

Use the test flight log below to record information about each paper airplane you test. Two sample flight entries are below.

Date	Airplane Name	Modification	Time	Notes
9/12	*The Dominator*	*None*	*2.5 s*	*Turned to the left and crashed*
9/12	*The Dominator*	*Bent rudder to the right*	*3 s*	*Flew straighter*

Our Best Airplane

Name: ______________________

1 Draw a picture of your team's most successful design, and be sure to
- include the plane's name,
- label any special features, and
- label the four forces of flight, using arrows to show the direction of each force.

2 What was your plane's best flight time? ______________

3 Why do you think this design worked better than the others you tried?

____

____

____

Down the Drain

Description

Learners keep track of their households' water use for one day, explore ways to conserve water, and then create a Water Watch campaign for school or home. They also discover that clean water is limited in many places on Earth and learn about how water use in Kenya differs from their own use.

Suggested Grade Levels: 3–6

Lesson Objectives Connecting to the *Framework*

Science and Engineering Practices

- Analyzing and interpreting data
- Obtaining, evaluating, and communicating information

Disciplinary Core Ideas

ESS3.A: Natural Resources

Crosscutting Concepts

- Cause and Effect

Featured Picture Books

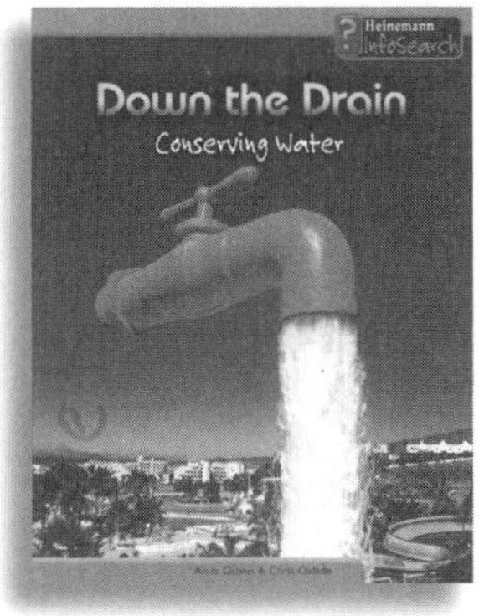

Title	***Down the Drain: Conserving Water***
Authors	**Anita Ganeri and Chris Oxlade**
Publisher	**Heinemann-Raintree**
Year	**2005**
Genre	**Nonnarrative Information**
Summary	**Explains why we need water, how much water we use, where water comes from, how we can save water, and why clean water is so important**

Title	***A Cool Drink of Water***
Author	**Barbara Kerley**
Publisher	**National Geographic Children's Books**
Year	**2006**
Genre	**Narrative Information**
Summary	**Beautifully illustrated with photographs, this book depicts people around the world collecting, chilling, and drinking water.**

Time Needed

This lesson will take several class periods. Suggested scheduling is as follows:

Day 1: **Engage** with Thinking About Water, and **Explore** with Water Diaries assignment (Day 1 should be done before a weekend or a holiday.)

Day 2: **Explain** with Where Did the Water Go? and *Down the Drain* read aloud

Day 3: **Elaborate** with *A Cool Drink of Water*

Day 4: **Evaluate** with Water Watch Campaign

Materials

- Water cards (1 set per pair)
- Sticky notes

Student Pages

- Water Diary
- Water in Kenya Narratives (1 set per team of 4)

Background

Fresh water is one of the most precious resources on Earth. It is essential for the survival of all living things. In developed countries like the United States, it is easy to take water for granted. Americans use more water per capita than anywhere else in the world, up to 100 gal a day. That's ten times the amount of water that an average person in Africa uses each day! Although the most dire water crises are in other parts of the world, scientists project that as the U.S. population grows, we may use water faster than it can be replenished. A misconception that students may have is that once we use water, it is gone. In reality, there is a fairly constant amount of water on our planet. The problem is that we tend to despoil our water supply faster than nature can clean it up. Therefore, humans must develop ways to both clean up the water supply and conserve it.

This lesson focuses on the importance of conserving water, ways in which water can be conserved, and how students can get involved in water conservation efforts, both locally and globally.

engage

Thinking About Water

Show students a paper bag with a gallon jug of water hidden inside. Tell them that inside the bag is the most precious resource in the world. It is even more important than gold or diamonds. Ask students to guess what it is. Then tell them every living thing on planet Earth needs this resource to survive. Have them guess again, then show them the container of water. Ask students to think of all of the ways in which they use water. Have them turn and talk with a partner. Pass out the Water Cards to each pair of students and ask them to order the cards from the activity they think uses the least amount of water to the activity they think uses the most. Give students the opportunity to explain why they ordered the cards they way they did.

ESTIMATING WATER USAGE

explore

Water Diaries

Next give each student a copy of the Water Diary student page and have students reorder their cards based on the information in the data table. Ask

- ? How did your guesses compare to the actual number of gallons used?
- ? What surprised you the most? Why?

Then tell the class that one way they can keep track of how they use water is by keeping a Water Diary. Ask them to fill in how many children and adults live in their household. Hold up a gallon jug of water for students to observe. Ask them to estimate on their student page how many total gallons of water their household uses in one day by flushing the toilet, taking showers and baths, using the dishwasher, washing hands, brushing teeth, and using the washing machine. Tell students that they are to take the Water Diary home and fill it in for one full day on a weekend or holiday. Explain that the individual results will be reported anonymously to calculate a class total, so no one can be singled out as a "water hog."

explain

Where Did the Water Go?

Ask students

- ? How did your predictions compare to the actual amount of water your households used in one day?
- ? What activity used the least amount of water in your household?
- ? What activity used the greatest amount of water in your household?

Ask students to look at the last column of the table on their Water Diaries (Total Water Used for Each Activity) and determine which activity used the most water in their household that day. Have each student write the name of that activity on a sticky note. On the board, create a bar graph titled "Biggest Water-Hogging Activity." Label the *x*-axis with the seven categories of water usage from the diary and the *y*-axis "Number of Households." Have students place their sticky notes above the appropriate category. When all students have placed their sticky notes on the graph, ask

? What was the biggest "water-hogging" activity for the class? (Answers will vary.)

? What are some ways to reduce the amount of water used for that activity?

Have students turn and talk.

Features of Nonfiction

Next show students the cover of the book *Down the Drain: Conserving Water.* Explain to them that this is a nonfiction book that can help them learn more about water use and conservation. Model for students the first thing a good reader does when getting ready to use a nonfiction book, reading through the table of contents. This allows the reader to know exactly what type of information the book contains. Read pages 4–9, about why we need water and how we use water, aloud. Discuss the reasons presented in the book for why we should conserve water. Have students look at their Water Diaries and brainstorm ways in which they could conserve water. Then show students on the table of contents that the section on page 16 is titled "How Can We Save Water at Home?" Read pages 16–21, about saving water at home and at school, aloud. Have students list several ways they could conserve water on the back of their Water Diaries.

elaborate

A Cool Drink of Water

Inferring

Show students the cover of *A Cool Drink of Water.* Read the book aloud, stopping periodically to ask students to infer from a photograph where it was taken and what was happening. Then read the location and photo descriptions found in the back of the book.

Synthesizing

Tell students that you are going to read the book again, but this time you want them to think hard about the overall message of the book. After reading, ask

? What is the overall message of this book?

Have students turn and talk. Then read the back jacket flap about the author, Barbara Kerley, and her reason for writing the book. She says, "This book was born of an idea that I really wanted to share with kids—how very basic water is to everyone's life. It's something we all have in common, whether we turn on the faucet above our kitchen sink or haul water home from the water tap. Water is something that unites us."

Explain that there is really no right answer to the question "What is the overall message of this book?" The reader's interpretation of a book can sometimes differ from the author's intended meaning because of the different past experiences from which the author and reader are drawing. Barbara Kerley gained a new perspective on water use while living on Guam and in Nepal, where she not only hauled her own drinking water but also boiled it and treated it. Ask

? Why do you think she had to boil and treat the water she carried to her home? (Answers will vary.)

Next read pages 23–24 of *Down the Drain,* titled "Why Is Clean Water So Important?" Point out the photo on page 23 of the village in Kenya. Locate Kenya on a map. Pass out the Water in Kenya narratives, one set of four cards to each team of four students. Explain that the narratives were written by Peace Corps volunteers. The Peace Corps is a U. S. government program devoted to world peace and friendship. Peace Corps volunteers spend about two years living and working with people in other countries to help them build a better life for themselves, their children, and their communities. The people who wrote these narratives were asked to write about how they obtain and use water while living in Kenya. Have students read the cards and discuss with a partner first, then join the other pair in the group to discuss all four narratives. After the reading, discuss the following questions:

- ? Where do the Peace Corps volunteers get their water?
- ? How does their daily water use compare to yours?
- ? How do they conserve their water?
- ? Have you ever thought about what it would be like not to have water so readily available?
- ? What things would you have to do differently?

FINDING THE CLOSEST WATER SOURCE

- ? If your school had no plumbing, where would you have to go to get water?

Finally, visit the Google Maps site *(http://maps.google.com)*, enter your school's address, and find the closest natural source of water for your location. Click on "Terrain" or "Satellite" for a better view of water sources. Calculate the distance to the source by using the "Get Directions" feature. Ask students to imagine what it

PASSING A BUCKET OF WATER

would be like to carry water from that source back to the school. How far would they have to walk? How many times would they need to fill a bucket? You may even want to have a bucket of water for them to pass around so they can feel how heavy it is. Remind students that it is not safe to drink water from a lake, river, or stream. The water would need to be boiled and filtered before drinking.

Tell students that because clean water is not available for millions of people in other countries, there are many organizations dedicated to solving that problem. You may want to share information on the following organizations that help people find ways to make their water supplies safer and more readily available:

Children's Safe Drinking Water Project
www.csdw.org/csdw/home.shtml

Q Drum: The Rollable Water Container for Developing Countries
www.qdrum.co.za

The Water Project
http://thewaterproject.org

POSTING A WATER CONSERVATION TIP

evaluate

Water Watch Campaign

Ask students

- ? Have your ideas changed about your own water use? How?

Tell students that there are many things they can do at home and school to conserve this precious resource. Have students revisit their Water Diaries to determine where their families might be wasting water, and reread the list of water conservation ideas they wrote on the back. Then have each student create a water conservation plan for his or her own household. They can make water conservation tips to post in key areas around their homes, such as over the bathroom sink, on the dishwasher, near the bathtub, and so on. They can also create posters with reasons to conserve water as well as ideas for saving water to display around their homes. As a class develop a plan for conserving water at school. Students can use suggestions from *Down the Drain* or the EPA's Water Sense for Kids website *(www.epa.gov/watersense/kids)* for their water watch campaigns.

Inquiry Place

Have students brainstorm questions about water, such as

- ? Do you use more water when you take a shower or when you take a bath? Measure and compare!
- ? What is "gray water" and how can it be used to conserve water? Research it!
- ? Are there places in the United States where people do not have access to clean, fresh water? Why? Research it!
- ? How can seawater be made safe for drinking? Research it!
- ? What could you invent to help people save water? Try it!

Then have students select a question to investigate, or have groups of students vote on the question they want to investigate as a team. Students can present their findings at a poster session or gallery walk.

Websites

The Water Project
http://thewaterproject.org

Children's Safe Drinking Water Project
www.csdw.org/csdw/home.shtml

Water in Africa
www.peacecorps.gov/wws/educators/enrichment/africa/resources/index.html

More Books to Read

Barnhill, K. 2009. *Do you know where your water has been? The disgusting story behind what you're drinking.* Mankato, MN: Capstone Press.
Summary: This book from the Sanitation Investigation series describes the history of human water treatment and modern water treatment systems.

Green, J. 2005. *Why should I save water?* Hauppauge, NY: Barron's Educational Series.
Summary: This book from the Why Should I? series explains why water is a precious resource and gives dozens of ideas for conserving water.

Wick, W. 1996. *A drop of water.* New York: Scholastic Press.
Summary: Spectacular photographs of water as ice, steam, frost, and dew will stimulate wonder. Readers can examine a drop of water as it falls from a faucet, see a drop of water as it splashes on a hard surface, count the points on a snowflake, and contemplate how drops of water form clouds.

References

Finding local water sources with Google maps is adapted from an activity from Reliance Products Educator Resources and the Children's Safe Drinking Water Project, *www.relianceproducts.info/educator_resources.html#.*

Water Cards

Directions: Cut out the cards and order them from the activity you think uses the least amount of water to the activity you think uses the greatest amount of water.

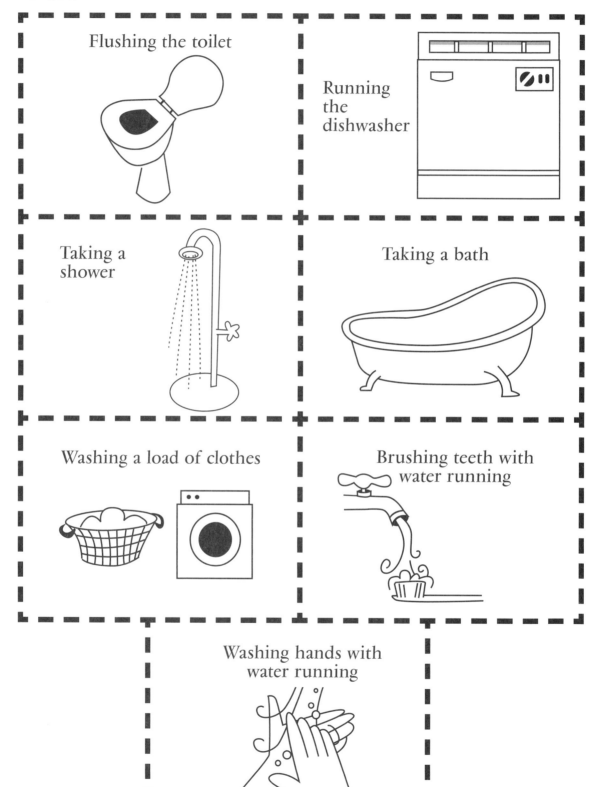

Flushing the toilet

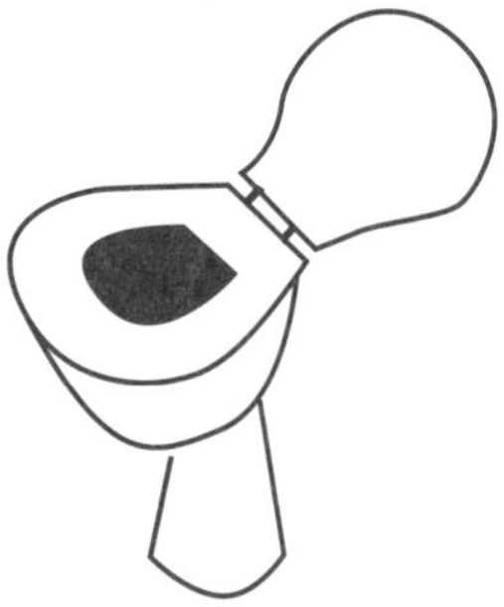

Running the dishwasher

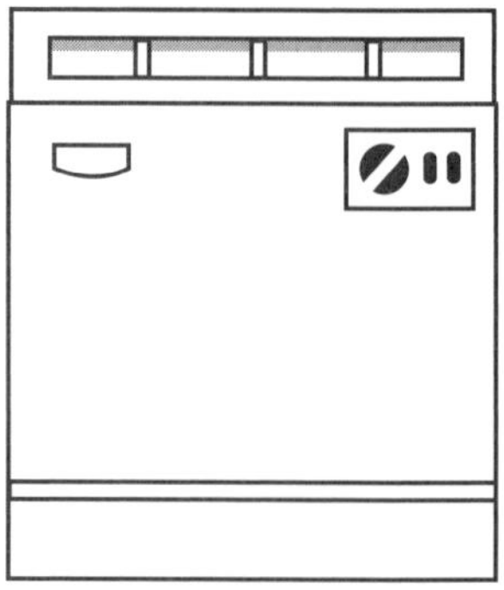

Taking a shower

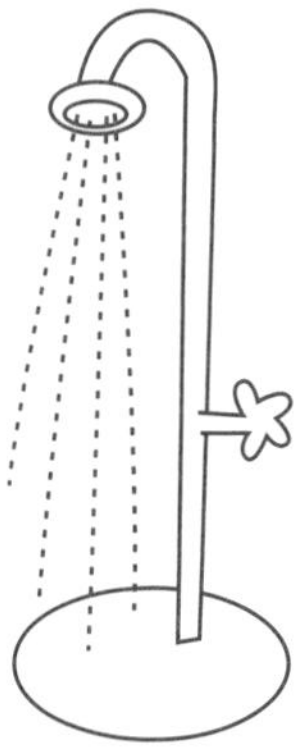

Taking a bath

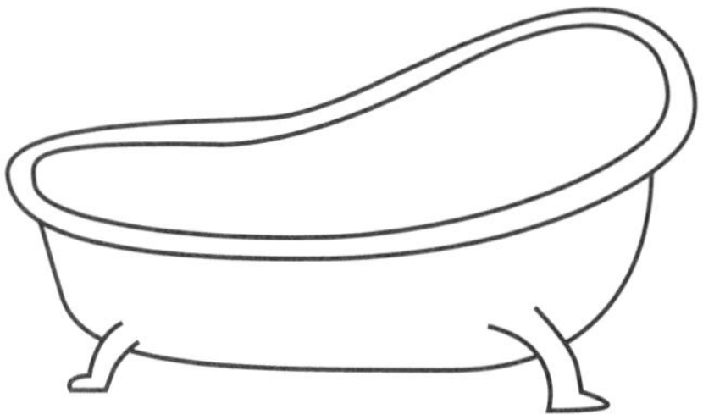

Washing a load of clothes

Brushing teeth with water running

Washing hands with water running

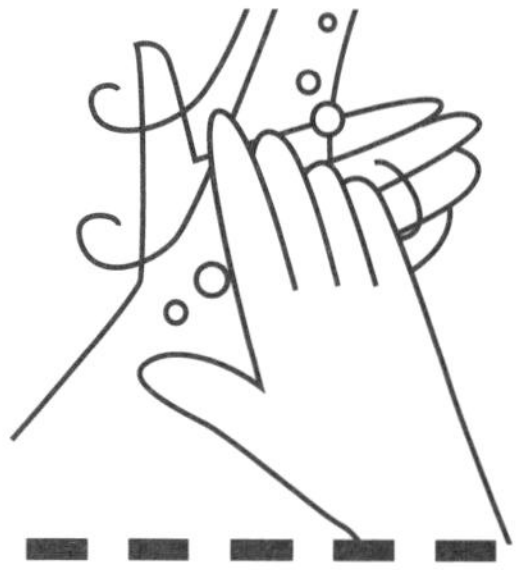

Name: ______________________________ Date: ____________

Water Diary

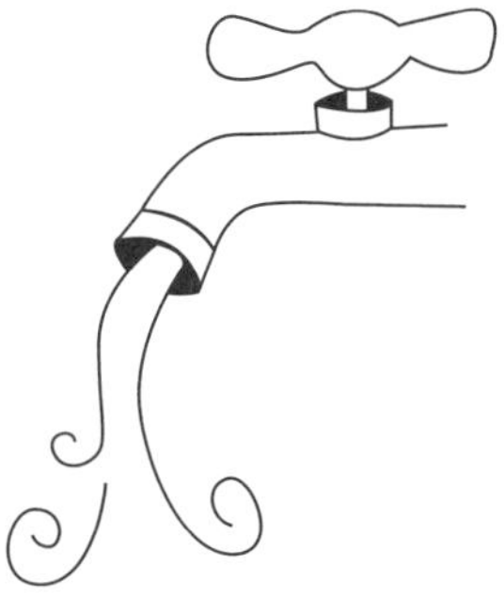

Number of people living in household: _____
How many gallons of water do you predict your household uses in one day? _________

Directions: During the day, make a tally mark in the appropriate row each time someone in your home uses water. Then calculate the total gallons your household used for each activity by multiplying the total number of times for each activity and the average amount of water used for that activity. Finally, calculate the total number of gallons your household actually used for the whole day by adding the water totals for each activity. (This total will be shared with the class anonymously.)

Water Use Activity	Number of Times (tally marks)	Total Number of Times (number)	Average Amount of Water Used (gallons)	Total Water Used for Each Activity
Washing machine			25	
Bath			20	
Dishwasher			20	
Shower			10	
Toilet flush			3	
Brushing teeth with water running			1	
Washing hands with water running			1	

Total gallons used in a day	
Number of people in your household	
Average water use per household member (Total gallons used ÷ number of people)	

How did your prediction compare to the actual amount of water your household used in one day? ____

Water in Kenya
Narratives

Melissa Perry, Oyugis, Kenya, writes: Before I came to Kenya to live as a Peace Corps volunteer, I never gave much thought to the water I used in the States. I just knew that if I needed water, all I had to do was turn on the faucet and there was safe, clean drinking water. Since I've come to Kenya, I understand more clearly what a luxury it is to have clean running water. In Kenya I get my water from a spring. If there hasn't been much rain, the water comes from a river nearby. I pay a boy 15 shillings (about 20 cents) to fetch the water from the spring. He brings the water in two 20 gal containers; the containers are placed on the back of his bicycle. The bike ride from the spring to town where I live is about two miles. He does this job every day and he makes around 10 to 15 trips a day. Therefore he earns around 150 to 225 shillings a day, which equals around 2 to 3 dollars. After I receive the water, I have to boil it to have drinking water. Most people in my town get their water this way.

Drew Denzin, Ololulunga, Kenya, writes: Our daily usage of water is extremely low compared to use in the United States. We have no running water and no flushing toilet, so we conserve quite a bit of water. In the morning, we brush our teeth using one cup of water, wash our faces with about two cups of water (we both use the same water), and are off to school. At school there also is no running water. Tea is served at 11 a.m., then we are home for lunch. We drink water (or Kool-Aid) with lunch, then return to teach. At night we cook with water (boiling noodles, rice, etc.) as well as boil water for bathing. We take the boiling water and add cold water until it is nice and warm, then "splash bathe" using 3 gal of water each. We collect the bath water and kitchen water in buckets to use it for watering our garden, so we reuse as much as possible.

Our community is much like us in terms of water usage. Our neighbors may go to the river to bathe or wash clothes. Water is scarce and it is safer to drink soda or tea rather than the river water. Everyone relies on rainwater for watering crops, and only the rich can afford to collect and store rainwater for personal use.

Patrick Campbell, Mombasa, Kenya,

writes: The first thing I do when I wake up is check whether or not I have running water. If I do, I fill my 3 l kettle and put it on my kerosene stove to boil drinking water for the day. And if I have water, I can shower. Otherwise I use water from my 100 l barrel, taking 3 l to boil and about 5 l to "splash bathe." I pour the 5 l into a basin, wet myself down, soap myself up, and rinse myself off. The key is to avoid getting soap in the water, otherwise you're stuck with soap in your eyes, trying to get water out of the barrel without getting soap into it, and polluting your only source of water (until the water comes back on). A very delicate operation, especially if you can't open your eyes.

I use water for many of the same things I did in the United States (drinking, bathing, washing clothes and dishes, and cleaning my house). The difference is that I use about one-fifth of the water for each of these tasks that I did in the States. For example, I can hand wash a load of clothes with about 10 l of water, quite a bit less than my washing machine at home would use. There are days, though, when I have sores on my knuckles from hand scrubbing clothes, that I still miss the washing machine.

Bryce Sitter, Mobile Clinic, Kajiado, Kenya,

writes: At a nearby technical school, students can learn a trade—metal work, plumbing, or carpentry. They live in dormitories, as they might in the States, but here they are given one to two buckets of water a week. Imagine how much water you use to bathe, wash your clothes, drink, and keep your dorm clean. The terrain is very dry and dusty. We have dust devils (miniature tornadoes) that spin through town and throw a dry "moon dust" everywhere. The soil is red and dirties clothes quickly.

I reside at the district hospital, where we can clean only once or twice a week due to water shortages. There are no toilets that can be flushed, and sanitation is a major problem. We use heavy solvents and cleaners to clean blood, sheets, and pit latrines. If you come to the hospital to deliver a baby or get stitches, you bring your own water. When you go to a restaurant, you often don't get the option of washing your hands before you eat. A simple pleasure is taking my Friday night "splash bath." I use less than a pitcher of water to wash my whole body, while standing in a large tub to collect the dirty runoff water. People sell water when they have access to a vehicle and can go to the next town and get it.

If I Built a Car

Description

Learners design their own dream cars, learn about different types of engineering and how engineers use the design process, and work with a team to design and build an assembly line to mass produce foam race cars. Learners then communicate the design process they used.

Suggested Grade Levels: 3–6

Lesson Objectives Connecting to the *Framework*

Science and Engineering Practices

- Asking questions (for science) and defining problems (for engineering)
- Constructing explanations (for science) and designing solutions (for engineering)

Disciplinary Core Ideas

ETS1.A: Defining and Delimiting Engineering Problems
ETS1.B: Developing Possible Solutions
ETS1.C: Optimizing the Design Solution

Crosscutting Concepts

- Systems and System Models

Featured Picture Books

Title	***If I Built a Car***
Author and Illustrator	**Chris Van Dusen**
Publisher	**Puffin**
Year	**2007**
Genre	**Story**
Summary	**Jack has designed the ultimate fantasy car. This whimsical take on the car of the future will ignite the imaginations of inventors of all ages.**

Title	***Inventing the Automobile***
Author	**Erinn Banting**
Publisher	**Crabtree**
Year	**2006**
Genre	**Nonnarrative Information**
Summary	**From the horse-drawn carriage to cars of the future, this book details the evolution of the automobile.**

Time Needed

This lesson will take several class periods. Suggested scheduling is as follows:

Day 1: **Engage** with *If I Built a Car* read aloud and **Explore** with Dream Cars

Day 2: **Explain** with What Do Engineers Do? and **Elaborate** Part 1: Mass Production

Day 3: *Inventing the Automobile* read aloud and **Elaborate** Part 2: Assembly Line Design

Day 4: **Evaluate** with Communicating the Design Process and The Little Car That Changed the World

Materials

(per team of 4–6 students)

- Foamies race car bucket
- 3 gallon-size zipper-close plastic bags

  (Note: Each bucket contains materials to make 18 cars. Teams will build only 12 cars, so you will have spare parts. Before the lesson, we suggest organizing each bucket into three separate gallon-size bags: one containing the wheels and axles, one containing the bodies, and another containing the sticky numbers. This way each team will have three zipper bags containing the parts from their bucket. After Part 1, they can disassemble the parts and put them back into the appropriate bags.)
- Plastic cup to use as scrap bucket
- MyChron silent student timers or stopwatches
- Mass Production Graph overhead (for teacher use)

Foamies race car buckets can be purchased at

www.amazon.com
(Darice Foamies 3D Activity Bucket, Race Cars)

www.craftsuppliesforless.com
(Item #: FRCB18)

MyChron Timers are available from

www.onlinesciencemall.com and *www.teachersource.com*

Student Pages

- My Dream Car
- What Do Engineers Do?
- Foamies Car Corporation Letter
- Assembly Line Design
- Communicating the Design Process
- The Little Car That Changed the World

Background

The design process in technology is the equivalent to inquiry in science. In scientific inquiry, students explore ideas and propose explanations about the natural world; in technological design, students identify a problem or need, design and implement a solution, evaluate a product or design, and communicate the design process. Students in grades 4–6 can begin to differentiate between science and technology by complementing their scientific investigations with activities that are meant to meet a human need, solve a problem, or develop a product.

The field that deals with designing materials, structures, products, and processes is known as *engineering*. Engineering is not the same as science. Science is about exploring the natural world, whereas engineering is about designing solutions to problems. In this lesson, teams of students learn to work together as engineers to design and test an assembly line. An *assembly line* is a carefully planned, sequential manufacturing process in which parts, usually carried along a mechanized conveyor, are added to a product. This process ensures that a large number of identical products can be made more cheaply and quickly than if they were individually handcrafted. Engineers are involved in all aspects of assembly line design, from analyzing the steps necessary to manufacture a product to controlling the quality of the products that roll off the line.

Many students think Henry Ford invented the car and the assembly line. He did neither. The first reliable, working automobiles were made in Germany in the late 1800s, one at a time and mostly by hand. The assembly sometimes took more than a year. This made the manufacturing process very expensive, and only the wealthy could afford to buy cars. In 1901, the American automobile manufacturer Olds Motor Works designed an assembly line in which workers moved from car to car to install a piece or system. This sped up the manufacturing process considerably. In 1913, Henry Ford perfected the assembly line by adding a moving conveyor belt to manufacture his Model T automobiles. Workers no longer had to move from car to car to add their parts; instead, the cars were attached to a conveyor that moved each vehicle past a stationary worker. By the 1920s, one Model T rolled off the assembly line every 24 sec.! Not only did this innovation make automobiles affordable for average working people, but it also transformed modern industry. Ford's mass production methods were eventually adopted by almost every other manufacturing industry. Now most of the products we use every day are manufactured on assembly lines.

Engage

If I Built a Car

Show students the cover of *If I Built a Car*. Tell them the book was written and illustrated by Chris Van Dusen. When he was a little boy, Chris Van Dusen's parents would pile all five of their kids into a car and drive three hours to visit their grandparents. This was before Game Boys and DVD players were invented, so the five brothers passed the time by playing games like "What would you change on this car?" That's what inspired him to write this book when he grew up. (For more information about Chris Van Dusen, go to *www.chrisvandusen.com.*)

Making Connections: Text-to-Self

Before reading, open the book cover to show students the first double-page spread of Jack's car designs. Then ask

? Have you ever sketched designs of cars, houses, clothes, or anything else? Turn and talk about the kinds of things you might like to design.

Read the book aloud. After reading, ask

? What would your dream car look like? What special features would it have? Turn and talk.

Tell students that some of their dream car ideas might not be far-fetched at all! Automotive designers, artists, and engineers work in teams to dream up new vehicles known as concept cars, and then prototypes are built. A *prototype* is the first full-size, usually working, model of an invention. Automakers unveil their concept car prototypes at conventions to demonstrate new ideas in car design and to see how people react to them. Tell students that you are going to show them some incredible and real concept cars.

VISUALIZING CONCEPT CARS

Visualizing

In advance, use large sticky notes to cover the pictures of the concept cars on pages 30 and 31 of *Inventing the Automobile* by Erinn Banting. With the pictures covered, read the first paragraph about the Mercedes-Benz Smart Fortwo car. Ask students to visualize what the car looks like. They may have already seen a smart car on the road. Then reveal the picture of the Smart Fortwo. Repeat for the other four concept cars. After reading about the Mercedes-Benz Bionic, you may want to show students the photo of the boxfish and Bionic side by side at *http://news.cnet.com/2300-11395_3-6130045-2.html.*

explore

Dream Cars

Making Connections: Text-to-Text

Tell students that all of these concept cars began with a drawing. Share the last double-page spread from *If I Built a Car,* showing the sketches of Jack's dream car. Describe how teams of designers, artists, and engineers always start with drawings of their ideas before their concept cars are built. Then pass out the My Dream Car student page and have students design their own dream cars on paper. They can give them catchy names and label any special features. When they are finished, have students share their car designs with two or three other students.

DREAM CAR DESIGNS

explain

What Do Engineers Do?

Tell students that in the real world, cars are designed by engineers and other design professionals using a step-by-step process. Ask

- ? Do you know anyone who is an engineer? What kinds of things do you think engineers do? Turn and talk.

Pairs Read

Tell students they are going to do a pairs read to find out what engineers do. Give each pair of students a copy of What Do Engineers Do? Have students take turns reading aloud from the article. While one partner reads a paragraph, the other should listen and then make comments ("I think ..."), ask questions ("I wonder ..."), or share any new learning (I didn't know ...").

Questioning

After students finish reading, ask them

- ? What are the steps of the design process? (identify a problem, design a solution, implement the design, evaluate the design, and communicate the process)
- ? What kind of engineer would design a car engine? (mechanical engineer)
- ? What kind of engineer would design a new type of headlight for a car? (electrical engineer)
- ? What kind of engineer would design a new fuel for a car? (chemical engineer)
- ? What kind of engineer would design an assembly line to build a car? (industrial engineer)
- ? What kind of engineer would design a highway for a car to drive on? (civil engineer)
- ? What kind of engineer would design the satellite that sends information to the car's GPS navigation system? (aerospace engineer)
- ? What characteristics do you think an engineer would need to have to be successful? (creativity, patience, logical thinking skills, ability to work with others, good communication skills, etc.)

A FOAMIE RACE CAR

- ? If you were going to be an engineer, what kind would you be and why?

elaborate

Part 1: Mass Production

Tell students that in the early 1900s, the first cars were built one at a time and almost entirely by hand. Ask

- ? How long do you think it took to build a car that way? (as long as a year to make one car)

Then explain that modern car companies can produce millions of nearly identical cars every year. This is known as *mass production*.

Next tell students that you have an exciting challenge for them! Pass out the letter from the fictional Foamies Car Corporation. Tell students that each team (of four to six students) will compete to win the Foamies Car Corporation's business. The team that can mass produce 12 cars the fastest will win! The letter details the criteria required by the Foamies Car Corporation to build their race cars. Have each team read the letter and brainstorm how they could quickly and efficiently build 12 cars according to the six criteria listed.

Mass producing Foamies race cars

(Note: It is important to let teams come up with their own processes for mass production at this point. Some teams may simply have each member build as many cars as they can. Some may come up with an assembly line design on their own, but don't give them any clues that might lead them to create an assembly line. In Part 2, they will learn how to design an assembly line and will compare that time to their Part 1 time.)

Next distribute the timers and let students practice using them. Remind students that you will be the chief quality control engineer, the person responsible for checking the quality of their cars after they have been manufactured. Then—with a "Ready, set, build!"—start the contest. (For fun, you may want to play some fast music during the competition.) When a team finishes and calls out "Time!" rush over to do a quick quality control check to make sure they have met all six criteria as outlined in the letter from the Foamies Car Corporation. If they haven't satisfactorily met all six criteria, have them resume timing and then call out again when they have corrected their quality issues. They will add the additional time it takes them to their original time. As teams finish, have them record their times on the Mass Production Graph overhead, Part 1. You will need to have students disassemble the cars and put the parts back in the appropriate plastic bags before beginning Part 2.

elaborate

Part 2: Assembly Line Design Determining Importance

Have students look at the results from Part 1 on the overhead graph. Then explain that car companies use a process that makes mass production very fast and efficient. Have students listen for the name of this invention (the moving assembly line) as you read aloud pages 12–13 of *Inventing the Automobile* by Erinn Banting (you may want to read the rest of this book aloud later). After reading the section titled "Henry Ford," show the photo of the moving assembly line at the top of page 13 and point out the track along which the cars move. Then ask

? What is the advantage of a moving assembly line? (Workers no longer need to move from car to car to add their parts; it saves time.)

? Why do you think cars are no longer handcrafted one at a time? (It takes a long time; it's expensive; each car might be a little different.)

Next you may want to show the 8 min. 54 sec. video of the Ford Mustang assembly line in action at *http://manufacturing.stanford.edu/hetm.html* by clicking on "Cars" on the left-hand menu. If you have a Discovery Education subscription, use the 4 min. 24 sec. assembly line video segment from "Greatest Inventions With Bill Nye: Math, Business, and Industry." Then tell students that Henry Ford once said, "Nothing is particularly hard if you divide it into small jobs." Ask

? What do you think he meant by that?

? How does this quote relate to the assembly line?

CELEBRATING ASSEMBLY LINE SUCCESS

- ? How could you divide up the steps it takes to build the Foamies race cars into small jobs?

Have them think about what job or jobs could be done by each person on their teams to build 12 cars faster than they did in Part 1. To get them thinking about all of the jobs involved, ask questions such as

- ? Which team member will start and stop the timer?
- ? Who will put the front wheels on?
- ? Who will put the side numbers on?
- ? Who will clean up the scraps?
- ? Who will line the cars up in order?

Then pass out the Assembly Line Design student page. Have team members describe the jobs and the name of the person who will perform each job or jobs on the Assembly Line Design page. They will need a check mark from you before they begin building their cars using the assembly line. After you have checked that all teams have a workable plan, have them organize their materials and get ready to build. Just as in Part 1, they will need to time how long it takes their teams to build 12 cars from start to finish. Then—with a "Ready, set, build!"—start Part 2 of the contest. You will be the chief quality control engineer again and will check the quality of their completed cars. Have students record their new times at the bottom of the Assembly Line Design page. Teams can then record their Part 2 (using a different color than they did for Part 1) time on the Mass Production Graph overhead.

After all teams have finished and recorded their times on their papers and on the overhead graph, ask

- ? Overall, did most of the teams complete the task faster in Part 1 or Part 2?
- ? Why do you think so?
- ? What are the advantages of mass producing cars on an assembly line? (It is faster and cheaper, and the cars will all look alike.)
- ? How well did you communicate with one another as you designed the assembly line?
- ? How well did your team work together during the competition?
- ? What could you do to work better as a team?
- ? What changes could you make to your assembly line design to manufacture 16 cars even faster? Turn and talk.
- ? Is there a limit to how fast an assembly line can produce products? Why or why not? (Yes, because there is a limit to how fast people and machines can move.)

For fun, show students a clip from the classic *I Love Lucy* episode where Lucy and Ethel can't keep up with the conveyor belt on the chocolate candy assembly line. This clip can be found by doing an internet search for "I Love Lucy assembly line."

evaluate

Communicating the Design Process and The Little Car That Changed the World

Have each student answer the design process questions on the Communicating the Design Process and The Little Car That Changed the World student pages. The answers for the first page will vary. The answers for The Little Car That Changed the World are as follows:

1. What was the problem Henry Ford wanted to solve? (He wanted to make a high-quality car that was more affordable.)
2. What solution did he design? (the Model T)
3. How did he evaluate the solution? (He test drove it and calculated how much it would cost to make.)
4. How did he know that he was successful in solving the problem? (In the first year, more than 10,000 Model Ts were sold; by 1918 half of the cars in the United States were Model Ts; or average working people could afford to buy them.)
5. How did Henry Ford's invention of the Model T change the world? (Answers will vary but should include the idea that more people can afford cars now or that cars have become a primary form of transportation.)

Inquiry Place

Have students brainstorm questions about designing, engineering, or manufacturing, such as

- ? Can you and your teammates design an assembly line to make a simple product like fortune-tellers, paper airplanes, or paper footballs? Try it!
- ? Can you design a bridge out of one sheet of paper? How many pennies can it hold? Try it!
- ? What's the tallest tower you can build using two sheets of newspaper? You may bend, fold, or tear the newspaper, but you cannot use glue, tape, or staples. Try it!
- ? How are some everyday things—such as crayons, pencils, or candy bars—made? Research it!
- ? What are the latest designs in concept cars? Research it!

Then have students select a question to investigate, or have groups of students vote on the question they want to investigate as a team. Students can present their findings at a poster session or gallery walk.

Websites

Discover Engineering
http://discoverengineering.org

Engineering for Middle School Girls
www.engineergirl.org

Engineer Your Life: A Guide to Engineering for High School Girls
www.engineeryourlife.org

How Everyday Things are Made
http://manufacturing.stanford.edu

More Books to Read

Beatty, A. 2013. *Rosie Revere, engineer.* New York: Harry N. Abrams.
Summary: Young Rosie dreams of being an engineer. Alone in her room at night, she constructs great inventions from odds and ends. Afraid of failure, Rosie hides her creations under her bed until a fateful visit from her great-great-Aunt Rose, who shows her a first flop is not something to fear. It's something to celebrate!

Miller, R. 2014. *Engineering close-up* series: *Engineering in our everyday lives, Engineers solve problems, Engineers build models.* New York: Crabtree Publishing Company.
Summary: This series provides an exciting and accessible introduction to the engineering professions and the engineering design process. It includes child-centered examples and opportunities for hands-on learning.

Rose, S. 2003. *How things are made: From automobiles to zippers.* New York: Black Dog and Leventhal.
Summary: Each page of this book for older readers features informative text followed by detailed, step-by-step descriptions of the manufacturing process for 34 different items. Interesting sidebars and simple black-and-white diagrams help tell the stories behind the things we sometimes take for granted but often wonder about.

Slavin, B. 2007. *Transformed: How everyday things are made.* Toronto: Kids Can Press.
Summary: Readers learn how 69 familiar items are made, including baseballs, toothpaste, and peanut butter. The raw materials used in the manufacturing processes are described, and the steps needed to manufacture each item are numbered in bold type so readers can follow along.

Smith, P. 2007. *See how it's made.* New York: DK Publishing.
Summary: From ice cream to T-shirts to electric guitars, this fascinating book follows the manufacture of a variety of everyday items from start to finish.

Time for Kids editors. 2008. *Henry Ford: Putting the world on wheels.* With D. El Nabli. New York: HarperCollins.
Summary: This mini-biography tells the story of Henry Ford, who as a young boy was fascinated by technology and how objects worked. His childhood interests led him to leave the Ford family farm in Michigan in search of a career with machinery. His innovations, including affordable automobiles and the first large-scale moving assembly line, changed the world.

My Dream Car

by ______________________

Name of Car ______________________

What Do Engineers Do?

The career that deals with designing materials, structures, products, and processes is known as engineering. Women and men in this field are known as engineers (not to be confused with the people who operate trains!). Some of the main types of engineers, as well as what they design, are listed in the chart below.

No matter what branch of engineering they are in, all engineers follow certain steps to design materials (like plastics), structures (like bridges), products (like tires), or processes (like assembly lines). Together, these steps are known as the design process. By working through these steps, engineers increase their odds that their concepts will work when built.

Types of Engineers	**Examples of What They Design**
Civil Engineer	Bridges, highways, stadiums, airports, water and sewer systems, race tracks
Electrical Engineer	Power grids, computers and parts, cell phones, video game components, lighting
Mechanical Engineer	Things that move: engines, motors, toys, tools, robot structures, space exploration vehicles
Chemical Engineer	Plastics, paints, medicines, fuels, dyes, and other chemical products
Industrial Engineer	Processes for making things: plant layouts, assembly lines, efficient work spaces
Aerospace Engineer	Airplanes, helicopters, spacecraft, missiles, satellites

Name: ______________________________

The steps of the design process are as follows:

- **Identify a problem or challenge.** What is the problem you are trying to solve? What are the constraints–in other words, are there certain size, weight, space, time, materials, or budget limitations for the design? Are there safety or environmental concerns you need to keep in mind? Talk to the people who will be using the product or process–do they have certain opinions or beliefs that you need to consider? After you find out all you can about the challenge (including what solutions have been designed before), you are ready to design!
- **Design a solution or product.** Brainstorm several ways to solve the problem, but keep in mind the constraints. Get feedback from other people, then choose your best idea and begin creating drawings, plans, or models. It is helpful to work with others as you are designing. Most engineers work in teams!
- **Implement a proposed design.** The only way to find out whether your design will work is to test it out. Collaborate with others to organize the materials and plan your work. Then try it!
- **Evaluate a completed design or product.** How well does your design meet the challenge or solve the problem? If your design doesn't successfully meet the challenge or fully solve the problem, you'll need to repeat the steps listed above. If your design was a success, go on to the next step!
- **Communicate the process.** What was the problem, and how did you solve it? Be ready to describe, in words or pictures, the process you went through and the solution you designed.

Look around you. Most of the things you use every day have been engineered in some way, from the pencil you hold in your hand to the sneakers you wear on your feet. Engineers use imagination and logic to invent, design, and build things that matter. Engineers are team players with independent minds who turn ideas into reality. By dreaming up practical solutions to all kinds of problems, engineers are changing the world every day.

Foamies
Car Corporation

Dear Engineers,

The Foamies Car Corporation is in need of a process to produce our Foamies Race Cars. We will award a manufacturing contract to the team of engineers who can produce 12 fully assembled Foamies race cars in the shortest amount of time.

The following criteria must be used in your design:

1. Your team must be made up of a minimum of four workers and a maximum of six workers.
2. Each completed car should have four wheels and two axles attached to a foam body.
3. Both sides of the cars should be numbered from 1 to 12. Blue cars may have only red or white numbers. Red cars may have only yellow or black numbers.
4. The cars must be lined up front to back. The numbers must be in order from 1 to 12.
5. There should be no scrap material anywhere on the assembly line after the 12 cars are assembled. All scraps must be placed in a scrap bucket for recycling.
6. Your teacher will be the chief quality control engineer, the person responsible for checking the quality of the cars your team manufactures. When you are finished, your team must call out "Time!" to signal the teacher that your cars are ready to be inspected.

May the best team win!

Sincerely,

Holden D. Cash

Holden D. Cash
Chairman of the Board
Foamies Car Corporation

Name: ______________________________

Mass Production Graph

Part 1 ☐
Part 2 ☐

Time (seconds)

0

Part 1	Part 2	Part 1	Part 2	Part 1	Part 2	Part 1	Part 2	Part 1	Part 2
Team Name		Team Name		Team Name		Team Name		Team Name	

Teams

Foamies

Car Corporation

Assembly Line Design

Team name: ______________________________

Team members: ____

1 Describe the job that will be done by each team member on the assembly line.

Job	Team Member

2 Teacher checkpoint ☐

3 Now organize your materials and get ready to build!

4 Time it took to build 12 cars using an assembly line (Part 2 time): ______

Name: ______________________________

Communicating the Design Process

Think about your team's assembly line and how you used the design process to create it. Then answer the questions below.

1 Identify the problem or challenge: What was the problem your team was trying to solve?

2 Design a solution or product: Describe your assembly line in words and/or labeled pictures.

3 Implement a proposed design: How did you organize your materials? How did you involve all team members?

Name: ______________________________

Communicating the Design Process cont.

4 Evaluate a completed design or product.

a How well did your assembly line design meet the challenge? (Think about your team's Part 2 time compared to your team's Part 1 time.)

b If you were going to make any changes to your design, what would you change so that the Foamies Car Corporation would want to use your assembly line?

Name: ______________________________

The Little Car That Changed the World

Read the following description of how Henry Ford used the design process to invent and manufacture the Model T automobile.

Library of Congress, Prints & Photographs Division [reproduction number, LC-USZ62-62258]

Before 1908, only wealthy people could afford to buy an automobile. Henry Ford wanted to create a high-quality car that more people could afford. In 1906, Ford set up a secret room at his plant in Detroit, Michigan, and he and a team of engineers began brainstorming ideas to make a more affordable car. They began by sketching out their ideas on blackboards and developing elaborate plans.

Finally, in 1908, they created a prototype. When Henry Ford brought the prototype out of the factory for its first test drive, he was too excited to drive it himself. An assistant had to take the wheel. After multiple test drives to see how well the car worked, and after calculating how much it would cost to make, many changes were made. Finally, success! Ford announced the invention of the little black car that would change the world–the Model T.

The first Model T was sold on October 1, 1908, and cost only $850. Cars sold by other companies at that time often cost $2,000 to $3,000. In its first year, more than 10,000 Model Ts were sold. This set a new record for automobile sales! Over the next several years, Ford continued to work on improving the Model T manufacturing process. In 1913, he perfected the assembly line by adding the moving conveyor belt. Workers no longer had to move from car to car to add their parts. Instead the cars were attached to a conveyor that moved each vehicle past a worker stationed in one place. Ford's moving assembly line allowed cars to be manufactured more quickly and cheaply than ever before. By 1918, half of all the cars sold in the United States were Model Ts. Henry Ford had changed the automobile from a luxury only the rich could afford to reliable transportation for average working people.

Name: ______________________________

The Little Car That Changed the World cont.

Answer the following questions about the design process used by Henry Ford:

1 What was the problem Henry Ford wanted to solve? ______________

____

____

____

2 What solution did he design? ______________________________

____

____

____

3 How did he evaluate the solution? ______________________________

____

____

____

4 How did he know that he was successful in solving the problem?

____

____

____

5 How did Henry Ford's invention of the Model T change the world?

____

____

____

Appendix 1

Connections Between Lessons and *A Framework for K–12 Science Education*

Chapter	Lesson Title	Grades	Science and Engineering Practices	Disciplinary Core Ideas	Crosscutting Concepts
6	Earth Hounds	3–6	• Obtaining, evaluating, and communicating information	**n/a**	• Scale, Proportion, and Quantity
7	Name That Shell!	3–5	• Constructing explanations (for science) and designing solutions (for engineering) • Obtaining, evaluating, and communicating information	**LS1.A:** Structure and Function	• Structure and Function
8	Rice Is Life	3–6	• Planning and carrying out investigations • Analyzing and interpreting data	**LS1.A:** Structure and Function **LS1.B:** Growth and Development of Organisms	• Structure and Function • Patterns
9	What's Poppin'?	5–6	• Planning and carrying out investigations • Analyzing and interpreting data	**n/a**	• Cause and Effect
10	Mystery Pellets	3–6	• Analyzing and interpreting data • Constructing explanations (for science) and designing solutions (for engineering) • Obtaining, evaluating, and communicating information	**LS2.A:** Interdependent Relationships in Ecosystems **LS2.B:** Cycles of Matter and Energy Transfer in Ecosystems	• Systems and System Models
11	Close Encounters of the Symbiotic Kind	3–6	• Constructing explanations (for science) and designing solutions (for engineering) • Obtaining, evaluating, and communicating information	**LS2.A:** Interdependent Relationships in Ecosystems	• Systems and System Models
12	Turtle Hurdles	3–5	• Developing and using models • Obtaining, evaluating, and communicating information	**LS4.D:** Biodiversity and Humans	• Cause and Effect
13	Oil Spill!	3–5	• Developing and using models • Planning and carrying out investigations • Analyzing and interpreting data	**LS4.D:** Biodiversity and Humans	• Cause and Effect
14	Sheep in a Jeep	3–5	• Planning and carrying out investigations • Analyzing and interpreting data	**PS2.A:** Forces and Motion **PS2.B:** Types of Interactions	• Cause and Effect
15	Sounds of Science	3–6	• Developing and using models • Constructing explanations (for science) and designing solutions (for engineering)	**PS3.A:** Definitions of Energy **PS4.A:** Wave Properties	• Energy and Matter
16	Chemical Change Café	3–5	• Constructing explanations (for science) and designing solutions (for engineering)	**PS1.B:** Chemical Reactions	• Cause and Effect

Appendix 1. Connections Between Lessons and *A Framework for K–12 Science Educatio*
(continued)

Chapter	Lesson Title	Grades	Science and Engineering Practices	Disciplinary Core Ideas	Crosscutting Concepts
17	The Changing Moon	3–5	• Asking questions (for science) and defining problems (for engineering) • Developing and using models • Analyzing and interpreting data	**ESS1.B:** Earth and the Solar System	• Patterns
18	Day and Night	3–5	• Asking questions (for science) and defining problems (for engineering) • Developing and using models • Analyzing and interpreting data	**ESS1.B:** Earth and the Solar System	• Patterns
19	Grand Canyon	3–6	• Developing and using models • Constructing explanations (for science) and designing solutions (for engineering) • Obtaining, evaluating, and communicating information	**ESS2.A:** Earth Materials and Systems	• Stability and Change
20	Brainstorms: From Idea to Invention	5–6	• Asking questions (for science) and defining problems (for engineering) • Planning and carrying out investigations • Constructing explanations (for science) and designing solutions (for engineering)	**ETS1.A:** Defining and Delimiting Engineering Problems **ETS1.B:** Developing Possible Solutions **ETS1.C:** Optimizing the Design Solution	• Structure and Function
21	Bugs!	3–5	• Constructing explanations (for science) and designing solutions (for engineering) • Obtaining, evaluating, and communicating information	**LS1.A:** Structure and Function	• Structure and Function
22	Batteries Included	3–5	• Asking questions (for science) and defining problems (for engineering) • Constructing explanations (for science) and designing solutions (for engineering)	**PS3.A:** Definitions of Energy **PS3.B:** Conservation of Energy and Energy Transfer	• Energy and Matter
23	The Secrets of Flight	3–6	• Asking questions (for science) and defining problems (for engineering) • Constructing explanations (for science) and designing solutions (for engineering)	**PS2.A:** Forces and Motion **PS2.B:** Types of Interactions **ETS1.A:** Defining and Delimiting Engineering Problems **ETS1.B:** Developing Possible Solutions **ETS1.C:** Optimizing the Design Solution	• Cause and Effect
24	Down the Drain	3–6	• Analyzing and interpreting data • Obtaining, evaluating, and communicating information	**ESS3.A:** Natural Resources	• Cause and Effect
25	If I Built a Car	3–6	• Asking questions (for science) and defining problems (for engineering) • Constructing explanations (for science) and designing solutions (for engineering)	**ETS1.A:** Defining and Delimiting Engineering Problems **ETS1.B:** Developing Possible Solutions **ETS1.C:** Optimizing the Design Solution	• Systems and System Models

Appendix 2

Correlations Between Lessons and *Common Core State Standards, English Language Arts (ELA)*

Lesson Title	Suggested Grade Levels	*Common Core State Standards, ELA*
Earth Hounds	3–6	***Grade 3*** **RL.3.1.** Ask and answer questions to demonstrate understanding of a text, referring explicitly to the text as the basis for the answers. **RL.3.2.** Recount stories, including fables, folktales, and myths from diverse cultures; determine the central message, lesson, or moral and explain how it is conveyed through key details in the text. **SL.3.1.** Engage effectively in a range of collaborative discussions (one-on-one, in groups, and teacher-led) with diverse partners on *grade 3 topics and texts*, building on others' ideas and expressing their own clearly. **SL.3.1.A.** Come to discussions prepared, having read or studied required material; explicitly draw on that preparation and other information known about the topic to explore ideas under discussion. **SL.3.1.B.** Follow agreed-upon rules for discussions (e.g., gaining the floor in respectful ways, listening to others with care, speaking one at a time about the topics and texts under discussion). **SL.3.1.C.** Ask questions to check understanding of information presented, stay on topic, and link their comments to the remarks of others. **SL.3.1.D.** Explain their own ideas and understanding in light of the discussion. **SL.3.2.** Determine the main ideas and supporting details of a text read aloud or information presented in diverse media and formats, including visually, quantitatively, and orally. **W.3.10.** Write routinely over extended time frames (time for research, reflection, and revision) and shorter time frames (a single sitting or a day or two) for a range of discipline-specific tasks, purposes, and audiences. **L.3.6.** Acquire and use accurately grade-appropriate conversational, general academic, and domain-specific words and phrases, including those that signal spatial and temporal relationships (e.g., *After dinner that night we went looking for them*). ***Grade 4*** **RL.4.1.** Refer to details and examples in a text when explaining what the text says explicitly and when drawing inferences from the text. **RL.4.2.** Determine a theme of a story, drama, or poem from details in the text; summarize the text. **SL.4.1.** Engage effectively in a range of collaborative discussions (one-on-one, in groups, and teacher-led) with diverse partners on *grade 4 topics and texts*, building on others' ideas and expressing their own clearly. **SL.4.1.A.** Come to discussions prepared, having read or studied required material; explicitly draw on that preparation and other information known about the topic to explore ideas under discussion. **SL.4.1.B.** Follow agreed-upon rules for discussions and carry out assigned roles. **SL.4.1.C.** Pose and respond to specific questions to clarify or follow up on information, and make comments that contribute to the discussion and link to the remarks of others. **SL.4.1.D.** Review the key ideas expressed and explain their own ideas and understanding in light of the discussion. **W.4.10.** Write routinely over extended time frames (time for research, reflection, and revision) and shorter time frames (a single sitting or a day or two) for a range of discipline-specific tasks, purposes, and audiences. **L.4.6.** Acquire and use accurately grade-appropriate general academic and domain-specific words and phrases, including those that signal precise actions, emotions, or states of being (e.g., quizzed, whined, stammered) and that are basic to a particular topic (e.g., *wildlife, conservation,* and *endangered* when discussing animal preservation). ***Grade 5*** **RL.5.1.** Quote accurately from a text when explaining what the text says explicitly and when drawing inferences from the text. **RL.5.2.** Determine a theme of a story, drama, or poem from details in the text, including how characters in a story or drama respond to challenges or how the speaker in a poem reflects upon a topic; summarize the text.

Appendix 2. Correlations Between Lessons and *Common Core State Standards, English Language Arts (ELA)* *(continued)*

Lesson Title	Suggested Grade Levels	*Common Core State Standards, ELA*
Earth Hounds *(continued)*	3–6	**SL.5.1.** Engage effectively in a range of collaborative discussions (one-on-one, in groups, and teacher-led) with diverse partners on *grade 5 topics and texts*, building on others' ideas and expressing their own clearly. **SL.5.1.A.** Come to discussions prepared, having read or studied required material; explicitly draw on that preparation and other information known about the topic to explore ideas under discussion. **SL.5.1.B.** Follow agreed-upon rules for discussions and carry out assigned roles. **SL.5.1.C.** Pose and respond to specific questions by making comments that contribute to the discussion and elaborate on the remarks of others. **SL.5.1.D.** Review the key ideas expressed and draw conclusions in light of information and knowledge gained from the discussions. **W.5.10.** Write routinely over extended time frames (time for research, reflection, and revision) and shorter time frames (a single sitting or a day or two) for a range of discipline-specific tasks, purposes, and audiences. **L.5.6.** Acquire and use accurately grade-appropriate general academic and domain-specific words and phrases, including those that signal contrast, addition, and other logical relationships (e.g., *however, although, nevertheless, similarly, moreover, in addition*). ***Grade 6*** **RL.6.1.** Cite textual evidence to support analysis of what the text says explicitly as well as inferences drawn from the text. **RL.6.2.** Determine a theme or central idea of a text and how it is conveyed through particular details; provide a summary of the text distinct from personal opinions or judgments. **SL.6.1.** Engage effectively in a range of collaborative discussions (one-on-one, in groups, and teacher-led) with diverse partners on grade 6 topics, texts, and issues, building on others' ideas and expressing their own clearly. **SL.6.1.A.** Come to discussions prepared, having read or studied required material; explicitly draw on that preparation by referring to evidence on the topic, text, or issue to probe and reflect on ideas under discussion. **SL.6.1.B.** Follow rules for collegial discussions, set specific goals and deadlines, and define individual roles as needed. **SL.6.1.C.** Pose and respond to specific questions with elaboration and detail by making comments that contribute to the topic, text, or issue under discussion. **SL.6.1.D.** Review the key ideas expressed and demonstrate understanding of multiple perspectives through reflection and paraphrasing. **W.6.10.** Write routinely over extended time frames (time for research, reflection, and revision) and shorter time frames (a single sitting or a day or two) for a range of discipline-specific tasks, purposes, and audiences. **L.6.6.** Acquire and use accurately grade-appropriate general academic and domain-specific words and phrases; gather vocabulary knowledge when considering a word or phrase important to comprehension or expression. **RST.6-8.3.** Follow precisely a multistep procedure when carrying out experiments, taking measurements, or performing technical tasks. **WHST.6-8.10.** Write routinely over extended time frames (time for reflection and revision) and shorter time frames (a single sitting or a day or two) for a range of discipline-specific tasks, purposes, and audiences.
Name That Shell!	3–5	***Grade 3*** **RL.3.1.** Ask and answer questions to demonstrate understanding of a text, referring explicitly to the text as the basis for the answers. **RL.3.2.** Recount stories, including fables, folktales, and myths from diverse cultures; determine the central message, lesson, or moral and explain how it is conveyed through key details in the text. **RL.3.4.** Determine the meaning of words and phrases as they are used in a text, distinguishing literal from nonliteral language. **SL.3.1.** Engage effectively in a range of collaborative discussions (one-on-one, in groups, and teacher-led) with diverse partners on *grade 3 topics and texts*, building on others' ideas and expressing their own clearly. **SL.3.1.A.** Come to discussions prepared, having read or studied required material; explicitly draw on that preparation and other information known about the topic to explore ideas under discussion. **SL.3.1.B.** Follow agreed-upon rules for discussions (e.g., gaining the floor in respectful ways, listening to others with care, speaking one at a time about the topics and texts under discussion). **SL.3.1.C.** Ask questions to check understanding of information presented, stay on topic, and link their comments to the remarks of others. **SL.3.1.D.** Explain their own ideas and understanding in light of the discussion.

Lesson Title	Suggested Grade Levels	*Common Core State Standards, ELA*
Name That Shell! *(continued)*	**3–5**	**SL.3.2.** Determine the main ideas and supporting details of a text read aloud or information presented in diverse media and formats, including visually, quantitatively, and orally. **W.3.10.** Write routinely over extended time frames (time for research, reflection, and revision) and shorter time frames (a single sitting or a day or two) for a range of discipline-specific tasks, purposes, and audiences. **L.3.6.** Acquire and use accurately grade-appropriate conversational, general academic, and domain-specific words and phrases, including those that signal spatial and temporal relationships (e.g., *After dinner that night we went looking for them*). ***Grade 4*** **RL.4.1.** Refer to details and examples in a text when explaining what the text says explicitly and when drawing inferences from the text. **RL.4.2.** Determine a theme of a story, drama, or poem from details in the text; summarize the text. **RL.4.4.** Determine the meaning of words and phrases as they are used in a text, including those that allude to significant characters found in mythology (e.g., Herculean). **SL.4.1.** Engage effectively in a range of collaborative discussions (one-on-one, in groups, and teacher-led) with diverse partners on *grade 4 topics and texts*, building on others' ideas and expressing their own clearly. **SL.4.1.A.** Come to discussions prepared, having read or studied required material; explicitly draw on that preparation and other information known about the topic to explore ideas under discussion. **SL.4.1.B.** Follow agreed-upon rules for discussions and carry out assigned roles. **SL.4.1.C.** Pose and respond to specific questions to clarify or follow up on information, and make comments that contribute to the discussion and link to the remarks of others. **SL.4.1.D.** Review the key ideas expressed and explain their own ideas and understanding in light of the discussion. **W.4.10.** Write routinely over extended time frames (time for research, reflection, and revision) and shorter time frames (a single sitting or a day or two) for a range of discipline-specific tasks, purposes, and audiences. **L.4.6.** Acquire and use accurately grade-appropriate general academic and domain-specific words and phrases, including those that signal precise actions, emotions, or states of being (e.g., quizzed, whined, stammered) and that are basic to a particular topic (e.g., *wildlife, conservation,* and *endangered* when discussing animal preservation). ***Grade 5*** **RL.5.1.** Quote accurately from a text when explaining what the text says explicitly and when drawing inferences from the text. **RL.5.2.** Determine a theme of a story, drama, or poem from details in the text, including how characters in a story or drama respond to challenges or how the speaker in a poem reflects upon a topic; summarize the text. **RL.5.4.** Determine the meaning of words and phrases as they are used in a text, including figurative language such as metaphors and similes. **SL.5.1.** Engage effectively in a range of collaborative discussions (one-on-one, in groups, and teacher-led) with diverse partners on *grade 5 topics and texts*, building on others' ideas and expressing their own clearly. **SL.5.1.A.** Come to discussions prepared, having read or studied required material; explicitly draw on that preparation and other information known about the topic to explore ideas under discussion. **SL.5.1.B.** Follow agreed-upon rules for discussions and carry out assigned roles. **SL.5.1.C.** Pose and respond to specific questions by making comments that contribute to the discussion and elaborate on the remarks of others. **SL.5.1.D.** Review the key ideas expressed and draw conclusions in light of information and knowledge gained from the discussions. **W.5.10.** Write routinely over extended time frames (time for research, reflection, and revision) and shorter time frames (a single sitting or a day or two) for a range of discipline-specific tasks, purposes, and audiences. **L.5.6.** Acquire and use accurately grade-appropriate general academic and domain-specific words and phrases, including those that signal contrast, addition, and other logical relationships (e.g., *however, although, nevertheless, similarly, moreover, in addition*).

Appendix 2. Correlations Between Lessons and *Common Core State Standards, English Language Arts* (*ELA*) *(continued)*

Lesson Title	Suggested Grade Levels	*Common Core State Standards, ELA*
Rice Is Life	3–6	***Grade 3*** **RL.3.1.** Ask and answer questions to demonstrate understanding of a text, referring explicitly to the text as the basis for the answers. **RL.3.2.** Recount stories, including fables, folktales, and myths from diverse cultures; determine the central message, lesson, or moral and explain how it is conveyed through key details in the text. **RL.3.4.** Determine the meaning of words and phrases as they are used in a text, distinguishing literal from nonliteral language. **RI.3.1.** Ask and answer questions to demonstrate understanding of a text, referring explicitly to the text as the basis for the answers. **RI.3.2.** Determine the main idea of a text; recount the key details and explain how they support the main idea. **RI.3.3.** Describe the relationship between a series of historical events, scientific ideas or concepts, or steps in technical procedures in a text, using language that pertains to time, sequence, and cause/effect. **RI.3.4.** Determine the meaning of general academic and domain-specific words and phrases in a text relevant to a *grade 3 topic or subject area*. **RI.3.5.** Use text features and search tools (e.g., key words, sidebars, hyperlinks) to locate information relevant to a given topic efficiently. **RI.3.7.** Use information gained from illustrations (e.g., maps, photographs) and the words in a text to demonstrate understanding of the text (e.g., where, when, why, and how key events occur). **RI.3.10.** By the end of the year, read and comprehend informational texts, including history/social studies, science, and technical texts, at the high end of the grades 2–3 text complexity band independently and proficiently. **SL.3.1.** Engage effectively in a range of collaborative discussions (one-on-one, in groups, and teacher-led) with diverse partners on *grade 3 topics and texts*, building on others' ideas and expressing their own clearly. **SL.3.1.A.** Come to discussions prepared, having read or studied required material; explicitly draw on that preparation and other information known about the topic to explore ideas under discussion. **SL.3.1.B.** Follow agreed-upon rules for discussions (e.g., gaining the floor in respectful ways, listening to others with care, speaking one at a time about the topics and texts under discussion). **SL.3.1.C.** Ask questions to check understanding of information presented, stay on topic, and link their comments to the remarks of others. **SL.3.1.D.** Explain their own ideas and understanding in light of the discussion. **SL.3.2.** Determine the main ideas and supporting details of a text read aloud or information presented in diverse media and formats, including visually, quantitatively, and orally. **W.3.10.** Write routinely over extended time frames (time for research, reflection, and revision) and shorter time frames (a single sitting or a day or two) for a range of discipline-specific tasks, purposes, and audiences. **L.3.6.** Acquire and use accurately grade-appropriate conversational, general academic, and domain-specific words and phrases, including those that signal spatial and temporal relationships (e.g., *After dinner that night we went looking for them*). ***Grade 4*** **RL.4.1.** Refer to details and examples in a text when explaining what the text says explicitly and when drawing inferences from the text. **RL.4.2.** Determine a theme of a story, drama, or poem from details in the text; summarize the text. **RI.4.1.** Refer to details and examples in a text when explaining what the text says explicitly and when drawing inferences from the text. **RI.4.2.** Determine the main idea of a text and explain how it is supported by key details; summarize the text. **RI.4.3.** Explain events, procedures, ideas, or concepts in a historical, scientific, or technical text, including what happened and why, based on specific information in the text. **RI.4.4.** Determine the meaning of general academic and domain-specific words or phrases in a text relevant to a *grade 4 topic or subject area*.

Lesson Title	Suggested Grade Levels	*Common Core State Standards, ELA*
Rice Is Life *(continued)*	3–6	**SL.4.1.** Engage effectively in a range of collaborative discussions (one-on-one, in groups, and teacher-led) with diverse partners on *grade 4 topics and texts*, building on others' ideas and expressing their own clearly. **SL.4.1.A.** Come to discussions prepared, having read or studied required material; explicitly draw on that preparation and other information known about the topic to explore ideas under discussion. **SL.4.1.B.** Follow agreed-upon rules for discussions and carry out assigned roles. **SL.4.1.C.** Pose and respond to specific questions to clarify or follow up on information, and make comments that contribute to the discussion and link to the remarks of others. **SL.4.1.D.** Review the key ideas expressed and explain their own ideas and understanding in light of the discussion. **W.4.10.** Write routinely over extended time frames (time for research, reflection, and revision) and shorter time frames (a single sitting or a day or two) for a range of discipline-specific tasks, purposes, and audiences. **L.4.6.** Acquire and use accurately grade-appropriate general academic and domain-specific words and phrases, including those that signal precise actions, emotions, or states of being (e.g., quizzed, whined, stammered) and that are basic to a particular topic (e.g., *wildlife, conservation,* and *endangered* when discussing animal preservation). ***Grade 5*** **RL.5.1.** Quote accurately from a text when explaining what the text says explicitly and when drawing inferences from the text. **RL.5.2.** Determine a theme of a story, drama, or poem from details in the text, including how characters in a story or drama respond to challenges or how the speaker in a poem reflects upon a topic; summarize the text. **RI.5.1.** Quote accurately from a text when explaining what the text says explicitly and when drawing inferences from the text. **RI.5.2.** Determine two or more main ideas of a text and explain how they are supported by key details; summarize the text. **RI.5.3.** Explain the relationships or interactions between two or more individuals, events, ideas, or concepts in a historical, scientific, or technical text based on specific information in the text. **RI.5.4.** Determine the meaning of general academic and domain-specific words and phrases in a text relevant to a *grade 5 topic or subject area*. **SL.5.1.** Engage effectively in a range of collaborative discussions (one-on-one, in groups, and teacher-led) with diverse partners on *grade 5 topics and texts*, building on others' ideas and expressing their own clearly. **SL.5.1.A.** Come to discussions prepared, having read or studied required material; explicitly draw on that preparation and other information known about the topic to explore ideas under discussion. **SL.5.1.B.** Follow agreed-upon rules for discussions and carry out assigned roles. **SL.5.1.C.** Pose and respond to specific questions by making comments that contribute to the discussion and elaborate on the remarks of others. **SL.5.1.D.** Review the key ideas expressed and draw conclusions in light of information and knowledge gained from the discussions. **W.5.10.** Write routinely over extended time frames (time for research, reflection, and revision) and shorter time frames (a single sitting or a day or two) for a range of discipline-specific tasks, purposes, and audiences. **L.5.6.** Acquire and use accurately grade-appropriate general academic and domain-specific words and phrases, including those that signal contrast, addition, and other logical relationships (e.g., *however, although, nevertheless, similarly, moreover, in addition*). ***Grade 6*** **RL.6.1.** Cite textual evidence to support analysis of what the text says explicitly as well as inferences drawn from the text. **RL.6.2.** Determine a theme or central idea of a text and how it is conveyed through particular details; provide a summary of the text distinct from personal opinions or judgments. **RI.6.1.** Cite textual evidence to support analysis of what the text says explicitly as well as inferences drawn from the text. **RI.6.2.** Determine a central idea of a text and how it is conveyed through particular details; provide a summary of the text distinct from personal opinions or judgments. **RI.6.4.** Determine the meaning of words and phrases as they are used in a text, including figurative, connotative, and technical meanings.

Appendix 2. Correlations Between Lessons and *Common Core State Standards, English Language Arts* (*ELA*) *(continued)*

Lesson Title	Suggested Grade Levels	*Common Core State Standards, ELA*
Rice Is Life *(continued)*	**3–6**	**SL.6.1.** Engage effectively in a range of collaborative discussions (one-on-one, in groups, and teacher-led) with diverse partners on grade 6 topics, texts, and issues, building on others' ideas and expressing their own clearly. **SL.6.1.A.** Come to discussions prepared, having read or studied required material; explicitly draw on that preparation by referring to evidence on the topic, text, or issue to probe and reflect on ideas under discussion. **SL.6.1.B.** Follow rules for collegial discussions, set specific goals and deadlines, and define individual roles as needed. **SL.6.1.C.** Pose and respond to specific questions with elaboration and detail by making comments that contribute to the topic, text, or issue under discussion. **SL.6.1.D.** Review the key ideas expressed and demonstrate understanding of multiple perspectives through reflection and paraphrasing. **W.6.10.** Write routinely over extended time frames (time for research, reflection, and revision) and shorter time frames (a single sitting or a day or two) for a range of discipline-specific tasks, purposes, and audiences. **L.6.6.** Acquire and use accurately grade-appropriate general academic and domain-specific words and phrases; gather vocabulary knowledge when considering a word or phrase important to comprehension or expression. **RST.6-8.1.** Cite specific textual evidence to support analysis of science and technical texts. **RST.6-8.2.** Determine the central ideas or conclusions of a text; provide an accurate summary of the text distinct from prior knowledge or opinions. **RST.6-8.3.** Follow precisely a multistep procedure when carrying out experiments, taking measurements, or performing technical tasks. **RST.6-8.4.** Determine the meaning of symbols, key terms, and other domain-specific words and phrases as they are used in a specific scientific or technical context relevant to *grades 6–8 texts and topics*. **WHST.6-8.10.** Write routinely over extended time frames (time for reflection and revision) and shorter time frames (a single sitting or a day or two) for a range of discipline-specific tasks, purposes, and audiences.
What's Poppin?	**5–6**	***Grade 5*** **RI.5.1.** Quote accurately from a text when explaining what the text says explicitly and when drawing inferences from the text. **RI.5.2.** Determine two or more main ideas of a text and explain how they are supported by key details; summarize the text. **W.5.10.** Write routinely over extended time frames (time for research, reflection, and revision) and shorter time frames (a single sitting or a day or two) for a range of discipline-specific tasks, purposes, and audiences. **SL.5.1.** Engage effectively in a range of collaborative discussions (one-on-one, in groups, and teacher-led) with diverse partners on *grade 5 topics and texts*, building on others' ideas and expressing their own clearly. **SL.5.1.A.** Come to discussions prepared, having read or studied required material; explicitly draw on that preparation and other information known about the topic to explore ideas under discussion. **SL.5.1.B.** Follow agreed-upon rules for discussions and carry out assigned roles. **SL.5.1.C.** Pose and respond to specific questions by making comments that contribute to the discussion and elaborate on the remarks of others. **SL.5.1.D.** Review the key ideas expressed and draw conclusions in light of information and knowledge gained from the discussions. **SL.5.4.** Report on a topic or text or present an opinion, sequencing ideas logically and using appropriate facts and relevant, descriptive details to support main ideas or themes; speak clearly at an understandable pace. **SL.5.5.** Include multimedia components (e.g., graphics, sound) and visual displays in presentations when appropriate to enhance the development of main ideas or themes. **L.5.6.** Acquire and use accurately grade-appropriate general academic and domain-specific words and phrases, including those that signal contrast, addition, and other logical relationships (e.g., *however, although, nevertheless, similarly, moreover, in addition*). ***Grade 6*** **RI.6.1.** Cite textual evidence to support analysis of what the text says explicitly as well as inferences drawn from the text. **RI.6.2.** Determine a central idea of a text and how it is conveyed through particular details; provide a summary of the text distinct from personal opinions or judgments. **W.6.10.** Write routinely over extended time frames (time for research, reflection, and revision) and shorter time frames (a single sitting or a day or two) for a range of discipline-specific tasks, purposes, and audiences.

Lesson Title	Suggested Grade Levels	*Common Core State Standards, ELA*
What's Poppin? *(continued)*	5–6	**SL.6.1.** Engage effectively in a range of collaborative discussions (one-on-one, in groups, and teacher-led) with diverse partners on grade 6 topics, texts, and issues, building on others' ideas and expressing their own clearly. **SL.6.1.A.** Come to discussions prepared, having read or studied required material; explicitly draw on that preparation by referring to evidence on the topic, text, or issue to probe and reflect on ideas under discussion. **SL.6.1.B.** Follow rules for collegial discussions, set specific goals and deadlines, and define individual roles as needed. **SL.6.1.C.** Pose and respond to specific questions with elaboration and detail by making comments that contribute to the topic, text, or issue under discussion. **SL.6.1.D.** Review the key ideas expressed and demonstrate understanding of multiple perspectives through reflection and paraphrasing. **SL.6.4.** Present claims and findings, sequencing ideas logically and using pertinent descriptions, facts, and details to accentuate main ideas or themes; use appropriate eye contact, adequate volume, and clear pronunciation. **SL.6.5.** Include multimedia components (e.g., graphics, images, music, sound) and visual displays in presentations to clarify information. **RST.6-8.1.** Cite specific textual evidence to support analysis of science and technical texts. **RST.6-8.2.** Determine the central ideas or conclusions of a text; provide an accurate summary of the text distinct from prior knowledge or opinions. **RST.6-8.3.** Follow precisely a multistep procedure when carrying out experiments, taking measurements, or performing technical tasks. **WHST.6-8.10.** Write routinely over extended time frames (time for reflection and revision) and shorter time frames (a single sitting or a day or two) for a range of discipline-specific tasks, purposes, and audiences. **L.6.6.** Acquire and use accurately grade-appropriate general academic and domain-specific words and phrases; gather vocabulary knowledge when considering a word or phrase important to comprehension or expression.
Mystery Pellets	3–6	***Grade 3*** **RL.3.1.** Ask and answer questions to demonstrate understanding of a text, referring explicitly to the text as the basis for the answers. **RL.3.2.** Recount stories, including fables, folktales, and myths from diverse cultures; determine the central message, lesson, or moral and explain how it is conveyed through key details in the text. **RL.3.4.** Determine the meaning of words and phrases as they are used in a text, distinguishing literal from nonliteral language. **RI.3.1.** Ask and answer questions to demonstrate understanding of a text, referring explicitly to the text as the basis for the answers. **RI.3.2.** Determine the main idea of a text; recount the key details and explain how they support the main idea. **RI.3.3.** Describe the relationship between a series of historical events, scientific ideas or concepts, or steps in technical procedures in a text, using language that pertains to time, sequence, and cause/effect. **RI.3.4.** Determine the meaning of general academic and domain-specific words and phrases in a text relevant to a *grade 3 topic or subject area*. **RI.3.7.** Use information gained from illustrations (e.g., maps, photographs) and the words in a text to demonstrate understanding of the text (e.g., where, when, why, and how key events occur). **SL.3.1.** Engage effectively in a range of collaborative discussions (one-on-one, in groups, and teacher-led) with diverse partners on *grade 3 topics and texts*, building on others' ideas and expressing their own clearly. **SL.3.1.A.** Come to discussions prepared, having read or studied required material; explicitly draw on that preparation and other information known about the topic to explore ideas under discussion. **SL.3.1.B.** Follow agreed-upon rules for discussions (e.g., gaining the floor in respectful ways, listening to others with care, speaking one at a time about the topics and texts under discussion). **SL.3.1.C.** Ask questions to check understanding of information presented, stay on topic, and link their comments to the remarks of others. **SL.3.1.D.** Explain their own ideas and understanding in light of the discussion. **SL.3.2.** Determine the main ideas and supporting details of a text read aloud or information presented in diverse media and formats, including visually, quantitatively, and orally. **SL.3.4.** Report on a topic or text, tell a story, or recount an experience with appropriate facts and relevant, descriptive details, speaking clearly at an understandable pace.

Appendix 2. Correlations Between Lessons and *Common Core State Standards, English Language Arts* (*ELA*) *(continued)*

Lesson Title	Suggested Grade Levels	*Common Core State Standards, ELA*
Mystery Pellets *(continued)*	3–6	**SL.3.6.** Speak in complete sentences when appropriate to task and situation in order to provide requested detail or clarification. **W.3.10.** Write routinely over extended time frames (time for research, reflection, and revision) and shorter time frames (a single sitting or a day or two) for a range of discipline-specific tasks, purposes, and audiences. **L.3.6.** Acquire and use accurately grade-appropriate conversational, general academic, and domain-specific words and phrases, including those that signal spatial and temporal relationships (e.g., *After dinner that night we went looking for them*). ***Grade 4*** **RL.4.1.** Refer to details and examples in a text when explaining what the text says explicitly and when drawing inferences from the text. **RL.4.2.** Determine a theme of a story, drama, or poem from details in the text; summarize the text. **RI.4.1.** Refer to details and examples in a text when explaining what the text says explicitly and when drawing inferences from the text. **RI.4.2.** Determine the main idea of a text and explain how it is supported by key details; summarize the text. **RI.4.3.** Explain events, procedures, ideas, or concepts in a historical, scientific, or technical text, including what happened and why, based on specific information in the text. **RI.4.4.** Determine the meaning of general academic and domain-specific words or phrases in a text relevant to a *grade 4 topic or subject area*. **SL.4.1.** Engage effectively in a range of collaborative discussions (one-on-one, in groups, and teacher-led) with diverse partners on *grade 4 topics and texts*, building on others' ideas and expressing their own clearly. **SL.4.1.A.** Come to discussions prepared, having read or studied required material; explicitly draw on that preparation and other information known about the topic to explore ideas under discussion. **SL.4.1.B.** Follow agreed-upon rules for discussions and carry out assigned roles. **SL.4.1.C.** Pose and respond to specific questions to clarify or follow up on information, and make comments that contribute to the discussion and link to the remarks of others. **SL.4.1.D.** Review the key ideas expressed and explain their own ideas and understanding in light of the discussion. **SL.4.4.** Report on a topic or text, tell a story, or recount an experience in an organized manner, using appropriate facts and relevant, descriptive details to support main ideas or themes; speak clearly at an understandable pace. **W.4.10.** Write routinely over extended time frames (time for research, reflection, and revision) and shorter time frames (a single sitting or a day or two) for a range of discipline-specific tasks, purposes, and audiences. **L.4.4.** Determine or clarify the meaning of unknown and multiple-meaning words and phrases based on grade 4 reading and content, choosing flexibly from a range of strategies. **L.4.4.A.** Use context (e.g., definitions, examples, or restatements in text) as a clue to the meaning of a word or phrase. **L.4.6.** Acquire and use accurately grade-appropriate general academic and domain-specific words and phrases, including those that signal precise actions, emotions, or states of being (e.g., quizzed, whined, stammered) and that are basic to a particular topic (e.g., *wildlife, conservation,* and *endangered* when discussing animal preservation). ***Grade 5*** **RL.5.1.** Quote accurately from a text when explaining what the text says explicitly and when drawing inferences from the text. **RL.5.2.** Determine a theme of a story, drama, or poem from details in the text, including how characters in a story or drama respond to challenges or how the speaker in a poem reflects upon a topic; summarize the text. **RI.5.1.** Quote accurately from a text when explaining what the text says explicitly and when drawing inferences from the text. **RI.5.2.** Determine two or more main ideas of a text and explain how they are supported by key details; summarize the text. **RI.5.3.** Explain the relationships or interactions between two or more individuals, events, ideas, or concepts in a historical, scientific, or technical text based on specific information in the text. **RI.5.4.** Determine the meaning of general academic and domain-specific words and phrases in a text relevant to a *grade 5 topic or subject area*.

Lesson Title	Suggested Grade Levels	*Common Core State Standards, ELA*
Mystery Pellets *(continued)*	3–6	**SL.5.1.** Engage effectively in a range of collaborative discussions (one-on-one, in groups, and teacher-led) with diverse partners on *grade 5 topics and texts*, building on others' ideas and expressing their own clearly. **SL.5.1.A.** Come to discussions prepared, having read or studied required material; explicitly draw on that preparation and other information known about the topic to explore ideas under discussion. **SL.5.1.B.** Follow agreed-upon rules for discussions and carry out assigned roles. **SL.5.1.C.** Pose and respond to specific questions by making comments that contribute to the discussion and elaborate on the remarks of others. **SL.5.1.D.** Review the key ideas expressed and draw conclusions in light of information and knowledge gained from the discussions. **SL.5.4.** Report on a topic or text or present an opinion, sequencing ideas logically and using appropriate facts and relevant, descriptive details to support main ideas or themes; speak clearly at an understandable pace. **W.5.10.** Write routinely over extended time frames (time for research, reflection, and revision) and shorter time frames (a single sitting or a day or two) for a range of discipline-specific tasks, purposes, and audiences. **L.5.4.** Determine or clarify the meaning of unknown and multiple-meaning words and phrases based on grade 5 reading and content, choosing flexibly from a range of strategies. **L.5.4.A.** Use context (e.g., cause/effect relationships and comparisons in text) as a clue to the meaning of a word or phrase. **L.5.6.** Acquire and use accurately grade-appropriate general academic and domain-specific words and phrases, including those that signal contrast, addition, and other logical relationships (e.g., *however, although, nevertheless, similarly, moreover, in addition*). ***Grade 6*** **RL.6.1.** Cite textual evidence to support analysis of what the text says explicitly as well as inferences drawn from the text. **RL.6.2.** Determine a theme or central idea of a text and how it is conveyed through particular details; provide a summary of the text distinct from personal opinions or judgments. **RI.6.1.** Cite textual evidence to support analysis of what the text says explicitly as well as inferences drawn from the text. **RI.6.2.** Determine a central idea of a text and how it is conveyed through particular details; provide a summary of the text distinct from personal opinions or judgments. **RI.6.4.** Determine the meaning of words and phrases as they are used in a text, including figurative, connotative, and technical meanings. **SL.6.1.** Engage effectively in a range of collaborative discussions (one-on-one, in groups, and teacher-led) with diverse partners on grade 6 topics, texts, and issues, building on others' ideas and expressing their own clearly. **SL.6.1.A.** Come to discussions prepared, having read or studied required material; explicitly draw on that preparation by referring to evidence on the topic, text, or issue to probe and reflect on ideas under discussion. **SL.6.1.B.** Follow rules for collegial discussions, set specific goals and deadlines, and define individual roles as needed. **SL.6.1.C.** Pose and respond to specific questions with elaboration and detail by making comments that contribute to the topic, text, or issue under discussion. **SL.6.1.D.** Review the key ideas expressed and demonstrate understanding of multiple perspectives through reflection and paraphrasing. **SL.6.4.** Present claims and findings, sequencing ideas logically and using pertinent descriptions, facts, and details to accentuate main ideas or themes; use appropriate eye contact, adequate volume, and clear pronunciation. **W.6.10.** Write routinely over extended time frames (time for research, reflection, and revision) and shorter time frames (a single sitting or a day or two) for a range of discipline-specific tasks, purposes, and audiences. **L.6.4.** Determine or clarify the meaning of unknown and multiple-meaning words and phrases based on grade 6 reading and content, choosing flexibly from a range of strategies. **L.6.4.A.** Use context (e.g., the overall meaning of a sentence or paragraph; a word's position or function in a sentence) as a clue to the meaning of a word or phrase. **L.6.6.** Acquire and use accurately grade-appropriate general academic and domain-specific words and phrases; gather vocabulary knowledge when considering a word or phrase important to comprehension or expression. **RST.6-8.1.** Cite specific textual evidence to support analysis of science and technical texts.

Appendix 2. Correlations Between Lessons and *Common Core State Standards, English Language Arts (ELA)* *(continued)*

Lesson Title	Suggested Grade Levels	*Common Core State Standards, ELA*
Mystery Pellets *(continued)*	3–6	**RST.6-8.2.** Determine the central ideas or conclusions of a text; provide an accurate summary of the text distinct from prior knowledge or opinions. **RST.6-8.3.** Follow precisely a multistep procedure when carrying out experiments, taking measurements, or performing technical tasks. **RST.6-8.4.** Determine the meaning of symbols, key terms, and other domain-specific words and phrases as they are used in a specific scientific or technical context relevant to *grades 6–8 texts and topics*. **WHST.6-8.10.** Write routinely over extended time frames (time for reflection and revision) and shorter time frames (a single sitting or a day or two) for a range of discipline-specific tasks, purposes, and audiences.
Close Encounters of the Symbiotic Kind	3–6	***Grade 3*** **RI.3.1.** Ask and answer questions to demonstrate understanding of a text, referring explicitly to the text as the basis for the answers. **RI.3.2.** Determine the main idea of a text; recount the key details and explain how they support the main idea. **RI.3.3.** Describe the relationship between a series of historical events, scientific ideas or concepts, or steps in technical procedures in a text, using language that pertains to time, sequence, and cause/effect. **RI.3.4.** Determine the meaning of general academic and domain-specific words and phrases in a text relevant to a *grade 3 topic or subject area*. **SL.3.1.** Engage effectively in a range of collaborative discussions (one-on-one, in groups, and teacher-led) with diverse partners on *grade 3 topics and texts*, building on others' ideas and expressing their own clearly. **SL.3.1.A.** Come to discussions prepared, having read or studied required material; explicitly draw on that preparation and other information known about the topic to explore ideas under discussion. **SL.3.1.B.** Follow agreed-upon rules for discussions (e.g., gaining the floor in respectful ways, listening to others with care, speaking one at a time about the topics and texts under discussion). **SL.3.1.C.** Ask questions to check understanding of information presented, stay on topic, and link their comments to the remarks of others. **SL.3.1.D.** Explain their own ideas and understanding in light of the discussion. **W.3.10.** Write routinely over extended time frames (time for research, reflection, and revision) and shorter time frames (a single sitting or a day or two) for a range of discipline-specific tasks, purposes, and audiences. **L.3.4.** Determine or clarify the meaning of unknown and multiple-meaning word and phrases based on *grade 3 reading and content,* choosing flexibly from a range of strategies. **L.3.4.A.** Use sentence-level context as a clue to the meaning of a word or phrase. **L.3.6.** Acquire and use accurately grade-appropriate conversational, general academic, and domain-specific words and phrases, including those that signal spatial and temporal relationships (e.g., *After dinner that night we went looking for them*). ***Grade 4*** **RI.4.1.** Refer to details and examples in a text when explaining what the text says explicitly and when drawing inferences from the text. **RI.4.2.** Determine the main idea of a text and explain how it is supported by key details; summarize the text. **RI.4.3.** Explain events, procedures, ideas, or concepts in a historical, scientific, or technical text, including what happened and why, based on specific information in the text. **RI.4.4.** Determine the meaning of general academic and domain-specific words or phrases in a text relevant to a *grade 4 topic or subject area*. **SL.4.1.** Engage effectively in a range of collaborative discussions (one-on-one, in groups, and teacher-led) with diverse partners on *grade 4 topics and texts*, building on others' ideas and expressing their own clearly. **SL.4.1.A.** Come to discussions prepared, having read or studied required material; explicitly draw on that preparation and other information known about the topic to explore ideas under discussion. **SL.4.1.B.** Follow agreed-upon rules for discussions and carry out assigned roles. **SL.4.1.C.** Pose and respond to specific questions to clarify or follow up on information, and make comments that contribute to the discussion and link to the remarks of others. **SL.4.1.D.** Review the key ideas expressed and explain their own ideas and understanding in light of the discussion. **W.4.10.** Write routinely over extended time frames (time for research, reflection, and revision) and shorter time frames (a single sitting or a day or two) for a range of discipline-specific tasks, purposes, and audiences. **L.4.4.** Determine or clarify the meaning of unknown and multiple-meaning words and phrases based on grade 4 reading and content, choosing flexibly from a range of strategies. **L.4.4.A.** Use context (e.g., definitions, examples, or restatements in text) as a clue to the meaning of a word or phrase.

Lesson Title	Suggested Grade Levels	*Common Core State Standards, ELA*
Close Encounters of the Symbiotic Kind *(continued)*	3–6	**L.4.6.** Acquire and use accurately grade-appropriate general academic and domain-specific words and phrases, including those that signal precise actions, emotions, or states of being (e.g., quizzed, whined, stammered) and that are basic to a particular topic (e.g., *wildlife, conservation,* and *endangered* when discussing animal preservation). ***Grade 5*** **RI.5.1.** Quote accurately from a text when explaining what the text says explicitly and when drawing inferences from the text. **RI.5.2.** Determine two or more main ideas of a text and explain how they are supported by key details; summarize the text. **RI.5.3.** Explain the relationships or interactions between two or more individuals, events, ideas, or concepts in a historical, scientific, or technical text based on specific information in the text. **RI.5.4.** Determine the meaning of general academic and domain-specific words and phrases in a text relevant to a *grade 5 topic or subject area.* **RI.5.10.** By the end of the year, read and comprehend informational texts, including history/social studies, science, and technical texts, at the high end of the grades 4–5 text complexity band independently and proficiently. **SL.5.1.** Engage effectively in a range of collaborative discussions (one-on-one, in groups, and teacher-led) with diverse partners on *grade 5 topics and texts*, building on others' ideas and expressing their own clearly. **SL.5.1.A.** Come to discussions prepared, having read or studied required material; explicitly draw on that preparation and other information known about the topic to explore ideas under discussion. **SL.5.1.B.** Follow agreed-upon rules for discussions and carry out assigned roles. **SL.5.1.C.** Pose and respond to specific questions by making comments that contribute to the discussion and elaborate on the remarks of others. **SL.5.1.D.** Review the key ideas expressed and draw conclusions in light of information and knowledge gained from the discussions. **W.5.10.** Write routinely over extended time frames (time for research, reflection, and revision) and shorter time frames (a single sitting or a day or two) for a range of discipline-specific tasks, purposes, and audiences. **L.5.4.** Determine or clarify the meaning of unknown and multiple-meaning words and phrases based on grade 5 reading and content, choosing flexibly from a range of strategies. **L.5.4.A.** Use context (e.g., cause/effect relationships and comparisons in text) as a clue to the meaning of a word or phrase. **L.5.6.** Acquire and use accurately grade-appropriate general academic and domain-specific words and phrases, including those that signal contrast, addition, and other logical relationships (e.g., *however, although, nevertheless, similarly, moreover, in addition*). ***Grade 6*** **RI.6.1.** Cite textual evidence to support analysis of what the text says explicitly as well as inferences drawn from the text. **RI.6.2.** Determine a central idea of a text and how it is conveyed through particular details; provide a summary of the text distinct from personal opinions or judgments. **RI.6.4.** Determine the meaning of words and phrases as they are used in a text, including figurative, connotative, and technical meanings. **RI.6.10.** By the end of the year, read and comprehend literary nonfiction in the grades 6–8 text complexity band proficiently, with scaffolding as needed at the high end of the range. **SL.6.1.** Engage effectively in a range of collaborative discussions (one-on-one, in groups, and teacher-led) with diverse partners on grade 6 topics, texts, and issues, building on others' ideas and expressing their own clearly. **SL.6.1.A.** Come to discussions prepared, having read or studied required material; explicitly draw on that preparation by referring to evidence on the topic, text, or issue to probe and reflect on ideas under discussion. **SL.6.1.B.** Follow rules for collegial discussions, set specific goals and deadlines, and define individual roles as needed. **SL.6.1.C.** Pose and respond to specific questions with elaboration and detail by making comments that contribute to the topic, text, or issue under discussion. **SL.6.1.D.** Review the key ideas expressed and demonstrate understanding of multiple perspectives through reflection and paraphrasing. **W.6.10.** Write routinely over extended time frames (time for research, reflection, and revision) and shorter time frames (a single sitting or a day or two) for a range of discipline-specific tasks, purposes, and audiences.

Appendix 2. Correlations Between Lessons and *Common Core State Standards, English Language Arts (ELA)* *(continued)*

Lesson Title	Suggested Grade Levels	*Common Core State Standards, ELA*
Close Encounters of the Symbiotic Kind *(continued)*	**3–6**	**L.6.4.** Determine or clarify the meaning of unknown and multiple-meaning words and phrases based on grade 6 reading and content, choosing flexibly from a range of strategies. **L.6.4.A.** Use context (e.g., the overall meaning of a sentence or paragraph; a word's position or function in a sentence) as a clue to the meaning of a word or phrase. **L.6.6.** Acquire and use accurately grade-appropriate general academic and domain-specific words and phrases; gather vocabulary knowledge when considering a word or phrase important to comprehension or expression. **RST.6-8.1.** Cite specific textual evidence to support analysis of science and technical texts. **RST.6-8.2.** Determine the central ideas or conclusions of a text; provide an accurate summary of the text distinct from prior knowledge or opinions. **RST.6-8.3.** Follow precisely a multistep procedure when carrying out experiments, taking measurements, or performing technical tasks. **RST.6-8.4.** Determine the meaning of symbols, key terms, and other domain-specific words and phrases as they are used in a specific scientific or technical context relevant to *grades 6–8 texts and topics*. **WHST.6-8.10.** Write routinely over extended time frames (time for reflection and revision) and shorter time frames (a single sitting or a day or two) for a range of discipline-specific tasks, purposes, and audiences.
Turtle Hurdles	**3–5**	***Grade 3*** **RL.3.1.** Ask and answer questions to demonstrate understanding of a text, referring explicitly to the text as the basis for the answers. **RL.3.2.** Recount stories, including fables, folktales, and myths from diverse cultures; determine the central message, lesson, or moral and explain how it is conveyed through key details in the text. **RI.3.1.** Ask and answer questions to demonstrate understanding of a text, referring explicitly to the text as the basis for the answers. **RI.3.2.** Determine the main idea of a text; recount the key details and explain how they support the main idea. **RI.3.3.** Describe the relationship between a series of historical events, scientific ideas or concepts, or steps in technical procedures in a text, using language that pertains to time, sequence, and cause/effect. **RI.3.7.** Use information gained from illustrations (e.g., maps, photographs) and the words in a text to demonstrate understanding of the text (e.g., where, when, why, and how key events occur). **SL.3.1.** Engage effectively in a range of collaborative discussions (one-on-one, in groups, and teacher-led) with diverse partners on *grade 3 topics and texts*, building on others' ideas and expressing their own clearly. **SL.3.1.A.** Come to discussions prepared, having read or studied required material; explicitly draw on that preparation and other information known about the topic to explore ideas under discussion. **SL.3.1.B.** Follow agreed-upon rules for discussions (e.g., gaining the floor in respectful ways, listening to others with care, speaking one at a time about the topics and texts under discussion). **SL.3.1.C.** Ask questions to check understanding of information presented, stay on topic, and link their comments to the remarks of others. **SL.3.1.D.** Explain their own ideas and understanding in light of the discussion. **SL.3.2.** Determine the main ideas and supporting details of a text read aloud or information presented in diverse media and formats, including visually, quantitatively, and orally. **W.3.4.** With guidance and support from adults, produce writing in which the development and organization are appropriate to task and purpose. **W.3.10.** Write routinely over extended time frames (time for research, reflection, and revision) and shorter time frames (a single sitting or a day or two) for a range of discipline-specific tasks, purposes, and audiences. **L.3.6.** Acquire and use accurately grade-appropriate conversational, general academic, and domain-specific words and phrases, including those that signal spatial and temporal relationships (e.g., *After dinner that night we went looking for them*). ***Grade 4*** **RL.4.1.** Refer to details and examples in a text when explaining what the text says explicitly and when drawing inferences from the text. **RL.4.2.** Determine a theme of a story, drama, or poem from details in the text; summarize the text. **RI.4.1.** Refer to details and examples in a text when explaining what the text says explicitly and when drawing inferences from the text. **RI.4.2.** Determine the main idea of a text and explain how it is supported by key details; summarize the text. **RI.4.3.** Explain events, procedures, ideas, or concepts in a historical, scientific, or technical text, including what happened and why, based on specific information in the text.

Lesson Title	Suggested Grade Levels	*Common Core State Standards, ELA*
Turtle Hurdles *(continued)*	3–5	**SL.4.1.** Engage effectively in a range of collaborative discussions (one-on-one, in groups, and teacher-led) with diverse partners on *grade 4 topics and texts*, building on others' ideas and expressing their own clearly. **SL.4.1.A.** Come to discussions prepared, having read or studied required material; explicitly draw on that preparation and other information known about the topic to explore ideas under discussion. **SL.4.1.B.** Follow agreed-upon rules for discussions and carry out assigned roles. **SL.4.1.C.** Pose and respond to specific questions to clarify or follow up on information, and make comments that contribute to the discussion and link to the remarks of others. **SL.4.1.D.** Review the key ideas expressed and explain their own ideas and understanding in light of the discussion. **W.4.4.** Produce clear and coherent writing in which the development and organization are appropriate to task, purpose, and audience. **W.4.10.** Write routinely over extended time frames (time for research, reflection, and revision) and shorter time frames (a single sitting or a day or two) for a range of discipline-specific tasks, purposes, and audiences. **L.4.6.** Acquire and use accurately grade-appropriate general academic and domain-specific words and phrases, including those that signal precise actions, emotions, or states of being (e.g., quizzed, whined, stammered) and that are basic to a particular topic (e.g., *wildlife, conservation,* and *endangered* when discussing animal preservation). ***Grade 5*** **RL.5.1.** Quote accurately from a text when explaining what the text says explicitly and when drawing inferences from the text. **RL.5.2.** Determine a theme of a story, drama, or poem from details in the text, including how characters in a story or drama respond to challenges or how the speaker in a poem reflects upon a topic; summarize the text. **RI.5.1.** Quote accurately from a text when explaining what the text says explicitly and when drawing inferences from the text. **RI.5.2.** Determine two or more main ideas of a text and explain how they are supported by key details; summarize the text. **RI.5.3.** Explain the relationships or interactions between two or more individuals, events, ideas, or concepts in a historical, scientific, or technical text based on specific information in the text. **RI.5.4.** Determine the meaning of general academic and domain-specific words and phrases in a text relevant to a *grade 5 topic or subject area*. **RI.5.10.** By the end of the year, read and comprehend informational texts, including history/social studies, science, and technical texts, at the high end of the grades 4–5 text complexity band independently and proficiently. **SL.5.1.** Engage effectively in a range of collaborative discussions (one-on-one, in groups, and teacher-led) with diverse partners on *grade 5 topics and texts*, building on others' ideas and expressing their own clearly. **SL.5.1.A.** Come to discussions prepared, having read or studied required material; explicitly draw on that preparation and other information known about the topic to explore ideas under discussion. **SL.5.1.B.** Follow agreed-upon rules for discussions and carry out assigned roles. **SL.5.1.C.** Pose and respond to specific questions by making comments that contribute to the discussion and elaborate on the remarks of others. **SL.5.1.D.** Review the key ideas expressed and draw conclusions in light of information and knowledge gained from the discussions. **W.5.10.** Write routinely over extended time frames (time for research, reflection, and revision) and shorter time frames (a single sitting or a day or two) for a range of discipline-specific tasks, purposes, and audiences. **L.5.4.** Determine or clarify the meaning of unknown and multiple-meaning words and phrases based on grade 5 reading and content, choosing flexibly from a range of strategies. **L.5.4.A.** Use context (e.g., cause/effect relationships and comparisons in text) as a clue to the meaning of a word or phrase. **L.5.6.** Acquire and use accurately grade-appropriate general academic and domain-specific words and phrases, including those that signal contrast, addition, and other logical relationships (e.g., *however, although, nevertheless, similarly, moreover, in addition*).

Appendix 2. Correlations Between Lessons and *Common Core State Standards, English Language Arts (ELA)* *(continued)*

Lesson Title	Suggested Grade Levels	*Common Core State Standards, ELA*
Oil Spill!	3–5	***Grade 3*** **RL.3.1.** Ask and answer questions to demonstrate understanding of a text, referring explicitly to the text as the basis for the answers. **RL.3.2.** Recount stories, including fables, folktales, and myths from diverse cultures; determine the central message, lesson, or moral and explain how it is conveyed through key details in the text. **RI.3.1.** Ask and answer questions to demonstrate understanding of a text, referring explicitly to the text as the basis for the answers. **RI.3.2.** Determine the main idea of a text; recount the key details and explain how they support the main idea. **RI.3.3.** Describe the relationship between a series of historical events, scientific ideas or concepts, or steps in technical procedures in a text, using language that pertains to time, sequence, and cause/effect. **RI.3.7.** Use information gained from illustrations (e.g., maps, photographs) and the words in a text to demonstrate understanding of the text (e.g., where, when, why, and how key events occur). **SL.3.1.** Engage effectively in a range of collaborative discussions (one-on-one, in groups, and teacher-led) with diverse partners on *grade 3 topics and texts*, building on others' ideas and expressing their own clearly. **SL.3.1.A.** Come to discussions prepared, having read or studied required material; explicitly draw on that preparation and other information known about the topic to explore ideas under discussion. **SL.3.1.B.** Follow agreed-upon rules for discussions (e.g., gaining the floor in respectful ways, listening to others with care, speaking one at a time about the topics and texts under discussion). **SL.3.1.C.** Ask questions to check understanding of information presented, stay on topic, and link their comments to the remarks of others. **SL.3.1.D.** Explain their own ideas and understanding in light of the discussion. **SL.3.2.** Determine the main ideas and supporting details of a text read aloud or information presented in diverse media and formats, including visually, quantitatively, and orally. **W.3.3.** Write narratives to develop real or imagined experiences or events using effective technique, descriptive details, and clear event sequences. **W.3.10.** Write routinely over extended time frames (time for research, reflection, and revision) and shorter time frames (a single sitting or a day or two) for a range of discipline-specific tasks, purposes, and audiences. **L.3.6.** Acquire and use accurately grade-appropriate conversational, general academic, and domain-specific words and phrases, including those that signal spatial and temporal relationships (e.g., *After dinner that night we went looking for them*). ***Grade 4*** **RL.4.1.** Refer to details and examples in a text when explaining what the text says explicitly and when drawing inferences from the text. **RL.4.2.** Determine a theme of a story, drama, or poem from details in the text; summarize the text. **RI.4.1.** Refer to details and examples in a text when explaining what the text says explicitly and when drawing inferences from the text. **RI.4.2.** Determine the main idea of a text and explain how it is supported by key details; summarize the text. **RI.4.3.** Explain events, procedures, ideas, or concepts in a historical, scientific, or technical text, including what happened and why, based on specific information in the text. **SL.4.1.** Engage effectively in a range of collaborative discussions (one-on-one, in groups, and teacher-led) with diverse partners on *grade 4 topics and texts*, building on others' ideas and expressing their own clearly. **SL.4.1.A.** Come to discussions prepared, having read or studied required material; explicitly draw on that preparation and other information known about the topic to explore ideas under discussion. **SL.4.1.B.** Follow agreed-upon rules for discussions and carry out assigned roles. **SL.4.1.C.** Pose and respond to specific questions to clarify or follow up on information, and make comments that contribute to the discussion and link to the remarks of others. **SL.4.1.D.** Review the key ideas expressed and explain their own ideas and understanding in light of the discussion. **W.4.3.** Write narratives to develop real or imagined experiences or events using effective technique, descriptive details, and clear event sequences. **W.4.10.** Write routinely over extended time frames (time for research, reflection, and revision) and shorter time frames (a single sitting or a day or two) for a range of discipline-specific tasks, purposes, and audiences.

Lesson Title	Suggested Grade Levels	*Common Core State Standards, ELA*
Oil Spill! *(continued)*	3–5	**L.4.6.** Acquire and use accurately grade-appropriate general academic and domain-specific words and phrases, including those that signal precise actions, emotions, or states of being (e.g., quizzed, whined, stammered) and that are basic to a particular topic (e.g., *wildlife, conservation,* and *endangered* when discussing animal preservation). ***Grade 5*** **RL.5.1.** Quote accurately from a text when explaining what the text says explicitly and when drawing inferences from the text. **RL.5.2.** Determine a theme of a story, drama, or poem from details in the text, including how characters in a story or drama respond to challenges or how the speaker in a poem reflects upon a topic; summarize the text. **RI.5.1.** Quote accurately from a text when explaining what the text says explicitly and when drawing inferences from the text. **RI.5.2.** Determine two or more main ideas of a text and explain how they are supported by key details; summarize the text. **RI.5.3.** Explain the relationships or interactions between two or more individuals, events, ideas, or concepts in a historical, scientific, or technical text based on specific information in the text. **SL.5.1.** Engage effectively in a range of collaborative discussions (one-on-one, in groups, and teacher-led) with diverse partners on *grade 5 topics and texts*, building on others' ideas and expressing their own clearly. **SL.5.1.A.** Come to discussions prepared, having read or studied required material; explicitly draw on that preparation and other information known about the topic to explore ideas under discussion. **SL.5.1.B.** Follow agreed-upon rules for discussions and carry out assigned roles. **SL.5.1.C.** Pose and respond to specific questions by making comments that contribute to the discussion and elaborate on the remarks of others. **SL.5.1.D.** Review the key ideas expressed and draw conclusions in light of information and knowledge gained from the discussions. **W.5.3.** Write narratives to develop real or imagined experiences or events using effective technique, descriptive details, and clear event sequences. **W.5.10.** Write routinely over extended time frames (time for research, reflection, and revision) and shorter time frames (a single sitting or a day or two) for a range of discipline-specific tasks, purposes, and audiences. **L.5.6.** Acquire and use accurately grade-appropriate general academic and domain-specific words and phrases, including those that signal contrast, addition, and other logical relationships (e.g., *however, although, nevertheless, similarly, moreover, in addition*).
Sheep in a Jeep	3–5	***Grade 3*** **RL.3.1.** Ask and answer questions to demonstrate understanding of a text, referring explicitly to the text as the basis for the answers. **RL.3.4.** Determine the meaning of words and phrases as they are used in a text, distinguishing literal from nonliteral language. **SL.3.1.** Engage effectively in a range of collaborative discussions (one-on-one, in groups, and teacher-led) with diverse partners on *grade 3 topics and texts*, building on others' ideas and expressing their own clearly. **SL.3.1.A.** Come to discussions prepared, having read or studied required material; explicitly draw on that preparation and other information known about the topic to explore ideas under discussion. **SL.3.1.B.** Follow agreed-upon rules for discussions (e.g., gaining the floor in respectful ways, listening to others with care, speaking one at a time about the topics and texts under discussion). **SL.3.1.C.** Ask questions to check understanding of information presented, stay on topic, and link their comments to the remarks of others. **SL.3.1.D.** Explain their own ideas and understanding in light of the discussion. **SL.3.2.** Determine the main ideas and supporting details of a text read aloud or information presented in diverse media and formats, including visually, quantitatively, and orally. **W.3.10.** Write routinely over extended time frames (time for research, reflection, and revision) and shorter time frames (a single sitting or a day or two) for a range of discipline-specific tasks, purposes, and audiences. **L.3.6.** Acquire and use accurately grade-appropriate conversational, general academic, and domain-specific words and phrases, including those that signal spatial and temporal relationships (e.g., *After dinner that night we went looking for them*). ***Grade 4*** **RL.4.1.** Refer to details and examples in a text when explaining what the text says explicitly and when drawing inferences from the text.

Appendix 2. Correlations Between Lessons and *Common Core State Standards, English Language Arts* (*ELA*) *(continued)*

Lesson Title	Suggested Grade Levels	*Common Core State Standards, ELA*
Sheep in a Jeep *(continued)*	3–5	**RL.4.4.** Determine the meaning of words and phrases as they are used in a text, including those that allude to significant characters found in mythology (e.g., Herculean). **SL.4.1.** Engage effectively in a range of collaborative discussions (one-on-one, in groups, and teacher-led) with diverse partners on *grade 4 topics and texts*, building on others' ideas and expressing their own clearly. **SL.4.1.A.** Come to discussions prepared, having read or studied required material; explicitly draw on that preparation and other information known about the topic to explore ideas under discussion. **SL.4.1.B.** Follow agreed-upon rules for discussions and carry out assigned roles. **SL.4.1.C.** Pose and respond to specific questions to clarify or follow up on information, and make comments that contribute to the discussion and link to the remarks of others. **SL.4.1.D.** Review the key ideas expressed and explain their own ideas and understanding in light of the discussion. **W.4.10.** Write routinely over extended time frames (time for research, reflection, and revision) and shorter time frames (a single sitting or a day or two) for a range of discipline-specific tasks, purposes, and audiences. **L.4.6.** Acquire and use accurately grade-appropriate general academic and domain-specific words and phrases, including those that signal precise actions, emotions, or states of being (e.g., quizzed, whined, stammered) and that are basic to a particular topic (e.g., *wildlife, conservation,* and *endangered* when discussing animal preservation). ***Grade 5*** **RL.5.1.** Quote accurately from a text when explaining what the text says explicitly and when drawing inferences from the text. **RL.5.2.** Determine a theme of a story, drama, or poem from details in the text, including how characters in a story or drama respond to challenges or how the speaker in a poem reflects upon a topic; summarize the text. **SL.5.1.** Engage effectively in a range of collaborative discussions (one-on-one, in groups, and teacher-led) with diverse partners on *grade 5 topics and texts*, building on others' ideas and expressing their own clearly. **SL.5.1.A.** Come to discussions prepared, having read or studied required material; explicitly draw on that preparation and other information known about the topic to explore ideas under discussion. **SL.5.1.B.** Follow agreed-upon rules for discussions and carry out assigned roles. **SL.5.1.C.** Pose and respond to specific questions by making comments that contribute to the discussion and elaborate on the remarks of others. **SL.5.1.D.** Review the key ideas expressed and draw conclusions in light of information and knowledge gained from the discussions. **W.5.10.** Write routinely over extended time frames (time for research, reflection, and revision) and shorter time frames (a single sitting or a day or two) for a range of discipline-specific tasks, purposes, and audiences. **L.5.6.** Acquire and use accurately grade-appropriate general academic and domain-specific words and phrases, including those that signal contrast, addition, and other logical relationships (e.g., *however, although, nevertheless, similarly, moreover, in addition*).
Sounds of Science	3–6	***Grade 3*** **RL.3.1.** Ask and answer questions to demonstrate understanding of a text, referring explicitly to the text as the basis for the answers. **RI.3.2.** Determine the main idea of a text; recount the key details and explain how they support the main idea. **RI.3.3.** Describe the relationship between a series of historical events, scientific ideas or concepts, or steps in technical procedures in a text, using language that pertains to time, sequence, and cause/effect. **RI.3.4.** Determine the meaning of general academic and domain-specific words and phrases in a text relevant to a *grade 3 topic or subject area*. **RI.3.5.** Use text features and search tools (e.g., key words, sidebars, hyperlinks) to locate information relevant to a given topic efficiently. **SL.3.1.** Engage effectively in a range of collaborative discussions (one-on-one, in groups, and teacher-led) with diverse partners on *grade 3 topics and texts*, building on others' ideas and expressing their own clearly. **SL.3.1.A.** Come to discussions prepared, having read or studied required material; explicitly draw on that preparation and other information known about the topic to explore ideas under discussion. **SL.3.1.B.** Follow agreed-upon rules for discussions (e.g., gaining the floor in respectful ways, listening to others with care, speaking one at a time about the topics and texts under discussion). **SL.3.1.C.** Ask questions to check understanding of information presented, stay on topic, and link their comments to the remarks of others. **SL.3.1.D.** Explain their own ideas and understanding in light of the discussion.

Lesson Title	Suggested Grade Levels	*Common Core State Standards, ELA*
Sounds of Science *(continued)*	**3–6**	**SL.3.2.** Determine the main ideas and supporting details of a text read aloud or information presented in diverse media and formats, including visually, quantitatively, and orally. **W.3.10.** Write routinely over extended time frames (time for research, reflection, and revision) and shorter time frames (a single sitting or a day or two) for a range of discipline-specific tasks, purposes, and audiences. **L.3.6.** Acquire and use accurately grade-appropriate conversational, general academic, and domain-specific words and phrases, including those that signal spatial and temporal relationships (e.g., *After dinner that night we went looking for them*). ***Grade 4*** **RL.4.1.** Refer to details and examples in a text when explaining what the text says explicitly and when drawing inferences from the text. **RI.4.1.** Refer to details and examples in a text when explaining what the text says explicitly and when drawing inferences from the text. **RI.4.2.** Determine the main idea of a text and explain how it is supported by key details; summarize the text. **RI.4.3.** Explain events, procedures, ideas, or concepts in a historical, scientific, or technical text, including what happened and why, based on specific information in the text. **RI.4.4.** Determine the meaning of general academic and domain-specific words or phrases in a text relevant to a *grade 4 topic or subject area*. **SL.4.1.** Engage effectively in a range of collaborative discussions (one-on-one, in groups, and teacher-led) with diverse partners on *grade 4 topics and texts*, building on others' ideas and expressing their own clearly. **SL.4.1.A.** Come to discussions prepared, having read or studied required material; explicitly draw on that preparation and other information known about the topic to explore ideas under discussion. **SL.4.1.B.** Follow agreed-upon rules for discussions and carry out assigned roles. **SL.4.1.C.** Pose and respond to specific questions to clarify or follow up on information, and make comments that contribute to the discussion and link to the remarks of others. **SL.4.1.D.** Review the key ideas expressed and explain their own ideas and understanding in light of the discussion. **W.4.10.** Write routinely over extended time frames (time for research, reflection, and revision) and shorter time frames (a single sitting or a day or two) for a range of discipline-specific tasks, purposes, and audiences. **L.4.6.** Acquire and use accurately grade-appropriate general academic and domain-specific words and phrases, including those that signal precise actions, emotions, or states of being (e.g., quizzed, whined, stammered) and that are basic to a particular topic (e.g., *wildlife, conservation,* and *endangered* when discussing animal preservation). ***Grade 5*** **RI.5.1.** Quote accurately from a text when explaining what the text says explicitly and when drawing inferences from the text. **RI.5.2.** Determine two or more main ideas of a text and explain how they are supported by key details; summarize the text. **RI.5.3.** Explain the relationships or interactions between two or more individuals, events, ideas, or concepts in a historical, scientific, or technical text based on specific information in the text. **RI.5.4.** Determine the meaning of general academic and domain-specific words and phrases in a text relevant to a *grade 5 topic or subject area*. **SL.5.1.** Engage effectively in a range of collaborative discussions (one-on-one, in groups, and teacher-led) with diverse partners on *grade 5 topics and texts*, building on others' ideas and expressing their own clearly. **SL.5.1.A.** Come to discussions prepared, having read or studied required material; explicitly draw on that preparation and other information known about the topic to explore ideas under discussion. **SL.5.1.B.** Follow agreed-upon rules for discussions and carry out assigned roles. **SL.5.1.C.** Pose and respond to specific questions by making comments that contribute to the discussion and elaborate on the remarks of others. **SL.5.1.D.** Review the key ideas expressed and draw conclusions in light of information and knowledge gained from the discussions. **W.5.10.** Write routinely over extended time frames (time for research, reflection, and revision) and shorter time frames (a single sitting or a day or two) for a range of discipline-specific tasks, purposes, and audiences. **L.5.6.** Acquire and use accurately grade-appropriate general academic and domain-specific words and phrases, including those that signal contrast, addition, and other logical relationships (e.g., *however, although, nevertheless, similarly, moreover, in addition*).

Appendix 2. Correlations Between Lessons and *Common Core State Standards, English Language Arts* (*ELA*) *(continued)*

Lesson Title	Suggested Grade Levels	*Common Core State Standards, ELA*
Sounds of Science *(continued)*	3–6	***Grade 6*** **RI.6.1.** Cite textual evidence to support analysis of what the text says explicitly as well as inferences drawn from the text. **RI.6.2.** Determine a central idea of a text and how it is conveyed through particular details; provide a summary of the text distinct from personal opinions or judgments. **RI.6.4.** Determine the meaning of words and phrases as they are used in a text, including figurative, connotative, and technical meanings. **SL.6.1.** Engage effectively in a range of collaborative discussions (one-on-one, in groups, and teacher-led) with diverse partners on grade 6 topics, texts, and issues, building on others' ideas and expressing their own clearly. **SL.6.1.A.** Come to discussions prepared, having read or studied required material; explicitly draw on that preparation by referring to evidence on the topic, text, or issue to probe and reflect on ideas under discussion. **SL.6.1.B.** Follow rules for collegial discussions, set specific goals and deadlines, and define individual roles as needed. **SL.6.1.C.** Pose and respond to specific questions with elaboration and detail by making comments that contribute to the topic, text, or issue under discussion. **SL.6.1.D.** Review the key ideas expressed and demonstrate understanding of multiple perspectives through reflection and paraphrasing. **W.6.10.** Write routinely over extended time frames (time for research, reflection, and revision) and shorter time frames (a single sitting or a day or two) for a range of discipline-specific tasks, purposes, and audiences. **L.6.6.** Acquire and use accurately grade-appropriate general academic and domain-specific words and phrases; gather vocabulary knowledge when considering a word or phrase important to comprehension or expression. **RST.6-8.1.** Cite specific textual evidence to support analysis of science and technical texts. **RST.6-8.2.** Determine the central ideas or conclusions of a text; provide an accurate summary of the text distinct from prior knowledge or opinions. **RST.6-8.4.** Determine the meaning of symbols, key terms, and other domain-specific words and phrases as they are used in a specific scientific or technical context relevant to *grades 6–8 texts and topics*. **WHST.6-8.10.** Write routinely over extended time frames (time for reflection and revision) and shorter time frames (a single sitting or a day or two) for a range of discipline-specific tasks, purposes, and audiences.
Chemical Change Café	3–5	***Grade 3*** **RL.3.1.** Ask and answer questions to demonstrate understanding of a text, referring explicitly to the text as the basis for the answers. **RI.3.1.** Ask and answer questions to demonstrate understanding of a text, referring explicitly to the text as the basis for the answers. **RI.3.2.** Determine the main idea of a text; recount the key details and explain how they support the main idea. **RI.3.3.** Describe the relationship between a series of historical events, scientific ideas or concepts, or steps in technical procedures in a text, using language that pertains to time, sequence, and cause/effect. **RI.3.4.** Determine the meaning of general academic and domain-specific words and phrases in a text relevant to a *grade 3 topic or subject area*. **RI.3.7.** Use information gained from illustrations (e.g., maps, photographs) and the words in a text to demonstrate understanding of the text (e.g., where, when, why, and how key events occur). **SL.3.1.** Engage effectively in a range of collaborative discussions (one-on-one, in groups, and teacher-led) with diverse partners on *grade 3 topics and texts*, building on others' ideas and expressing their own clearly. **SL.3.1.A.** Come to discussions prepared, having read or studied required material; explicitly draw on that preparation and other information known about the topic to explore ideas under discussion. **SL.3.1.B.** Follow agreed-upon rules for discussions (e.g., gaining the floor in respectful ways, listening to others with care, speaking one at a time about the topics and texts under discussion). **SL.3.1.C.** Ask questions to check understanding of information presented, stay on topic, and link their comments to the remarks of others. **SL.3.1.D.** Explain their own ideas and understanding in light of the discussion. **SL.3.2.** Determine the main ideas and supporting details of a text read aloud or information presented in diverse media and formats, including visually, quantitatively, and orally. **W.3.10.** Write routinely over extended time frames (time for research, reflection, and revision) and shorter time frames (a single sitting or a day or two) for a range of discipline-specific tasks, purposes, and audiences.

Lesson Title	Suggested Grade Levels	*Common Core State Standards, ELA*
Chemical Change Café *(continued)*	3–5	**L.3.6.** Acquire and use accurately grade-appropriate conversational, general academic, and domain-specific words and phrases, including those that signal spatial and temporal relationships (e.g., *After dinner that night we went looking for them*). ***Grade 4*** **RL.4.1.** Refer to details and examples in a text when explaining what the text says explicitly and when drawing inferences from the text. **RI.4.1.** Refer to details and examples in a text when explaining what the text says explicitly and when drawing inferences from the text. **RI.4.2.** Determine the main idea of a text and explain how it is supported by key details; summarize the text. **RI.4.3.** Explain events, procedures, ideas, or concepts in a historical, scientific, or technical text, including what happened and why, based on specific information in the text. **RI.4.4.** Determine the meaning of general academic and domain-specific words or phrases in a text relevant to a *grade 4 topic or subject area*. **SL.4.1.** Engage effectively in a range of collaborative discussions (one-on-one, in groups, and teacher-led) with diverse partners on *grade 4 topics and texts*, building on others' ideas and expressing their own clearly. **SL.4.1.A.** Come to discussions prepared, having read or studied required material; explicitly draw on that preparation and other information known about the topic to explore ideas under discussion. **SL.4.1.B.** Follow agreed-upon rules for discussions and carry out assigned roles. **SL.4.1.C.** Pose and respond to specific questions to clarify or follow up on information, and make comments that contribute to the discussion and link to the remarks of others. **SL.4.1.D.** Review the key ideas expressed and explain their own ideas and understanding in light of the discussion. **W.4.10.** Write routinely over extended time frames (time for research, reflection, and revision) and shorter time frames (a single sitting or a day or two) for a range of discipline-specific tasks, purposes, and audiences. **L.4.6.** Acquire and use accurately grade-appropriate general academic and domain-specific words and phrases, including those that signal precise actions, emotions, or states of being (e.g., quizzed, whined, stammered) and that are basic to a particular topic (e.g., *wildlife, conservation,* and *endangered* when discussing animal preservation). ***Grade 5*** **RL.5.1.** Quote accurately from a text when explaining what the text says explicitly and when drawing inferences from the text. **RI.5.1.** Quote accurately from a text when explaining what the text says explicitly and when drawing inferences from the text. **RI.5.2.** Determine two or more main ideas of a text and explain how they are supported by key details; summarize the text. **RI.5.3.** Explain the relationships or interactions between two or more individuals, events, ideas, or concepts in a historical, scientific, or technical text based on specific information in the text. **RI.5.4.** Determine the meaning of general academic and domain-specific words and phrases in a text relevant to a *grade 5 topic or subject area*. **SL.5.1.** Engage effectively in a range of collaborative discussions (one-on-one, in groups, and teacher-led) with diverse partners on *grade 5 topics and texts*, building on others' ideas and expressing their own clearly. **SL.5.1.A.** Come to discussions prepared, having read or studied required material; explicitly draw on that preparation and other information known about the topic to explore ideas under discussion. **SL.5.1.B.** Follow agreed-upon rules for discussions and carry out assigned roles. **SL.5.1.C.** Pose and respond to specific questions by making comments that contribute to the discussion and elaborate on the remarks of others. **SL.5.1.D.** Review the key ideas expressed and draw conclusions in light of information and knowledge gained from the discussions. **W.5.10.** Write routinely over extended time frames (time for research, reflection, and revision) and shorter time frames (a single sitting or a day or two) for a range of discipline-specific tasks, purposes, and audiences. **L.5.6.** Acquire and use accurately grade-appropriate general academic and domain-specific words and phrases, including those that signal contrast, addition, and other logical relationships (e.g., *however, although, nevertheless, similarly, moreover, in addition*).

Appendix 2. Correlations Between Lessons and *Common Core State Standards, English Language Arts* (*ELA*) *(continued)*

Lesson Title	Suggested Grade Levels	*Common Core State Standards, ELA*
The Changing Moon	**3–5**	***Grade 3*** **RL.3.1.** Ask and answer questions to demonstrate understanding of a text, referring explicitly to the text as the basis for the answers. **RL.3.4.** Determine the meaning of words and phrases as they are used in a text, distinguishing literal from nonliteral language. **RI.3.1.** Ask and answer questions to demonstrate understanding of a text, referring explicitly to the text as the basis for the answers. **RI.3.2.** Determine the main idea of a text; recount the key details and explain how they support the main idea. **RI.3.3.** Describe the relationship between a series of historical events, scientific ideas or concepts, or steps in technical procedures in a text, using language that pertains to time, sequence, and cause/effect. **RI.3.4.** Determine the meaning of general academic and domain-specific words and phrases in a text relevant to a *grade 3 topic or subject area*. **RI.3.7.** Use information gained from illustrations (e.g., maps, photographs) and the words in a text to demonstrate understanding of the text (e.g., where, when, why, and how key events occur). **SL.3.1.** Engage effectively in a range of collaborative discussions (one-on-one, in groups, and teacher-led) with diverse partners on *grade 3 topics and texts*, building on others' ideas and expressing their own clearly. **SL.3.1.A.** Come to discussions prepared, having read or studied required material; explicitly draw on that preparation and other information known about the topic to explore ideas under discussion. **SL.3.1.B.** Follow agreed-upon rules for discussions (e.g., gaining the floor in respectful ways, listening to others with care, speaking one at a time about the topics and texts under discussion). **SL.3.1.C.** Ask questions to check understanding of information presented, stay on topic, and link their comments to the remarks of others. **SL.3.1.D.** Explain their own ideas and understanding in light of the discussion. **SL.3.2.** Determine the main ideas and supporting details of a text read aloud or information presented in diverse media and formats, including visually, quantitatively, and orally. **W.3.10.** Write routinely over extended time frames (time for research, reflection, and revision) and shorter time frames (a single sitting or a day or two) for a range of discipline-specific tasks, purposes, and audiences. **L.3.6.** Acquire and use accurately grade-appropriate conversational, general academic, and domain-specific words and phrases, including those that signal spatial and temporal relationships (e.g., *After dinner that night we went looking for them*). ***Grade 4*** **RL.4.1.** Refer to details and examples in a text when explaining what the text says explicitly and when drawing inferences from the text. **RI.4.1.** Refer to details and examples in a text when explaining what the text says explicitly and when drawing inferences from the text. **RI.4.2.** Determine the main idea of a text and explain how it is supported by key details; summarize the text. **RI.4.3.** Explain events, procedures, ideas, or concepts in a historical, scientific, or technical text, including what happened and why, based on specific information in the text. **RI.4.4.** Determine the meaning of general academic and domain-specific words or phrases in a text relevant to a *grade 4 topic or subject area*. **SL.4.1.** Engage effectively in a range of collaborative discussions (one-on-one, in groups, and teacher-led) with diverse partners on *grade 4 topics and texts*, building on others' ideas and expressing their own clearly. **SL.4.1.A.** Come to discussions prepared, having read or studied required material; explicitly draw on that preparation and other information known about the topic to explore ideas under discussion. **SL.4.1.B.** Follow agreed-upon rules for discussions and carry out assigned roles. **SL.4.1.C.** Pose and respond to specific questions to clarify or follow up on information, and make comments that contribute to the discussion and link to the remarks of others. **SL.4.1.D.** Review the key ideas expressed and explain their own ideas and understanding in light of the discussion. **W.4.10.** Write routinely over extended time frames (time for research, reflection, and revision) and shorter time frames (a single sitting or a day or two) for a range of discipline-specific tasks, purposes, and audiences. **L.4.6.** Acquire and use accurately grade-appropriate general academic and domain-specific words and phrases, including those that signal precise actions, emotions, or states of being (e.g., quizzed, whined, stammered) and that are basic to a particular topic (e.g., *wildlife, conservation,* and *endangered* when discussing animal preservation).

Lesson Title	Suggested Grade Levels	*Common Core State Standards, ELA*
The Changing Moon *(continued)*	3–5	***Grade 5*** **RL.5.1.** Quote accurately from a text when explaining what the text says explicitly and when drawing inferences from the text. **RL.5.2.** Determine a theme of a story, drama, or poem from details in the text, including how characters in a story or drama respond to challenges or how the speaker in a poem reflects upon a topic; summarize the text. **RI.5.1.** Quote accurately from a text when explaining what the text says explicitly and when drawing inferences from the text. **RI.5.2.** Determine two or more main ideas of a text and explain how they are supported by key details; summarize the text. **RI.5.3.** Explain the relationships or interactions between two or more individuals, events, ideas, or concepts in a historical, scientific, or technical text based on specific information in the text. **RI.5.4.** Determine the meaning of general academic and domain-specific words and phrases in a text relevant to a *grade 5 topic or subject area.* **SL.5.1.** Engage effectively in a range of collaborative discussions (one-on-one, in groups, and teacher-led) with diverse partners on *grade 5 topics and texts*, building on others' ideas and expressing their own clearly. **SL.5.1.A.** Come to discussions prepared, having read or studied required material; explicitly draw on that preparation and other information known about the topic to explore ideas under discussion. **SL.5.1.B.** Follow agreed-upon rules for discussions and carry out assigned roles. **SL.5.1.C.** Pose and respond to specific questions by making comments that contribute to the discussion and elaborate on the remarks of others. **SL.5.1.D.** Review the key ideas expressed and draw conclusions in light of information and knowledge gained from the discussions. **W.5.10.** Write routinely over extended time frames (time for research, reflection, and revision) and shorter time frames (a single sitting or a day or two) for a range of discipline-specific tasks, purposes, and audiences. **L.5.6.** Acquire and use accurately grade-appropriate general academic and domain-specific words and phrases, including those that signal contrast, addition, and other logical relationships (e.g., *however, although, nevertheless, similarly, moreover, in addition*).
Day and Night	3–5	***Grade 3*** **RL.3.1.** Ask and answer questions to demonstrate understanding of a text, referring explicitly to the text as the basis for the answers. **RL.3.4.** Determine the meaning of words and phrases as they are used in a text, distinguishing literal from nonliteral language. **RI.3.1.** Ask and answer questions to demonstrate understanding of a text, referring explicitly to the text as the basis for the answers. **RI.3.2.** Determine the main idea of a text; recount the key details and explain how they support the main idea. **RI.3.3.** Describe the relationship between a series of historical events, scientific ideas or concepts, or steps in technical procedures in a text, using language that pertains to time, sequence, and cause/effect. **RI.3.4.** Determine the meaning of general academic and domain-specific words and phrases in a text relevant to a *grade 3 topic or subject area*. **RI.3.7.** Use information gained from illustrations (e.g., maps, photographs) and the words in a text to demonstrate understanding of the text (e.g., where, when, why, and how key events occur). **SL.3.1.** Engage effectively in a range of collaborative discussions (one-on-one, in groups, and teacher-led) with diverse partners on *grade 3 topics and texts*, building on others' ideas and expressing their own clearly. **SL.3.1.A.** Come to discussions prepared, having read or studied required material; explicitly draw on that preparation and other information known about the topic to explore ideas under discussion. **SL.3.1.B.** Follow agreed-upon rules for discussions (e.g., gaining the floor in respectful ways, listening to others with care, speaking one at a time about the topics and texts under discussion). **SL.3.1.C.** Ask questions to check understanding of information presented, stay on topic, and link their comments to the remarks of others. **SL.3.1.D.** Explain their own ideas and understanding in light of the discussion. **SL.3.2.** Determine the main ideas and supporting details of a text read aloud or information presented in diverse media and formats, including visually, quantitatively, and orally. **W.3.10.** Write routinely over extended time frames (time for research, reflection, and revision) and shorter time frames (a single sitting or a day or two) for a range of discipline-specific tasks, purposes, and audiences.

Appendix 2. Correlations Between Lessons and *Common Core State Standards, English Language Arts* (*ELA*) *(continued)*

Lesson Title	Suggested Grade Levels	*Common Core State Standards, ELA*
Day and Night *(continued)*	3–5	**L.3.6.** Acquire and use accurately grade-appropriate conversational, general academic, and domain-specific words and phrases, including those that signal spatial and temporal relationships (e.g., *After dinner that night we went looking for them*). ***Grade 4*** **RL.4.1.** Refer to details and examples in a text when explaining what the text says explicitly and when drawing inferences from the text. **RI.4.1.** Refer to details and examples in a text when explaining what the text says explicitly and when drawing inferences from the text. **RI.4.2.** Determine the main idea of a text and explain how it is supported by key details; summarize the text. **RI.4.3.** Explain events, procedures, ideas, or concepts in a historical, scientific, or technical text, including what happened and why, based on specific information in the text. **RI.4.4.** Determine the meaning of general academic and domain-specific words or phrases in a text relevant to a *grade 4 topic or subject area.* **SL.4.1.** Engage effectively in a range of collaborative discussions (one-on-one, in groups, and teacher-led) with diverse partners on *grade 4 topics and texts*, building on others' ideas and expressing their own clearly. **SL.4.1.A.** Come to discussions prepared, having read or studied required material; explicitly draw on that preparation and other information known about the topic to explore ideas under discussion. **SL.4.1.B.** Follow agreed-upon rules for discussions and carry out assigned roles. **SL.4.1.C.** Pose and respond to specific questions to clarify or follow up on information, and make comments that contribute to the discussion and link to the remarks of others. **SL.4.1.D.** Review the key ideas expressed and explain their own ideas and understanding in light of the discussion. **W.4.10.** Write routinely over extended time frames (time for research, reflection, and revision) and shorter time frames (a single sitting or a day or two) for a range of discipline-specific tasks, purposes, and audiences. **L.4.6.** Acquire and use accurately grade-appropriate general academic and domain-specific words and phrases, including those that signal precise actions, emotions, or states of being (e.g., quizzed, whined, stammered) and that are basic to a particular topic (e.g., *wildlife, conservation,* and *endangered* when discussing animal preservation). ***Grade 5*** **RL.5.1.** Quote accurately from a text when explaining what the text says explicitly and when drawing inferences from the text. **RL.5.2.** Determine a theme of a story, drama, or poem from details in the text, including how characters in a story or drama respond to challenges or how the speaker in a poem reflects upon a topic; summarize the text. **RI.5.1.** Quote accurately from a text when explaining what the text says explicitly and when drawing inferences from the text. **RI.5.2.** Determine two or more main ideas of a text and explain how they are supported by key details; summarize the text. **RI.5.3.** Explain the relationships or interactions between two or more individuals, events, ideas, or concepts in a historical, scientific, or technical text based on specific information in the text. **RI.5.4.** Determine the meaning of general academic and domain-specific words and phrases in a text relevant to a *grade 5 topic or subject area.* **SL.5.1.** Engage effectively in a range of collaborative discussions (one-on-one, in groups, and teacher-led) with diverse partners on *grade 5 topics and texts*, building on others' ideas and expressing their own clearly. **SL.5.1.A.** Come to discussions prepared, having read or studied required material; explicitly draw on that preparation and other information known about the topic to explore ideas under discussion. **SL.5.1.B.** Follow agreed-upon rules for discussions and carry out assigned roles. **SL.5.1.C.** Pose and respond to specific questions by making comments that contribute to the discussion and elaborate on the remarks of others. **SL.5.1.D.** Review the key ideas expressed and draw conclusions in light of information and knowledge gained from the discussions. **W.5.10.** Write routinely over extended time frames (time for research, reflection, and revision) and shorter time frames (a single sitting or a day or two) for a range of discipline-specific tasks, purposes, and audiences. **L.5.6.** Acquire and use accurately grade-appropriate general academic and domain-specific words and phrases, including those that signal contrast, addition, and other logical relationships (e.g., *however, although, nevertheless, similarly, moreover, in addition*).

Lesson Title	Suggested Grade Levels	*Common Core State Standards, ELA*
Grand Canyon	**3–6**	***Grade 3*** **RI.3.1.** Ask and answer questions to demonstrate understanding of a text, referring explicitly to the text as the basis for the answers. **RI.3.2.** Determine the main idea of a text; recount the key details and explain how they support the main idea. **RI.3.3.** Describe the relationship between a series of historical events, scientific ideas or concepts, or steps in technical procedures in a text, using language that pertains to time, sequence, and cause/effect. **RI.3.4.** Determine the meaning of general academic and domain-specific words and phrases in a text relevant to a *grade 3 topic or subject area*. **RI.3.5.** Use text features and search tools (e.g., key words, sidebars, hyperlinks) to locate information relevant to a given topic efficiently. **RI.3.7.** Use information gained from illustrations (e.g., maps, photographs) and the words in a text to demonstrate understanding of the text (e.g., where, when, why, and how key events occur). **SL.3.1.** Engage effectively in a range of collaborative discussions (one-on-one, in groups, and teacher-led) with diverse partners on *grade 3 topics and texts*, building on others' ideas and expressing their own clearly. **SL.3.1.A.** Come to discussions prepared, having read or studied required material; explicitly draw on that preparation and other information known about the topic to explore ideas under discussion. **SL.3.1.B.** Follow agreed-upon rules for discussions (e.g., gaining the floor in respectful ways, listening to others with care, speaking one at a time about the topics and texts under discussion). **SL.3.1.C.** Ask questions to check understanding of information presented, stay on topic, and link their comments to the remarks of others. **SL.3.1.D.** Explain their own ideas and understanding in light of the discussion. **SL.3.2.** Determine the main ideas and supporting details of a text read aloud or information presented in diverse media and formats, including visually, quantitatively, and orally. **W.3.10.** Write routinely over extended time frames (time for research, reflection, and revision) and shorter time frames (a single sitting or a day or two) for a range of discipline-specific tasks, purposes, and audiences. **L.3.4.** Determine or clarify the meaning of unknown and multiple-meaning word and phrases based on grade 3 reading and content, choosing flexibly from a range of strategies. **L.3.4.A.** Use sentence-level context as a clue to the meaning of a word or phrase. **L.3.6.** Acquire and use accurately grade-appropriate conversational, general academic, and domain-specific words and phrases, including those that signal spatial and temporal relationships (e.g., *After dinner that night we went looking for them*). ***Grade 4*** **RI.4.1.** Refer to details and examples in a text when explaining what the text says explicitly and when drawing inferences from the text. **RI.4.2.** Determine the main idea of a text and explain how it is supported by key details; summarize the text. **RI.4.3.** Explain events, procedures, ideas, or concepts in a historical, scientific, or technical text, including what happened and why, based on specific information in the text. **RI.4.4.** Determine the meaning of general academic and domain-specific words or phrases in a text relevant to a *grade 4 topic or subject area*. **SL.4.1.** Engage effectively in a range of collaborative discussions (one-on-one, in groups, and teacher-led) with diverse partners on *grade 4 topics and texts*, building on others' ideas and expressing their own clearly. **SL.4.1.A.** Come to discussions prepared, having read or studied required material; explicitly draw on that preparation and other information known about the topic to explore ideas under discussion. **SL.4.1.B.** Follow agreed-upon rules for discussions and carry out assigned roles. **SL.4.1.C.** Pose and respond to specific questions to clarify or follow up on information, and make comments that contribute to the discussion and link to the remarks of others. **SL.4.1.D.** Review the key ideas expressed and explain their own ideas and understanding in light of the discussion. **W.4.10.** Write routinely over extended time frames (time for research, reflection, and revision) and shorter time frames (a single sitting or a day or two) for a range of discipline-specific tasks, purposes, and audiences. **L.4.4.** Determine or clarify the meaning of unknown and multiple-meaning words and phrases based on grade 4 reading and content, choosing flexibly from a range of strategies. **L.4.4.A.** Use context (e.g., definitions, examples, or restatements in text) as a clue to the meaning of a word or phrase.

Appendix 2. Correlations Between Lessons and *Common Core State Standards, English Language Arts* (*ELA*) *(continued)*

Lesson Title	Suggested Grade Levels	*Common Core State Standards, ELA*
Grand Canyon *(continued)*	**3–6**	**L.4.6.** Acquire and use accurately grade-appropriate general academic and domain-specific words and phrases, including those that signal precise actions, emotions, or states of being (e.g., quizzed, whined, stammered) and that are basic to a particular topic (e.g., *wildlife, conservation,* and *endangered* when discussing animal preservation). ***Grade 5*** **RI.5.1.** Quote accurately from a text when explaining what the text says explicitly and when drawing inferences from the text. **RI.5.2.** Determine two or more main ideas of a text and explain how they are supported by key details; summarize the text. **RI.5.3.** Explain the relationships or interactions between two or more individuals, events, ideas, or concepts in a historical, scientific, or technical text based on specific information in the text. **RI.5.4.** Determine the meaning of general academic and domain-specific words and phrases in a text relevant to a *grade 5 topic or subject area*. **SL.5.1.** Engage effectively in a range of collaborative discussions (one-on-one, in groups, and teacher-led) with diverse partners on *grade 5 topics and texts*, building on others' ideas and expressing their own clearly. **SL.5.1.A.** Come to discussions prepared, having read or studied required material; explicitly draw on that preparation and other information known about the topic to explore ideas under discussion. **SL.5.1.B.** Follow agreed-upon rules for discussions and carry out assigned roles. **SL.5.1.C.** Pose and respond to specific questions by making comments that contribute to the discussion and elaborate on the remarks of others. **SL.5.1.D.** Review the key ideas expressed and draw conclusions in light of information and knowledge gained from the discussions. **W.5.10.** Write routinely over extended time frames (time for research, reflection, and revision) and shorter time frames (a single sitting or a day or two) for a range of discipline-specific tasks, purposes, and audiences. **L.5.4.** Determine or clarify the meaning of unknown and multiple-meaning words and phrases based on grade 5 reading and content, choosing flexibly from a range of strategies. **L.5.4.A.** Use context (e.g., cause/effect relationships and comparisons in text) as a clue to the meaning of a word or phrase. **L.5.6.** Acquire and use accurately grade-appropriate general academic and domain-specific words and phrases, including those that signal contrast, addition, and other logical relationships (e.g., *however, although, nevertheless, similarly, moreover, in addition*). ***Grade 6*** **RI.6.1.** Cite textual evidence to support analysis of what the text says explicitly as well as inferences drawn from the text. **RI.6.2.** Determine a central idea of a text and how it is conveyed through particular details; provide a summary of the text distinct from personal opinions or judgments. **RI.6.4.** Determine the meaning of words and phrases as they are used in a text, including figurative, connotative, and technical meanings. **SL.6.1.** Engage effectively in a range of collaborative discussions (one-on-one, in groups, and teacher-led) with diverse partners on grade 6 topics, texts, and issues, building on others' ideas and expressing their own clearly. **SL.6.1.A.** Come to discussions prepared, having read or studied required material; explicitly draw on that preparation by referring to evidence on the topic, text, or issue to probe and reflect on ideas under discussion. **SL.6.1.B.** Follow rules for collegial discussions, set specific goals and deadlines, and define individual roles as needed. **SL.6.1.C.** Pose and respond to specific questions with elaboration and detail by making comments that contribute to the topic, text, or issue under discussion. **SL.6.1.D.** Review the key ideas expressed and demonstrate understanding of multiple perspectives through reflection and paraphrasing. **W.6.10.** Write routinely over extended time frames (time for research, reflection, and revision) and shorter time frames (a single sitting or a day or two) for a range of discipline-specific tasks, purposes, and audiences. **L.6.4.** Determine or clarify the meaning of unknown and multiple-meaning words and phrases based on grade 6 reading and content, choosing flexibly from a range of strategies. **L.6.4.A.** Use context (e.g., the overall meaning of a sentence or paragraph; a word's position or function in a sentence) as a clue to the meaning of a word or phrase.

Lesson Title	Suggested Grade Levels	*Common Core State Standards, ELA*
Grand Canyon *(continued)*	3–6	**L.6.6.** Acquire and use accurately grade-appropriate general academic and domain-specific words and phrases; gather vocabulary knowledge when considering a word or phrase important to comprehension or expression. **RST.6-8.1.** Cite specific textual evidence to support analysis of science and technical texts. **RST.6-8.2.** Determine the central ideas or conclusions of a text; provide an accurate summary of the text distinct from prior knowledge or opinions. **RST.6-8.3.** Follow precisely a multistep procedure when carrying out experiments, taking measurements, or performing technical tasks. **RST.6-8.4.** Determine the meaning of symbols, key terms, and other domain-specific words and phrases as they are used in a specific scientific or technical context relevant to *grades 6–8 texts and topics*. **WHST.6-8.10.** Write routinely over extended time frames (time for reflection and revision) and shorter time frames (a single sitting or a day or two) for a range of discipline-specific tasks, purposes, and audiences.
Brainstorms: From Idea to Invention	5–6	***Grade 5*** **RI.5.1.** Quote accurately from a text when explaining what the text says explicitly and when drawing inferences from the text. **RI.5.2.** Determine two or more main ideas of a text and explain how they are supported by key details; summarize the text. **RI.5.3.** Explain the relationships or interactions between two or more individuals, events, ideas, or concepts in a historical, scientific, or technical text based on specific information in the text. **RI.5.4.** Determine the meaning of general academic and domain-specific words in a text relevant to a *grade 5 topic or subject area.* **SL.5.1.** Engage effectively in a range of collaborative discussions (one-on-one, in groups, and teacher-led) with diverse partners on *grade 5 topics and texts*, building on others' ideas and expressing their own clearly. **SL.5.1.A.** Come to discussions prepared, having read or studied required material; explicitly draw on that preparation and other information known about the topic to explore ideas under discussion. **SL.5.1.B.** Follow agreed-upon rules for discussions and carry out assigned roles. **SL.5.1.C.** Pose and respond to specific questions by making comments that contribute to the discussion and elaborate on the remarks of others. **SL.5.1.D.** Review the key ideas expressed and draw conclusions in light of information and knowledge gained from the discussions. **W.5.10.** Write routinely over extended time frames (time for research, reflection, and revision) and shorter time frames (a single sitting or a day or two) for a range of discipline-specific tasks, purposes, and audiences. **L.5.6.** Acquire and use accurately grade-appropriate general academic and domain-specific words and phrases, including those that signal contrast, addition, and other logical relationships (e.g., *however, although, nevertheless, similarly, moreover, in addition*). ***Grade 6*** **RI.6.1.** Cite textual evidence to support analysis of what the text says explicitly as well as inferences drawn from the text. **RI.6.2.** Determine a central idea of a text and how it is conveyed through particular details; provide a summary of the text distinct from personal opinions or judgments. **RI.6.4.** Determine the meaning of words and phrases as they are used in a text, including figurative, connotative, and technical meanings. **SL.6.1.** Engage effectively in a range of collaborative discussions (one-on-one, in groups, and teacher-led) with diverse partners on grade 6 topics, texts, and issues, building on others' ideas and expressing their own clearly. **SL.6.1.A.** Come to discussions prepared, having read or studied required material; explicitly draw on that preparation by referring to evidence on the topic, text, or issue to probe and reflect on ideas under discussion. **SL.6.1.B.** Follow rules for collegial discussions, set specific goals and deadlines, and define individual roles as needed. **SL.6.1.C.** Pose and respond to specific questions with elaboration and detail by making comments that contribute to the topic, text, or issue under discussion. **SL.6.1.D.** Review the key ideas expressed and demonstrate understanding of multiple perspectives through reflection and paraphrasing. **W.6.10.** Write routinely over extended time frames (time for research, reflection, and revision) and shorter time frames (a single sitting or a day or two) for a range of discipline-specific tasks, purposes, and audiences.

Appendix 2. Correlations Between Lessons and *Common Core State Standards, English Language Arts* (*ELA*) *(continued)*

Lesson Title	Suggested Grade Levels	*Common Core State Standards, ELA*
Brainstorms: From Idea to Invention *(continued)*	5–6	**L.6.6.** Acquire and use accurately grade-appropriate general academic and domain-specific words and phrases; gather vocabulary knowledge when considering a word or phrase important to comprehension or expression. **RST.6-8.1.** Cite specific textual evidence to support analysis of science and technical texts. **RST.6-8.2.** Determine the central ideas or conclusions of a text; provide an accurate summary of the text distinct from prior knowledge or opinions. **RST.6-8.3.** Follow precisely a multistep procedure when carrying out experiments, taking measurements, or performing technical tasks. **RST.6-8.4.** Determine the meaning of symbols, key terms, and other domain-specific words and phrases as they are used in a specific scientific or technical context relevant to *grades 6–8 texts and topics*. **WHST.6-8.10.** Write routinely over extended time frames (time for reflection and revision) and shorter time frames (a single sitting or a day or two) for a range of discipline-specific tasks, purposes, and audiences.
Bugs!	3–5	***Grade 3*** **RL.3.1.** Ask and answer questions to demonstrate understanding of a text, referring explicitly to the text as the basis for the answers. **RL.3.4.** Determine the meaning of words and phrases as they are used in a text, distinguishing literal from nonliteral language. **RI.3.1.** Ask and answer questions to demonstrate understanding of a text, referring explicitly to the text as the basis for the answers. **RI.3.2.** Determine the main idea of a text; recount the key details and explain how they support the main idea. **RI.3.3.** Describe the relationship between a series of historical events, scientific ideas or concepts, or steps in technical procedures in a text, using language that pertains to time, sequence, and cause/effect. **RI.3.4.** Determine the meaning of general academic and domain-specific words and phrases in a text relevant to a *grade 3 topic or subject area*. **RI.3.7.** Use information gained from illustrations (e.g., maps, photographs) and the words in a text to demonstrate understanding of the text (e.g., where, when, why, and how key events occur). **SL.3.1.** Engage effectively in a range of collaborative discussions (one-on-one, in groups, and teacher-led) with diverse partners on *grade 3 topics and texts*, building on others' ideas and expressing their own clearly. **SL.3.1.A.** Come to discussions prepared, having read or studied required material; explicitly draw on that preparation and other information known about the topic to explore ideas under discussion. **SL.3.1.B.** Follow agreed-upon rules for discussions (e.g., gaining the floor in respectful ways, listening to others with care, speaking one at a time about the topics and texts under discussion). **SL.3.1.C.** Ask questions to check understanding of information presented, stay on topic, and link their comments to the remarks of others. **SL.3.1.D.** Explain their own ideas and understanding in light of the discussion. **SL.3.2.** Determine the main ideas and supporting details of a text read aloud or information presented in diverse media and formats, including visually, quantitatively, and orally. **SL.3.4.** Report on a topic or text, tell a story, or recount an experience with appropriate facts and relevant, descriptive details, speaking clearly at an understandable pace. **W.3.10.** Write routinely over extended time frames (time for research, reflection, and revision) and shorter time frames (a single sitting or a day or two) for a range of discipline-specific tasks, purposes, and audiences. **L.3.6.** Acquire and use accurately grade-appropriate conversational, general academic, and domain-specific words and phrases, including those that signal spatial and temporal relationships (e.g., *After dinner that night we went looking for them*). ***Grade 4*** **RL.4.1.** Refer to details and examples in a text when explaining what the text says explicitly and when drawing inferences from the text. **RI.4.1.** Refer to details and examples in a text when explaining what the text says explicitly and when drawing inferences from the text. **RI.4.2.** Determine the main idea of a text and explain how it is supported by key details; summarize the text. **RI.4.3.** Explain events, procedures, ideas, or concepts in a historical, scientific, or technical text, including what happened and why, based on specific information in the text. **RI.4.4.** Determine the meaning of general academic and domain-specific words or phrases in a text relevant to a *grade 4 topic or subject area*.

Lesson Title	Suggested Grade Levels	*Common Core State Standards, ELA*
Bugs! *(continued)*	3–5	**SL.4.1.** Engage effectively in a range of collaborative discussions (one-on-one, in groups, and teacher-led) with diverse partners on *grade 4 topics and texts*, building on others' ideas and expressing their own clearly. **SL.4.1.A.** Come to discussions prepared, having read or studied required material; explicitly draw on that preparation and other information known about the topic to explore ideas under discussion. **SL.4.1.B.** Follow agreed-upon rules for discussions and carry out assigned roles. **SL.4.1.C.** Pose and respond to specific questions to clarify or follow up on information, and make comments that contribute to the discussion and link to the remarks of others. **SL.4.1.D.** Review the key ideas expressed and explain their own ideas and understanding in light of the discussion. **SL.4.4.** Report on a topic or text, tell a story, or recount an experience in an organized manner, using appropriate facts and relevant, descriptive details to support main ideas or themes; speak clearly at an understandable pace. **W.4.10.** Write routinely over extended time frames (time for research, reflection, and revision) and shorter time frames (a single sitting or a day or two) for a range of discipline-specific tasks, purposes, and audiences. **L.4.6.** Acquire and use accurately grade-appropriate general academic and domain-specific words and phrases, including those that signal precise actions, emotions, or states of being (e.g., quizzed, whined, stammered) and that are basic to a particular topic (e.g., *wildlife, conservation,* and *endangered* when discussing animal preservation). ***Grade 5*** **RL.5.1.** Quote accurately from a text when explaining what the text says explicitly and when drawing inferences from the text. **RI.5.1.** Quote accurately from a text when explaining what the text says explicitly and when drawing inferences from the text. **RI.5.2.** Determine two or more main ideas of a text and explain how they are supported by key details; summarize the text. **RI.5.3.** Explain the relationships or interactions between two or more individuals, events, ideas, or concepts in a historical, scientific, or technical text based on specific information in the text. **RI.5.4.** Determine the meaning of general academic and domain-specific words and phrases in a text relevant to a *grade 5 topic or subject area.* **SL.5.1.** Engage effectively in a range of collaborative discussions (one-on-one, in groups, and teacher-led) with diverse partners on *grade 5 topics and texts*, building on others' ideas and expressing their own clearly. **SL.5.1.A.** Come to discussions prepared, having read or studied required material; explicitly draw on that preparation and other information known about the topic to explore ideas under discussion. **SL.5.1.B.** Follow agreed-upon rules for discussions and carry out assigned roles. **SL.5.1.C.** Pose and respond to specific questions by making comments that contribute to the discussion and elaborate on the remarks of others. **SL.5.1.D.** Review the key ideas expressed and draw conclusions in light of information and knowledge gained from the discussions. **SL.5.4.** Report on a topic or text or present an opinion, sequencing ideas logically and using appropriate facts and relevant, descriptive details to support main ideas or themes; speak clearly at an understandable pace. **W.5.10.** Write routinely over extended time frames (time for research, reflection, and revision) and shorter time frames (a single sitting or a day or two) for a range of discipline-specific tasks, purposes, and audiences. **L.5.6.** Acquire and use accurately grade-appropriate general academic and domain-specific words and phrases, including those that signal contrast, addition, and other logical relationships (e.g., *however, although, nevertheless, similarly, moreover, in addition*).
Batteries Included	3–5	***Grade 3*** **RL.3.1.** Ask and answer questions to demonstrate understanding of a text, referring explicitly to the text as the basis for the answers. **RI.3.1.** Ask and answer questions to demonstrate understanding of a text, referring explicitly to the text as the basis for the answers. **RI.3.2.** Determine the main idea of a text; recount the key details and explain how they support the main idea. **RI.3.3.** Describe the relationship between a series of historical events, scientific ideas or concepts, or steps in technical procedures in a text, using language that pertains to time, sequence, and cause/effect. **RI.3.4.** Determine the meaning of general academic and domain-specific words and phrases in a text relevant to a *grade 3 topic or subject area*.

Appendix 2. Correlations Between Lessons and *Common Core State Standards, English Language Arts* (*ELA*) *(continued)*

Lesson Title	Suggested Grade Levels	*Common Core State Standards, ELA*
Batteries Included *(continued)*	**3–5**	**SL.3.1.** Engage effectively in a range of collaborative discussions (one-on-one, in groups, and teacher-led) with diverse partners on *grade 3 topics and texts*, building on others' ideas and expressing their own clearly. **SL.3.1.A.** Come to discussions prepared, having read or studied required material; explicitly draw on that preparation and other information known about the topic to explore ideas under discussion. **SL.3.1.B.** Follow agreed-upon rules for discussions (e.g., gaining the floor in respectful ways, listening to others with care, speaking one at a time about the topics and texts under discussion). **SL.3.1.C.** Ask questions to check understanding of information presented, stay on topic, and link their comments to the remarks of others. **SL.3.1.D.** Explain their own ideas and understanding in light of the discussion. **W.3.10.** Write routinely over extended time frames (time for research, reflection, and revision) and shorter time frames (a single sitting or a day or two) for a range of discipline-specific tasks, purposes, and audiences. **L.3.4.** Determine or clarify the meaning of unknown and multiple-meaning word and phrases based on grade 3 reading and content, choosing flexibly from a range of strategies. **L.3.6.** Acquire and use accurately grade-appropriate conversational, general academic, and domain-specific words and phrases, including those that signal spatial and temporal relationships (e.g., *After dinner that night we went looking for them*). ***Grade 4*** **RL.4.1.** Refer to details and examples in a text when explaining what the text says explicitly and when drawing inferences from the text. **RI.4.1.** Refer to details and examples in a text when explaining what the text says explicitly and when drawing inferences from the text. **RI.4.2.** Determine the main idea of a text and explain how it is supported by key details; summarize the text. **RI.4.3.** Explain events, procedures, ideas, or concepts in a historical, scientific, or technical text, including what happened and why, based on specific information in the text. **RI.4.4.** Determine the meaning of general academic and domain-specific words or phrases in a text relevant to a *grade 4 topic or subject area*. **SL.4.1.** Engage effectively in a range of collaborative discussions (one-on-one, in groups, and teacher-led) with diverse partners on *grade 4 topics and texts*, building on others' ideas and expressing their own clearly. **SL.4.1.A.** Come to discussions prepared, having read or studied required material; explicitly draw on that preparation and other information known about the topic to explore ideas under discussion. **SL.4.1.B.** Follow agreed-upon rules for discussions and carry out assigned roles. **SL.4.1.C.** Pose and respond to specific questions to clarify or follow up on information, and make comments that contribute to the discussion and link to the remarks of others. **SL.4.1.D.** Review the key ideas expressed and explain their own ideas and understanding in light of the discussion. **W.4.10.** Write routinely over extended time frames (time for research, reflection, and revision) and shorter time frames (a single sitting or a day or two) for a range of discipline-specific tasks, purposes, and audiences. **L.4.4.** Determine or clarify the meaning of unknown and multiple-meaning words and phrases based on grade 4 reading and content, choosing flexibly from a range of strategies. **L.4.4.A.** Use context (e.g., definitions, examples, or restatements in text) as a clue to the meaning of a word or phrase. **L.4.6.** Acquire and use accurately grade-appropriate general academic and domain-specific words and phrases, including those that signal precise actions, emotions, or states of being (e.g., quizzed, whined, stammered) and that are basic to a particular topic (e.g., *wildlife, conservation,* and *endangered* when discussing animal preservation). ***Grade 5*** **RL.5.1.** Quote accurately from a text when explaining what the text says explicitly and when drawing inferences from the text. **RL.5.2.** Determine a theme of a story, drama, or poem from details in the text, including how characters in a story or drama respond to challenges or how the speaker in a poem reflects upon a topic; summarize the text. **RI.5.1.** Quote accurately from a text when explaining what the text says explicitly and when drawing inferences from the text. **RI.5.2.** Determine two or more main ideas of a text and explain how they are supported by key details; summarize the text.

Lesson Title	Suggested Grade Levels	*Common Core State Standards, ELA*
Batteries Included *(continued)*	3–5	**RI.5.3.** Explain the relationships or interactions between two or more individuals, events, ideas, or concepts in a historical, scientific, or technical text based on specific information in the text. **RI.5.4.** Determine the meaning of general academic and domain-specific words and phrases in a text relevant to a *grade 5 topic or subject area*. **SL.5.1.** Engage effectively in a range of collaborative discussions (one-on-one, in groups, and teacher-led) with diverse partners on *grade 5 topics and texts*, building on others' ideas and expressing their own clearly. **SL.5.1.A.** Come to discussions prepared, having read or studied required material; explicitly draw on that preparation and other information known about the topic to explore ideas under discussion. **SL.5.1.B.** Follow agreed-upon rules for discussions and carry out assigned roles. **SL.5.1.C.** Pose and respond to specific questions by making comments that contribute to the discussion and elaborate on the remarks of others. **SL.5.1.D.** Review the key ideas expressed and draw conclusions in light of information and knowledge gained from the discussions. **W.5.10.** Write routinely over extended time frames (time for research, reflection, and revision) and shorter time frames (a single sitting or a day or two) for a range of discipline-specific tasks, purposes, and audiences. **L.5.4.** Determine or clarify the meaning of unknown and multiple-meaning words and phrases based on grade 5 reading and content, choosing flexibly from a range of strategies. **L.5.4.A.** Use context (e.g., cause/effect relationships and comparisons in text) as a clue to the meaning of a word or phrase. **L.5.6.** Acquire and use accurately grade-appropriate general academic and domain-specific words and phrases, including those that signal contrast, addition, and other logical relationships (e.g., *however, although, nevertheless, similarly, moreover, in addition*).
The Secrets of Flight	3–6	***Grade 3*** **RI.3.1.** Ask and answer questions to demonstrate understanding of a text, referring explicitly to the text as the basis for the answers. **RI.3.2.** Determine the main idea of a text; recount the key details and explain how they support the main idea. **RI.3.3.** Describe the relationship between a series of historical events, scientific ideas or concepts, or steps in technical procedures in a text, using language that pertains to time, sequence, and cause/effect. **RI.3.4.** Determine the meaning of general academic and domain-specific words and phrases in a text relevant to a *grade 3 topic or subject area*. **RI.3.7.** Use information gained from illustrations (e.g., maps, photographs) and the words in a text to demonstrate understanding of the text (e.g., where, when, why, and how key events occur). **SL.3.1.** Engage effectively in a range of collaborative discussions (one-on-one, in groups, and teacher-led) with diverse partners on *grade 3 topics and texts*, building on others' ideas and expressing their own clearly. **SL.3.1.A.** Come to discussions prepared, having read or studied required material; explicitly draw on that preparation and other information known about the topic to explore ideas under discussion. **SL.3.1.B.** Follow agreed-upon rules for discussions (e.g., gaining the floor in respectful ways, listening to others with care, speaking one at a time about the topics and texts under discussion). **SL.3.1.C.** Ask questions to check understanding of information presented, stay on topic, and link their comments to the remarks of others. **SL.3.1.D.** Explain their own ideas and understanding in light of the discussion. **SL.3.2.** Determine the main ideas and supporting details of a text read aloud or information presented in diverse media and formats, including visually, quantitatively, and orally. **W.3.10.** Write routinely over extended time frames (time for research, reflection, and revision) and shorter time frames (a single sitting or a day or two) for a range of discipline-specific tasks, purposes, and audiences. **L.3.6.** Acquire and use accurately grade-appropriate conversational, general academic, and domain-specific words and phrases, including those that signal spatial and temporal relationships (e.g., *After dinner that night we went looking for them*). ***Grade 4*** **RI.4.1.** Refer to details and examples in a text when explaining what the text says explicitly and when drawing inferences from the text. **RI.4.2.** Determine the main idea of a text and explain how it is supported by key details; summarize the text. **RI.4.3.** Explain events, procedures, ideas, or concepts in a historical, scientific, or technical text, including what happened and why, based on specific information in the text.

Appendix 2. Correlations Between Lessons and *Common Core State Standards, English Language Arts* (*ELA*) *(continued)*

Lesson Title	Suggested Grade Levels	*Common Core State Standards, ELA*
The Secrets of Flight *(continued)*	**3–6**	**RI.4.4.** Determine the meaning of general academic and domain-specific words or phrases in a text relevant to a *grade 4 topic or subject area.* **SL.4.1.** Engage effectively in a range of collaborative discussions (one-on-one, in groups, and teacher-led) with diverse partners on *grade 4 topics and texts*, building on others' ideas and expressing their own clearly. **SL.4.1.A.** Come to discussions prepared, having read or studied required material; explicitly draw on that preparation and other information known about the topic to explore ideas under discussion. **SL.4.1.B.** Follow agreed-upon rules for discussions and carry out assigned roles. **SL.4.1.C.** Pose and respond to specific questions to clarify or follow up on information, and make comments that contribute to the discussion and link to the remarks of others. **SL.4.1.D.** Review the key ideas expressed and explain their own ideas and understanding in light of the discussion. **W.4.10.** Write routinely over extended time frames (time for research, reflection, and revision) and shorter time frames (a single sitting or a day or two) for a range of discipline-specific tasks, purposes, and audiences. **L.4.6.** Acquire and use accurately grade-appropriate general academic and domain-specific words and phrases, including those that signal precise actions, emotions, or states of being (e.g., quizzed, whined, stammered) and that are basic to a particular topic (e.g., *wildlife, conservation,* and *endangered* when discussing animal preservation). ***Grade 5*** **RI.5.1.** Quote accurately from a text when explaining what the text says explicitly and when drawing inferences from the text. **RI.5.2.** Determine two or more main ideas of a text and explain how they are supported by key details; summarize the text. **RI.5.3.** Explain the relationships or interactions between two or more individuals, events, ideas, or concepts in a historical, scientific, or technical text based on specific information in the text. **RI.5.4.** Determine the meaning of general academic and domain-specific words and phrases in a text relevant to a *grade 5 topic or subject area.* **SL.5.1.** Engage effectively in a range of collaborative discussions (one-on-one, in groups, and teacher-led) with diverse partners on *grade 5 topics and texts*, building on others' ideas and expressing their own clearly. **SL.5.1.A.** Come to discussions prepared, having read or studied required material; explicitly draw on that preparation and other information known about the topic to explore ideas under discussion. **SL.5.1.B.** Follow agreed-upon rules for discussions and carry out assigned roles. **SL.5.1.C.** Pose and respond to specific questions by making comments that contribute to the discussion and elaborate on the remarks of others. **SL.5.1.D.** Review the key ideas expressed and draw conclusions in light of information and knowledge gained from the discussions. **W.5.10.** Write routinely over extended time frames (time for research, reflection, and revision) and shorter time frames (a single sitting or a day or two) for a range of discipline-specific tasks, purposes, and audiences. **L.5.6.** Acquire and use accurately grade-appropriate general academic and domain-specific words and phrases, including those that signal contrast, addition, and other logical relationships (e.g., *however, although, nevertheless, similarly, moreover, in addition*). ***Grade 6*** **RI.6.1.** Cite textual evidence to support analysis of what the text says explicitly as well as inferences drawn from the text. **RI.6.2.** Determine a central idea of a text and how it is conveyed through particular details; provide a summary of the text distinct from personal opinions or judgments. **RI.6.4.** Determine the meaning of words and phrases as they are used in a text, including figurative, connotative, and technical meanings.

Lesson Title	Suggested Grade Levels	*Common Core State Standards, ELA*
The Secrets of Flight *(continued)*	3–6	**SL.6.1.** Engage effectively in a range of collaborative discussions (one-on-one, in groups, and teacher-led) with diverse partners on grade 6 topics, texts, and issues, building on others' ideas and expressing their own clearly. **SL.6.1.A.** Come to discussions prepared, having read or studied required material; explicitly draw on that preparation by referring to evidence on the topic, text, or issue to probe and reflect on ideas under discussion. **SL.6.1.B.** Follow rules for collegial discussions, set specific goals and deadlines, and define individual roles as needed. **SL.6.1.C.** Pose and respond to specific questions with elaboration and detail by making comments that contribute to the topic, text, or issue under discussion. **SL.6.1.D.** Review the key ideas expressed and demonstrate understanding of multiple perspectives through reflection and paraphrasing. **W.6.10.** Write routinely over extended time frames (time for research, reflection, and revision) and shorter time frames (a single sitting or a day or two) for a range of discipline-specific tasks, purposes, and audiences. **L.6.6.** Acquire and use accurately grade-appropriate general academic and domain-specific words and phrases; gather vocabulary knowledge when considering a word or phrase important to comprehension or expression. **RST.6-8.1.** Cite specific textual evidence to support analysis of science and technical texts. **RST.6-8.2.** Determine the central ideas or conclusions of a text; provide an accurate summary of the text distinct from prior knowledge or opinions. **RST.6-8.3.** Follow precisely a multistep procedure when carrying out experiments, taking measurements, or performing technical tasks. **RST.6-8.4.** Determine the meaning of symbols, key terms, and other domain-specific words and phrases as they are used in a specific scientific or technical context relevant to *grades 6–8 texts and topics*. **WHST.6-8.10.** Write routinely over extended time frames (time for reflection and revision) and shorter time frames (a single sitting or a day or two) for a range of discipline-specific tasks, purposes, and audiences.
Down the Drain	3–6	*Grade 3* **RI.3.1.** Ask and answer questions to demonstrate understanding of a text, referring explicitly to the text as the basis for the answers. **RI.3.2.** Determine the main idea of a text; recount the key details and explain how they support the main idea. **RI.3.3.** Describe the relationship between a series of historical events, scientific ideas or concepts, or steps in technical procedures in a text, using language that pertains to time, sequence, and cause/effect. **RI.3.5.** Use text features and search tools (e.g., key words, sidebars, hyperlinks) to locate information relevant to a given topic efficiently. **RI.3.7.** Use information gained from illustrations (e.g., maps, photographs) and the words in a text to demonstrate understanding of the text (e.g., where, when, why, and how key events occur). **SL.3.1.** Engage effectively in a range of collaborative discussions (one-on-one, in groups, and teacher-led) with diverse partners on *grade 3 topics and texts*, building on others' ideas and expressing their own clearly. **SL.3.1.A.** Come to discussions prepared, having read or studied required material; explicitly draw on that preparation and other information known about the topic to explore ideas under discussion. **SL.3.1.B.** Follow agreed-upon rules for discussions (e.g., gaining the floor in respectful ways, listening to others with care, speaking one at a time about the topics and texts under discussion). **SL.3.1.C.** Ask questions to check understanding of information presented, stay on topic, and link their comments to the remarks of others. **SL.3.1.D.** Explain their own ideas and understanding in light of the discussion. **SL.3.2.** Determine the main ideas and supporting details of a text read aloud or information presented in diverse media and formats, including visually, quantitatively, and orally. **W.3.10.** Write routinely over extended time frames (time for research, reflection, and revision) and shorter time frames (a single sitting or a day or two) for a range of discipline-specific tasks, purposes, and audiences. **L.3.6.** Acquire and use accurately grade-appropriate conversational, general academic, and domain-specific words and phrases, including those that signal spatial and temporal relationships (e.g., *After dinner that night we went looking for them*).

Appendix 2. Correlations Between Lessons and *Common Core State Standards, English Language Arts* (*ELA*) *(continued)*

<table>
<tr><th>Lesson Title</th><th>Suggested Grade Levels</th><th>Common Core State Standards, ELA</th></tr>
<tr><td>Down the Drain
(continued)</td><td>3–6</td><td>Grade 4
RI.4.1. Refer to details and examples in a text when explaining what the text says explicitly and when drawing inferences from the text.
RI.4.2. Determine the main idea of a text and explain how it is supported by key details; summarize the text.
RI.4.3. Explain events, procedures, ideas, or concepts in a historical, scientific, or technical text, including what happened and why, based on specific information in the text.
RI.4.9. Integrate information from two texts on the same topic in order to write or speak about the subject knowledgeably.
SL.4.1. Engage effectively in a range of collaborative discussions (one-on-one, in groups, and teacher-led) with diverse partners on grade 4 topics and texts, building on others' ideas and expressing their own clearly.
SL.4.1.A. Come to discussions prepared, having read or studied required material; explicitly draw on that preparation and other information known about the topic to explore ideas under discussion.
SL.4.1.B. Follow agreed-upon rules for discussions and carry out assigned roles.
SL.4.1.C. Pose and respond to specific questions to clarify or follow up on information, and make comments that contribute to the discussion and link to the remarks of others.
SL.4.1.D. Review the key ideas expressed and explain their own ideas and understanding in light of the discussion.
W.4.10. Write routinely over extended time frames (time for research, reflection, and revision) and shorter time frames (a single sitting or a day or two) for a range of discipline-specific tasks, purposes, and audiences.
L.4.6. Acquire and use accurately grade-appropriate general academic and domain-specific words and phrases, including those that signal precise actions, emotions, or states of being (e.g., quizzed, whined, stammered) and that are basic to a particular topic (e.g., wildlife, conservation, and endangered when discussing animal preservation).

Grade 5
RI.5.1. Quote accurately from a text when explaining what the text says explicitly and when drawing inferences from the text.
RI.5.2. Determine two or more main ideas of a text and explain how they are supported by key details; summarize the text.
RI.5.3. Explain the relationships or interactions between two or more individuals, events, ideas, or concepts in a historical, scientific, or technical text based on specific information in the text.
RI.5.9. Integrate information from several texts on the same topic in order to write or speak about the subject knowledgeably.
SL.5.1. Engage effectively in a range of collaborative discussions (one-on-one, in groups, and teacher-led) with diverse partners on grade 5 topics and texts, building on others' ideas and expressing their own clearly.
SL.5.1.A. Come to discussions prepared, having read or studied required material; explicitly draw on that preparation and other information known about the topic to explore ideas under discussion.
SL.5.1.B. Follow agreed-upon rules for discussions and carry out assigned roles.
SL.5.1.C. Pose and respond to specific questions by making comments that contribute to the discussion and elaborate on the remarks of others.
SL.5.1.D. Review the key ideas expressed and draw conclusions in light of information and knowledge gained from the discussions.
W.5.10. Write routinely over extended time frames (time for research, reflection, and revision) and shorter time frames (a single sitting or a day or two) for a range of discipline-specific tasks, purposes, and audiences.
L.5.6. Acquire and use accurately grade-appropriate general academic and domain-specific words and phrases, including those that signal contrast, addition, and other logical relationships (e.g., however, although, nevertheless, similarly, moreover, in addition).

Grade 6
RI.6.1. Cite textual evidence to support analysis of what the text says explicitly as well as inferences drawn from the text.
RI.6.2. Determine a central idea of a text and how it is conveyed through particular details; provide a summary of the text distinct from personal opinions or judgments.
RI.6.9. Compare and contrast one author's presentation of events with that of another (e.g., a memoir written by and a biography on the same person).</td></tr>
</table>

Lesson Title	Suggested Grade Levels	*Common Core State Standards, ELA*
Down the Drain *(continued)*	**3–6**	**L.6.6.** Acquire and use accurately grade-appropriate general academic and domain-specific words and phrases; gather vocabulary knowledge when considering a word or phrase important to comprehension or expression. **SL.6.1.** Engage effectively in a range of collaborative discussions (one-on-one, in groups, and teacher-led) with diverse partners on grade 6 topics, texts, and issues, building on others' ideas and expressing their own clearly. **SL.6.1.A.** Come to discussions prepared, having read or studied required material; explicitly draw on that preparation by referring to evidence on the topic, text, or issue to probe and reflect on ideas under discussion. **SL.6.1.B.** Follow rules for collegial discussions, set specific goals and deadlines, and define individual roles as needed. **SL.6.1.C.** Pose and respond to specific questions with elaboration and detail by making comments that contribute to the topic, text, or issue under discussion. **SL.6.1.D.** Review the key ideas expressed and demonstrate understanding of multiple perspectives through reflection and paraphrasing. **RST.6-8.1.** Cite specific textual evidence to support analysis of science and technical texts. **RST.6-8.2.** Determine the central ideas or conclusions of a text; provide an accurate summary of the text distinct from prior knowledge or opinions. **RST.6-8.3.** Follow precisely a multistep procedure when carrying out experiments, taking measurements, or performing technical tasks. **RST.6-8.4.** Determine the meaning of symbols, key terms, and other domain-specific words and phrases as they are used in a specific scientific or technical context relevant to *grades 6–8 texts and topics*. **WHST.6-8.10.** Write routinely over extended time frames (time for reflection and revision) and shorter time frames (a single sitting or a day or two) for a range of discipline-specific tasks, purposes, and audiences.
If I Built a Car	**3–6**	***Grade 3*** **RL.3.1.** Ask and answer questions to demonstrate understanding of a text, referring explicitly to the text as the basis for the answers. **RI.3.1.** Ask and answer questions to demonstrate understanding of a text, referring explicitly to the text as the basis for the answers. **RI.3.2.** Determine the main idea of a text; recount the key details and explain how they support the main idea. **RI.3.3.** Describe the relationship between a series of historical events, scientific ideas or concepts, or steps in technical procedures in a text, using language that pertains to time, sequence, and cause/effect. **RI.3.4.** Determine the meaning of general academic and domain-specific words and phrases in a text relevant to a *grade 3 topic or subject area*. **SL.3.1.** Engage effectively in a range of collaborative discussions (one-on-one, in groups, and teacher-led) with diverse partners on *grade 3 topics and texts*, building on others' ideas and expressing their own clearly. **SL.3.1.A.** Come to discussions prepared, having read or studied required material; explicitly draw on that preparation and other information known about the topic to explore ideas under discussion. **SL.3.1.B.** Follow agreed-upon rules for discussions (e.g., gaining the floor in respectful ways, listening to others with care, speaking one at a time about the topics and texts under discussion). **SL.3.1.C.** Ask questions to check understanding of information presented, stay on topic, and link their comments to the remarks of others. **SL.3.1.D.** Explain their own ideas and understanding in light of the discussion. **SL.3.2.** Determine the main ideas and supporting details of a text read aloud or information presented in diverse media and formats, including visually, quantitatively, and orally. **W.3.10.** Write routinely over extended time frames (time for research, reflection, and revision) and shorter time frames (a single sitting or a day or two) for a range of discipline-specific tasks, purposes, and audiences. **L.3.6.** Acquire and use accurately grade-appropriate conversational, general academic, and domain-specific words and phrases, including those that signal spatial and temporal relationships (e.g., *After dinner that night we went looking for them*). ***Grade 4*** **RL.4.1.** Refer to details and examples in a text when explaining what the text says explicitly and when drawing inferences from the text. **RI.4.1.** Refer to details and examples in a text when explaining what the text says explicitly and when drawing inferences from the text.

Lesson Title	Suggested Grade Levels	*Common Core State Standards, ELA*
If I Built a Car *(continued)*	**3–6**	**RI.4.2.** Determine the main idea of a text and explain how it is supported by key details; summarize the text. **RI.4.3.** Explain events, procedures, ideas, or concepts in a historical, scientific, or technical text, including what happened and why, based on specific information in the text. **RI.4.4.** Determine the meaning of general academic and domain-specific words or phrases in a text relevant to a *grade 4 topic or subject area.* **SL.4.1.** Engage effectively in a range of collaborative discussions (one-on-one, in groups, and teacher-led) with diverse partners on *grade 4 topics and texts*, building on others' ideas and expressing their own clearly. **SL.4.1.A.** Come to discussions prepared, having read or studied required material; explicitly draw on that preparation and other information known about the topic to explore ideas under discussion. **SL.4.1.B.** Follow agreed-upon rules for discussions and carry out assigned roles. **SL.4.1.C.** Pose and respond to specific questions to clarify or follow up on information, and make comments that contribute to the discussion and link to the remarks of others. **SL.4.1.D.** Review the key ideas expressed and explain their own ideas and understanding in light of the discussion. **W.4.10.** Write routinely over extended time frames (time for research, reflection, and revision) and shorter time frames (a single sitting or a day or two) for a range of discipline-specific tasks, purposes, and audiences. **L.4.6.** Acquire and use accurately grade-appropriate general academic and domain-specific words and phrases, including those that signal precise actions, emotions, or states of being (e.g., quizzed, whined, stammered) and that are basic to a particular topic (e.g., *wildlife, conservation,* and *endangered* when discussing animal preservation). ***Grade 5*** **RL.5.1.** Quote accurately from a text when explaining what the text says explicitly and when drawing inferences from the text. **RI.5.1.** Quote accurately from a text when explaining what the text says explicitly and when drawing inferences from the text. **RI.5.2.** Determine two or more main ideas of a text and explain how they are supported by key details; summarize the text. **RI.5.3.** Explain the relationships or interactions between two or more individuals, events, ideas, or concepts in a historical, scientific, or technical text based on specific information in the text. **RI.5.4.** Determine the meaning of general academic and domain-specific words and phrases in a text relevant to a *grade 5 topic or subject area.* **SL.5.1.** Engage effectively in a range of collaborative discussions (one-on-one, in groups, and teacher-led) with diverse partners on *grade 5 topics and texts*, building on others' ideas and expressing their own clearly. **SL.5.1.A.** Come to discussions prepared, having read or studied required material; explicitly draw on that preparation and other information known about the topic to explore ideas under discussion. **SL.5.1.B.** Follow agreed-upon rules for discussions and carry out assigned roles. **SL.5.1.C.** Pose and respond to specific questions by making comments that contribute to the discussion and elaborate on the remarks of others. **SL.5.1.D.** Review the key ideas expressed and draw conclusions in light of information and knowledge gained from the discussions. **W.5.10.** Write routinely over extended time frames (time for research, reflection, and revision) and shorter time frames (a single sitting or a day or two) for a range of discipline-specific tasks, purposes, and audiences. **L.5.6.** Acquire and use accurately grade-appropriate general academic and domain-specific words and phrases, including those that signal contrast, addition, and other logical relationships (e.g., *however, although, nevertheless, similarly, moreover, in addition*). ***Grade 6*** **RL.6.1.** Cite textual evidence to support analysis of what the text says explicitly as well as inferences drawn from the text. **RI.6.1.** Cite textual evidence to support analysis of what the text says explicitly as well as inferences drawn from the text. **RI.6.2.** Determine a central idea of a text and how it is conveyed through particular details; provide a summary of the text distinct from personal opinions or judgments.

Lesson Title	Suggested Grade Levels	*Common Core State Standards, ELA*
If I Built a Car *(continued)*	3–6	**RI.6.4.** Determine the meaning of words and phrases as they are used in a text, including figurative, connotative, and technical meanings. **SL.6.1.** Engage effectively in a range of collaborative discussions (one-on-one, in groups, and teacher-led) with diverse partners on grade 6 topics, texts, and issues, building on others' ideas and expressing their own clearly. **SL.6.1.A.** Come to discussions prepared, having read or studied required material; explicitly draw on that preparation by referring to evidence on the topic, text, or issue to probe and reflect on ideas under discussion. **SL.6.1.B.** Follow rules for collegial discussions, set specific goals and deadlines, and define individual roles as needed. **SL.6.1.C.** Pose and respond to specific questions with elaboration and detail by making comments that contribute to the topic, text, or issue under discussion. **SL.6.1.D.** Review the key ideas expressed and demonstrate understanding of multiple perspectives through reflection and paraphrasing. **W.6.10.** Write routinely over extended time frames (time for research, reflection, and revision) and shorter time frames (a single sitting or a day or two) for a range of discipline-specific tasks, purposes, and audiences. **L.6.6.** Acquire and use accurately grade-appropriate general academic and domain-specific words and phrases; gather vocabulary knowledge when considering a word or phrase important to comprehension or expression. **RST.6-8.1.** Cite specific textual evidence to support analysis of science and technical texts. **RST.6-8.2.** Determine the central ideas or conclusions of a text; provide an accurate summary of the text distinct from prior knowledge or opinions. **RST.6-8.3.** Follow precisely a multistep procedure when carrying out experiments, taking measurements, or performing technical tasks. **RST.6-8.4.** Determine the meaning of symbols, key terms, and other domain-specific words and phrases as they are used in a specific scientific or technical context relevant to *grades 6–8 texts and topics*. **WHST.6-8.10.** Write routinely over extended time frames (time for reflection and revision) and shorter time frames (a single sitting or a day or two) for a range of discipline-specific tasks, purposes, and audiences.

© Copyright 2010 National Governors Association Center for Best Practices and Council of Chief State School Officers. All rights reserved.

Glossary

Note: All definitions attributed to (Colburn 2003) are verbatim from the book referenced at the end of the glossary.

Anticipation guides—Sets of questions that serve as a pre- or post-reading activity for a text, anticipation guides can activate and assess prior knowledge, determine misconceptions, focus thinking on the reading, and motivate reluctant readers by stimulating interest in the topic.

Assessment—"Assessment, broadly defined, means information gathering. Grading (or evaluating) students is certainly one type of assessment. Tests, portfolios, and lab practicals are all assessment devices. However, teachers assess students in other ways. When teachers check for understanding, to determine whether or not to continue teaching about a particular idea and where to go next with instruction, they are also assessing their students. Ungraded pretests and self-tests likewise represent assessment. Any information that helps the teacher make instructional decisions is assessment.

"Assessment is valuable to students as well as teachers (not to mention parents and other education stakeholders) because it helps students figure out what they do and don't understand and where they need to place their efforts to maximize learning. Assessment is also used to sort or rank students, letting them know how their performance compares to others, both for placement purposes and as a way to ensure minimum competencies in those who have passed particular tests." (Colburn 2003, p. 37)

Checkpoint labs—One way to manage a guided inquiry is to use a checkpoint lab. This type of lab is divided into written sections, with a small box located at the end of each section for a teacher check mark or stamp. Students work in teams, each one proceeding at its own pace. Teams use a red cup and a green cup taped together at their bottoms to signal the teacher—green on top when a team is working and red on top when a team has a question or reaches a checkpoint at which it needs the teacher's approval to continue.

Chunking—Chunking, just like it sounds, is dividing the text into manageable sections and reading only one section at any one time.

Cloze—Cloze is an activity to help readers infer the meanings of unfamiliar words. In the cloze strategy, key words are deleted in a passage, and students fill in the blanks with words that make sense and sound right.

Constructivism—"Constructivism has multiple meanings, and it's important that when people discuss the concept they be sure they're talking about the same thing! Much of the confusion stems from the fact that constructivism refers to both an explanation (theory) about how people learn and a philosophical position related to the nature of learning (see Matthews 1994, 137–39). Increasingly, people are also using the term to refer to teaching techniques designed to build on what students already know, for example, open-ended, hands-on inquiry (Brooks and Brooks 1993).

"I'd like to focus on constructivism as an explanation about learning; that's probably what is most relevant to readers. In this context, 'constructivism' refers to the concept that learners always bring with them to the classroom (or any other place where learning takes place) ideas about how the world works—including ideas related to whatever may be in today's lesson. Most of the time learners are unaware they even have these ideas! The ideas come from life experiences combined with what people have learned elsewhere.

"According to constructivist learning theory, learners test new ideas against that which they already believe to be true. If the new ideas seem to fit in with their pictures of the world, they have little difficulty learning the ideas. There's no guarantee, though, that they will fit the ideas into their pictures of how the world works with the kind of meaning the teacher intends. ...

"On the other hand, if the new ideas don't seem to fit the learner's picture of reality then they won't seem to make sense. Learners may dismiss them, learn them well enough to please the teacher (but never fully accept the ideas), or eventually accommodate the new ideas and change the way they understand the world. As you might guess, this third outcome is most difficult to achieve, although it's what teachers most often desire in students.

"Seen this way, teaching is a process of trying to get people to change their minds—difficult enough as is, but made even more difficult by the fact that learners may not even know they hold an opinion about the idea in question! People who study learning and cognition often contrast constructivism with the more classical idea that students in our classes are 'blank slates' who know nothing about the topics they are being taught. From this perspective, the teacher 'transmits' new information to students, who mentally store it away. In contrast, constructivist learning theory says that students are not blank slates; learning is sometimes a process whereby new ideas help students to 'rewrite' the misconceptions already on their slates." (Colburn 2003, pp. 58–59)

Dual-purpose books—Intended to serve two purposes, present a story and provide facts, dual-purpose books employ a format that allows readers to use the book as a storybook or as a nonnarrative information book. Sometimes information can be found in the running text, but more frequently it appears in insets and diagrams. Readers can enter on any page to access specific facts or read the book through as a story.

Elaborate—See 5E model of instruction.

Engage—See 5E model of instruction.

Evaluate—See 5E model of instruction.

Explain—See 5E model of instruction.

Explore—See 5E model of instruction.

Features of nonfiction—Many nonfiction books include a table of contents, index, glossary, bold-print words, picture captions, diagrams, and charts that provide valuable information. Modeling how to interpret the information is important because children often skip over these features.

5E model of instruction—"The 5E model of instruction is a variation on the learning cycle model, pioneered by the Biological Sciences Curriculum Study (BSCS 1993). The five Es of the model are *engage, explore, explain, elaborate*, and *evaluate*. *Engage* refers to beginning instruction with something that both catches students' attention and helps them relate what is to come with what they already know. *Explore* is virtually identical with the exploration phase of the learning cycle, as *explain* is the concept- or term-introduction phase and *elaborate* is the application phase. *Evaluation* is both formative and summative since it helps determine whether instruction should continue or whether students need more time and teaching to learn the unit's key points." (Colburn 2003, p. 23)

Frayer model—A Frayer model is one of several organizers that can help learners activate prior knowledge, organize thinking, understand the essential characteristics of concepts, and see relationships among concepts. It can be used for pre-reading, for assessment, or for summarizing or reviewing material. See also *I Wonder/I Learned chart, O-W-L chart, T-chart, semantic map,* and *personal vocabulary list.* See Chapters 6 and 16 for examples.

Genre—Picture books are a genre in themselves, but in this text, genre refers to types of picture books: storybooks, nonnarrative information book, narrative information books, and dual-purpose books.

Guided inquiry activity—"In a guided inquiry activity, the teacher gives students only the problem to investigate (and the materials to use for the investigation). Students must figure out how to answer the investigation's question and then generalize from the data collected." (Colburn 2003, pp. 20–21)

Inquiry—"Historically, discussions of inquiry generally have fallen within two broad classes. Sometimes people talk about inquiry as describing what scientists do and sometimes as a teaching and learning process. Authors of the *National Science Education Standards* (NRC 1996) seemed to recognize this dichotomy:

Scientific inquiry refers to the diverse ways in which scientists study the natural world and propose explanations based on the evidence derived from their work. Inquiry also *refers to the activities of students in which they develop knowledge and understanding of scientific ideas, as well as an understanding of how scientists study the natural world.* [emphasis added] (23)

"To make this distinction less confusing, people also sometimes use the phrase 'inquiry-based instruction.' This term refers to the creation of a classroom where students are engaged in (essentially) open-ended, student-centered, hands-on activities. This means that students must make at least some decisions about what they are doing and what their work means—thinking along the way.

"While most people in the science education community would probably think of inquiry as hands-on, it's also true that many educators would 'count' as inquiry any activity where students are analyzing real-life data—even if the information were simply given to students on paper, without any hands-on activity on their part.

"As readers can begin to see, inquiry and inquiry-based instruction represent ideas with broad definitions and occasional disagreements about their meaning. Two people advocating inquiry-based instruction may not be advocating for the same methods! Some define 'inquiry' (instruction) in terms of open-ended, hands-on instruction; others define the term in terms of formally teaching students inquiry skills (trying to teach students how to observe or make hypotheses, for example); and some define inquiry so broadly as to represent any hands-on activity." (Colburn 2003, pp. 19–20)

I Wonder/I Learned chart—An I Wonder/I Learned chart is one of several organizers that can help learners activate prior knowledge, organize their thinking, understand the essential characteristics of concepts, and see relationships among concepts. It can be used for pre-reading, for assessment, or for summarizing or reviewing material. See also *O-W-L chart, Frayer model, T-chart, semantic map,* and *personal vocabulary list.* See Chapter 9 for an example.

Learning cycle—"Different versions of the learning cycle exist today. However, the general pattern is to begin instruction with students engaged in an activity designed to provide experience with a new idea. The idea behind this exploratory phase of the cycle is that learning of new ideas is maximized when students have had relevant, concrete experience with an idea before being formally introduced to it (Barman and Kotar 1989).

"This exploratory phase is ideally followed by a concept- or term-introduction phase. That phase generally begins with class discussion about student findings and thoughts following the previous part of the cycle. Sometimes the teacher can then go on to simply provide names for ideas that students previously discovered or experienced.

"Finally, students expand on the idea in an application phase of instruction in which they use the new idea(s) in a different context. Using a new idea in a new context is an important part of maximizing learning. In addition, some students don't begin to truly understand an idea until they've had the time to work with it for a while, in different ways. The learning cycle model provides these students with time and opportunities that help them learn.

"Ideally, the application phase of the cycle also introduces students to a new idea. In this sense, the application phase of one learning cycle is also the exploratory phase of another learning cycle—hence the 'cycle' part of 'learning cycle.' (Notice that the previous sentence began with the word 'ideally'; sometimes it's difficult for an application phase activity to also encourage students to explore other ideas.)" (Colburn 2003, p. 22)

Misconceptions—"[L]earners always bring preconceived ideas with them to the classroom about how the world works. Misconceptions, in the field of science education, are preconceived ideas that differ from those currently accepted by the scientific community. Educators use a variety of phrases synonymously with 'misconceptions,' including 'naive conceptions,' 'prior conceptions,' 'alternate conceptions,' and 'preconceptions.' Many people have interviewed students to discover commonly held scientific ideas (Driver, Guesne, and Tiberghien 1985; Osborne and Freyberg 1985)." Colburn 2003, p. 59)

Narrative information books—Narrative information books communicate a sequence of factual events over time and sometimes recount the events of a specific case to generalize to all cases. Teachers should establish a purpose for reading so students focus on the science content rather than the storyline. Teachers may want to read the book through one time for the aesthetic components and a second time for specific science content.

National Science Education Standards—"The National Science Education Standards were published in 1996, after a lengthy commentary period from many interested citizens and groups. ...

"The Standards were designed to be achievable by all students, no matter their background or characteristics. ...

"Beside standards for science content and for science teaching, the *National Science Education Standards* includes standards for professional development for science teachers, science education programs, and even science education systems. Finally, the document also addresses what some consider the bottom line for educational reform—standards for assessment in science education.

"Although the information in the *National Science Education Standards* is often written in a rather general manner, the resulting document provides a far-reaching and generally agreed upon comprehensive starting place for people interested in changing the U.S. science educational system." (Colburn 2003, pp. 81–82)

Nonnarrative information books—Factual texts that introduce a topic, describe the attributes of the topic, or describe typical events that occur are considered nonnarrative information books. The focus is on the subject matter, not specific characters. The vocabulary is typically technical, and readers can enter the text at any point in the book.

Open inquiry activity—"Open inquiry, in many ways, is analogous to doing science. Problem-based learning and science fair activities are often open inquiry experiences for students. Basically, in an open inquiry activity students must figure out pretty much everything. They determine questions to investigate, procedures to address their questions, data to generate, and what the data mean." (Colburn 2003, p. 21)

O-W-L chart—An O-W-L chart ("Observations, Wonderings, Learnings") is one of several organizers that can help learners activate prior knowledge, organize their thinking, understand the essential characteristics of concepts, and see relationships among concepts. It can be used for pre-reading, for assessment, or for summarizing or reviewing material. See also *I Wonder/I Learned chart, Frayer model, T-chart, semantic map,* and *personal vocabulary list.* See Chapters 10 and 11 for examples.

Pairs read—In a pairs read, one learner reads aloud, while the other listens and then summarizes the main idea. Benefits include increased reader involvement, attention, and collaboration and students who become more independent learners.

Personal vocabulary list—A personal vocabulary list is one of several organizers that can help learners activate prior knowledge, organize their thinking, understand the essential characteristics of concepts, and see relationships among concepts. It can be used for pre-reading, for assessment, or for summarizing or reviewing material. See also *I Wonder/I Learned chart, O-W-L chart, Frayer model, T-chart,* and *semantic map.* See Chapter 19 for a variation of a personal vocabulary list.

Reading aloud—Being read to builds knowledge for success in reading and increases interest in reading and literature and in overall academic achievement. See Chapter 2 for more on reading aloud, including 10 tips on how to do it.

Reading comprehension strategies—The six key reading comprehension strategies featured in *Strategies That Work* (Harvey and Goudvis 2000) are *making connections, questioning, visualizing, inferring, determining importance,* and *synthesizing.* See Chapter 2 for fuller explanations.

Rereading—Nonfiction text is often full of unfamiliar ideas and difficult vocabulary. Rereading content for clarification is an essential skill of proficient readers, and you should model this frequently. Rereading for a different purpose can aid comprehension. For example, a teacher might read aloud for enjoyment and then revisit the text to focus on science content.

Semantic map—A semantic map is one of several organizers that can help learners activate prior knowledge, organize their thinking, understand the essential characteristics of concepts, and see relationships among concepts. It can be used for pre-reading, for assessment, or for summarizing or reviewing material. See also *I Wonder/I Learned chart, O-W-L chart, Frayer model, T-chart,* and *personal vocabulary list.* See Chapter 8 for an example.

Sketch to stretch—Learners pause briefly to reflect on the text and do a comprehension self-assessment by drawing on paper the images they visualize in their heads during reading. Teachers should have students use pencils so they understand the focus should be on collecting their thoughts rather than creating a piece of art. You may want to use a timer.

Stop and jot—Learners stop and think about the reading and then jot down a thought. If they use sticky notes, the notes can be added to a whole-class chart to connect past and future learning.

Storybooks—Storybooks center on specific characters who work to resolve conflicts or problems. The major purpose of stories is to entertain. The vocabulary is typically commonsense, everyday language. A storybook can spark interest in a science topic and move students toward informational texts to answer questions inspired by the story.

Structured inquiry activity—"In a structured inquiry activity, the teacher gives students a (usually) hands-on problem they are to investigate, and the methods and materials to use for the investigation, but not expected outcomes. Students are to discover a relationship and generalize from data collected.

"The main difference between a structured inquiry activity and verification lab (or 'cookbook activity') lies in what students do with the data they generate. In structured inquiry activities, students are largely responsible for figuring out what the data might mean—that is, they analyze and interpret the data. Students may ultimately interpret the data differently; different students may come to somewhat different conclusions. In a verification lab, on the other hand, all students are expected to arrive at the same conclusion—there's a definite right answer that students are supposed to be finding during the lab activity." (Colburn 2003, p. 20)

T-chart—A T-chart is one of several organizers that can help learners activate prior knowledge, organize their thinking, understand the essential characteristics of concepts, and see relationships among concepts. It can be used for prereading, for assessment, or for summarizing or reviewing material. See also *I Wonder/I Learned chart, O-W-L chart, Frayer model, semantic map,* and *personal vocabulary list*. See Chapters 6, 12, and 14 for examples.

Turn and talk—Learners pair up with a partner to share ideas, explain concepts in their own words, or tell about a connection they have to the book. This method allows each child to be involved as either a talker or a listener.

Word sorts—Word sorts help learners understand the relationships among key concepts and help teach classification. Used as a pre-reading activity, they can reveal misconceptions. In an *open sort,* learners sort the words into categories of their own making. In a *closed sort,* the teacher gives learners the categories for sorting.

References

Barman, C. R., and M. Kotar. 1989. The learning cycle. *Science and Children* 26 (7): 30–32.

Biological Sciences Curriculum Study (BSCS). 1993. *Developing biological literacy.* Dubuque, IA: Kendall/Hunt.

Brooks, J. G., and M. G. Brooks. 1993. *In search of understanding: The case for constructivist classrooms.* Alexandria, VA: Association for Supervision and Curriculum Development.

Colburn, A. 2003. *The lingo of learning: 88 education terms every science teacher should know.* Arlington, VA: NSTA Press.

Driver, R., E. Guesne, and A. Tiberghien. 1985. *Children's ideas in science.* Buckingham, England: Open University Press.

Harvey, S., and A. Goudvis. 2000. *Strategies that work: Teaching comprehension to enhance understanding.* York, ME: Stenhouse Publishers

Matthews, M. R. 1994. *Science teaching: The role of history and philosophy of science.* New York: Routledge.

National Research Council (NRC). 1996. *National science education standards.* Washington, DC: National Academies Press.

Osborne, R., and P. Freyberg. 1985. *Learning in science.* Portsmouth, NH: Heinemann.

Index

*Page numbers in **boldface** type refer to figures or tables. Those followed by "n" refer to footnotes.*

Franklin Pierce University
00210211